GANGS
AND SOCIETY

GANGS

AND SOCIETY

ALTERNATIVE PERSPECTIVES

EDITED BY LOUIS KONTOS,

DAVID BROTHERTON, **AND**

LUIS BARRIOS

COLUMBIA UNIVERSITY PRESS / NEW YORK

COLUMBIA UNIVERSITY PRESS

Publishers Since 1893

New York   Chichester, West Sussex

© 2003 Columbia University Press

All rights reserved

The photographs in chapter 13 © Robert Yager

The photographs in chapter 14 © Donna De Cesare

Library of Congress Cataloging-in-Publication Data

Gangs and society : alternative perspectives / edited by
   Louis Kontos, David Brotherton, and Luis Barrios.
      p.   cm.
   Includes bibliographical references and index.
   ISBN 978-0-231-12140-8 (cloth : alk. paper) —
   ISBN 978-0-231-12141-5 (paper : alk. paper)
   1. Gangs — United States. 1. Kontos, Louis.
   II. Brotherton, David. III. Barrios, Luis.

HV6439.U5 G3597 2003
302.3'4 — dc21
                                                            2002035038

Columbia University Press books are printed
on permanent and durable acid-free paper.
Printed in the United States of America

CONTENTS

INTRODUCTION

This collection will show throughout that the complexity of gangs mirrors the complexity of the communities in which they are found. One dimension of the complexity of the latter is the diversity of opinion that normally exists within it. With regard to the "gang problem," there are competing definitions—not only of its nature, but also of appropriate solutions to it. In addition, attempts to represent and speak for the community serve to problematize the concept as a unit of analysis. Is the community a concrete space—for instance, a collection of neighborhoods? Or is it instead a matter of collective identity, a "symbolic" community that extends only as far as people can be found who share a particular cultural identity or system of beliefs or "collective representations" (Hunter 1974)? To address these questions and the substantive issues concerning the relationship between gangs and communities, we have brought together the following eclectic range of textual representations, modes, and subjects of inquiry and theoretical positions related to the question of gangs. The reader will notice that there is no attempt to produce a uniform statement, but instead to provide a forum for critical issues as a way of advancing a nonreductive understanding of gangs. In our view, in order to broaden the understanding of gangs it is necessary to problematize the systemic references that make sociological explanation canonical rather than reflective and critical. We hope this volume will make some headway in that endeavor.

THEORY AND METHODOLOGY

Each of the chapters in part 1 involves an attempt to show the limits of conventional theorizing about gangs. In the first reading, Sudhir Venkatesh points out that gang research and theorizing continue to be defined by the "ecology perspective," originally adopted by the Chicago School. Focusing on immigrant groups in Chicago in the 1920s and 1930s, which were assumed to be both disenfranchised and poorly organized, researchers like Thrasher (1927) and Shaw and McKay (1931) argued that second-generation immigrant gangs formed deviant subcultures in relative isolation from mainstream society. Unlike what is typically perceived by contemporary researchers, however, the disparate works of the Chicago School did not pathologize the notion of subculture. Rather, the concern was with the creation of social identity through symbolic systems of communication—folklore, songs, and poetry—which were deemed significant sources of motivation and bond, regardless of the extent of crime and mayhem. Venkatesh points out that although such concepts as "disorganization" are elemental (under various headings) to contemporary social research, the concern with the social identity of gang members initiated by the Chicago School has not been maintained, save for a few exceptions. The cultural dimension of gangs, according to Venkatesh, is especially relevant in contemporary society, which he characterizes as post-Fordist (referring to the crisis of capitalist accumulation that occurred after World War II). The corresponding shift in the locus of social identity from production to consumption is not unique to gang members, but instead is part of the environment to which they must respond. In turn, it is important to understand the nature of that response, rather than depicting gang members as passive or merely reactive. In addition, Venkatesh underlines the need to take into account the cultural and political dimensions of the gang scene. This involves not only a greater focus on symbolic codes and styles but also a more specific focus on the full range of activities of gang members.

In chapter 2, Avelardo Valdez addresses the issues of variation and change in Mexican gangs around San Antonio. Although "Chicano" gangs have traditionally been more territorial than other kinds, Valdez points out that the growth in lethal violence and well-organized criminal activities marks a break with a well-documented territorial ethos. Increased male joblessness and decreased government services for the poor also create a situation in which large numbers of adults can be found in gangs. Those adults, according to Valdez, play a mostly negative role, largely determining the degree to which an organization is criminally oriented. Unlike earlier times when the presence of adults made the gang more of a family, as when the "cholo" lifestyle was passed down from generation to generation beginning in the 1940s on the west coast, today in the San Antonio area at least, they are more important in maintaining a drug supply. And they are more able and willing to use instrumental violence in order to maintain obedience within the organization and to keep competition away. Valdez also finds several different types of gangs and substantial variation within types, as determined by commitment to goals, degree of organization, and constitution of their membership. In contrast to Venkatesh, Valdez does not find any-

thing positive in his sample of gangs, but instead a deterioration of proso-
cial elements that previously existed.

Ric Curtis (chapter 3) illustrates the turning points in the development of
the gang scene in New York City. During the 1960s, the city experienced a
mass exodus of its predominantly white middle class followed by most of its
industrial sector. Social services were drastically reduced, even as unemployment skyrocketed. It was in this context that New York developed a heroin
"epidemic" that caught the attention of the whole country. Going into the
1980s, the epidemic seemed to subside. Yet, as Curtis points out, the drug
trade was merely consolidated in the hands of a few "owners" who ran drug
crews. Ethnic tensions developed in the process between the owners, who
were predominantly Dominican, and the workers, who were predominantly
Puerto Rican. Aggressive buy-and-bust tactics in the 1980s served to exacer-
bate this tension. Street-level dealers took the fall and subsequently came to
rely on each other for protection in prison. It was out of this situation that
the Latino "supergangs" emerged. Groups like the Almighty Latin King and
Queen Nation (ALKQN) and the Asociación Ñeta developed "a culture of
resistance," something lacking from the "drug crew" phenomenon. But as
the organizations grew, the state was systematically dismantling their leadership, resulting in the rapid growth of loosely structured street organizations. As Curtis demonstrates, those groups were not interested in taking
over the drug trade, but instead represented an attempt to impose order on
what had become an unmanageable situation. During the mid-1990s, they
became better organized and more oppositional, articulating a message that
was simultaneously antidrugs and antiviolence, and that gave voice to the
grievances of young people in the Latino community.

In chapter 4, Kevin McDonald's study of homeless youth in Australia
contrasts their mode of organization to that of "gangs" and other forms of
"youth culture." Youth culture is understood as a mode of response and
adaptation to dominant social trends that affect young people especially.
The American "gang" is understood as a unique phenomenon that emerges
in the context of industrial capitalism marked by sustained waves of immigration, ethnic conflict, and machine politics. Contemporary capitalism, by
contrast, is increasingly global and unrestrained in nature, effectively sub-
verting regional and cultural distinctions. Thus young people throughout
the urban world are confronted with similar problems, including unpre-
dictability, uncertainty, and an ever-present "demand for self-esteem." One

consequence of this mode of organization, according to McDonald, is the emergence of a form of violence in which the goal is success at any cost, without "reciprocal" limits.

GANGS AND POLITICS

Although the reason to be concerned with the criminal aspect of gangs is self-explanatory, a concern with anything else regarding them requires explanation. Yet gangs are not criminal organizations in the strict sense of the term. That is to say, the existence of "other," noncriminal dimensions is not only a matter of what some groups have in some form or another and that others are lacking. Rather, given a range of members with conflicting and contradictory goals, there are always noncriminal reasons for joining and noncriminal agendas that surface periodically. In addition, the ultimate form that any gang takes at any particular time also depends on outside factors that need to be brought into view, including the nature of its relationship to activist groups, politicians, patrons, and other parts of the community.

In the language of Albert DiChiara and Russell Chabot (chapter 5), gangs exist on several continua that include not only a range of activities but also commitments to specific goals. The authors point out that a range of goals, criminal and noncriminal, emerges naturally from these types of organizations. The relationship among disparate goals and between goals and means is neither straightforward nor fixed. That is, gangs will find both criminal and noncriminal ways to achieve goals that are criminal, noncriminal, or some mixture of the two. The important fact is that gang formation is lucid and reflects local concerns. To the same extent, the group must be able to elicit some degree of support, or at least sympathy, from the community. Thus the formulation of goals often involves extensive planning, depending on the nature of the group, its goals, and its relationship to the community organizations and leaders. Inasmuch as goals involve attempts to develop and coordinate resources and establish consensus, they can be referred to as "projects." The group that the authors describe, Los Solidos, one of the biggest gangs in Hartford, sees itself as a political organization, "albeit one that saw fit to use criminal activities to further the interests of its members." Unlike earlier times when political boss machines operated on elaborate systems of patronage, the authors point out, gangs now have reason to be suspicious of the motives of politicians. In its literature, the Los Solidos gang depicts politicians variously as self-interested, inept, corrupt, and "sell-outs." At the same time, it maintains alliances with certain community leaders who occasionally serve in the role of "patrons." (The "frame" with the greatest resonance between members and outsiders is that of "institutional failure." Thus, in the Los Solidos handbook, a future worth striving for involves members opening up businesses, becoming doctors and lawyers, and broadening the self-help function—erasing the distinction between the group and the community.) Overwhelming pressures of the street undermine the gang's ability and desire to become more involved in the civic affairs of the community.

Juan Esteva (chapter 6) also examines the relationship between gangs and politics, focusing on the development of "street activism" among one of the largest and most sophisticated gangs in the country—the Bloods. This research project takes place around a series of events that occurred during the spring of 1999. The New York ALKQN was locked in a feud with a newly created Bloods faction, which appeared to be the aggressor. This created a dilemma for the Kings, because any attempt at retaliation would discredit their claim that they were no longer a gang. But the situation seemed only to get worse. In response, the Kings established contact with the west-coast Bloods and asked for assistance to negotiate a peace treaty with the group in New York. One of the leaders, Bloodhound, was flown in for that purpose. With the cooperation of Bloodhound, Esteva was introduced to a world in which politics and gangsterism are closely related. As the author points out, many of the older gang members and ex-members see themselves as "street activists." The important facts, in this respect, are that the gang subculture contains elements that support politicization, and that a certain authenticity and moral legitimacy is granted to reformers who have paid their dues in those organizations. Indeed, all of Esteva's respondents appear to have developed a political consciousness in prison, where they were exposed to political texts and politically oriented associations like the Black Muslims. The effectiveness of such activists is also predicated on their ability to go where others cannot. A wide range of political objectives and strategies are documented in this study.

GANGS, AGENCY, AND AT-RISK YOUTH

In the entire literature on gangs, there is hardly an attempt to explore the spiritual dimension and practices of gang membership (the exceptions are

Campbell 1984 and Conquergood 1993). Yet, as Luis Barrios points out in chapter 7, a substantial part of the culture of the ALKQN involves interpretations of spiritual texts and religious belief systems. Those texts circumscribe rituals as well as, over the last few years, the formulation and legitimation of specific political objectives. In addition, King Tone, the leader, has a Pentecostal background and the ability to deliver "sermons" to large crowds of people in which religion and politics are seamlessly interwoven. Barrios approaches his analysis of the texts, rituals, symbols, and imagery of the group through the framework of liberation theology and argues for a reading of the group as an example of popular cultural religion.

Chapter 8 provides ethnographic data on two groups in New York City, the ALKQN and the Asociación Ñeta, focusing on members' quest for individual and collective empowerment alongside attempts to incorporate alternative forms of learning in their rituals and routine activities. David Brotherton examines the evolution of these groups from violent street gangs into what he calls "street organizations"—groups that are engaged in recovering, appropriating, and creating social and political spaces without becoming political groups in any formal sense. He notes that few gang studies have paid attention to education as a source of consciousness development, rather than simply a tool of socialization and social control. Contrary to the assumption that gang members are opposed to learning anything other than delinquency, he finds that, in the case of the ALKQN and the Ñetas, they maintain both formal and informal pedagogical structures and practices while placing a premium on the pursuit of "knowledge" that they consider practical or liberating.

WOMEN AND GANGS

Although much has been written about gangs, there are only a handful of published studies on female gangs and the role of females in gangs generally. Consequently, not enough is known about why they join and in what ways their participation differs from that of their male counterparts. As the authors in part 4 point out, many of the reasons for joining are the same—namely, camaraderie, protection, and making money. But unique circumstances, particularly family backgrounds, dependent children, and the various forms of harassment and discrimination they must regularly confront are clearly manifest in the decisions and activities of the female gang member.

Dana Nurge's study (chapter 9) of female gangs and "cliques" in Boston takes up the debate of whether female gangs are becoming more like male gangs because of loosening societal restrictions on women—the so-called liberation hypothesis—or whether instead contemporary female gangs resemble their predecessors and are merely treated differently than before, when masculine bias in the criminal justice system was stronger. In Nurge's study, female gangs appear to provide tangible benefits that often include the ability to make money and help with child rearing. Ultimately, the author concludes that the dichotomy applied to female gang members is a false one. Those members cannot be described as liberated as long as they are forced to raise children without sufficient social and economic resources. Nor can it be said that they are mere appendages of men and male gangs.

Many of these findings are confirmed by David Brotherton and Camila Salazar-Atias in their chapter on the Latin Queens in New York (chapter 10). The authors examine the motives for joining and the extent to which those motives are realized in the organization. Their study begins in 1996, shortly after the Queens had started to expand and gain a greater role within the group. Many of the women in this study were found to have suffered high levels of abuse and neglect both from their families and from the state's multilayered child welfare system. They appeared to turn to the ALKQN for social, emotional, and economic support—something that provided a strong impetus for the eventual semiautonomous development of the Latin Queens within the organization.

GANGS AND SOCIAL CONTROL

Social policies designed to remedy the "gang problem" are increasingly justified by the claim that the problem is getting worse and more drastic measures are necessary. An increasingly popular policy initiative, as Loren Siegel points out in chapter 11, is the use of gang injunctions. In this essay, the author traces the history of injunctions to vagrancy laws, which, in earlier times, were aimed directly at the criminalization of poverty. The problem with such laws, from a legal standpoint, is that an exception to constitutionally protected rights, including the right to assembly, is made for gang members. From a broader social policy standpoint, they do not appear to be very effective. Rather, the appearance of increased safety from gangs is bought at the cost of engagement. This is to say that such laws work to create pariah groups—not only to reinforce the status of pariah, as is normally the case with antigang laws. For instance, the antigang injunction law enacted in Chicago a few years ago (which was eventually struck down after being challenged by the ACLU) made it a criminal act subject to prosecution for one to talk to a "known" gang member. This would potentially include researchers, journalists, and ministers, among others who have legitimate reasons for such talk. Siegel also demonstrates that "injunction" laws have historically been used typically to work around existing laws and constitutional rights, rather than reinforce them. For example, in the 1930s, after the passage of the Labor Relations Act, companies issued injunctions. Now, after a number of Supreme Court decisions that serve to extend numerous civil rights to marginalized urban populations, many city governments are apparently looking for a way around them.

Phillip Kassel (chapter 12) examines the policy of differential treatment and segregation of gang members in prison. Like other policies that target gang members, there are issues of effectiveness and constitutionality. But, here, there are also administrative and procedural problems that are deemed insurmountable without significant changes in the current system. The most significant problem is shown to be the misidentification of gang members. Because there is little engagement with gang members, identification tends to be impressionistic, lacking uniform criteria and oversight procedures. Kassel also points out that the perception of unfairness heightens antagonisms between guards and prisoners, which makes violence more likely. In addition, it creates a situation in which inmates can violate regulations unintentionally, resulting in unequal treatment and further segregation. For instance, one common stipulation for prisoners that Kassel mentions is nonassociation with "known" gang members. This might make sense if prisoners had some way of knowing for certain who the gang members are—which is more difficult than it seems, given that most gang members in prison are deemed to be loosely associated rather than "hard-core" members.

GANG PHOTOJOURNALISM

As the contributors to part 6 demonstrate, gang photography is not only a form of knowledge, it is also a political art form. Whereas photographic images of gangs are often dramatic, the photographer has to make calculated decisions about what to focus on from a stream of disparate activities and how to contextualize "the image." This puts the photographer in the role of the ethnographer. But the dramatic image revolves around stereotype—precisely what the ethnographer seeks to subvert by going beneath the surface to capture something essential but not obvious. In addition, the end product is very different, because the photographic image carries an aura of authenticity and appears self-explanatory. The seeming obviousness of certain images of gangs is problematic to the extent to which the goal in producing them is dramatic effect rather than an attempt to address their complexity.

As Richard Rodríguez says (chapter 13), very few images stick in the mind as much as that of the young Latino gang member with a menacing look and a gun. This image, endlessly repeated, takes on an iconic status that also affects the way gang members look at themselves. A particular "look" is cultivated that instills fear in the mind of the observer. But the gang member presents a different self to different observers. For example, he is relaxed with his friends. He is reverential to parents. And he "poses" for pictures with an attitude that demonstrates "self-respect" and demands "respect from others." A different kind of image is produced by photographers who get to know the gang. In this case, "poses" are more representative of the range of attitudes and activities that constitute life in the gang. This approach serves not only to humanize the subject of photography, but also to capture something real.

In chapter 14, award-winning photojournalist Donna DeCesare provides an elaborate series of photos of Salvadoran gang members on the west coast. This is accompanied by written text that contextualizes the imagery in the Salvadoran civil war, which produced a mass exodus to the United States. Thousands of children of refugees who fled for their lives often found themselves joining the Mara Salvatrucha (MS-13) and Eighteenth Street gangs. In the early 1990s, a policy of mass deportation for gang members convicted of crimes brought American gang culture to El Salvador. Within very little time, "acculturated" members began to appear on the west coast and eventually the east. DeCesare's essay and photos illustrate the many sides of this phenomenon, focusing on the life and death of two brothers whose mother brought them to the United States after being threatened by government forces as a result of her husband's membership with the guerilla movement.

In chapter 15, Steve Hart and David Brotherton provide a visual depiction of the ALKQN during its reform years in New York City. In contrast to most media images of the time, which either cast doubt on the group's self-reform goals or reported its efforts at political engagement with a mixture of paternalism and cynicism, the authors show members of the group as inspired, complex social agents. Focusing on group rituals, organizational activities, and catalytic moments in the group's history, they provide a sense of the complexity behind this subcultural phenomenon that fascinated youth both locally and nationwide in the late 1990s.

REFERENCES

Campbell, Anne. 1984. *The Girls in the Gang.* New York: Basil Blackwell.

Conquergood, Dwight. 1993. "Homeboys and Hoods: Gang Communication and Cultural Space." In *Group Communication in Context: Studies of Natural Groups,* edited by Larry Frey. Hillsdale, N.J.: Lawrence Erlbaum.

Hunter, Albert, ed. 1974. *Symbolic Communities: The Persistence and Change of Chicago's Local Communities.* Chicago and London: The University of Chicago Press.

Shaw, Clifford R., and Henry McKay. 1931. "Social Factors in Juvenile Delinquency." National Commission on Law Observation and Enforcement, no. 13. *Report on the Causes of Crime.* Vol. 2. Washington, D.C.: U.S. Government Printing Office.

Thrasher, F. 1927. *The Gang: A Study of 1,313 Gangs in Chicago.* Chicago: Chicago University Press.

PART 1
THEORY AND
METHODOLOGY

1

A NOTE ON SOCIAL THEORY AND THE AMERICAN STREET GANG

SUDHIR VENKATESH

Theory in street gang research continues to be defined by the human ecology paradigm, a perspective on urban social relationships formulated in the mid-twentieth century by social scientists at the University of Chicago. At that time, the urban gang was one of several agent provocateurs that researchers identified as deleteriously affecting the process of social integration: Social scientists understood gangs, to some degree, as emblematic of disenfranchised members of European ethnic groups and southern black migrants who were seeking their future in the industrial city. Gangs were publicly manifest signs that communities were poorly organized—specifically, "socially disorganized" beyond the capacities of their local institutions of control and integration.

The character of gang activity has changed significantly since that time. Apart from a period of fertile research in the postwar era, in which social psychology was imported into the study of gang activity, there have been few consistent attempts to theorize the novel aspects of gang activity in the post-

Fordist age.[1] For that matter, researchers have also not adequately explained why certain aspects of street gangs have remained relatively unchanged despite a continuously changing urban social order. Two modifications are briefly suggested here that will be necessary as the entrepreneurial, political, and social activities of modern gangs are analyzed. First, the paradigm of deviance needs to be altered in order to take into account the cultural and political aspects of contemporary gang activity; specifically, conceptualizations of the social practices of gang members should move beyond the adaptation model that remains in place and see gang activity as contingent and meaningful, perhaps even resistant on occasion. Second, the gang qua organization is not a monolithic entity; within any gang there may be considerable diversity of opinion and expectation, and any single individual may be pulled by multiple ideologies and motivations.

THE POVERTY OF THE DEVIANT ADAPTATIONS

In *Islands in the Street*, a study of thirty-seven street gangs in three American cities, Martin Jankowski (1991) argues that gangs have been incorrectly conflated with contexts of poverty, thereby limiting the range of analytic materials that might be brought to bear on them. In his own work, Jankowski incorporates theories of organizational behavior to account for the internal relations among members, the variations in gang activity within and across cities, and the impact of organizational structure on the gangs' relationship to their "local and larger" neighborhood. Understandably, with its focus on breadth, *Islands in the Street* did not fully pursue each topic for any single gang; nevertheless, it is an important document that has helped to push the field of street gang research away from the dogma of criminology.

Why is criminology limited for an understanding of gangs? Are not urban gangs criminal entities by most legal definitions? Although many social groups may adhere to legal and scholarly definitions of "gang," the process by which appellations become attached is neither value free nor politically neutral. Peggy Sanday's (1990) research on American fraternities has raised the thorny question, "why are fraternities not considered to be gangs?" In legal cases, judges and prosecutors have overlooked fraternal misconduct as youthful aberrations, and such groups have been absolved from possible qualification as collective actors intent on promoting criminal activity. Yet examples abound that lend credence to the notion that fraternities exist to perpetuate social transgressions; if this sounds alarmist, one should consider the weight of fraternal pedagogy—sometimes literally in manifestos and charters—around issues such as theft, vandalism, sexual conquest (read: harassment) and the imbibing of alcohol (read: underage drinking). The specter of labeling theory haunts the field of sociology of deviance (of which criminology is a subfield), and scholars—the exception being Dwight Conquergood—have not adequately applied the lessons of Erving Goffman, Aaron Cicourel, Howard Becker, and others who studied the organization of deviance, in their study of the gang.

Based in the human ecology paradigm, the sociologists who pioneered the study of deviance (e.g., Shaw and McKay; Thrasher) tended to see such activity as a community-level process that is rooted in the relative capacities of individuals, families, and organizations to transmit values (deterring behavior) and sanction behavior (transgressing values). With respect to gangs, this dual social control process, through the unspecified notion of "values," was intended to deter gang formation. This basic proposition is laudable and has yielded much insight into the behavior of the gang. Yet socially destabilizing processes—for example, poor employment opportunities, diminished political clout, or lapsing city services—rendered this theory of delinquency and this comparative index of neighborhood capacities for delinquency prevention largely irrelevant, because neighborhoods differed in terms of their basic material resources.

To use an extreme example, a community with no police enforcement will probably have lower rates of criminal activity than one with a disproportionately high police presence. To offer another example: In the sixties, a broad range of youth-based groups were labeled by social scientists as gangs and deviants—groups that ranged from the Blackstone Rangers street gang in Chicago, to the Black Panther Party, to youth chapters of the Congress of Racial Equality. For the most part, these researchers did not concede the political dimensions of these actions; instead they accounted for the rising tide of youth anger and street-based mobilization somewhat myopically as "social deviance" (Marable 1988:101)—that is, as collective dysfunctionality. Yielding no quarrel, Marable remarked somewhat sardonically that even the great "rebellions" of the late 1960s were not enough for "sociologists and politicians . . . to confront their own theoretical inadequacies" and thereby suspend their "social deviance" perspective (101). To claim that a single community is disorganized would miss the mark if the area in question does not have equitable resources and services with which to respond to delinquent and criminal activity. To claim that an actor in the community is "deviant" may be valid from the point of view that his or her action flouts social codes or laws, but it fails to capture both the very real inequity that may exist among the communities as well as the numerous nondelinquent aspects of the activity (e.g., resource distribution, political resistance, articulation of a belief or ideal). Because such disparities exist among contemporary urban communities, one should apply the paradigm of social deviance with caution.

Ironically, since its initial formulation, important dimensions of the deviance perspective have not been retained in contemporary scholarship on the gang. Most important, gang researchers pay relatively little attention to community-level processes that have an impact on gang activity, where once this was the norm. Few studies exist—Jankowski (1991) is an exception—that examine the social relationships of gang members with parents, schoolteachers, church leaders, social service agency directors, and so on. The consequence has been to dilute some of the most impressive contributions of the early human ecological theorists: specifically, the model of social control that signaled the power of the community institutions to mediate the effects (and likelihood) of social delinquency has not been central in contemporary research (exceptions include Sampson and Groves 1989; Spergel 1995).

In the last two decades, several researchers have developed innovative techniques to analyze the historical novelty of contemporary gang activity and to reconcile structural constraints with individual decision making. They have drawn on critical Marxist theories of cultural reproduction and resistance theory to highlight aspects of street gang activity that are not fully grasped by the categories of "crime" and "delinquency." Philippe Bourgois's (1995) ethnographic study of entrepreneurial gang members' attempts to withdraw from the "street culture" into that of the "mainstream" demonstrates that they are perpetually blocked—so street-based drug dealing becomes the only option to continue earning money. Bourgois is careful not to claim that his informants are passive victims, and part of the blockage is motivated by their own identities: the streets become the preferred sites for those informants in which to realize ideals of masculinity, because they consider office work as domestic or emasculated labor.

Bourgois builds on an established field of cultural studies research, emanating from the British Isles. Known popularly as the "British school" of

cultural studies, this research paradigm was noteworthy for applying semi-
otic analysis to studies of ostensibly deviant processes: Like ethnomethod-
ologists in America, but with the verve of Marxism, the researchers demonstrated that politically motivated (and charged) processes often labeled
certain activities as "deviant" in order to deemphasize their political or cultural dimensions; "cultural studies" scholars paid attention to the range of
beliefs and ideals of gang members and at-risk youth in order to highlight
the complex aspirations that informed youth practice. Whereas eth-
nomethodologists tended to study social institutions from the perspective of
microinteraction, the cultural studies scholars made compelling arguments
at the macrosocial level: They suggested that certain groups and power blocs
may have structural interests in portraying the behavior of minority youth
as social deviance; they showed why certain deviant activities (e.g., property theft—economically motivated crime) will continually be reproduced in
a capitalist society.

One of the insights that derives from Bourgois's work concerns the conceptualization of everyday practice among street gangs. By paying attention
to the aspirations of his actors, Bourgois is able to mediate the relationship
of social structure and individual agency in a way that respects the contin-
gency and nuance of human social practice. Most gang research, from
Thrasher to the "underclass school" of Hagedorn (1988) and Taylor (1990),
has viewed forms of gang activity as responses to structural constraints—
that is, as "adaptations" or "survival strategies" in contexts of limited resources. The argument that persons innovate when normative paths and institutional resources are not present is plausible, but can often be too
mechanistic. For example, hardship cannot by itself explain why a particular mode of gang organization arises at a specific time nor why it is put into
place by a particular group; for example, both Latino and African American
groups could "adapt" to poor labor force conditions by selling narcotics, but
research clearly shows that Latino gangs do not actively take this path
(Block and Block 1993). As Bourgois (1995, and Paul Willis before him in
Learning to Labor, 1977) demonstrates, individuals' responses to poverty are
mediated by their own ideologies and systems of meaning that orient their
action. The adaptation paradigm tends to ignore the cultural aspects of
gang activity—that is, the "totality of signs and relations" (Comaroff and
Comaroff 1997) that shape gang members' participation in this economic
sphere. Whereas one would expect Bourgois's informants to work diligent-

ly at their office jobs given that there are few other alternatives, this is not the case: They are in fact not adapting in pace with scholarly expectation, but resisting the compunction to respond to their structural predicament in a predictable way. Office work is "woman's work," so they prefer instead to work on the streets and, in their perspective, successfully retain their male identity. Not only Bourgois, but Jankowski (1991) and Padilla (1992) both make clear that involvement in gang-related economic activities is motivated by expectations of future gain, by perceptions of one's cultural capital in mainstream and illegitimate labor markets, and by one's engagement with socially dominant ideologies that structure material gain as well as conspicuous consumption.

DIVERSITY WITHIN THE GANG

In the postwar era, Albert Cohen, James Short, and Fred Strotdbeck (and others influenced by social-psychology and subculture theory) attempted to document the diversity within the gang. Their findings, elegantly phrased in terms of taxonomies of ideal types of delinquent propensities, suggested that within any gang there could be competing and entirely conflicting understandings and expectations of gang activity circulating among the members (see Fagan 1996 for an excellent discussion of variation within a gang). Their crucial insight has been lost in much of contemporary scholarship in which the gang may be depicted as a monolithic entity, with a single-mindedness of purpose and outlook. Taking the insight of the postwar researchers into the contemporary period, much of the entrepreneurial activity of gangs must be seen as a social achievement, on many different levels: Individuals must adhere to the purpose of the group as a moneymaking enterprise, even if this conflicts with other social or psychological benefits they derive; the group must successfully balance the interests of the individual in order to create cohesive action; and, like other organizations, it must take care to handle exigencies of leadership coup d'états, personality conflicts, and so on. The most fertile and destabilizing conflict is between the principle that the gang must act like a "business" (i.e., the corporatist ethos) and "collectivist ideologies" (Padilla 1992) such as "family" that prioritize the social support and peer affirmation that the gang can offer. Collective action, then, is a contingent process in which agents with differing conceptions of the gang's commercial activity must either reach a working consensus or a proportion of the membership must concede to the wishes of their leader(s)—a process carefully documented in Jankowski's (1991) research.

Scholars have paid relatively less attention to the internal conflicts, expectations, and preference structures within any single gang member. The pull of different ideologies may also be located within the same person so that the system of predispositions that orient action—"habitus" in Bourdieu's terminology—may reflect varying and possibly discordant cultural structures (1977:87). That is, not only will the gang as a social group display variance in terms of the motives and interests of its members, but any one individual affiliated with the group may have different reasons for investing time and energy. And, these may change over time, especially over the life course as youth mature and move in and through other social institutions. This basic principle of sociological reasoning, the hallmark in life-course research, has been missing in street gang scholarship. The methodological reasons are not surprising: Research contact with gangs is difficult, and to create lasting ties that would enable longitudinal research to develop is an even greater challenge. Few have been able to follow gangs over time. Theoretically, the factors may be traced to the lack of historical perspective in the study of deviance in general. Although the communities in which gang members operate have been seen as changing, declining, eviscerating, and so on, less often has the group been studied in terms of its own changes (or those of its members). In Jürgen Habermas's terms, change in urban poverty scholarship in general, and gang research in particular, tends to be perceived as "systemic integration," wherein macrosocial institutions are in flux; individual, group, or community change (i.e., change at the level of "lifeworld") is seen as a response to systemic movements instead of possessing its own generative dynamics.

Even within a successful drug-selling gang there may be divergent beliefs held by members; some will prefer social activities and participate in economic activities minimally and reluctantly, while others will try to detour the gang away from recreational pursuits and into new markets and new underground economies. In Padilla's (1992) terms, "family" and "business" will create tensions among the membership to which leaders must be attentive in order to ensure group cohesion over time. Among Chicago's African American gangs, there are clear distinctions between the expectations of members acculturated into street gang life in the late seventies and those who arose in the mid-eighties. Among the former, gang-based entrepreneurialism is often a sidebar; an occasional remedy to the loss of income in the legitimate labor market. The more-steady benefit of the gang is in terms of social support and peer-group affirmation. For the younger cohorts whose labor market horizons have been fully eclipsed by the lack of adequate blue-collar or manufacturing work, "gangland" is a viable employer, a competitor with the menial service-sector jobs available throughout the city. Their voices indicate repeatedly that the possibility for exit out of gang entrepreneurial activities is not merely a "legit job" per se, but one that has the possibility to push them down a road of mobility. In other words, the true test of legitimate labor market opportunities is whether they offer the potential of "career" development, not merely income. While they wait, they are immersed in gang entrepreneurial structures in which such long-term prospects are perceptible, albeit the chances of any single individual "making it" to the top of the food chain are quite low (see Levitt and Venkatesh 2000).

NOTE

1. Post-Fordism is, at root, the crisis in capitalist accumulation that manifested after World War II—specifically after 1968.

REFERENCES

Block, C. B., and R. Block. 1993. "Street Gang Crime in Chicago." In *Research in Brief*. Washington, D.C.:National Institute of Justice, Office of Justice Programs, U.S. Department of Justice.

Bourdieu, P. 1977. *Outline of a Theory of Practice*. Cambridge: Cambridge University Press.

Bourgois, P. 1995. *In Search of Respect: Selling Crack in El Barrio*. Cambridge: Cambridge University Press.

Comaroff, Jean, and John Comaroff. 1997. Vol. 2 of *Of Revelation and Revolution*. Chicago: University of Chicago Press.

Fagan, J. 1996. "Gangs, Drugs, and Neighborhood Change." In *Gangs in America*, 2d ed., 39–74. Edited by C. Ronald Huff. Newbury Park: Sage.

Hagedorn, J. 1988. *People Folks: Gangs, Crime, and the Underclass in a Rustbelt City*. Chicago: Lake View Press.

Jankowski, M. S. 1991. *Islands in the Street: Gangs and American Urban Society*. Berkeley: University of California Press.

Levitt, Steven, and Sudhir Venkatesh. 2000. "The Financial Activities of a Street Gang." *Quarterly Journal of Economics* vol. 115, no. 3 (August): 755–789.

Marable, M. 1988. *Race, Reform, and Rebellion: The Second Reconstruction in Black America, 1945–1982*. Jackson: University of Mississippi Press.

Padilla, F. 1992. *The Gang as an American Enterprise*. New Brunswick, N.J.: Rutgers University Press.

Sampson, R. J., and W. Byron Groves. 1989. "Community Structure and Crime: Testing Social Disorganization Theory." *American Journal of Sociology* 94 (4): 774–802.

Sanday, Peggy Reeves. 1990. *Fraternity Gang Rape: Sex, Brotherhood, and Privilege on Campus*. New York: New York University Press.

Spergel, I. A. 1995. *The Youth Gang Problem: A Community Approach*. New York: Oxford University Press.

Taylor, C. S. 1990. *Dangerous Society*. East Lansing: Michigan State University.

Willis, Paul. 1977. *Learning to Labor: How Working Class Kids Get Working Class Jobs*. New York: Columbia University Press.

2

TOWARD A TYPOLOGY OF CONTEMPORARY MEXICAN AMERICAN YOUTH GANGS

AVELARDO VALDEZ

There have been increases in street violence, drug trafficking, homicides, organized criminal activities, and use of sophisticated weaponry among delinquent youth during the 1980s and 1990s. Most of these activities have been associated with African American, Latino, and Asian youth gangs in large metropolitan areas of the United States. In an attempt to understand the extent and nature of those gangs, researchers have proposed a variety of classifications. However, Spergel states, "Gang typologies and classifications suggest a bewildering array, complexity, and variability of structures, purposes, and behavioral characteristics of gangs, with these dimensions not clearly identified or interrelated" (1995:79).

The purpose of this chapter is to develop a typology of Mexican American gangs within the evolving social context of the Mexican-origin population of the United States. Mexican American gangs are assumed to be similar to those described in research conducted in previous decades (Heller 1966; Moore 1978; and Vigil 1988). Generally, these gangs were found to be territorially oriented, spread over multiple generations, and embedded in a "cholo" lifestyle. As a result, perceptions of contemporary gangs are often based on these studies, without awareness of the wide differences and diversity that exist today. This situation makes it difficult for researchers to distinguish among the variety of existing Mexican American gangs, and to make valid comparisons of gangs across ethnic, racial, and subcultural groups.

This classification or typology is important in that it provides a structural framework by which to analyze the diversity of Mexican American gangs. This diversity is linked to the relative growth of this ethnic group, its young age distribution, and the increased economic decline of its urban poor. The appearance of gangs in Mexican American neighborhoods is often related to increases in street violence, juvenile crime, and illegal drug markets. Yet we understand little about the types of gangs that are emerging in Mexican Americans communities and the roles of its members. Moreover, there is a scarcity of information on how these gangs are integrated into existing criminal networks. Ultimately, knowing more about the variety of gangs, membership roles, and activities provides the opportunity for policy makers to develop programs that may divert gang members from a life trajectory that often yields hardened adult criminals.

This study presents a typology of gangs derived from a community-based research project among twenty-six active Mexican American gangs in San Antonio, Texas. Five specific research dimensions are used to develop this classification: illegal activities, gang organization, drug use patterns, adult influences, and violence. In the tradition of the Chicago School of community field studies, this typology is based on qualitative data derived from actual interaction with the study subjects. This community field study method, discussed more extensively in the methodology section, allowed for the discovery of the research dimensions used in the construction of the typology. This methodology allows us to acquire an understanding that goes beyond that of most studies on gangs, which are often more narrow in their methodological approaches.

CONTEMPORARY GANG TYPES AND ORGANIZATIONS

Researchers have used a variety of social factors for classifying and typing youth gangs (Fagan 1989; Taylor 1990; Jankowski 1991; Hagedorn 1994; Spergel 1995). Some have classified gangs according to the group's major activity. Categories include social gangs that are extensions of delinquent peer groups formed in ethnic communities, such as the gangs that thrived during the 1950s and 1960s (Yablonsky 1962). Cultural gangs place greater importance on activities that emphasize styles of dress, speech, gestures, and tattoos, often with a subcultural or ethnic context. Delinquent gangs focus on the commission of delinquent activities that reinforce identity and solidarity. A distinction is often made between these types of gangs and more criminally centered gangs. There also exist contemporary gangs that are primarily party gangs that are involved in various levels of delinquent activity and drug and alcohol use (Taylor 1990). Brotherton's (1999) recent study of New York Puerto Rican gangs argues that in the 1990s, the gangs he studied "began to transform themselves into street organizations or cultural associations for self and community empowerment."

Other researchers have classified gangs according to their level of organization (Jankowski 1991; Hagedorn 1994; and Spergel 1995). Organizationally, gangs have been found to vary from the loosely knit to the highly hierarchical. These gangs may have a discernable leadership or one that is highly diffuse. Building upon the earlier work of the New York City Youth Board, Jankowski (1991) developed a gang organizational model that included the vertical/horizontal, the horizontal/commission, and the influential type of gang. Knox (1991) proposes a more dynamic organizational model that begins with an emergent gang that crystallizes into a formal gang organization with satellite units, goals, stable leadership, and diverse sources of criminal income. Taylor's (1990) and Padilla's (1992) studies in Detroit and Chicago, respectively, identified "organized" or "corporate" gangs that are characterized by elaborate and cohesive leadership structures. These types of gangs develop a formal organizational structure to strengthen and defend their economic interests. There are also gangs that are organizationally unstable and tend to engage in more impulsive behavior. Both Taylor and Padilla argue that these groups will be more prone to erratic, impulsive, and violent behavior.

Exemplifying the same selective research focus, researchers have categorized gangs according to their respective stages of development or organizational history (Spergel 1995). This requires the classification of gangs on a continuum that may span from the gang's early formation to its decline. Gangs have also been categorized by their level of permanency, and/or their transitory nature. Differences in types of membership may also be a criterion used to identify gangs with memberships that may include original gangsters (older members, veterans), regulars (stable members), marginal members, rascals or "pee-wees"(young members), and "wanna-bes" (potential gang members). Membership may also be multigenerational, especially for gangs historically associated with specific neighborhoods (Moore 1978).

Gangs can also be grouped by the nature and degree of criminality, such as the seriousness of the offenses. The primary illegal activity of some gangs is centered on drug selling and trafficking, either collectively or individually (Fagan 1989; Taylor 1990). There are gangs whose criminality is focused on other organized criminal activities such as selling stolen vehicles, burglaries, and dealing in stolen property. Others are extensively involved in more violent offenses such as assault, drive-by shooting, car jacking, and homicide (Fagan 1989; Anderson 1990). Many territorial gangs commit low-level delinquent acts similar to the gangs of earlier decades. In these "territorial" gangs, criminality is linked to maintaining control of neighborhood and turf, which they defend from outsiders and territorial adversaries (Fagan 1996).

Gangs also may be typed according to the extensiveness of rules and rituals. Some gangs place high importance on monikers, colors, symbols, and hand signs, which are used for self-identification. Although this type of gang may be involved in illegal activities such as drug dealing, its primary goal is to protect the gang's honor, turf, and solidarity (Spergel 1995).

There are several consistent patterns across these various types of gangs. Although substance-use patterns may vary among gangs, almost all have engaged in some level of drug and alcohol use. Violence is also consistent among gangs. The extent and nature of the violence varies depending on the status of the gang. Most gangs will use some form of violence to protect their interests, honor, or turf. Most are engaged in some form of drug dealing; however, this varies by locale and ethnicity. One fact that emerges is that although many gangs are involved in drug dealing, they are not the major importers of drugs into the communities (Kornblum 1993).

Many contemporary gangs in large urban areas have a high propensity for violence committed with sophisticated firearms. One of the distinguishing features of these new gangs is that they seem more disconnected from com-

munity-based family networks and sanctions. This phenomenon may be related to the changing economic status of many urban minority communities
(Wilson 1996).

MINORITY GANGS: AFRICAN AMERICANS, ASIANS, AND LATINOS

Minority group members make up an overwhelming number of existing
gangs due to the large proportion of them living in communities characterized by unemployment, poverty, welfare dependency, single-headed households, and other socioeconomic characteristics associated with the underclass.[1] However, minority gangs are often distinct from each other,
reflecting differences in economic situation, social status, generations, and
cultural characteristics. Historically, African Americans have been more
negatively affected by the nation's economic transformations than other minority groups (Wilson 1987). As a result, more street gangs of greater variation have emerged in the black community compared to others. Taylor
(1990) argues that most black gangs are geared toward a "corporate structure" organization whose main focus is making money illegally. This may be
due to the extreme economic isolation of African American inner-city communities in which underground economies thrive (Wilson 1999). Asian
gangs are distinct in that they are linked to the semilegal businesses involved
in criminal-gain activities such as extortion and heroin distribution (Chin
1995). Often, these Asian gangs are associated with adult gangs such as
Tongs, Triad groups, and other Asian community organizations.

Latino gangs in the United States generally comprise Puerto Ricans,
Central Americans, and Mexican Americans. They have distinctive characteristics associated with the special circumstances of the populations from
which their membership is drawn. The Puerto Rican population is concentrated in northeastern and midwestern urban areas severely affected by deindustrialization. The socioeconomic conditions experienced by Puerto Ricans have forced many gangs to focus on the drug trade for economic
survival. In this sense, Puerto Rican gangs are similar in structure and activities to those in the African American community. Central American
gangs consist of recent immigrants residing primarily in multiethnic and
racial urban areas in Southern California. These gangs are more territorial
and are less involved in organized criminal activities than are other ethnic

gangs. Most of their activities revolve around protecting themselves from other ethnic gangs and youth in their neighborhoods.

MEXICAN AMERICAN GANGS

The majority of research on Latino gangs has focused on Mexican Americans in the Southwest (Spergel 1995). Mexican Americans have a long gang tradition that is focused in Southern California. Many of the street gangs in Southern California have existed within particular localities as extended families or clans for three or more generations (Moore 1978; Vigil 1988). Some of these gangs have evolved into highly organized criminal networks engaged in heroin distribution (Moore 1991). Other gangs have evolved into adult prison gangs whose illegal activities now extend beyond correctional institutions. The majority, however, were territorially based gangs concerned with protecting their turfs from rival Mexican American gangs. A distinguishing characteristic of early Mexican American gangs was their connection to family networks and community-based institutions.

Chicano gangs are distinct from other ethnic gangs in their style of dress, language, gestures, tattoos, and graffiti. Vigil (1988) claims that the Chicano gang lifestyle is embedded in and representative of the larger *cholo* subculture to which many Chicano youth subscribe. This *cholo* subculture has its roots in the "pachuco" lifestyle of the 1940s and 1950s. The *cholo* lifestyle is related to what has been described as "defiant individualism" (Jankowski 1991), *carnalismo* (brotherhood), and machismo (masculinity) (Vigil 1988). Many Mexican American youths outside the gang arena adopt the *cholo* subculture. Unfortunately, the adoption of such styles by these nongang youths invites the gang member label from school and law enforcement officials. This parallels urban Black "gangsta" styles that are being adopted by mainstream popular youth culture.

During the 1990s, Chicano gangs began to exhibit characteristics that were different from the gangs of earlier periods. Although the gang continues to be territorial and provide an identity, contemporary gangs are associated with increased incidents of episodic and lethal violence such as drive-by shootings. Similar to earlier periods, these gangs are turf oriented, and are known for using more lethal violence to protect their territory (Sanders 1994). Other Chicano gangs are involved in organized criminal activities such as drug dealing—often in association with adult gangs. Moreover, contemporary gangs are more transitory, existing for shorter periods of time than earlier gangs.

The Mexican-origin population, during this period, was experiencing declines in economic status similar to African Americans in large urban areas such as Los Angeles, Houston, San Francisco-Oakland, and Chicago. The "concentration effects" of increased male joblessness, welfare dependency, single-headed households, and decreases in governmental services have had a devastating impact on poor and working-class segments of the Mexican American population. Among the effects was the loss of the Mexican American middle class, which fled to higher-status neighborhoods and suburbs leaving traditional barrios to poor Mexican Americans and recent (and impoverished) Mexican and Central American immigrants.

Chicano youth became increasingly marginalized as a result of this economic transformation. Reduced economic opportunities forced many youths and young adults to turn to the underground economy as a means of material subsistence. During the 1980s and 1990s, a greater proportion of these youths was drawn to criminal activity associated with street gangs and the attractiveness and resources associated with gang enterprises, especially those associated with drug dealing.

METHODOLOGY

The study upon which this article is based examined the epidemiology of violence and drugs among twenty-six Mexican American gangs. This three-year study extended the community field studies approach suggested in works by Moore (1978), Hagedorn (1994), and Akins and Beschner (1980). This approach consists of conducting field observations, interviews, and interacting on a day-to-day basis with the subject population. Much of the data presented in this chapter, however, is based on 150 life-history/intensive interviews.

The study was focused on two geographical areas (south and west) of San Antonio. These two areas have the highest concentration of San Antonio's Mexican American population. These areas also have the highest rate of delinquent behavior and Mexican American gang activity (Yin et al. 1996; Valdez and Kaplan 1999). After identification of these areas, community field workers associated with the project began collecting data about distinct communities and neighborhoods. They also began acquainting themselves with gang members and community/neighborhood gatekeepers, and collecting data on key gangs and gang activity. Extensive efforts were made to gain access, entrée, and rapport with these persons (Yin et al. 1996). Due to the delinquent, deviant, criminal, or déclassé nature of some gang activities, it was often difficult to accurately and reliably identify gang members and gain information.Unstructured individual and group interview data were collected as the schedules and routines of fieldworkers permitted.

Fieldwork for the study was largely collected by two indigenous parapro-fessionals who had "privileged access" to these gangs. These workers were able to establish rapport with subjects, which was important in that it en-hanced the researcher's ability to acquire a deeper understanding of the so-cial context of these subjects. After gaining entrée and trust, community field researchers began to collect observational data set in recreational centers, housing projects, downtown areas, gang hangouts, and other public areas, including corner stores and parks. All efforts were made to not rely on insti-tutional agencies or agents of social control (school officials or police) as a means for contact. Given the limited number of field-workers, each com-munity researcher designated his or her own area, contacts, and networks.

CONSTRUCTION OF THE GANG TYPOLOGY

Building upon existing research (Bailey 1994), four classifications of Mexi-can American gangs were constructed from the analysis. The classifications included criminal adult-dependent gangs, criminal non-adult-dependent gangs, barrio-territorial gangs, and transitional gangs. This gang typology is multidimensional and conceptual in that its construction was based on five distinct dimensions or variables. They are: illegal activities, gang organiza-tion, drug-use patterns, adult influences, and violent behavior. These di-mensions were used to distinguish the variation of gangs found in San An-tonio's Mexican American community. This analysis produced four polythetic classes of gangs that share an overall similarity around these di-mensions. What follows is a description of these dimensions as they were applied to the construction of the typology.

ILLEGAL ACTIVITIES

Each gang in this study reported participation in various criminal activities including drug dealing, auto theft, burglary, car jacking, robbery, fencing, and weapon sales. Gangs differed on the basis of whether the illegal activities were controlled by the gang as an organization or more on an individual basis. Organized gangs were identified as having a distinct division of labor that assigned members specific tasks associated with criminal operations. Profits were dispersed according to each member's status, role, and also the needs of the gang. Unlike these organized gangs, other gangs engaged in criminal activity that was more individually based. In some cases, there were groups of individuals, or crews, that functioned as a subset of the gang. In these types of gangs, the gang provided a cover for the activities of the individual or crew. For instance, it provided protection within a physical territory or market in which they were operating. The subset typically kept the profits; however, those members were obligated to contribute to the gang for organizational needs such as the purchase of guns.

GANG ORGANIZATION

The organizational structure was based on type of leadership, hierarchy, and the rules among gangs in this study. The types of gang leadership may range from very diffuse to highly structured (Jankowski 1991). The twenty-six gangs in this study varied regarding the existence and enforcement of rules and regulations, violations and sanctions, cliques and sets, frequency of meetings, collection of money (dues), and division of labor and territory.

DRUG-USE PATTERNS

A third dimension was the extent and nature of each gang's drug-use patterns. On an individual level, they had exceptionally high rates of lifetime use of most controlled substances. For example, the majority had tried marijuana (98 percent), cocaine (90 percent), heroin (57 percent), hallucinogens, and various prescription pills such as Rohypnol, Valium, and Xanax. However, gang members differed on current use patterns by frequency and type of drug. Marijuana was consumed daily by a majority of gang members along with alcohol as part of their everyday routine. There was little variation among gangs on this type of substance use. Cocaine and heroin use and abuse were perceived differently by individual gangs. Some gangs had strict regulations prohibiting the use of heroin, seriously sanctioning members who violated this rule. Sanctions included severe beatings by other members. Other gangs tolerated the use of heroin as long as it did not interfere with the individual's responsibility to the gang. Other gangs generally were known for partying and polydrug use, including cocaine and heroin.

ADULT INFLUENCE

Another characteristic used to construct this typology was the extent to which the gang's illegal activities were adult dependent. The level of dependency on adults influenced the nature of the gangs' illegal activities and organization. Typically, those types of gangs that closely associated with adults displayed higher levels of organization and sophistication with regard to criminality. These gangs were organized more as criminal enterprises than as delinquent groups.

VIOLENCE

Finally, the construction of this typology included the type of violence committed by members of these gangs. Violent incidents were differentiated as purposeful (expressive) versus random (personal) acts of violence. Purposeful violence is planned or premeditated. Such acts were often associated with illegal activities and the customers who refused to pay drug debts. Other acts of violence tended to be more spontaneous and gratuitous, often centered on perceived acts of disrespect. Consideration was also given to the severity of the violence with emphasis on the use of weapons. Attention was paid to the frequency of the violence committed.

GANG TYPOLOGY

CRIMINAL ADULT DEPENDENT

Of the twenty-six gangs in this study, four were identified as *criminal adult dependent*. In these gangs, adults provided access to illegal drugs, weapons, drug-dealing networks, and national and international (Mexican) markets for stolen merchandise. Adults provided other important services such as protection against rival gang members and adult criminals. Drug dealing was this type of gang's major source of income, especially heroin. Relative to other gangs in the community, these gangs are highly organized in that they are based more on a criminal enterprise with a distinct hierarchy and a distinct leadership structure. Heroin use was generally discouraged, although, as the gangs began to deal heroin, many members became addicted. Violence among these types of gangs was more purposeful and revolved around business transactions.

There are two types of adult criminal networks associated with gangs in this community. One type of criminal network consists of relatives of gang members such as fathers, uncles, in-laws, common-law relations and other extended-family members. In some cases, the adult may have been a long-term neighborhood associate. Another type of criminal adult network consists of organized prison gang members who operate in the Mexican American community. The prison gang controls a significant segment of the heroin market in specific neighborhoods through direct sales. They impose a surcharge on drugs sold by others in areas they control.

THE NINE-BALL CREW: PRISON GANG DEPENDENT The Nine-Ball Crew is located in one of the major housing projects in San Antonio. This gang was distinct from other adult gangs in its direct ties to a Chicano prison gang that controlled the heroin trade in this community. The gang leader's stepfather was one of the heads in the prison gang called the Chicano Brotherhood. The Brotherhood began in the Texas prison system nearly fifteen years ago among Chicano prisoners. Over the last decade, they have established a criminal network outside the prison that controls the heroin trade in San Antonio and other South Texas cities. On the West Side of San Antonio, it is common knowledge among heroin dealers that they must contribute 10 percent of all sales to the Chicano Brotherhood. Over the last few years, they have recruited several youth gangs to sell heroin for them. The control they have over the Nine-Ball Crew is their most successful.

The Nine-Ball Crew is highly organized, with a leader and two second-heads (or lieutenants), a hard-core membership of twenty members, and approximately thirty others. The leader of this gang is Juan, who rules it tightly. He is twenty-three years old and has been described as "cold-blooded and vicious." His control of the gang is solidified by the support of his five brothers who are active in the gang.

The selling of drugs is coordinated by one of Juan's brothers and another member identified as a hard-core member or original gangster (OG). The hard-core membership, under the direct supervision of the two second-heads, is responsible for the distribution and sale of the drugs. Most of these transactions occur in the Carranza Courts and the nearby vicinity. When one of the Nine-Ball Crew members was asked if any one person was in charge of the drug selling, he responded:

> There is one guy in charge of selling. Yeah, he's the main guy that controls the drugs. He says who is going to sell and who ain't going to sell. If you're selling without permission and don't bring money to him you're going to get in trouble, get a V [a violation, a punishment].

The Nine-Ball Crew is also used by the Chicano Brotherhood against gangs who refuse to cooperate. For example, the leader of the Chicano Boyz, one of the largest gangs in the area, was shot by a rival gang for refusing to pay the Brotherhood a percentage of his profit. The hit was an attempt by them to solidify their control of the drug trade in this area. The Chicano Boyz at this time was one of the largest gangs on the West Side and selling large quantities of heroin. If the Chicano Brotherhood could control this gang, they would assume control of most of the heroin and cocaine trade in this area of the city.

THE GANGSTERS: ADULT CRIMINAL GANG DEPENDENT The Gangsters had previously been known as one of the most violent gangs in the city. The Gangsters identified themselves in interviews as having ties to a Chicago-based gang, although this was never substantiated. The gang had evolved into a highly organized drug-dealing criminal enterprise with several independent cliques. Each of these cliques had a head that was responsible for the operation of that group. Every clique operated relatively independently from each other, but they did answer to the Gangsters' leader. At the time of this study, the gang was experiencing a crisis in that many of the gang's hard-core members and leadership had been incarcerated. Allegedly, the leader was running the gang from prison. However, according to members that were interviewed, several of the cliques were breaking away from the Gangsters and were forming their own gangs. One Gangster, commenting on several of the cliques forming their own gangs, stated:

> To hell with the S. Perez Boys, Dallas St. Killers. Screw all of them. That's why there is so much problems in the organization . . . because of shit like that. They got to have their own gang.

The Gangsters' constituency is among the emerging Mexican American and Mexican immigrant neighborhoods forming on the fringes of the diminishing Black community on the east side of the city. The gang's membership is distinct in that it has a mixture of Mexican Americans, Blacks, and Anglos. The gang operates in areas adjacent to territories controlled by two black gangs: Crips and the Bloods. Nonetheless, there did not seem to be any conflict between the Gangsters and these two gangs.

Unlike the Nine-Ball Crew, which associated with adult prison gang members, the Gangsters were highly dependent on adult family criminal connections in the South Texas region. The fathers of the two founders of this gang were both well-known underground figures with extensive criminal records including sentences in the state and federal penitentiaries. These relatives provided the gang with access to a network of adult criminals not as accessible to other gangs. These contacts facilitated the acquisition of criminal resources such as illegal drugs and markets for stolen goods. One of the Gangster's uncles was a high-level drug dealer in South Texas and Mexico. This provided the gang a safe and consistent source of marijuana, cocaine, and heroin directly from Mexican dealers. Moreover, the Gangsters were purchasing these drugs at wholesale prices, often on consignment. This level of accessibility to illegal drugs gave them an advantage over other drug-dealing gangs. The adult relatives were a key factor in the evolution of the gang from one whose primary illegal activity was the fencing of stolen property (e.g., weapons, audio and video equipment) to a powerful drug-dealing gang.

The Gangsters were distinct from other gangs in that they were not concerned with territorial issues such as turf violations or random personal violence. For instance, little importance was placed on identifying their territory with gang tags, or preventing other gangs from tagging their neighborhoods. One Gangster likened tagging to a "dog pissing on a fire hydrant. Another dog is going to walk by and piss on it too. At least we know who's pissing on the wall." In other words, the Gangsters utilized tagging as a vehicle to determine "who's in our hood and who to look out for." Tagging itself was often a source of violent conflict among other San Antonio gangs. The Gangsters generally viewed tagging as a distraction from their illegal activities.

The Gangsters perceived themselves as a criminal organization that was primarily concerned with making money. One Gangster expressed these views:

You're not going to be a Gangster unless you got some sense. You ain't gonna just be a thug. I mean there is no such thing as a thug [in the Gangsters]. If you ain't making money . . . bringing something to the boys that's profitable for everyone, then we don't need you. If you don't want to be productive for yourself, then you won't be a Gangster.

This attitude gave the Gangsters an advantage over other drug-dealing gangs.

The Gangsters were distinct from most other gangs in several other ways. The gang leadership discouraged the use of heroin. One member of the Gangsters described his gang's feelings toward heroin. "We don't do it, but we can sell it. . . . We don't want to be known as *tecatos*. We don't want to be like the Chicano Boyz." As opposed to other gangs, there was not a high value placed on heavy drug use or alcohol consumption. *Tecato* is a derogatory term used by Mexican Americans to identify injecting heroin users.

The Gangsters were also distinct from other gangs by the nature of their activities. Although they had a reputation as a violent gang, their violence was highly instrumental and often related to drug dealing. Members were discouraged from engaging in more expressive acts of violence such as drive-by shootings, random assaults, and personal fights. According to several members, these types of violent acts tended to draw unnecessary attention from the police, which could disrupt their sophisticated drug-dealing operations. One member stated:

We're not evil. I mean hell, we're just like any other man out there. We got to fight for what we can get. You know nothing is free. I know it's not right to go out and steal, but we're not going to go out and shoot somebody, just to shoot them. People think that we drive around, just to shoot someone. Like we ain't got nothing else better to do. There is always two sides to the story. Don't think that somebody is sitting on their porch and just got shot. That's bullshit, they're not an innocent bystander.

CRIMINAL NON-ADULT DEPENDENT

Criminal non-adult-dependent gangs are similar in organizational structure to the criminal adult-dependent gangs, but they are more loosely knit with a flexible leadership structure. There are a total of five gangs in this category. They differ from the previous group in that they are not as influenced by adults. They are involved in more independent and personal (non-adult-dependent) illegal activities such as drug dealing, stolen cars, robberies, and car jacking. The gangs offer an organizational structure to protect the interests of individual gang members, not as a centralized criminal enterprise. Members display higher rates of drug and alcohol abuse, especially heroin. The members are involved in more minor personal fights within the gang and with rival gang members. Often their level of drug dealing will determine the purposefulness of the violence. Such gangs may be more territorially based than those described previously.

There are two categories of criminal non-adult-dependent gangs. One of these is loosely organized with a weak leadership structure. The other is highly structured with a clear hierarchy and strong membership.

CHICANO BOYZ: "LOOSELY" ORGANIZED CRIMINAL NON-ADULT DEPENDENT

The Chicano Boyz were one of the largest and most violent gangs on the west side of San Antonio. There were approximately fifty-nine members at the time of the study. This gang controls a large portion of the heroin and cocaine market in a large West Side public housing unit. The Chicano Boyz are organized into five main sets/cliques that make up the main core of the gang. Each of these sets has a head (leader), hard-core members, and others, including beginners and marginal members. The set is under the control of the head who, in turn, answers to the leader of the gang.

The leader of the Chicano Boyz is Mark Sanchez, who took control of the gang after the previous leader (Ernest) was sent to prison for attempted murder. Sanchez has a reputation in the community as being extremely violent. In the initial months of his leadership he had a physical confrontation with two adult members of a notorious adult prison gang whom he viciously beat with a wooden two-by-four. Subsequently, he "kicked a lot of the younger members' asses," which consolidated his control of the gang by gaining loyalty among the set's heads.

The Chicano Boyz is organized as a federation, whose primary activities are drug distribution and dealing. These illegal activities are conducted on an individual or subgroup basis, not as an organized gang. Therefore gang members are not expected to share their profits with the gang as a whole. The gang provides a drug market within a geographic territory that it protects through intimidation and violence. Members are expected to support and defend the gang's collective interests often through violence. Violating this expectation could be serious as one field-worker's notes recount:

Last night an ex-Chicano Boyz who turned Brotherhood got an order to jump on a Chicano Boyz who broke a car window of a sister of a sergeant in the Brotherhood. He went to do his work, and he took his best friend, who is still a Chicano Boy, with him. He did his job, and roughed up Tony, the one who broke the window. The Chicano Boyz who went along, Robert, didn't do anything but observe the situation. This all happened around 9:00 p.m. At 11:00 p.m., Mark, the head of Chicano, sent a group of seven boys to find Jesse, the ex-Chicano now Brotherhood, and beat him. The group did find him, and did beat him. They also found Robert, and beat him for watching.

Members may be required to participate in a drive-by shooting, an assault, or a gang fight. One member of the Chicano Boyz described this incident about catching a rival gang member selling drugs in their area:

This dude was from another gang. We had already kicked his ass I don't know how many times. . . . We were saying "fuck your gang" and all this shit. We started laughing. We let him get up. He took off and started running. . . . My homeboy took out an AK from the truck, my other homeboy took out a 9 mm. My homeboy got on his knee, aiming at him. He shot him in the head. My other homeboy just ran up and shot him in the back too.

In some circumstances, the gang members are required to contribute monies (pitch in) to purchase weapons or other gang needs. This usually takes the form of an informal "pitch in" by all the members present. In most instances the gang gets to keep all their illegal income. One member stated: "Everybody is making their own money. So you don't have to be giving money to the gang. You just have to pay for your drugs and that's it."

The heads of the sets and the leader met occasionally to discuss important issues affecting the gang and violations of gang rules. The Chicano Boyz had specific rules to which it expected its gang members to adhere. One of the rules that was often mentioned was the "no fighting with fellow gang members" rule. One member commented: "Everybody knows about it, it's been established. If there is any fighting, it's one on one. Not everyone has to be there, just the heads and the guys that are going to fight. Nobody wins, it's just settled." At a typical meeting of one of the sets:

Jake and Carlos begin the meeting by talking about the drug profit or loss for the past week. The money is counted and given to someone to hold. The plan is to buy a *cuete* (gun) next week. A few other matters are discussed, who's messing up at Rosedale [high school], the prison gang's 10 percent, violations for Xanax abuse, etc. After about an hour of chatting the meeting is closed.

Gang members were restricted from instrumental acts of violence against rival gang members without permission from the leader. Members needed approval of the leader to commit a drive-by against another gang. Such acts were likely to precipitate a war with the other gang, which would disrupt the drug trade. In other situations, the gang made a conscious decision to commit an act of violence against another gang, understanding the consequences.

The gang initially had rules against the use of heroin and inhalants. Both drugs were highly stigmatized, but for different reasons. The use of inhalants was thought to cause people to lose control and do "stupid things." No one seemed to have much respect for "spray heads." Additionally, most gang members believed that using inhalants caused brain damage. When asked about the heroin rule one member stated:

> Because if they do heroin, they get too fucked up. They start stealing shit from one another. They start stealing from their own people. Doing all kinds of shit. We don't want them doing none of the shit. We start losing.

One veteran member expressed the ambiguity of the gang's drug rule:

> You can do cocaine and weed. Heroin is something that is up and down with us. Sometimes we say nah, you can't use it. But, they use it anyway. What can you do? Les gusta [They like it]. They can't stop, so that's something we live with. You just try not to let the "juniors" get involved.

In reality, many of the original gangsters (OGs) were regular users of heroin and had become addicted. One rival gang member, commenting on the demise of the Chicano Boyz, stated, "They're nothing anymore because of the heroin."

One of the distinctions of the Chicano Boyz was its independence from the adult prison gang that operated in the same area as this gang. The prison gang over the years has attempted to control the Chicano Boyz— particularly its drug trade. The leader of the gang, Mark Sanchez, was one of the few gang leaders in that community to stand up to them. He did this through his own violent behavior and the loyalty of several hard-core Chicano Boyz who were not intimidated by these adults. Only recently did this independence begin to waver when Sanchez was seriously injured in an aborted attempt on his life by a rival gang associated with the Chicano Brotherhood. Nonetheless, the ability and willingness of the Chicano Boyz to stand up to the adult prison gang financially benefited those members who were involved in drug dealing, especially heroin.

VARRIO LA PALOMA: STRONG LEADERSHIP A second type of non-adult-dependent, criminal-enterprise gang is that with a dominating hierarchical leadership. An example of this type of gang is the Varrio La Paloma (VLP) located in the San Miguel housing project and the Indigo River subdivision. This is an older established gang that has multigenerational ties. It is one of the few gangs that actually had parents and relatives who have in the past participated in this gang. The San Miguel projects have been traditionally identified as the territory of Varrio La Paloma. The Indigo River faction is a more recent development that occurred after families were displaced from the San Miguel housing project to the working-class suburb by public housing authorities.

There are approximately one hundred hard-core and eighty marginal members in the Varrio La Paloma gang. These gang members are generally characterized as polydrug users with daily marijuana and alcohol use, and occasional use of cocaine and heroin. Most of the activity described by the members includes the use of drugs.

Organizationally, the gang has several sets. One principal set is located in the Carranza Courts and another in the Indigo River subdivision. Each of the sets has a head that is under the command of the leader of the gang. This is a highly organized gang with a distinct division of labor among its members. There are several cliques of members who are responsible for various tasks associated with the gang's business. For instance, there is a drug-dealing clique that is responsible for the distribution and dealing of drugs. There is also a shooting clique that coordinates all the organized violence that is initiated by the gang, including retaliation against rival gang members.

During the three years of this study, the gang was involved in a war with a rival gang located in the residential neighborhood adjacent to the San Miguel projects. One respondent describes an incident with this gang:

In the beginning of January, one of the homeboys got jumped there outside the neighborhood by a couple of Nine-Balls. We caught one of the guys and beat him up pretty bad with a lead pipe and car jack. If we would have had a gun, we would have killed him. But, there were too many bystanders around.

Several individuals from both sides were murdered as a result of this conflict. They were also involved in a serious conflict with the adult prison gang, which was attempting to take control of the heroin market in Carranza Courts. Two adult gang members were murdered by a VLP member when they refused to cooperate with him. One of our field-workers described the time he met this VLP member soon after the shootout incident:

> Georgie walked with the help of two crutches as he approached the car. The Brotherhood put out a contract on him because he refused to pay the 10 percent commission on his drug sales. Georgie had started out selling dime bags of heroin. Shortly thereafter, he was selling three to four ounces of heroin and coke a week. That's when Brotherhood started asking for their 10 percent. He said, "They sent two hit men. The men shot first hitting me in the thigh and the knee. I was shooting on the way down and killed them both. I gave the gun to Ray-Ray, who stashed it before the police got there." Georgie was upset because none of the VLP got down for him.

Eventually, the VLP reached a compromise with the adult gang. The VLP would be allowed to sell cocaine and marijuana, but the heroin trade would be the exclusive right of the prison gang.

The distribution and dealing of drugs by the gang were largely controlled by its leader and its close gang associates. The associates were older hard-core members, including two of the leader's brothers. These individuals had connections to wholesale drug distributors that were associated with independent adult criminals with ties to Mexico. The actual drug dealing was conducted by other gang members who were fronted the drugs by the gang's leadership. Except for a small percentage of the total, profits were turned over to the heads, who passed them on to the leader of the VLP.

Control of the VLP membership was maintained through the strong leadership of Charlie, the leader of the gang. The leader held periodic meetings with the San Miguel set to discuss any problems either internally or with rival gang members. As in other highly organized gangs, the group had strict rules that they had to abide by to retain their privileges. Breaking the rules would result in a violation that may warrant a physical beating from other gang members. During the study, Charlie was able to defuse a potentially violent situation when two Chicano Boyz beat up some VLP members in the Indigo River area.

Charlie explained in a meeting to a researcher in his apartment, "[I] don't want to take care of this with guns." But Charlie emphasized that he would encourage his own people to "strap it on" with members of the Chicano Boyz if they confronted them again. He added that the prison gang told him that "if there is any crossfire in the courts they will take care of the VLP and the Chicano Boyz."

BARRIO-TERRITORIAL GANGS

Barrio-territorial gangs are traditional territory-based gangs located in various types of neighborhoods ranging from public housing to residential single-family home neighborhoods. Twelve gangs are categorized as this type. These are not as hierarchical as the above-mentioned groups, but they still adhere to gang rituals and so on. Criminal activities include drug dealing, auto theft, burglary, robbery, vandalism, criminal mischief, and other petty crime. These crimes tend to be more individual, less organized, and less gang directed. Violent behavior tends to be more random and personal. Except for gang turf disputes, most violence is centered on interpersonal fights and random situational acts of violence often associated with male bravado. Even gang drive-by shootings tend to be more spontaneous, and predicated on issues such as defending the gang's honor. The use of drugs by barrio-territorial gangs is similar to that of the other types of gangs, with the exception of the low prevalence of heroin use. These gangs tend to operate independently of any adult gang influence. Territorial gangs constitute the majority of the gangs in this study.

THE INVADERS: TERRITORIAL GANG The Invaders are located in a low-income residential area characterized by modest single-family homes in ecologically segregated neighborhoods with long-term residents. The neighborhood is accessible by car through a couple of major streets, making it difficult for rival gang members to enter the area unobtrusively. The gang consists of approximately twenty members ranging in age from fourteen to eighteen years old. This gang is relatively young compared to the gangs described previously. Various sources generated by project researchers indicated that the gang is in its second generation, with many of the previous generations either maturing out or incarcerated.

The gang seems to have a loosely organized structure. Although members claim that it does not have a leader, two individuals appear to make major decisions regarding the gang. The gang will hold an occasional meeting if it is necessary, but they do so reluctantly because the cops tend to hassle them if they are seen in large numbers in public. The gang has some informal rules that include the prohibition of heroin use, spray use, and "ganking" each other. "Ganking" loosely refers to robbing fellow gang members. "Violations" are formal sanctions used against gang members who break these and other rules. The violations usually consist of a beating by fellow gang members for a designated amount of time.

At the meetings, the gang may require that members "pitch in" if the gang needs to purchase guns or other things. The gang's major criminal activities center on car theft, robbery, and burglary. For instance, one Invader recalls how they stole a low-rider bicycle from a rival gang:

> We were drinking that night and took a drive downtown. I was drunk. We saw three Crowns who had shot my friend. I went to the first one that was closest to me. He threw down his bike. I just popped him and told him, "fuck the Crowns." We started fighting and three of my homeboys jumped in and started beating him. My friend started hitting one with a hammer on the head. He just fell down. We threw two of the bikes in the truck and hit the highway.

This type of random violence is not seen among the more criminal gangs described above. It is not seen as economically smart and often results in arrests and convictions.

A few members of the Invaders are involved in small-time drug dealing, primarily marijuana sales. Drug dealing is done on an individual basis, as opposed to collectively. The gang activity that seems to occupy most of the member's illegal creativity is "gang-banging." This includes protecting the gang's turf from rival gangs, drive-by shootings, fights, and assaults. When asked why they committed a particular drive-by, a member responded, "At the time they were our main rival. After we shot them, they stayed low. Then the Vatos Locos came up. They became our main enemy." Many members are heavily armed with high-caliber assault weapons. Their rival gang is the Vatos Locos with whom they had numerous violent incidents during the course of the study. Their other main rival gang is the Crowns, the largest and most violent active Mexican American gang in the city. However, that rivalry has diminished after several violent altercations left members of both sides seriously wounded.

The Invaders also have a reputation as a party gang. The members are known to be heavy users of marijuana, cocaine, and alcohol. What distinguishes them from the more criminal gangs is that partying is often the gang's central activity. In fact, members often discuss how a night of partying usually results in committing an act of violence. The following describes how one such night resulted in a shooting:

> I: Okay so lets back up a little bit. So you guys were, you and a *camarada* were in a stolen car?
>
> R: Yeah we had it was like 3 o'clock in the morning.
>
> I: Okay.
>
> R: We were already all wasted and shit.
>
> I: Where were you in what, in your 'hood, or somebody else's 'hood?
>
> R: In somebody else's 'hood.
>
> R: I just started shooting.
>
> I: Okay so your reaction was, you know, you just started shooting?
>
> R: Yeah.
>
> I: So you shot a few times and then you guys took off and went down the street?
>
> R: Yeah.

TRANSITIONAL

The *transitional* category encompasses several gangs in transition relative to a trajectory—that is, growing in membership and reputation, or fading organizationally.[2] In some cases, the gang is a temporary phenomenon, such as only when school is in session. The six gangs that fit into this category were usually smaller and were semiorganized with a loose hierarchy and loose leadership structure. Often, such gangs center on a charismatic leader. The formation of these groups may be based on residential factors such as living in the same building or subarea of the projects or neighborhood. There is a lot of partying with alcohol and drugs. Criminal activities, such as drug dealing, auto theft, and burglaries, are individually based as opposed to more organized gang activity. In some cases, certain gangs may have relationships with adult criminals that supply them with guns or drugs. These adults are often parents or other relatives of gang members.

School-based gangs are a subset of the smaller, less-structured gangs. These gangs are formed and maintained in the junior high and high schools. Membership is geographically more dispersed. Violence revolves primarily around personal fights and girl-boy differences. Many of their activities occur in school-related settings (i.e., after-school hangouts, parties with school friends).

UP AND ABOVE: DELINQUENT GROUP TO GANG Up and Above (UAA) is a gang that in the initial months of the research project had been classified as a "tagging crew." This is a group of individuals whose major activity focuses on spray painting walls, alleyways, street signs, and buildings in a highly individualistic style described as "graffiti art." Tagging crew art is often confused for gang graffiti by the general public and school and police authorities. In fact, tagging crew art is much more elaborate than gang graffiti, which is primarily used to mark off territory. The primary objective of tagging crews is to display their artistic ability. Tagging crews are often in competition with each other for the most elaborate tags and for the best location. Prestige is bestowed on those that display their art in the highest places (e.g., tops of buildings).

Members of tagging crews vary according to the roles played in the organization. At the top of the tagging hierarchy is the "bomber," who does large-scale colorful paintings with spray paint, markers, or chalk on public and private buildings. Crew members are those that assist the bombers in their work. There are also members who are the "partyers." These members are attracted to the gang because of the group's social activities, which include the frequent use of marijuana and alcohol, and the occasional use of cocaine.

On one occasion, a rival gang accused an Up and Above member of painting over their gang signs and operating in their neighborhood without permission. As the tension mounted, UAA members began to organize themselves more as a gang. They identified a leader and began to recruit persons to their crew for factors other than their artistic talent. As the crew began to diversify, the group's activities expanded into more illegal activities such as drug dealing. The crew's identity as a gang was solidified when they successfully defended themselves in a gang fight with one of the most notorious gangs in the area.

Up and Above began to evolve into a gang as it was forced to physically protect itself from other gangs. One member talks about an incident with a local black gang:

> We were cruising in our van with the rims. We cruised in it all the time before it got stolen. Some black Crips pulled up next to us. They thought we were Crownz because we were dressed in black. They were talking shit and threw their fucking beer bottles at the van. We were like "fuck, you meet us over there.." . . We both parked and all started getting out. And one of them looked like he was going to reach for a gun. We were like, "ah damn man!" So, I was in the back. I hooked one of the UAAs with a Tech 9 that my uncle got for me. So we fired on the whole car and they took off. We only shot a couple of rounds, just enough to scare them.

Incidents such as this have transformed this tagging crew into a full-fledged gang.

THE KILLING CREW: DECLINE OF A GANG The Killing Crew is a gang that experienced a significant decline during the course of this study. They started out as a territorial gang located in a public housing project (Martin Homes) and the adjacent residential area. At the height of their organizational career, the gang had at least twenty members, including a large number of "little rascals" who were considered too young to be full-fledged members. Gang members were involved in a wide range of illegal activities focusing primarily on drug dealing and arms sales. The gang has been known to protect its territory from encroachment by rival gang members violently.

The gang's organizational structure was not highly evolved. Most of the members functioned independently of the gang structure. One of the leaders mentioned the following about their meetings:

> Yeah, we have meetings every month. But, the guys don't want to get together. They're too busy or don't have time. It's kinda too impossible. I mean, not everyone shows up.

The gang had two exceptionally strong leaders whose functions seemed to be drawn toward coordinating instrumental acts of violence against other gangs. They would also mediate problems as they arose among Killing Crew members. There were no distinct sets or cliques with heads that answered to the gang leaders. Meetings were held when an assault or a more coordinated act of violence was needed to protect their drug markets and territory against violations by rival gang members.

The Killing Crew was known primarily by Martin Homes residents as the sole source of marijuana and weapons. Guns were not only sold, they were also used by gang members. One member involved in the gang's gun trade said:

> We do a lot of gun smuggling. We get many different arms, like grenades and armor-piercing bullets and guns like "cop killers" and AK-47s. A lot of these guns we use ourselves. Once we get busted, they start taking away the guns. Guys start fucking up. By the time I know it, I look into the case and there is nothing there no more.

The gun trade described is controlled by the above-mentioned individual and the gang's sergeant at arms. The sergeant at arms makes sure there is enough money and acts as a bodyguard to the gun dealer, who knows where to purchase the weapons.

Members sold marijuana individually or in small groups to area residents in the courts and adjacent neighborhoods. Profits were not distributed to other gang members, nor to the two gang leaders who themselves were known to sell large volumes of marijuana. As long as the gang only dealt marijuana and not cocaine or heroin, it did not draw the attention of the adult gangs in the area. This is how they were able to maintain their independence from other adults. Marijuana dealing was organized in the same manner as the weapons; it was a business that was conducted by individual members, not collectively.

A combination of factors led to the demise of the Killing Crew. The severity of the violence associated with the Killing Crew coupled with the arms dealing attracted the attention of the police. As a result, the police made special efforts to break up this gang by arresting and convicting the leaders, Phillip and Eddie. They were both given lengthy prison sentences for drug dealing. At the same time, other more veteran members began to mature out of the gang. Of more importance, the gang's base of operation was being undermined by the city's housing authority, who decided that the Martin Homes were to be demolished and the families relocated to other neighborhoods.

With the two leaders in prison and older members leaving the gang, the group's "little rascals" were not so eager to "drop their rags" (give up their gang affiliation). They decided to change the name of the gang to the Martin Thugs. The gang went by this name for almost two years, until the Martin Homes were completely demolished, and no reports have surfaced to indicate that they still exist.

There are also groups of youths that reside in these types of neighborhoods who engage in activities similar to the gangs, but are not gang members. They are described as delinquent youth. Throughout the neighborhoods (barrios, projects) these non-gang-affiliated youths use and deal drugs, engage in violent behavior, and commit other crimes. They are able to avoid conflict and coexist with the gangs by not self-identifying as one.

DISCUSSION

Contemporary Chicano gangs exhibit as wide a spectrum of types as exist among other racial and ethnic gangs described in the current literature. The majority of Chicano gangs are involved in illegal activities such as theft, drug dealing, and violence. Today, gangs are more likely to use lethal violence than in the past, although they tend to be judicious in the actual use of weapons. The use of high-powered weapons is facilitated by their ready availability. A gang's organizational hierarchy varies depending on the need for such a structure. Obviously, gangs described as criminal enterprises are more in need of a sophisticated structure than barrio-based gangs. The severity of drug use and abuse varies among gangs, but all are heavy users of marijuana and alcohol. Most are occasional users of cocaine, and a minority of mostly older gang members inject heroin. However, almost half of the study sample reported noninjecting heroin use, which has serious implications for future related health and social problems.

The gangs we studied seem to represent a means by which to fulfill an economic need generated by the structural position in society rather than a social need, as was more the case in the past. However, some of the barrio-based gangs may be more social in nature than the more criminal gangs. The resources generated by the gangs, especially through drug sales and markets, are related to their relationships with criminal adults. In cases where the gang is generating high volumes of drug sales and income, adults tend to get involved as either partners or competitors. Competitive adult relationships often result in high-profile violent incidents. Differences are almost always quickly resolved, because this type of phenomenon often draws the attention of police, which disrupts the drug trade.

In the past, Mexican American gangs existed, but they differed from those that operate today. These earlier urban gangs were linked multigenerationally, just as the European ethnic gangs described by Whyte (1943) and others. Among the benefits of these multigenerational ties was the existence of indigenous social control mechanisms such as extended family members and long-term neighbors. These mechanisms managed to moderate the extreme behavior of these delinquent groups and gangs by their supervision. However, this generational connectiveness broke down as a result, in part, of greater economic and urban ecological factors that increasingly marginalized low-income Chicano communities in large southwestern cities (Soja, Morales, and Wolff 1984; Moore 1988; Vigil 1988; Morales 2001). These processes also created conditions that nurtured the environments in which contemporary Mexican American gangs began to flourish. These are the same economic processes that affected low-income Black communities in the northeast (Wilson 1987, 1996).

The result of this social process is the emergence of the different categories of Chicano gangs illustrated in this typology. Although not entirely exhaustive, this study does offer a classification of gangs that mirrors disparate experiences of contemporary Mexican American urban youth. The reality is that the Mexican American population in the United States is highly diversified and the typology may have to be adapted for communities with distinct characteristics, such as those where the majority of youths are immigrants or those along the U.S.-Mexico border, with its set of particular binational characteristics. Nonetheless, the findings from this study can be generalized to other Mexican American gangs located in most Southwestern communities, and they can be used to better understand gangs in other ethnic and racial communities.

NOTES

   1. This is not to suggest that underclass characteristics solely explain the emergence of drug markets in urban minority ghettos and barrios. We concur with

William Kornblum (1993) that the ghetto/barrio containment has "stimulated the creation of thriving illicit markets and illegal economic institutions."
2. See Spergel (1995:75) for a discussion on variations of transitional gangs.

REFERENCES

Akins, C., and G. Beschner. 1980. *Ethnography: A Research Tool for Policymakers in the Drug and Alcohol Fields*. Rockville, Md.: National Institute on Drug Abuse.

Anderson, E. 1990. *Streetwise: Race, Class, and Change in an Urban Community*. Chicago: University of Chicago Press.

Bailey, K. B. 1994. *Typologies and Taxonomies: An Introduction to Classification Techniques*. Thousand Oaks, Calif.: Sage Publications.

Brotherton, D. 1999. Old heads tell their stories. *Free Inquiry in Creative Sociology*, 27 (1): 1–15.

Chin, K. L. 1995. Chinese gangs and extortion. In M. W. Klein, C. L. Maxson, and J. Miller, eds., *The Modern Gang Reader*, pp. 46–52. Los Angeles, Calif.: Roxbury Publishing.

Fagan, J. 1989. The social organization of drug use and drug dealing among urban gangs. *Criminology*, 27 (4): 633–667.

———. 1996. Gangs, drugs, and neighborhood change. In C. R. Huff, ed., *Gangs in America*. Newbury Park, Calif.: Sage.

Hagedorn, J. M. 1994. Neighborhoods, markets, and gang drug organization. *Journal of Research in Crime and Delinquency*, 31 (3): 264–294.

Heller, C. S. 1966. *Mexican American Youth: Forgotten Youth at the Crossroads*. New York: Random House.

Jankowski, M. S. 1991. *Islands in the Street: Gangs and American Urban Society*. Berkeley: University of California Press.

Knox, G. W. 1991. *An Introduction to Gangs*. Barrien Springs, Mich.: Vande Vere Publishing.

Kornblum, W. 1993. Drug legalization and minority poor. In R. Bayer and G. M. Oppenheimer, eds., *Confronting Drug Policy: Illicit Drugs in a Free Society*. New York: Cambridge University Press.

Moore, J. W. 1978. *Homeboys: Gangs, Drugs, and Prison in the Barrios of Los Angeles*. Philadelphia: Temple University Press.

———. 1988. Introduction: Gangs and the underclass: A comparative perspective. In J. M. Hagedorn, ed., *People and Folks: Gangs, Crime, and the Underclass in a Rustbelt City*. Chicago: Lake View.

———. 1991. *Going down to the Barrio: Homeboys and Homegirls in Change*. Philadelphia: Temple University Press.

Morales, Armando, T. 2001. "Urban and Suburban Gangs: The Psychosocial Crisis Spreads." In Armando T. Morales and Bradford W. Sheafor, eds., *Social Work: A Profession of Many Faces*, pp. 397–433. 9th ed. Boston: Allyn and Bacon.

Padilla, F. M. 1992. *The Gang as an American Enterprise*. New Brunswick, N.J.: Rutgers University Press.

Sanders, W. B. 1994. *Gangbangs and Drive-Bys*. New York: Aldine de Gruyter.

Soja, E., R. Morales, and G. Wolff. 1984. Urban restructuring: An analysis of social and spatial change in Los Angeles. *Economic Geography*, 60: 195–230.

Spergel, I. A. 1995. *The Youth Gang Problem: A Community Approach*. New York: Oxford University Press.

Taylor, C. 1990. *Dangerous Society*. East Lansing: Michigan State University Press.

Valdez, A., and C. D. Kaplan. 1999. Reducing selection bias in the use of focus groups in investigating hidden populations: The case of Mexican-American gang members from South Texas. *Drugs and Society*, 14 (1/2): 209–224.

Vigil, D. 1988. *Barrio Gangs: Street Life and Identity in Southern California*. Austin: University of Texas Press.

Whyte, William F. 1943. *Street Gang Society*. Chicago: University of Chicago Press.

Wilson, W. J. 1987. *The Truly Disadvantaged: The Inner City, The Underclass, and Public Policy*. Chicago: University of Chicago Press.

———. 1996. *When the Work Disappears: The World of the New Urban Poor*. New York: Alfred A. Knopf.

———. 1999. *The Bridge over the Racial Divide*. Berkeley: The University of California Press.

Yablonsky, L. 1962. *The Violent Gang*. New York: Macmillan.

Yin, Z., A. Valdez, A. G. Mata Jr., and C. Kaplan. 1996. Developing a field-intensive methodology for generating a randomized sample for gang research. *Free Inquiry—Special Issue: Gangs, Drugs, and Violence*, 24 (2): 195–204.

3

THE NEGLIGIBLE ROLE OF GANGS IN DRUG DISTRIBUTION IN NEW YORK CITY IN THE 1990S

RIC CURTIS

The widespread belief that there is an intimate and enduring connection between gangs and drug distribution and use is deeply rooted in the perceptions of law enforcement officials, media representations, and academic studies that document their existence (Fagan 1989). Firmly entrenched in the public imagination, gangs and drugs form an inseparable pair. Although gangs have been connected to drug distribution in the popular imagination during the last fifteen years, particularly in the wake of the crack "epidemic," empirical evidence has shown the relationship to be very uneven. Some researchers have identified the emergence of corporate-style gangs (Taylor 1990; Jankowski 1991; Skolnick 1992; Venkatesh 2000) that have sprung up in the deindustrialized inner cities of Chicago, Detroit, and Los Angeles, while other researchers have found gangs to be far less organized, with gang members involved in the drug economy on an individual and informal basis (Fagan 1995; Decker, Bynum, and Wiesel 1998).

This chapter uses ethnographic data collected in a Brooklyn, New York neighborhood over a ten-year period (1990–2000) to describe the involvement of street gangs in drug distribution and consumption. If we simply looked at the "gangs" that have been identified in New York City over the last several years, many instances of drug distribution and use could certainly be documented among its members. On the basis of these cases, we might readily agree with the prevailing view that gangs and drugs are intimately connected. On the other hand, the evidence that we have collected over nearly twenty years of ethnographic research on drug markets throughout New York City neighborhoods suggests that such a perception would be misleading. In our view, gang involvement in drug distribution has been largely inconsequential with respect to the overall market. Despite exceptional cases that occasionally garner media headlines, gangs have not played a major role as distributors in New York City's drug markets.

Unlike the gangs that have recently appeared in many American cities—which researchers have tended to interpret as the result of a diffusion of ideas, styles, and organized drug distribution originating on the West coast—we view many of the so-called gangs in New York City as arising from specific conditions and events that have taken place in its inner-city neighborhoods, especially as an outcome of the war on drugs. This chapter uses two case studies of drug dealers/users who became members of the Almighty Latin King and Queen Nation (ALKQN) in the early and mid-1990s, to examine and illuminate the processes that energized and transformed social relations in Latino neighborhoods during this period. By situating these new "gangs" in the wider contexts of changes in the social, cultural, economic, and political character of New York City and its neighborhoods—especially changes in the illegal drug business—this chapter will reveal how the state's attempts to control "dangerous" populations led to their politicization and to the rapid emergence of alternative modes of resistance.

METHODS

The data used in this paper were collected in North Brooklyn from 1990 to 2000, focusing especially on drug distributors and use.[1] Ethnography is often employed to describe populations and social environments that are hidden from normal observation (see, e.g., Weppner 1977; Lambert 1990), and it is indispensable when exploring emergent phenomena. A principal strength of ethnography rests on the physical presence of researchers at activities and events—using their privileged position to "test" the accuracy and truthfulness of what they hear and see. As such, fieldwork in this instance involved extensive observations in sites such as the homes of study participants, their kin, and others; in parks, playgrounds, and street corners; at schools, in clubs, near clinics and treatment centers; in places where drug use and distribution took place; and many other neighborhood locales. The combination of direct observation and ethnographic interviews (of which there were more than four hundred available for analysis in this paper) serves as a built-in cross-check of information and helps synthesize multiple viewpoints, heavily contextualizing each phenomenon to facilitate arrival at a holistic and accurate rendering of reality (Bernard 1994).

The research teams from the various projects listed above focused their efforts on describing and analyzing changes in patterns of drug distribution and use in New York City neighborhoods over the last ten years. As Latino gangs—street organizations—grew in popularity in the early and mid-1990s, their presence was observed and documented in the same neighborhoods where drug researchers had a well-established presence. In conducting the various research projects mentioned above over this ten-year period, one remarkable finding was the degree to which "gang" members, who had been largely recruited from the ranks of incarcerated drug dealers and users, were not involved in the drug scene upon their release from jail or prison. Of the more than four hundred interviews with active drug dealers and users, less than ten were with men and women who claimed current gang membership. Yet, because so many young men and women from these neighborhoods had been steeped in drugs throughout their lives, it is unrealistic to imagine that the members of these nascent groups would be able to completely divest themselves of any involvement in the drug scene. This chapter uses two case studies to examine the difficult transitions that many young men and women made from drug dealer/user to gang member, and the relationship that these growing organizations had to street-level drug markets.

THE DEMISE OF GANGS AND THE ASCENDANCY OF DRUG DISTRIBUTION IN NEW YORK CITY: 1950–92

The history of gangs in New York City has differed somewhat from the national norm. From the 1950s to the mid-1970s, gangs were found in many of the city's ethnic neighborhoods (Gilbert 1986). Their ubiquity commanded the attention of social scientists (Cohen 1955; Miller 1958; Cloward and Ohlin 1960; Matza and Sykes 1961; Yablonsky 1962; Becker 1963; Geis 1965). The most common type was the territorially based youth gang, which was said to govern the social lives of alienated youths in affected neighborhoods. This youth culture, however, was soon altered. In the early 1960s, many New York City neighborhoods experienced a radical transformation that originated in the period's restructuring of global, national, and regional socioeconomic arrangements (Braverman 1970; Mandel 1975; Sutton 1979; McCullough 1983; Durnin 1987; Sviridoff et al. 1992). Neighborhoods that had once been populated by European Americans were rapidly evacuated and repopulated by migrants from Latin America and the Caribbean, where U.S.-directed modernization and development programs had transformed indigenous economies, causing malintegration between economic sectors, unemployment, and new waves of migration (Wallerstein 1974; Koslofsky 1981; Sassen-Koob 1989). But as European Americans deserted the city, more than one-half million manufacturing jobs fled with them, and as the city's tax base shrank, expenditure on public services was sharply reduced (Mollenkopf and Castells 1991; Kasarda 1992). Although a few large manufacturers have remained, the typical local company in 1996 intermittently employs workers in nonunion, low-skill, low-wage, and high-risk jobs. The economy had stopped guaranteeing economic prosperity and security and offered high unemployment and underemployment instead.

The malign neglect of government had allowed and sometimes promoted the deterioration of the infrastructure and social fabric of many inner-city neighborhoods. It was not simply a turnover in population and departing jobs that changed these neighborhoods, they were also physically transformed, and by the 1970s, many observers were describing the inner city as resembling "Dresden after the war" (Wallace 1990; Hamid 1990; Verghara 1991). Other neighborhoods, like Bushwick, Brooklyn experienced unprecedented levels of arson by homeowners seeking to collect insurance monies when they could not sell their houses. By 1977, more than one thousand lots were empty, fully one-fifth of the neighborhood (Curtis et al. 1994). As the neighborhood literally went up in flames, smoldering racial/ethnic relations also caught fire and many stabilizing neighborhood social institutions—block associations, clubs, and church groups—were significantly weakened or disappeared altogether (Curtis and Maher 1992).

Thus a significant proportion of new immigrants were isolated in steadily deteriorating neighborhoods by unemployment and the lack of low-income housing. For newly arriving minority youths, therefore, there were few loyalties or enduring ties to a worthwhile territorial base. The paucity of gang studies in New York City during the 1970s and 1980s (Campbell 1987; Jankowski 1991) suggests that, during this period, drug distribution organizations had supplanted gangs as the primary units of association for younger persons in low-income, minority neighborhoods (Curtis and Maher 1992). What had proved more attractive to youths than gang membership were drugs and the "fast" money circulating in drug markets.

The evolution of street-level drug markets (heroin and marijuana in the 1970s and cocaine and crack in the 1980s) and the societal responses to them (an enlarged police force, more incarcerated persons, drug-related stigmatization) had rapidly transformed the urban landscape. Latino neighborhoods, like Williamsburg and Bushwick in Brooklyn, the Lower East Side of Manhattan, or the South Bronx, became centers of retail heroin and cocaine distribution (Zimmer 1985, 1990; Courtwright, Joseph, and Des Jarlais 1989; Belenko, Nickerson, and Ruberstein 1990; Curtis and Maher 1992; Sviridoff et al. 1992). By the mid-1970s, many of these neighborhoods had witnessed the evaporation of institutional and neighborhood-level controls, a vacuum that enabled corporate-style drug distribution organizations to emerge and operate with impunity. Near the end of the heroin "epidemic" that had begun in the early 1970s, a few "owners" (largely Puerto Ricans) had consolidated the market and their businesses had grown into monolithic, corporate-style enterprises that tightly integrated wholesale, mid-level, and street-level markets. The street-level drug businesses that were prominent during this period operated on a two-tiered system, much like those economies discussed in segmented labor market theory: A core of "good" jobs exist for a privileged few, while the majority were consigned to low-wage, high-risk, dead-end jobs. Like many corporations in the formal economy, the corporate-style drug distribution organizations generally operated in a fashion that disregarded the welfare of the communities in which they were located. The damages that this style of drug distribution inflicted upon neighborhoods included such things as further lowering property values, a greater incidence of drug misuse, alarmingly high rates of incarceration among local youth, and a legacy of violence. Their impact was deeply etched on the psyches of local youths: Throughout the 1980s, inner-city youth culture was dominated by a style popularized by the corporate-style distributors whose ultra-hedonistic image and discourse was replete with violence and callousness toward others. The depth of their wickedness was epitomized in an episode that took place in Williamsburg in the late 1980s: When the police arrested one of the local corporate-style heroin owners, they discovered a jar of human teeth inside his home. The teeth had been yanked from the mouths of employees who had been disloyal to the business. The jar had been kept on the mantle to instill fear in others.

THE END OF CORPORATE-STYLE DRUG DISTRIBUTION IN NEW YORK CITY: 1993

Law enforcement initiatives that began in the late 1980s (Sviridoff et al. 1992; Curtis 1996) fatefully affected the succession of ethnic and national groups in some drug markets. There had been a long history of rivalry between Puerto Ricans and Dominicans in New York City, but this animosity was especially pronounced in the drug business. For example, as police campaigns clamped down on the Puerto Rican "owners" in Latino neighborhoods, Dominicans entered the competition and displaced them. As the campaign against crack markets mounted steadily after the mid-1980s, courts and prisons (Belenko, Nickerson, and Ruberstein 1990) were overwhelmed, and the effects were soon apparent in many neighborhoods: A deep rift between the new Dominican owners and a disaffected, largely Puerto Rican labor force tore apart many of these corporate-style enterprises (Curtis and Maher 1992).

It is often thought that, to protect their interests, successful street-level drug businesses hire lookouts, steerers, and touts in addition to those who handle and sell the product. By the early 1990s, however, the structure of drug markets was such that management refused to hire additional workers beyond what was absolutely necessary to move the product. The reserve pool of potential sellers was so large that they could easily replace workers who were arrested and thus managers found it unnecessary to hire extra help such as lookouts. Although drug sellers preferred to have lookouts watching the corners for oncoming patrol cars, they could rarely afford to pay for such a person out of their meager earnings. Sometimes, groups of sellers would combine resources and pay someone to act as a lookout during their shift.

Through the use of aggressive buy-and-bust tactics, the police ratcheted up the pressure on the large street-level drug markets that had become geographically concentrated. For example, between 1988 and 1992, more than 8,200 persons were arrested on drug-related charges in Bushwick alone, an outcome that served to widen the growing rift between management and labor over the harshness of working conditions. Management sought to insulate themselves from the streets while employees were steadily and systematically moved from streets to jail, where they were abandoned by the people whose businesses had put them there. In response to the increasingly uncaring attitudes that the large drug organizations exhibited toward their labor force, many employees began to abscond with product if given the opportunity. Mounting business losses due to police seizures and/or worker theft saw mid-level managers being held accountable for productivity and profits, and they, in turn, placed increased pressure on workers to toe the line. Much of the increase in drug-related violence during this period was directly attributable to these changes in the relationship between management and labor.

The large drug-selling organizations had once been seen as lucrative businesses that offered minorities economic opportunities that were denied to them in the legitimate world of work. Furthermore, participation in drug markets had always carried with it a subversive quality, an element of resistance to the state's attempt to regulate and control unruly, working-class minorities who live in the inner city (Burroughs 1958; Brown 1965; Bourgois 1989; Malcolm X 1992; etc.). In the early 1990s, however, the structure of corporate-style drug distribution precluded the formation of any type of culture of resistance, especially when pressured by the police. Instead, it had led to a culture of subjugation and fear. The large corporate drug businesses had employed many local people and generated large amounts of money, but when the NYPD began focusing on them, the beleaguered owners and managers showed nothing but disregard for the community, and, in turn, few residents expressed sympathy for them. The shift in local attitudes toward the illegal drug markets that dominated these neighborhoods was evident in the increasingly frequent public displays of violence between managers and workers in the late 1980s and early 1990s. Adding to their sense that these drug distributors had betrayed the community, residents stood witness as building after building was run down by the incessant drum beat of business; the streets were constantly filthy with drug paraphernalia from the heavy traffic; children could not play on sidewalks as distributors and users stood shoulder to shoulder until late into the night; vicious fights were a daily occurrence; and most of the young men from the neighborhood had been locked up and left to fend for themselves as an outcome of their involvement with the businesses. The taste of drug money had clearly soured in many people's mouths, and there was no longer any illusion that working for the drug organizations was, in any fashion, a type of resistance to the state.

In October 1992, following an embarrassing two-part report in the *New York Times* about the blatancy of street-level drug markets in Bushwick (Tabor 1992), the New York Police Department began a massive assault on them, a maneuver that earned them both praise and resentment among neighborhood residents. The war of attrition had shifted into high gear. A mobile command post placed in a nearby park symbolized the NYPD's commitment to reclaiming the territory by brute force. In addition to increasing the frequency of buy-and-bust operations, a heavy saturation of uniformed officers was combined with horse-mounted police to patrol the parks and drug "hot spots" in the area. Helicopters gave additional support to officers pursuing suspects on foot. Police officers stopped and questioned all pedestrians on these blocks and asked for their identification and destination. Nonresidents were told to stay out of the area. The heaviest drug trafficking streets were blocked with wooden barricades and police vans, vehicles were diverted to other streets where they were stopped and searched. When evening came, large flatbed trucks with generators and flood lights were brought to strategic corners to illuminate entire blocks. For the next eighteen months, the entire area was an occupation zone.

As police initiatives waged a war of attrition on the street-level Puerto Rican labor force, a common joke was that "Rikers [Island] has turned into a Bushwick [or Williamsburg or Lower East Side] block party" (Curtis et al. 1994). The Latin Kings and other prison gangs had long been present in those facilities, but they had never enjoyed mass appeal, until now. Where the Latin Kings had once been a marginal organization that appealed to a select few, in the charged atmosphere of Rikers Island in the early 1990s, it served to focus and galvanize the anger and frustrations of the many captives in the war on drugs. Quite suddenly, it was "cool" to be a King or a Ñeta and flaunt your national heritage.

By 1993, a tipping point was reached in Bushwick and other Latino neighborhoods, and remarkable transformations began to take place among the populace, especially its youth (Curtis 1996). As the "gang" phenomenon burst into public view that summer, many drug distributors and users told of dramatic transformations in their personas, going from being a drain on the neighborhood to do-gooder almost overnight. Increasingly embittered by their experiences in drug distribution, and as crack sales stagnated in the early 1990s, Latino youths found that their street-level drug dealing had stopped providing the "fast money" that had attracted their predecessors (Golub and Johnson 1997; Hamid et al. 1997). In Bushwick, following on the heels of the massive police initiative begun in September 1992, which jailed hundreds of neighborhood youths, sizeable groups of Latin Kings and Ñetas began to appear and assert their influence over some blocks, especially those that had been characterized by large street-level drug markets and unchecked violence. These youth, predominantly of Puerto Rican descent, reported that they had experienced a genuine rebirth (usually in jail) and in leaving behind the past, their new goal was to "uplift the Latino community." As former street-level drug workers who had suffered at the hands of their Dominican bosses and the police, they were disillusioned. Though they had long realized their limitations in American society, they at last also appreciated the shallowness of the drug distribution organizations that had employed them. The Dominican "owners" did not bail them out of jail, hire lawyers, look after family, or compensate them for the time in prison. They remained indifferent to Puerto Rican sensibilities, although mainly Puerto Ricans suffered the brunt of the war on drugs. King Psyche, a former street-level drug seller, described the source of his bitter feelings:

> During my time on Rikers Island, I was going to court. My bail was only $5,000. My foster mother spoke to the [Dominican] owner and asked if he could bail me out. At that time, I had $10,000 out there in the streets that different people owed me. He said, "well, whoever works for me and gets arrested has got to be a man. Do the crime, do the time." That right there pissed me off. Eventually, I came home. I wanted to get even with this guy 'cause he played me. All that time, I could have been at home. I could have fought the case outside. Five thousand dollars, you're telling me that you couldn't bail me out? I don't want to hear that.

For many youths arrested during this period, the experience of going to jail—Rikers Island—meant many years of frustration, violence, and abuse. It was in jail that many youths made a remarkable turnaround; the Latin

Kings gave them a new identity that stressed community building, and in striving toward those goals it provided them a means by which they could repudiate the past. Participation in corporate-style drug distribution had come to symbolize adherence to a destructive hedonism that was blind to community suffering. For many young men and women, the Latin Kings and Queens and the Ñetas articulated thoughts and feelings—a class consciousness—that had been pent up and percolating for years. As King Psyche noted:

> Before I was a King, I was a knucklehead. My temper got me kicked out of school. I used to fight a lot with teachers. I used to sell drugs a lot inside school. During my time on Rikers Island, I was in the position of changing myself: stop selling drugs. I started seeing the light more and wanted to follow a more spiritual path. It's not all about selling drugs anymore. It's not all about taking. It's all about giving back to the community. I took so much; now, it's time to give back.

In the aftermath of the war on drugs, gang life—or more accurately, grassroots political mobilizations that were responsive to specific local conditions and circumstances—revived after a dormancy of nearly two decades, sparked, at least initially, by the bulging numbers of convicted drug distributors and users in jails and prisons and the increasing reports of police brutality and corruption (see, for example, the Mollen Commission report that appeared during this period: City of New York 1994). The Latin Kings and Queens solved many of the difficulties of young Puerto Rican men and women. For those who were incarcerated, the most pressing was protection from other inmates. For a first-time arrestee, membership in an organization that applied blanket protection throughout the prison system was a blessing. It bestowed status and prestige and allowed disputes with other members to be arbitrated peacefully. Gang membership was also advantageous on return to civilian life. Where many members' households were chaotic, the gang functioned as an alternative family that prescribed rules and justifications for behavior, thereby bringing order and structure into potentially unmanageable social and emotional situations. For those who had histories of substance abuse or who were infected with HIV, the gangs functioned as vital support networks. As one member of the Asociación Ñeta explained:

> A lot of members have had a history with drugs. Like myself, I sold, I used. We recognize the difficulty that some people have had and what leads them to these

things. So, before they go and fall, we go and pick them up as quick as possible. In order to help somebody, you've got to be more than concerned. You can call yourself a friend if you're only there some of the time. But if you're a family member, you have to be there 24/7. If we found out that a member was shooting dope, we'd go after him, and talk with him, and make sure that he did something with his life. We'd try and change it for him. We'd try and get him off it. And if we can't, then he can't be a Ñeta. But we'd give him a chance to get his shit together. Other people don't do that, they want it right there and then.

After more than two decades of unimpeded violence perpetrated by the state and callous corporate-style drug dealers, the Latin Kings and Queens and the Ñetas represented an indigenous attempt to impose order and structure on what had become an unmanageable situation. Operating within a larger historical context and discourse of violence, their efforts to manage its arbitrary and seemingly random application resonated with a wide swath of residents in Latino neighborhoods. Especially attracted to these organizations were the pawns of the drug wars—local youths—who repudiated both sides (the police/state and the dealers) as they refocused attention and energy on their emergent notion of community.

One irony is that just as the Latin Kings and Queens and the Ñetas began to attract large numbers of new members, the state was systematically dismantling their leadership (see chapters 5–8, 10, and 15 of this volume). One outcome of this confluence of events was that there was a rapid growth in these loosely structured street organizations, but they often lacked direction and coherence. The central and legitimate concerns that animated these organizations attracted many neighborhood youths (and a considerable number of older members as well), but their broad umbrella was, at least initially, spread too wide. As the Latin Kings/Queens and the Ñetas skyrocketed to popularity, their rolls swelled to include a wide variety of members who would later be winnowed out as the organizations sought to better define themselves. Among those who were systematically weeded out over the next several years were young teens, whose impulsive tendencies brought too many headaches for the newly formed leadership. Also included were those for whom membership was calculated for personal gain more than the collective betterment of the community, particularly those who explicitly used their gang membership to engage in blatant drug distribution or use.

RETRENCHMENT IN THE DRUG BUSINESS AND THE GANGS: 1992–94

Interviews with many drug-selling youths during this period tended to highlight the perception about the Latin Kings that although there were serious tensions and disputes between members in leadership positions, the organization did little to oversee the everyday activities of many low-level or marginal members, and membership in the "Nation" often seemed to be self-determined in these early days of organizing. There were many young men and women who, in the early 1990s, were loosely affiliated with the Latin Kings and Queens or other street organizations, but who seemed to drift in and out of the "Nation" without much notice or fanfare. The organizations had substantial core memberships who regularly attended formal meetings, but they also had significant numbers of sympathizers who, if not full-fledged or official members, adopted styles that signified their support. Lacking a well-formed leadership, there were few attempts by the organizations to impose or monitor behavioral standards upon members during this period. In this rapid growth phase, it was sometimes difficult to discern who was or was not a Latin King or a Ñeta. By 1993, so many local youths had begun wearing the colors associated with Latin Kings or Ñetas, that the organizations found it necessary to standardize their symbols. The Latin Kings began to insist that members use a particular type of gold bead (the transparent ones) in their signature black-and-gold-beaded necklaces so that bona fide members could differentiate themselves from the "wanna-bes." For example, Macho was a nineteen-year-old occasional drug seller in Bushwick who, for a period of time, wore Latin King colors, but was clearly peripheral to the organization:

> Fieldnotes: The interview was almost complete when I asked Macho about the yellow and black beads he was wearing—a necklace, bracelet, and ring. He said that he was a Latin King, but the beads were not the clear type that Kings are supposed to wear these days. When I asked him what chapter he belonged to, he was evasive: "I attend meetings, but I don't know the name of the tribe. We're starting a new one around here," he told me. I don't think that he's really a King and I wondered why he made a public display of the beads.

Macho was a sad case: a decent enough kid who had the barest minimum of education, no job skills, a shaky family life, few friends, no girlfriend, no money, and no real aspirations that were evident. He survived by occasionally selling drugs (though his heart was not in it) and doing robberies (which made him uncomfortable). Not interested in dope, coke, or crack, he's content to smoke weed and chill out, but with no money, he can barely afford to smoke a blunt a day. At nineteen, it is hard to imagine where he might end up, but he says that he's chilling out and leading a boring life because he doesn't want to end up in prison.

Street vendors in Latino neighborhoods, where young men like Macho bought their clothing accessories, were important barometers of the ascendancy of gang styles: From 1988 to 1990, the hottest selling items were marijuana symbols, particularly Philly Blunt T-shirts and sweatshirts. Beginning in 1993, however, the most popular item was beaded necklaces of the Puerto Rican flag. Marijuana had been a potent symbol of anticrack sentiment in these ravaged neighborhoods, but as local discontent with both sides in the drug war grew in its intensity, popular sentiment relegated marijuana to the back burner as community consciousness (expressed here as nationalist sentiment, "Puerto Rican pride") became prominently displayed on every street corner.

Even though the emergence of Latino street organizations gave expression to local people's disgust with the police/state and the corporate drug barons, the drug business still underwrote much of the economic activity in these neighborhoods. For many people, the ideal of "uplifting" the Latino community still had to give way to paying the rent and putting food on the table. Acknowledging this apparent contradiction, the Latin Kings in Bushwick, for example, allowed drug dealers to become members of the "Nation," but they were required to pay extra dues and were not allowed to wear their "colors" while working. This accommodation by street organizations to the material needs of their members was important in that it served to undermine the organizations' ability to make good on their rhetoric, but also served the needs of the police by providing them with enough arrests of "gang members" to "spin" the idea through the media that the drug business was being taken over by the Latin Kings, the Ñetas, and later, the Bloods and the Crips. By this time, however, the drug business had begun to change in response to its protracted war with the police, and street-level drug dealers were far less visible than the corporate drug hawkers had been. The idea that gangs were taking over the drug business made great headlines and justified greater funding for the NYPD's gang intelligence unit, but it was a story without legs.

Worn down by incessant and aggressive policing, stung by the loss of neighborhood support, and suffering from a general stagnation in heroin and cocaine sales, many of the remaining drug businesses in the neighborhood adapted their operations to fit these new realities. The reconfigured businesses no longer conducted transactions in the street and sold almost exclusively to consumers they knew. In moving to indoor locations such as bodegas, delis, poolrooms, the lobbies of buildings, and in apartments, fewer operatives were needed to run the businesses and their blatancy was greatly reduced. The more successful businesses in the postcorporate era explicitly sought to integrate themselves into the neighborhood and continued to operate with little trouble in a climate that had adversely affected the corporate sellers (Curtis and Wendel 2000). One crack dealer contrasted his discreet operation with the corporate-style distributors who had once controlled business several blocks away:

> This [my area] is the suburbs. That's [the corporate area] like New York, do you know what I'm saying? This is the suburbs, and that is like a pile of shit down there. And, you know, this is like this because I maintain it like this. I demand this to be like this. I don't want my workers fucking around with people. Do you notice how many people walk by, and not one of these people called the police on my guys? You don't disrespect nobody. My guys don't make sales in front of kids or wives. You stop, let the customer wait, let the pedestrian pass by, make sure it is clear, and then you make your sale. Respect. That is all it is. You have to respect people, especially when you are in a dirty game. You have to. There is no ifs, or buts, or maybes. Work with me, you have to respect, if not, go work for [the corporate guys] and go to jail.

If gangs were to make inroads into the drug business, this period of retooling would have been the perfect time: The drug market was in chaos and few could have challenged newcomers, and the Latino gangs were making strides toward better organizing themselves in the wake of wholesale changes in their leadership structure. Latino gangs during this period, however, were not interested in taking over the drug markets; instead, they were recruiting members on the strength of an antidrug, anticrime, antiviolence, prohealth, proeducation, and culturally affirming platform. Giving a coherent voice to the grievances that had initially filled their ranks, the Latin Kings/Queens and the Ñetas were actively reaching out to community intellectuals in search of guidance and legitimacy. As one former drug user and dealer remarked:

From the time I became a Ñeta, I found a change in my life. I now had a purpose and I was doing something. My position in the *capítulo* is to go out and talk with people in authority like police and community leaders. And then, I would talk with the brothers and sisters. I would teach them, tell them about how things were and what I did, how jail used to be, how jails can be if we stick together and know how to live with each other. Since I've been in this *capítulo*, we've tried to help people. We want to be there for the people 'cause there's nobody out here for them. And for a lot of them, when things turn real bad, they seem to turn to drugs or start to drink. But if people have people who are concerned about what they are doing and are going to go out there for them, they'll accept you. We have contacted other helping organizations in the community, like the National Congress for Puerto Rico, and we work with them. A lot of our leaders work with them and help them politically. We do a lot of things like help with voter registration. We help out. We do a lot of things. Sometimes, a lot of community organizations call us when they have rallies. And we go with them on marches.

During the mid-1990s, the rapidly expanding street organizations were focused on rebuilding their leadership structure, and, consequently, individual members who felt that they had to earn income via drug sales were afforded considerable latitude by the organizations. Rather than closely monitoring the behavior of group members, aspiring leaders within the movements devoted considerable time and energy to reconnecting themselves to their ancestors (e.g., the Young Lords) and giving an articulate voice to the concerns that had attracted so many young people to their ranks. Individual members, however, constantly struggled to find a balance between the ghosts of the past, the needs of the present, and their visions of the future. The need to impose structure, make money, and do something "positive" was a daily challenge for many members of the Latin Kings/Queens and the Ñetas.

DISCUSSION

At first glance, the "gang" phenomenon in New York City seems paradoxical: It occurred precisely at a time when crime and violence had fallen to unprecedented lows (Krauss 1996; Butterfield 1997). The sound-bite-driven analyses by the media and the reductionist approaches by many academics credited the mayor and his police department for achieving what many had thought impossible, taming the unruly people who live in the unmanageable neighborhoods. But despite their ballyhooed successes in combating crime and restoring "quality of life" to neighborhoods, the "gang problem" was a nagging fly in the ointment. To many, this was a disturbing trend that defied explanation: If the mayor had the city under "lockdown," and conditions at the local level were improving, then why were gangs becoming more popular in these neighborhoods?

What is not understood or appreciated by these observers is how the Latin Kings and the Ñetas were transformed in the early to mid-1990s as they moved from the jails to the streets, and the significance that these types of organizations had for young men and women who lived in neighborhoods that had been the primary battlegrounds in the war on drugs, a war that pitted heavily armed police against ruthless corporate-style drug-dealing organizations. The Latin Kings, the Ñetas, and other street organizations gained popularity in New York City in the early and mid-1990s as a response to the unparalleled levels of violence via the war on drugs, which threatened to traumatize an entire generation of youth who lived there, and more fundamentally, as a forward-looking response to the social, economic, and political deterioration that afflicted their neighborhoods.

The gangs fulfilled many functions for these young men and women, but perhaps paramount in their eyes was their attempt to restore order and structure in what had become a chaotic situation. One hallmark of the gang movement that emerged in the early and mid-1990s was the extraordinarily high level of individual and collective agency in response to the dynamics of their changing social, political, and economic circumstances. Initially, the Latin Kings and the Ñetas recruited many of their members among disillusioned Puerto Rican youths, incarcerated in the war on drugs, who were ready to repudiate a way of life that had visibly distracted them from their families and neighborhoods. As the movements matured, however, ethnic exclusivity and competition increasingly gave way to ethnic incorporation, and youths from many backgrounds were recruited, including Dominicans and South and Central Americans. In becoming a Latin King/Queen or a Ñeta, these young men and women tried to reconstitute their lives, gain self-esteem, and "uplift the Latino community." Just as the construction of moderate- and low-income housing came to symbolize the rebuilding of the infrastructure of inner-city neighborhoods, these grassroots movements represent a reawakening and reorientation of working-class people's collective resistance to the state and other oppressors.

The street organizations that emerged in the early and mid-1990s served to galvanize and focus the discontent that had been slowly building in these neighborhoods for years and channel it into individual and collective action. Many observers, like the police and corrections officials, were mystified and alarmed at how quickly these organizations seemed to materialize—seemingly out of nowhere. As the large corporate-style drug-dealing organizations were methodically targeted and dismantled by the police, leaving a vacuum in the market, there was an assumption that these gangs would, quite naturally, fill the void. This was, after all, what nearly everyone says that gangs are supposed to do. The assumption was further reinforced by the fact that many of the young men and women who had been the main "quarry" in the war on drugs (i.e., the street-level operatives) were switching allegiances and becoming gang members. Even if the assumptions made about these gangs lacked empirical evidence to support them, they provided a convenient and credible excuse for the city to institute harsh "preventive" measures.

Although public officials, the police, and the media misread the signals with respect to these emergent street organizations (a thoroughly cynical interpretation would be that they knew exactly what was going on), the sea change that they represented in the attitudes and orientations of young people was clear to all but the most clueless of local residents. The majority of local young people did not become gang members during this period, but the significance of their message was reflected in the degree to which gang styles and sensibilities came to dominate youth discourse.

In some ways, it is remarkable that the gangs did not attempt to fill the vacuum that the demise of the corporate drug dealing organizations had created in the early 1990s. After all, many of the young men and women who joined street organizations were unemployed and had served time in jail or prison, so legal employment was less of an option to them. Although the potential profits from drug sales were attractive to many members, several factors mitigated against their involvement during this period, not the least of which was the massive buildup of antinarcotics police who were engaged in a search-and-destroy mission aimed at street-level drug markets in their neighborhoods. As drugs receded from public view, the reconfiguration of drug markets during this period saw the emergence of new forms of

retail drug dealing, especially delivery services (Curtis and Wendel 2000)—
forms of distribution that were dependent upon greater intimacy between
sellers and buyers and, in many respects, antithetical to the kind of large-
scale operations that gangs might have brought with them. The discreetness
of these new markets and the shift to private venues for consuming drugs
also stood in contrast with the very public displays that characterized gangs
during this period. As drug dealers and users were ducking for cover, members of the Latin Kings and the Ñetas were, by their own choice, highly visible in local affairs.

NOTE

1. The various sponsors of research over this period have included: the Social
   Ecology of Crime and Drug Use in American Cities: Social Structure and
   Neighborhood Dynamics (Social Science Research Council); Social Factors
   and HIV Risk (NIDA no. DA06723); HIV Risk Among Youth (National
   Institute of Allergy and Infectious Diseases no. A134723); Latin Kings and
   Gang Violence (Harry Frank Guggenheim Foundation); the Natural History
   of Crack Distribution (NIDA no. DA05126-05); Drug Use and HIV Risk
   among Youth (NIDA no. DA10411); and Heroin in the Twenty-first Century (NIDA no. DA10105-02).

REFERENCES

Becker, H. S. 1963. *Outsiders*. New York: Free Press.
Belenko, S., G. Nickerson, and T. Ruberstein. 1990. *Crack and the New York
    Courts: A Study of Judicial Responses and Attitudes*. New York: New York City
    Criminal Justice Agency.
Bernard, H. 1994. *Research Methods in Anthropology: Qualitative and Quantitative
    Approaches*. 2d ed. Thousand Oaks, Calif.: Sage.
Bourgois, P. 1989. In search of Horatio Alger: Culture and Ideology in the Crack
    Economy. *Contemporary Drug Problems*, 16: 619–649.
Braverman, H. 1970. *Monopoly Capital*. New York: Monthly Review Press.
Brown, C. 1965. *Manchild in the Promised Land*. New York: Macmillan.
Burroughs, W. S. 1958. *Junkie*. New York: Harcourt, Brace, Jovanovich.
Butterfield, F. 1997. Number of Victims of Crime Fell Again in '96, Study Says:
    Lowest Level since Reports Began in 1973. *New York Times*, 16 November,
    p. A18.
Campbell, A. 1987. *Girls in the Gang*. New York: Basil Blackwell.
City of New York, Mollen Commission. 1994. Commission Report: Commission
    to Investigate Allegations of Police Corruption and the Anti-corruption Proce-
    dures of the Police Department, 7 July.

Cloward, R. A., and L. B. Ohlin. 1960. *Delinquency and Opportunity: A Theory of Delinquent Gangs*. New York: Free Press.

Cohen, A. K. 1955. *Delinquent Boys: The Culture of Gangs*. Glencoe, Ill.: Free Press.

Courtwright, D., H. Joseph, and D. Des Jarlais. 1989. *Addicts Who Survived: An Oral History of Narcotic Use in America, 1923–1965*. Knoxville: University of Tennessee Press.

Curtis, R. 1996. The War on Drugs in Brooklyn, New York: Street Level Drug Markets and the Tactical Narcotics Team. Ph.D. diss., Teachers College, Columbia University, New York.

Curtis, R., and L. Maher. 1992. Highly Structured Drug Markets on Williamsburg's Southside. Paper prepared under contract with the Social Science Research Council. Working Group on the Social Ecology of Drugs and Crime.

Curtis, R., and T. Wendel. 2000. Toward the Development of a Typology of Illegal Drug Markets. In M. Natarajan and M. Hough, eds., *Illegal Drug Markets: From Research to Prevention Policy*, vol. 11 of *Crime Prevention Studies*. Monsey, N.Y.: Criminal Justice Press.

Curtis R., S. R. Friedman, A. Neaigus, B. Jose, and M. Goldstein. 1994. Emerging Patterns of Drug Use among Youth in a Neighborhood with High HIV Seroprevalence. Paper presented at the annual meeting of the American Public Health Association, Washington, D.C., December.

Decker, S., T. Bynum, and D. Weisel. 1998. A Tale of Two Cities: Gangs as Organized Crime Groups. *Justice Quarterly*, 15: 295–425.

Durnin, R. L. 1987. *Erasmus Hall Academy and High School: 200 Years*. New York: City College of New York.

Fagan, J. 1989. The Social Organization of Drug Use and Drug Dealing among Urban Gangs. *Criminology*, 27 (4): 633–669.

———. 1995. Gangs, Drugs, and Neighborhood Change. In C. Ronald Huff, ed., *Gangs in America*. 2d ed. New York: Sage.

Geis, G. 1965. *Juvenile Gangs*. Washington, D.C.: President's Committee on Juvenile Delinquency and Youth Crime.

Gilbert, J. 1986. *A Cycle of Outrage*. New York: Oxford University Press.

Golub, A., and B. Johnson. (1997). Crack's Decline: Some Surprises among U.S. Cities. National Institute of Justice, Research in Brief, July 1997. Washington, D.C.: National Institute of Justice.

Hamid, A. 1990. The Political Economy of Crack-related Violence. *Contemporary Drug Problems*, 17 (1): 31–78.

Hamid, A., R. Curtis, K. McCoy, J. McGuire, A. Conde, W. Bushell, R. Lindenmayer, K. Brimberg, S. Maia, S. Abdur-Rashid, and J. Settembrino. 1997. The Heroin Epidemic in New York City: Current Status and Prognoses. *Journal of Psychological Drugs*, 29 (4): 375–391.

Jankowski, M. S. 1991. *Islands in the Street: Gangs and American Urban Society*. Berkeley: University of California Press.

Kasarda, J.D. 1992. The Severely Distressed in Economically Transforming Cities.

In A. D. Harrell and G. E. Peterson, eds., *Drugs, Crime, and Social Isolation: Barriers to Urban Opportunity.* Washington, D.C.: Urban Institute Press.

Koslofsky, J. 1981. Going Foreign: Causes of Jamaican Migration. North American Congress on Latin America (NACLA) Report on the Americas, vol. 15, no. 1 (January–February).

Krauss, C. 1996. Crime Rate Plummets to Levels Not Seen in 30 Years. *New York Times.* 20 December, p. A1.

Lambert, E. 1990. *The Collection and Interpretation of Data from Hidden Populations.* NIDA Research Monograph 98. Rockville, Md.: National Institute on Drug Abuse.

Malcolm X. 1992. *The Autobiography of Malcolm X.* New York: Ballantine.

Mandel, E. 1975. *Late Capitalism.* Rev. ed. Atlantic Highlands, N.J.: Humanities Press.

Matza, D., and G. M. Sykes. 1961. Juvenile Delinquency and Subterranean Values. *American Sociological Review,* 26: 712–719.

McCullough, D. 1983. *Brooklyn—And How It Got That Way.* New York: Dial Press.

Miller, W. 1958. Lower Class Culture as a Generating Milieu of Gang Delinquency. *Journal of Social Issues,* 14: 5–19.

Mollenkopf, J. H., and M. Castells. 1991. *Dual City: Restructuring New York.* New York: Russell Sage Foundation.

Sassen-Koob, S. 1989. New York City's Informal Economy. In A. Portes, M. Castells, and L. A. Benton, eds., *The Informal Economy: Studies in Advanced and Less Developed Countries.* Baltimore: Johns Hopkins University Press.

Skolnick, J. 1992. Gangs in the Post-industrial Ghetto. *American Prospect,* vol. 3, no. 8 (1 January): 109–120.

Sutton, J. 1979. *Aleppo-in-Flatbush: The Story of a Unique Jewish Ethnic Community.* New York: Thayer-Jacoby.

Sviridoff, M., S. Sadd, R. Curtis, and R. Grinc. 1992. *The Neighborhood Effects of New York City's Tactical Narcotics Team on Three Brooklyn Precincts.* Vera Institute of Justice.

Tabor, M. 1992. The World of a Drug Bazaar, Where Hope Has Burned Out. *New York Times.* 1 October, p. B1.

Taylor, C. 1990. *Dangerous Society.* East Lansing: Michigan State University Press.

Venkatesh, S. 2000. *American Project.* Cambridge: Harvard University Press.

Verghara, C. 1991. New York's Ghettos. *The Nation* (17 June): 804–810.

Wallace, R. 1990. Urban Desertification, Public Health, and Public Order: Planned Shrinkage, Violent Death, Substance Abuse, and AIDS in the Bronx. *Social Science and Medicine,* 31 (7): 801–813.

Wallerstein, E. 1974. *The Modern World System: Capitalist Agriculture and the Origins of the European World-Economy in the Sixteenth Century.* New York: Academic Press.

Weppner, R. S. 1977. *Street Ethnography: Selected Studies of Crime and Drug Use in Natural Settings*. Beverly Hills: Sage Publications.

Yablonsky, L. 1962. *The Violent Gang*. New York: Macmillan.

Zimmer, L. 1985. *Operation Pressure Point: The Disruption of Street-level Drug Trade on New York's Lower East Side*. New York: New York University School of Law.

———. 1990. Proactive Policing against Street-level Drug Trafficking. *American Journal of Police*, 9 (1): 43–74.

4

MARGINAL YOUTH, PERSONAL IDENTITY, AND THE CONTEMPORARY GANG: RECONSTRUCTING THE SOCIAL WORLD?

KEVIN MCDONALD

We are witnessing a profound transformation in contemporary youth experience. But with this awareness comes an increasing difficulty in making sense of what is happening. Older models of youth constructed in terms of a more or less linear transition from childhood to adulthood no longer seem to make sense in a network society, where culture is oriented to the present, not to the future (Laidi 2000). Images of young people seem to oscillate from one extreme to the other, from potential victim to potential threat, while youth experience seems to express increasingly urgent social anxieties, from the danger of anomic violence and the threat of social disconnection to an increasingly pervasive illegal economy organized in terms of personal relationships.

During the 1980s, it seemed that the social world was becoming so fragmented and our theoretical tools so inadequate that social analysis had become impossible—a context that led to the all-pervasive theme of "post-modernity" in the social sciences. But this period of deconstruction of older frameworks of analysis is over. Social life is reconstructing: New social relationships are emerging, new forms of suffering, conflict, and possibility are taking shape. A century ago, the sociologist Max Weber attempted to make sense of the shift from familial to bureaucratic-industrial capitalism. Today we face no less of a challenge—attempting to make sense of the shift from bureaucratic-industrial capitalism to network capitalism (Boltanski and Chiapello 1999). And here the experience of young people is critical. Young people more than any other group live the new world of network capitalism—its culture, its freedoms, its forms of conflict; but also its forms of suffering and destruction of the person.

In this chapter, I consider some dimensions of the social world of marginal young people—young people in gang experiences, graffiti writers, and other marginal situations—as a lens to explore this wider social reality. In turn, I consider dimensions of this new social pattern as a way to explore changes in the experience of marginal young people. This highlights young people constructing defensive worlds in response to the new modes of personality increasingly demanded in network capitalism. But we encounter more than just defensive worlds—the experience of these young people points as well to forms of conflict that may point to a reconstruction of social life.

NETWORK CAPITALISM AND SELF-IDENTITY

Sociologists are increasingly analyzing shifts in contemporary social life within a context framed by the development of network capitalism. Industrial capitalist society was based on the principles of the assembly line (or Fordism—after Henry Ford, whose automobile factories pioneered this mode of production); it was a form of social organization based on the separation of public and private (bureaucratic organization), strong roles, a culture of the future, and an emphasis on function, hierarchy, and predictability. Today we live in a social world organized around radically different principles: Complexity and uncertainty replace standardization and predictability, network replaces hierarchy, communication replaces function.

There is now an extensive body of literature exploring the social patterns associated with network capitalism (see, for example, Castells 1997). Most of this focuses on the new patterns of social polarization emerging in the context of "post-Fordism" (as societies are no longer organized around mass production)—in particular, the new patterns of spatial polarization associated with the development of "global cities" (Sassen 1991). These new forms of spatial division are critical to make sense of emerging urban youth cultures and identities, underlining new forms of urban segregation represented by the "gated community" (Blakely and Snyder 1997) and the decline of a form of urban culture that sustains the encounter with the stranger.

But if we want to understand emerging urban youth cultures, we need to move beyond these analyses of social polarization and begin to explore the forms of individuality and connection that also characterize this emerging global/network culture. French sociologist Alain Ehrenberg (1995) underlines the extent to which contemporary social transformation involves a radical transformation of individuality itself. We have moved from a model of selfhood constructed in terms of discipline, duty, sacrifice, and security—a cultural model at the center of the assembly line—to one constructed in terms of risk, challenge, initiative, decision, competition, and the extreme. The new paradigm of individual action and self-creation is characterized by uncertainty, weak roles, and a culture of communication. It demands self-esteem and the ability to enter into relationships with the other, rather than obedience and fulfilling roles (McDonald 1999). In his exploration of the cultural models associated with "flexible capitalism," Richard Sennett underlines the increasing demands to reinvent oneself and is concerned that the culture of the short term is undermining the ability to construct long-term relationships (1997). If traditional societies are oriented to the past, and industrial society is oriented to the future, then network society is oriented to the present (Laidi 2000). Networks do not project into the future, in contrast to the imagination of industrial society and the assembly line. We can see the importance of the "now" in contemporary culture, from extreme sports that amplify the present to the succession of presents that make up the music video clip.

Arguably, young people live this model more intensely than other groups because they are the first generation to have to negotiate the transition from childhood to adulthood in this new context. We can see this in the weakening place of roles and institutions in the experience of young people. Important dimensions of this are illustrated in the school context. In the institutional school, roles are clear, and the mode of learning involves learning by internalization. In the contemporary school, learning is increasingly personalized, it is project based, and the successful student is one who is able to turn learning into a vector of self-discovery, to use it to establish a positive relationship with oneself. In the emerging social model, self-esteem is a condition for successful negotiation of the social world. In the contemporary school, the learning experience is far freer, but it also causes the student to directly confront the self. We can see this in studies of the experience of assessment—in the institutional school, organized in terms of roles, students understand that it is their work that is being assessed. In the contemporary school, increasingly students feel that it is their personality, their subjectivity, that is being assessed. Here the costs of failure are much higher (Barrère 2000).

This underscores a critical dimension to exploring the social world of marginal young people today: Although social roles constrain, they also protect. If the contemporary school is freer for the student today, with less of the constraint associated with the institutional school, the student's personality is subsequently more exposed (Dubet 1997). With the new freedom comes a new imperative—establishing a positive relationship with oneself as a medium for negotiating the social world and entering into a relationship with the other. As Richard Sennett emphasizes (1997), in the contemporary social world of flexible capitalism, we are all confronted with reinventing ourselves—turning our lives into an original story. The demand to produce identity is being pushed back on the person, it is less the product of institutions. This involves new freedoms, celebrated in the culture of risk and extremes. But it also involves new vulnerabilities, evident in increasing rates of depression or forms of personal fragmentation and disconnection.

If the new social model demands self-esteem, the capacity to enter into communication with the other, and the production of a coherent identity, the experience of young people today underlines the increasingly unequal distribution of the social and cultural resources necessary to construct such an identity. This is at the center of contemporary urban youth cultures. We can see this when we compare contemporary experiences to the social model associated with the classical gang.

THE CLASSICAL GANG

The concept of "gang" was constructed by sociologists to make sense of a form of youth experience marked by a specific time, place, and social process. As a sociological concept, "the gang" was used to explore the social patterns and conflicts emerging in American cities at the time of immigration and industrialization—the paradigm case being Chicago in the 1920s, studied by Thrasher (1927). The studies undertaken by the sociologists who would later become known as the "Chicago School" focused on several critical dimensions to the gang experience. First, the gang was a form of social organization, associated with experiences of migration to the city, which involved competition for control over a territory. Second, this competition with other gangs reinforced loyalty to the group—in that sense, external competition reinforced internal loyalty and identity. Third, the gang structure is characterized by hierarchy, with a clearly defined set of roles within the gang. Fourth, the gang is a producer of identity—it has a significant ritual dimension, from rites of initiation to rites of exclusion. Fifth, the gang emerges in social and spatial contexts characterized by the weakening of traditional forms of community authority (linked to the loss of status of parents, particularly the father, as a result of the immigration experience), and finally, in a context involving barriers to fully participating in the new society—these could be the school system, racism, or other forms of stigmatization.

These studies allow us to underscore two dimensions as critical to the gang experience. First, the gang is a response to *social disorganization:* It produces order in a world of disorder. Second, the gang is a response to barriers to participation, or to *social exclusion:* Excluded from society, the members of the gang fall back on a territory or a turf and make it their own. The gang can thus be seen as a spatial response to social exclusion (Dubet 1987). This classical sociological approach regards the gang as a transitional form of social organization, one associated with the experience of the children of immigrants who confront both barriers to participation in society and the weakening of traditional forms of authority. Important elements of this traditional form of authority, involving a culture of honor and personal loyalty, are reinvented in the gang, with its culture of hierarchy based on violence.

For most of the twentieth century, the gang was regarded by many sociologists as a particularly American form of social organization, associated with the ethnic spatial patterns found in American cities and the weaker class integration and high levels of immigration characterizing the United States. For sociologists, the gang was a form of social organization that would develop in the early stages of industrialization, an "in-between" experience where traditional community was disorganized and where young people from these communities found themselves excluded from the benefits of the country they had migrated to. The core social process that the gang points to, for the classical model, is the convergence of social exclusion and social disorganization that one would expect to find associated with the early period of industrialization and immigration. As industrial society develops, this model predicts that the incidence of gangs will decline, with social class becoming the more important basis of identity, conflict, and integration.

For much of the second half of the twentieth century, this seemed to be the case. The studies of the Chicago School—focused on the city, immigration, the gang, and questions of social integration—did not seem to capture the dramas being lived by the United States in the second half of the twentieth century. Although the lower incidence of immigration and the importance of social class meant that gang experiences remained marginal in most European countries, in the case of Australia, an emphasis on assimilation, full employment, and trade unionism meant that the forms of gang experience associated with pre-1945 United States did not emerge. The gang, from a sociological point of view, seemed a specific form of social experience associated with pre-1945 industrialization.

But during the 1980s, it became clear that something new was happening—across a series of countries, not just the United States, forms of street-level culture and organization seemed to point to a return of the gang—but this time in a very different context. For the Chicago School sociologists, the experience of marginalized young people told a great deal about broader social organization. This is a very important idea for us today: What does the contemporary experience of marginalized young people tell us about the emerging social model? Are we witnessing a return to the patterns of social organization of 1920s Chicago, or are we confronting a new set of questions?

MARGINAL YOUTH, PERSONAL IDENTITY, AND THE CONTEMPORARY GANG

Is the concept of "gang" of any use in making sense of the issues involved today where young people construct identity in relation to territory? It seems to me that there are significant continuities, but also very important differences. The core ideas of "social disorganization" and "social exclusion" remain critical to understanding these experiences—but at the same time we need to recognize the new questions posed in a context where the meanings of place and identity are radically transformed.

In the case of homeless young people in Melbourne, Australia, there are very clear continuities with the gang experience. Many of these young people have constructed worlds where they share a collective identity—defined in terms of the control of territory. They have developed rituals and tests of initiation where the potential members have to prove themselves worthy of joining, and once a member, the young person is bound by a strong code of loyalty to the group. This is manifested by a strong culture of hierarchy, and by competition with neighboring groups for the control of territory. But significantly, this territory most often is the local shopping mall, where different groups will attempt to deny access to the others. This points to the extent to which the global city, with its movement of people and weaker borders, involves a weakening of the idea of "neighborhood." It is the shopping mall, the symbol of consumption, freedom, and identity, rather than the borders to the suburb, that is the identity resource that these young people claim as their own.

We can see a similar transformation in the relationship to territory in the case of graffiti writers. They too have constructed a world of hierarchy, one with "kings" at the top and "toys" at the bottom, but the city is experienced in terms of flow and movement. The "writers" have colonized the train system, they occupy an urban space of movement and image, and have developed an aesthetic style that values complexity and flow. Their city is a network of signs and traces, not the defense of a bordered territory. They seek to leave a trace of themselves—otherwise, "you'll be forgotten" (McDonald 1999).

The continuities with the classical gang are clear. The gang of homeless young people is a strategy that produces order in a world of chaos; it produces predictability in a context where living on the streets (moving from squat to squat) means being in a situation that is highly vulnerable. The gang is involved in violence, but this violence is predictable and to some extent, it is governed by rules that make being part of the gang far more secure than being outside it. In the words of Tina—the leader of a gang of homeless young people in Melbourne—the gang is "routine" (McDonald 1999).

But just as the nature of relationships in network capitalism is changing, involving a greater personalization, so too in the contemporary gang. In the case I am referring to, the leader is a young woman. This illustrates a more general change in the nature of authority within the contemporary gang.

Pascal Duret (1998) explores contemporary gang cultures in France and detects a similar transformation. He underlines a shift from a model of "virile authority" based on physical force and unilateral respect, to a more fluid form of relationship based on a demand for reciprocity—a relational model based more on admiration than on fear. The group not only honors the fighting ability of the leader, but also his or her capacity for verbal jousting and joking—this reinforces group complicity. Being "smart" or manipulating others through cunning is not a source of dishonor, but a sign of ability, of not being a "loser." Older forms of deferring to the authority of the chief have weakened in a context where the chief has to demonstrate verbal ability—in a context where gang culture underlines that lack of success in education is not the result of lack of ability, but a path that is chosen. Although Tina refers to the fact that she is a good fighter, she constantly emphasizes that she is smarter than the members of her gang—this is the basis of her authority. Thus while the contemporary gang is structured in terms of hierarchy, the basis of authority has undergone a real transformation. We can see just how critically important this is when we explore the medium of exchange in contemporary gang relationships—"respect."

Respect is at the center of the gang experience, from the relationships in Tina's gang of homeless youths to the social world of graffiti writers, where "you get respect and you give respect." The phenomenon of respect is a universal in the cultures of marginal young people, and is the key to understanding a new social reality.

The classical gangs fell back on the neighborhood, defending it as their social world. Gans's study of an Italian American gang in the 1950s reveals a context wherein the young people of the Italian neighborhood would avoid contact with the middle class to avoid situations that would mark them as inferior (1962). The contemporary context is very different. The culture of the gang is not based on a strong neighborhood culture, and we see constant affirmations of the imperative of being recognized as belonging to society as a whole. Thus the importance of "brand-name" clothing—so critical to gang cultures. Whether in France, the United States, Brazil, or Australia, the brand emphasizes belonging to the broader consumer society, not the local community. The brand involves a search for respect that is constructed in relation to the dominant culture. In the case of marginal young people, the extent that the demand for recognition of full social participation takes this form leads to a constant fragility of identity—both personal and collective—in a context where identity must be constantly reaffirmed through the regard of the other, and where the self is constantly vulnerable to the lack of respect (see Vidal 2000 for an excellent discussion of the role of respect in interpersonal relationships among slum dwellers in Brazil).

The contemporary gang is a strategy to defend subjectivity in a culture where social domination is increasingly experienced in terms of personal failure (Ehrenberg 1995; McDonald 1999). But it is not a retreat into a community culture. We can see this in the paradoxical example of young people who reject school as an experience that threatens their subjectivity while embracing the forms of status offered by consumer culture. But this embracing of brand culture is always associated with the cultivation of microdifferences that allows an affirmation of belonging to join an affirmation of individuality.

The culture of respect is also at the center of the contemporary experience of violence in the world of marginal young people. The world of the classical gang was structured in terms of a code of honor, an ethic of one-on-one, and to break this ethic was a source of dishonor. The contemporary experience is radically different. Violence between gangs is no longer based on an ethic of one-on-one (the loyal contest), and there is no loss of honor for a group to beat up an individual. But the form of violence that takes place between members of the same gang is governed by quite different principles. Where a fight occurs among members of the same gang, it is important that the victor not humiliate the vanquished: The victor wishes to win the respect of the vanquished, and it is not possible to respect someone who has destroyed your own self-esteem. Thus intragroup violence will pay great attention to reaffirming the dignity of the defeated ("you fought well"), while violence between groups will have as a critical dimension the humiliation of the other. As Pascal Duret observes, "one can get over defeat, but not insult. It guarantees a future exchange of violence" (1998:43).

The violence of the classical gang was regulated by an ethic similar to that regulating the physical exchange in contact sports, while also being effectively regulated by the community—the older generation would step in if things started getting out of hand—and this community-based authority was recognized by the young people (Dubet 1992). The violence that takes place in the contemporary gang is of a different nature. The community is much more fragmented and diverse, to the extent that the parents of one youth are unlikely to know many neighbors of their own generation, much less their children. And as the sense of being part of a common world is much weaker, so too is any authority that older people can exercise vis-à-vis young people. Thus violence reflects a weakening of community and its integration.

Understanding the social meaning of contemporary violence is critical to any understanding of the gang experience. On the one hand, violence reflects a weakening of social regulation, a fragmentation of community. But on the other, violence serves as a medium of relationship. Tina describes the "buzz" of power she feels in the fear of the other, when people cross over to the other side of the street to let her and her gang pass. As Lapeyronnie argues, in a context of social stigmatization, violence enables its authors to reassure themselves of their social status through the social reduction of the other (1999). This is central to the forms of violence to which many young people are subject, such as having a cap or running shoes stolen, particularly in a public place such as the train system. This is not a form of instrumental theft. Significantly, the cap and the running shoes are signs of belonging to the culture of consumption—being dispossessed of them in public is a ritual that symbolically immobilizes the person, sending them back to a community that can visibly no longer protect them (older people often witness this form of theft on the transport system and rarely attempt to intervene). Such violence is a medium of disrespect, not only for the victim, but also for the community, which is powerless to stop it. This process points to a mode of urban experience that opposes those who have access to consumption and mobility and those who are trapped in poverty and neighborhood, and it points to the relationships of competition for the scarce resource of respect. This form of urban violence, as Lapeyronnie argues, emerges in a context wherein, unable to be recognized as an individual, the person can only exist as part of a group that imposes its power on specific urban spaces—violence becomes the norm of a group (1999:56).

It is wrong to read this violence in terms competition for relative levels on a status hierarchy. Although this could account for the violence of the classical gang, violence in the world of marginal young people is much more about securing self-esteem in a social world that makes increasingly powerful demands for it, while unequally distributing the resources necessary to achieve it. In this context, the demand for self-esteem sustains a strategy that seeks esteem from the other, and through this, one can achieve esteem in one's own eyes. This is the drama at the center of the contemporary gang experience, captured in the theme of respect, that makes it radically different from the context of the classical gang. In the contemporary global city, the increasing demand for self-esteem is accompanied by both increasing social segregation and increasing stigmatization that undermines both self-identity and the sense of belonging to a shared world. Violence responds to both processes—it is a strategy to achieve respect and to constitute a shared world. These are central to the development of the illegal economy, particularly the role of the drug economy in poor neighborhoods (Bourgois 1995).

RECONSTRUCTING THE SOCIAL

The imperative of self-esteem is essential for participation in the network society. It is central to the theme of "respect," which forms the foundation of the street cultures that have developed over the past twenty years. This imperative is the basis of new forms of gangs and of the role violence plays in the lives of marginal young people.

Beyond reflecting a weakening community and being a medium of affirming one's own identity through the denial of the other's, there is a third meaning of violence, a search for an encounter with an "other" that can constitute a limit, and in the process, allow the person to construct a boundary to one's experience. Lagrange underlines this dimension of the role of violence in the world of marginal young people when he argues "violence is less a refusal of limits that are imposed upon us than a search for limits, and as such, for a distinct identity" (2000:141). In this way, violence emerges where young people are unable to construct an experience of individuality—which is increasingly the case in the context of neighborhoods with rising concentrations of poverty.

In this context, the critical question for the reconstruction of a social world becomes: Under what conditions can the unilateral demand for respect through violence take the shape of a reciprocal respect—one based on mutual recognition? This is the question at the center of the contemporary experience of street cultures—Is it possible that the demand for self-respect can be sustained through an ethic of respect for the difference of the other?

At one level, the development of street cultures points to increasingly closed and self-referential worlds. But on another level, these cultures converge on conditions essential to the constitution of self-identity in a new form of society. This is not a psychological problem, but it underscores the unequal distribution of the resources necessary to construct coherent identity in this social model. Contemporary forms of conflict in the world of street cultures can lead to reactions of fear and recourse to the legal system. But there is much more at stake. On the one hand, we are confronted with the rising difficulty of constituting identity in network capitalism, and the increasingly unequal distribution of the resources needed to achieve this. On the other, we are confronted with different forms of social practice to achieve respect. And herein marginal youth cultures confront the dilemma at the very center of contemporary social life—constituting an ethic of respect based on the recognition of difference (see Taylor 1997).

In practical terms, what does this dilemma imply? We must recognize that although criminalizing street youth cultures may respond to community anxiety, it is not a response to the processes of social polarization and stigmatization, which are at the center of the contemporary gang experience. Nor can criminalization respond to the cultures of social connection and risk that sustain the illegal economy (the effect of increasing stigmatization actually serves to stimulate this economy). Didier Lapeyronnie (1999) underlines the extent to which the logic of belonging through consumption (which sustains both the gang and the wider illegal economy) emerges in a context where groups have been deprived of a political language to explore other forms of social connection and relationship—in particular, where localities and neighborhoods are controlled by machine politics, which dispossess people of any local autonomy, and where institutions such as the school are shaped by a middle-class culture and definition of social problems. In this context, he argues, the populations of poor neighborhoods experience a condition of "colonization," or nonrecognition to the point of nonexistence—leaving the inhabitants of these neighborhoods with the choice of accepting these middle-class models, or rejecting them through violence, which leads to an inevitable ghettoization.

These unfavorable choices suggest a counterresponse—one that emphasizes instead a process of transforming social demands (recognition, identity, respect) into political demands, and creates forms of public culture that can give localities and neighborhoods the opportunity to give them content and shape. This involves responding to the new challenges for democracy—in a social world where conflicts increasingly take place around the distribution of meaning rather than goods (Melucci 1996). Just as labor movements played a key role in reshaping the horizons of democracy at the beginning of the twentieth century, forging an ethic of justice grounded in work, new forms of street cultures may be central to reinventing democracy today, confronting us all with the challenge of respect in a society that simultaneously demands and denies individuality.

REFERENCES

Barrère, A. 2000. *Les léceens au travail*. Paris: Presses Universitaires de France.

Blakely, E., and M. Snyder. 1997. *Fortress America : Gated Communities in the United States*. Washington: Brookings Institution Press.

Boltanski, L., and E. Chiapello. 1999. Le nouvel esprit du capitalisme. Paris: Gallimard.

Bourgois, P. 1995. *In Search of Respect*. New York: Cambridge University Press.

Castells, M. 1997. *The Network Society*. Oxford: Blackwell.

Dubet, F. 1987. *La galère: jeunes en survie*. Paris: Fayard.

———. 1992. A propos de la violence des jeunes. *Cultures et Conflits*, 6: 7–24.

———. 1997. Le travail comme equivalent démocratique du jugement scolaire. In J. Ion and M. Pironi, eds., *Engagement publique et exposition de la personne*. Paris: Editions de l'Aube.

Duret, P. 1998. L'autorité virile dans les bandes, d'hier à aujourd'hui. *Migrants-Formations*, 112: 40–48.

Ehrenberg, A. 1995. *Le culte de la performance*. Paris: Calman-Levy.

Gans, H. 1962. *The Urban Villagers: Group and Class in the Life of Italo-Americans*. New York: Free Press.

Lagrange, H. 2000. Reconnaissance, délinquance, et violences collectives. *Esprit*, 10 (October): 131–152.

Laidi, Z. 2000. Le sacre du present. Paris: Flammarion.

Lapeyronnie, D. 1999. Contre-monde: Imitation, opposition, exclusion. *Les Annales de la Recherche Urbaine*, 83/84: 53–58.

McDonald, K. 1999. *Struggles for Subjectivity: Identity, Action, and Youth Experience*. Cambridge: Cambridge University Press.

Melucci, A. 1996. *The Playing Self*. Cambridge: Cambridge University Press.

Sassen, S. 1991. *The Global City*. Princeton: Princeton University Press.

Sennett, R. 1997. *The Corrosion of Character*. New York: Norton.

Taylor, C. 1997. *The Politics of Recognition*. Cambridge: Harvard University Press.

Thrasher, F. 1927. *The Gang: A Study of 1,313 Gangs in Chicago*. Chicago: Chicago University Press.

Vidal, D. 2000. Le respect: catégorie du social, catégorie du politique dans une fafela de Recife. *Cultures et Conflits*, 35: 95–124.

PART 2
GANGS AND POLITICS

5

GANGS AND THE CONTEMPORARY URBAN STRUGGLE: AN UNAPPRECIATED ASPECT OF GANGS

ALBERT DICHIARA AND RUSSELL CHABOT

GANGS AS A SOCIOLOGICAL PHENOMENON

Stereotypes dominate the debate about gangs. The most popular stereotypes are those that emphasize the criminal tendencies of gangs and the social and personal pathology of gang members. This is no less true for academic criminology, because the leaders of this field have adopted the control ideology of criminal justice agencies (Klein 1995). But it is important to remember that as sociological and criminological phenomena, gangs exist on several continua. Gangs vary in terms of criminality, social organization, ideological foundations, and degree of alienation. Gang members, too, range from the "wanna-be" to the "OG" (original gangster), from the irresponsible street soldier to the politically motivated and responsible street leader. Many say that claims by gangs that they can serve positive functions in the community are nothing more than spin used to relieve short-term problems with the police. Yet gang-sponsored positive activities, those that do not conform to dominant constructions of "the gang," should be viewed with a less cynical eye.

Our fieldwork with one gang in Hartford, Connecticut has convinced us that the multiple realities and contradictions that characterize gangs as social groups, and gang members as "outlaws" and community members, must be accounted for in any intellectually honest conceptualization of gangs. Ignoring the full range of activities sponsored by a gang leads one to a limited conclusion about gangs as social groups. Some gangs organize only criminal activities, others organize voter registration drives, community cleanups, and cultural awareness. The crime-oriented view of gangs may be useful for getting federal funding for research, but it tends to omit from analysis other important aspects of gangs—namely, their roots in a community that is wounded in one or several ways. The gang response to the social forces that negatively affect their community, sometimes in the form of positive activities and political activism, is a truly organic feature of the urban gang.

It is equally wrong to see gang formation and behavior as being totally reactive to poverty. No one disputes the effect of social forces on behavior among those who live in poverty and isolation. Yet if gang formation is a response to poverty and alienation, it should be viewed as a matter of degrees and not as "either-or." This is because a wide range of cultural artifacts (e.g., style, local gang folklore, national media influences) are used by gang members to *create* and *re-create* the gang. The process of gang social organization is influenced also by local concerns, either police or other gangs, and by expressive factors such as subcultural style. This complexity often reflects many contradictions, the most common contradiction being the claim by certain gangs that they can serve to further the political needs of the poor. Thus gang formation, organization, and change are both reactive and proactive to social forces and the gang members' perception of social reality—in terms of both individual and collective perceptions, as are sometimes elaborated in the gang's official ideology, its codified rules and regulations, or other group understandings. Clearly, some gangs maintain a proactive strategy that anticipates the needs of its members and the available resources that meet those needs. In this way, it can be said that some gangs exist in society as the institutionalization of alienation and cultural resistance.

Although the criminological literature includes many well-documented cases of gangs functioning as cultural and social resistance organizations, this view has not found a home in the dominant strands of criminological thinking about gangs. This paper examines the positive activities of Los

Solidos, one of the largest gangs in Hartford, Connecticut. The information and events reported here are based on both an ethnography of the gang (involving close interaction with the members for several years) and active involvement (helping with some of the gang's political activities in the mid-1990s). The research began in 1992 and continues, but the material reported here is limited to the period 1992–96.

As we will subsequently illustrate, the events presented here show that Los Solidos considered itself a political organization, albeit one that saw fit to use criminal activities to further the interests of its members. The positive activities of the Los Solidos organization served as a forum to express the needs of its members and, by implication, all urban minority youth. Rather than moving underground when negative publicity about the gang was presented, Los Solidos actively sought publicity and support for its positive activities. It facilitated communication between the membership, the gang's patrons, and even the police and the city. It pursued and secured funding for its initiatives and injected the gang into local economic and political debates.

The blanket indictment of gangs as criminal organizations is both intellectually dishonest and sociologically baseless. One cannot generalize about all gangs, but it is important to recognize that some gang activity is an expression of the struggles of the urban underclass (cf., Hobsbawm 1965). It is also important to recognize that urban gangs form in the context of deprivation, police repression, institutional failure, and personal disorganization. Some gangs—for example, the Almighty Latin King and Queen Nation of New York City and Chicago's Gangster Disciples—have moved to a point where political awareness motivates action.

To illustrate, Gangster Disciples has published a number of documents on its ideology and plans. According to the Gangster Disciples, the current gang structure is the core form of social organization for youth in the slums. Gangster Disciples statements indicate their view that Chicago gangs are in a decades-long power struggle with the white leaders of Chicago. They situate this conflict in the context of the struggle of disenfranchised African Americans to create their community on their terms and not on the terms of mainstream African American leaders. According to Nehemiah Russell, a spokesman for the Gangster Disciples, "the gangs have created a paradigm shift across the nation. Traditionally, African Americans functioned as house negroes or field negroes. Gang members do not consider themselves as house or field negroes. They consider themselves as runaway Africans" (no date:14).

Within this context of police oppression and the perceived "sell-out" by their leaders, gangs formed to fill social vacuums and create an alternative social order. Russell says "The movement toward [Black] freedom came to a halt in the 1970s, but the desire for full rights can never be satisfied outside victory to achieve that goal. Those years of hope when we were unafraid to recognize that all people group and define themselves and have a right to do so, were the years that the gang structures anchored in inner cities. *The residue of the freedom struggles of the 20th century in the African American community is, indeed, the gang structure*" (no date:1–2, emphasis in original) and the gang structure is the only "liberating structure" (13) available to poor, urban African Americans.

These views show that the Gangster Disciples are fighting for the power of self-identity and community control. So the modern gang is not "prepolitical"; in fact, contemporary gangs have had the opportunity to draw from political and popular culture to establish the parameters that express their discontent. Unlike the gangs of the Progressive Era, today's gangs are not as well connected to political bosses who can help focus gang energy toward positive ends. And to the extent that gangs have patrons in the community, they are often themselves members of relatively powerless and marginalized groups.

However, other gangs (for example, Hartford's Los Solidos) are in an embryonic stage wherein crime and political activities coexist. Concerning this point, it is important to realize that some gangs, although formally constituted and structured, are really emergent social formations that must continually respond to a variety of situational challenges and social forces. The fluid nature of gangs has been long appreciated, but fluidity has been wrongly understood as meaning impermanence, as in Yablonsky's idea of the "near group" (1959). As "emergent" social groups, it would be unrealistic to consider gangs as formal organizations because the nature of the social world of the gang is precarious and requires quick changes to deal with new events and realities. Yet the precarious social world affords an opportunity to explore how a gang develops and uses a political agenda and the social responses to their efforts.

It is important to respect the somewhat tenuous nature of gangs and to remember that external factors, both positive and negative, often change the gang's needs, motivations, and the response strategies used by the gang. At any given time, the gang will be this or that—a drug operation, or a source of ethnic pride, girls, parties, and jobs. Sometimes the gang is threatened, then it is dominating the local gang scene; it may be in need of more members—later, it is expelling other members; it is factionalized, and then unified. It should be accepted that not all gangs define themselves as criminal organizations, and recent events suggest more variety in gang activities than media do and police reports would suggest. Because of this complexity, Ruth Horowitz's advice is that it is "necessary to explore the social as a more continuing, evolving, and situationally constructed experience" (1990:42). The gang is many different things in its life as an organization; it changes to meet short-term exigencies, the changing needs of its members, and its changing goals. Thus the "gang" is not so much a thing as it is the totality of a series of ongoing "projects"—some criminal, others not.

Russell Chabot offers a framework in which to conduct such studies. He says the study of marginalized cultural worlds is best approached by paying attention to the contradictory, transient, and contingent nature of social relationships in those worlds. The notion of *projects* derives from work done in interpretative sociology, and the term *project* is defined as a fusion of conception and action in an interactional setting and is the social process by which objects of consciousness (for example, a gang) become "concrete in action" (1992:79). In such worlds, goals are only contingently defined, because the exigencies of life make them so tenuous. So in a situation where police, rival gangs, and others intrude on gang life, the actual day-to-day functioning as a social group is often redirected, stopped, or redefined as needed.

Correspondingly, in this study, we view the gang as a contingently defined social group making its collective way through the world, often responding to a variety of transitory and contradictory social situations. We ignore dominant notions of what is a gang so that the baggage of crime, violence, and other negative socially constructed images will be treated as a variation in behavior, not a defining property of the group (Ball and Curry 1995).

FRAMING THE LOS SOLIDOS MOVEMENT

In the period of this research, Los Solidos worked on four distinct projects: a gangster project, a family project, a business project, and a civic project. Support and resources from a collection of community patrons helped the gang develop and recast certain aspects of their positive projects, but the gang itself developed its business and civic obligations in its early years. The projects represented both long-term goals and short-term accommodations to social reality and the help offered by patrons.

Larry Beauvais, the acknowledged "godfather" of the Los Solidos, wrote the Los Solidos Handbook. Even though he is incarcerated, he still exerts influence on the gang through his continued leadership of the gang's Executive Council. His vision of the Los Solidos Nation grew from his experiences on the streets in the 1980s, his understanding of the decline in the Puerto Rican community in Hartford, and the limited chances of Puerto Rican youth. In both the handbook and in its daily activities, the gang was constituted as a set of four relatively well-articulated initiatives—short-term economic survival through drug sales, family support, community development, and eventual movement into the legitimate community. The gang's patrons emphasized similar themes and stressed the need for self-help and community building. One of the first challenges for the gang was to engage in both the social construction of reality and the creation of an image that would work to achieve its ends (both criminal and legitimate). The gang sought to offer a compelling story from which to gain public support and understanding. It did so by making its problems and complaints generalizable to the whole community, turning a common-held image of personal troubles into a useful political tool.

The evolution and transformation of the gangster project is illustrative of the gang's changing social construction of reality. The former president of OFO (Original Family Organization), the junior branch of Los Solidos, said that in 1991–92, when the local gangs were not yet a public or media concern, the Solids (as they are called in English) chose to present themselves as a gang in the most stereotypical sense.[1] The gang took the role of "badasses" as a challenge and deterrent to other gangs. In the early years, the "badass" frame was necessary in order for Los Solidos to claim a place in the Hartford gang scene.

In 1993, after things quieted down, Los Solidos organized a community cleanup day in which all members were required to work and this event is often mentioned as evidence of the true nature of Los Solidos. The leadership often expressed frustration that the community never fully appreciated the meaning of the gesture. In 1996, two superiors of Los Solidos attended a meeting of a local civic association's plans to create a youth center. When

asked why they were there, one responded " it's important that we participate in all efforts to help the community. A Solid at every meeting!" This
shift in "frame" from negative to positive, and from predatory to activist,
may be a core characteristic of gangs in the intermediate stages of change.

The Solids benefited because Hartford has a history of activist gangs. In
the 1970s, the Magnificent 20s established a youth disco, sponsored
Thanksgiving turkey giveaways, and donated money to community organizations. Eventually, they were approached by state and city agencies to help
with programs for delinquent and at-risk youth. In the 1990s, positive factions of the Solids were able to draw from this cache of "gang prehistory" to
establish an identity as a legitimate community constituency. The Solids
became friendly with former gang members and used the ideological and
organizational foundations of the older gangs as a source of edgy re-
spectability among some members of the community. The former gang
leaders also formed a network of streetwise patrons to augment and influence the work of the gang's patrons in the clergy, education, and academia.

In carrying on in this tradition, the Los Solidos Handbook describes the
gang as a family, details the organization of the illegal drug operation and
other criminal activities, and presents a call for legitimacy. For example, the
handbook expresses the following organizational goal that indicated the
gang's noncriminal projects:

> Our main objective at this point is to expand our Family into the mainstream of
> society. Therefore it would be good for you to bring your cousins, uncles, broth-
> ers, and friends into the Family so we can secure the backbone of our empire.
> In the process, we will be cleaning up our community by making them into one
> big Family and giving our children a safer environment to grow up in.
>
> *(Los Solidos Nation, no date)*

THE ROLE OF PATRONS

Having patrons in the community greatly helped the Solids to frame the
gang in an effective manner, and to move along on their positive projects.
Certainly the gang's leadership initiates a change in frame, but often change
may be motivated by patrons also. Patrons can facilitate the bridging of
frames through outreach efforts, help to clarify and reinvigorate frames, and
extend the boundaries of a frame to make it more powerful—for example,

making the gang problem a general problem of minority, disaffected, and poor youths (see Snow et al. 1986 for similarities in resource mobilization theory). The Solids' patrons helped to locate space for meetings, organize press conferences, and locate funding sources. They also worked closely with Los Solidos members rehearsing speeches for various groups, developing phrasing, an appropriate terminology, and other vocabularies that served the purposes of the gang. The patrons worked from themes and ideas generated by the gang and refined them for presentation. However, the work of the patrons is difficult to separate from the totality of the Solids' positive efforts.

Turning to projects, they are first and foremost the work of "organic intellectuals" within the gang. They are rooted in the life experiences and beliefs of the street youth that created and reproduce the gang. Patrons in the community are useful in helping to elaborate and polish the presentation of grievances, and in many cases they were essential in initiating positive projects through their access to funds and important individuals, and due to their reputations in the city. It is wrong to see the development of frames and projects as a unilinear or progressive movement. In reality, frames and their related projects are constrained and altered by situational factors, which imparts to them a less predictable quality. In addition, frames and projects may coexist in conflict, as in the coexistence of the gangster and civic projects. Such contradictions reflect the often confusing reality of the lives of Los Solidos members.

LOS SOLIDOS: FRAMING THE GOOD AND BAD

The idea of frames and fields provides a useful strategy for understanding the positive activities of Los Solidos and its work to realize the success of its projects. Most generally, the Los Solidos organization is framed by its complaint that their families and the community had failed them, thus forcing youth toward the streets and crime. Frames are important because they are used to define reality, provide legitimation for courses of action, and offer ideological support for a gang's projects. The community rejected many of the Solids' claims and demands, but others were embraced. Los Solidos claims that it was rejected and alienated by some members of the community in Frog Hollow because they, too, felt alienated. High levels of family dysfunction and a strong sense of being ignored by the city among Frog

Hollow residents made the Solids' frame of family and institutional failure appear plausible, and the Solids offered a personal story of such failure to anyone who would listen. The gang mounted a publicity campaign that included gang spokespersons appearing on television and radio shows, at churches and civic organizations, and organizing two conferences. These framed their presentation to the community to provide a rationale for their actions, deflect responsibility, and elicit the highest degree of support and sympathy. Migi, a veteran member who was active in the publicity efforts of the gang, provided the most compelling example of how family crisis leads to the gang life.

The "family" project has been a major aspect of the public comments of Migi, and she has been especially eloquent in presenting this idea to audiences (some of her comments are in the *Tampa Tribune*, Crachere 1995:17 and in Alexander 1996). Migi says she joined the gang to find a sense of family after suffering several sexual assaults at the hands of stepbrothers—a common situation, as we learned. In 1995, a group of six female Solids discussed their family life and each one reported sexual victimization in their extended families. For each woman, the gang was sought out based on its reputation for protecting women and providing social and financial support for those in need. Several female members commented that the gang showed its concern for the safety of women and youth. They noted that the gang enforced a curfew for female members, established rules of comportment while members were in public, and provided funds to members for emergencies—in one case paying for the funeral of a member's mother. Migi says that Los Solidos stands up for the poor and for kids who need a place to grow and develop into positive adults. She is aware of the drug dealing and violence, but says that it is a necessary evil.

The Los Solidos Handbook clearly indicates that a principle goal of the organization is to support the Puerto Rican community. On a local radio show, Los Solidos spokesperson Smurf once said that the gang could more effectively control its members than the police could. He added that Los Solidos was organized to serve as the major source of informal social control of youth on the streets. He said the gang's self imposed "red light," whereby all intergang violence is banned, and the gang's policy of forcing members to be more discreet in their drug sales was proof of this. He noted that the gang had made peace on its own and that this was a sign of the gang's potential. He concluded that with jobs and access to education, Los

Solidos could become a major source of legitimate entrepreneurship and commitment to the community. Unfortunately, the overwhelming pressures of the streets on youth often undermined the gang's ability and desire to become more involved in the civic affairs of the community.

The literature is clear in the economic foundations of gang development (Hagedorn 1988; Taylor 1990; Moore 1991), and this is no less true in the case of Los Solidos. Los Solidos made economic dislocation an element of its "cultural ideology" (Padilla 1992). The group argued that its members were victims of neglect, and that neglect explains and legitimates the persistence of the gang's criminal behavior (compare this with the notion of "choloization" in Vigil 1990). At a public forum on gangs, G., a female member of the executive committee, said that if members of Los Solidos were white and "living in a dorm or frat house," their drug dealing would be viewed as nothing more than "a youthful indiscretion." She said racism against Puerto Ricans and a bias against poor youths make the public more fearful of street youths when their behavior, while criminal in some cases, is not much different than what one finds in the suburbs. More directly, the cultural ideology of Los Solidos also emphasizes Puerto Rican nationalism and resistance to American cultural domination. For example, Los Solidos member Big Bird idolizes Los Macheteros, the Puerto Rican liberation group that committed a multimillion-dollar robbery in West Hartford. He once claimed Los Macheteros were more dangerous than the Italian Mafia because they had a political agenda as the foundation for their crime. He said that just like other ethnic groups, Los Solidos had to use crime to further its social and political agenda.

The organization and functioning of Los Solidos is characterized by this fundamental duality, what we refer to as the negative (gangster) project and the positive (family, civic, business) projects. The gang uses its feelings of alienation from the community to legitimate both its criminal and noncriminal activities; the gang emerges from its environment reflecting and embodying all the local dysfunctions in its organization and structure. Smurf, the speaker of Los Solidos, says crime, especially drug dealing, was the result of an unresponsive community and was a necessity due to the lack of jobs. He also argued that Los Solidos was the only place for street youth to find direction, caring, and a way to become productive members of the community. In other words, the gang was necessary to provide both an alternative opportunity system and an alternative support network for alienated youth.

A CLOSER LOOK AT THE FAMILY, BUSINESS, AND CIVIC PROJECTS

The Solids, and their local rivals, the Latin Kings and 20 Love, all refer to their respective organizations as "families," resent being referred to as "gangs," and have observed numerous incidents of public denial that the organizations were anything other than "gangs." Of course this "nongang status" is an idea that is rejected by the police, but it is institutionalized by the Solids in their ideology. The Los Solidos Handbook offers a fairly well-developed theory of how the gang works as a family:

> The family and friends you grew up with are now addicted to drugs. Don't turn your back on them. Look out for them, put them in rehab, and give them a reason to better themselves. Show them there is someone who cares for them and a family they can belong to if they straighten themselves out. The majority of young males in our communities today don't have any family. That's why they're out running around and acting all crazy and foolish.
>
> *(Los Solidos Nation, no date)*

An older member of the gang offered a theory of the origins of the family project. He said that the workers from publicly funded social programs of the 1960s and 1970s stressed to inner-city residents the importance of, and the need for, an extended family as an effective support network and source for financial aid. When federal money was cut off in the 1980s, the people who relied on the federal family support system were now without the funds, leadership, and programs to help to meet those needs. He said the gangs filled this vacuum by forming extended families.

Smurf states that the Solids are members of a "family" with a sense of social order, offices, and the regular means of rotating members in and out of leadership positions. Members are referred to as "brother" and "sister," similar to Keiser's (1969) notion of the "brotherhood ideology." The Los Solidos "family" is interested in helping the community, especially those like themselves who are left out of the affairs of the community and whose voices are not heard. It would be incorrect to say that all members have the same sense of family as do the members of the positive factions, nor would it be correct to say that all superiors accept the notion of family developed here. Factions exist within the gang, and there are those in Los Solidos who prefer gang-banging and life in the underworld. Yet the existence of these negative factions should not cloud the clear message that, for its members, Los Solidos functions as a family.

It is well known that many gangs refer to themselves as families, but it is important not to cynically reject this as merely a front to establish legitimacy. Doing so ignores the fact that the notion of family is central to the self-definition of the gangs. Moreover, to reject this notion is unsociological, and makes it impossible to explore the ways in which marginalized populations build community and survive.

When it was stated to Big Bird that people in the community said the crimes of Los Solidos contradicted all the rhetoric about family, he referred to the U.S. government's use of spies and assassins. He said "we need a few knuckleheads in the organization to do the dirty work." The Solids believe they are driven to criminal behavior but are not overly troubled by being linked to drug sales because they see it as an activity that goes on in the suburbs and in colleges without the kind of criticism inner-city drug dealing receives. Carlos said he has no problem with recreational drug use or sales, but it is violence that is the problem. He said that although he is "no angel," he is also not "an animal." In other words, for Carlos and others in the Solids, drug crime is considered natural in their social world and is a less serious crime than those committed by devils and animals—such as rape and murder—crimes that truly threaten the community.

Smurf summarized the Los Solidos theory of gang formation, one that is reflected in much of the extant gang literature. The gang was a place for a person to find physical safety, financial support, and cultural pride. According to Smurf, gangs were the result of dysfunctional families, lack of support from teachers and other adult role models, and of youth being denied involvement in community matters. According to Los Solidos public statements on television, radio, and the newspapers, their gang was created to provide street youth with protection from victimization by other gangs, and to help deal with the negative personal and social effects of poverty. In interviews, personal conversations, and observations, we learned about the range of services the gang promised and provided. Many female members have told us that the gang protected them from street predators and rival gang members and often provided funds for burials, bail, or to pay rent. This gang was to be more than an opportunity to make money from crime—serving a number of functions for the members.

Los Solidos claimed that the only way to control the growth and danger of gangs was to find a meaningful role for the street youths that are likely to join gangs. The long-term goal of the group is to eventually move away from crime, take a place in the affairs of the community, and work for the interests of their members. What held them back was their perceived need to sell drugs, because it was their only real option for money—the economic lifeblood of the organization.

The Los Solidos Handbook clearly describes the gang's legitimate business project. The handbook outlines plans for the future that include "a chain of stores, have Brothers (members) [become] lawyers, doctors, and politicians, and have our families be well off. . . . The main objective at this point is to expand our Family into the mainstream of society" (Los Solidos Nation, no date). In 1996, the gang worked with a local community group for funds to get training in how to create business plans and secure business loans. Funds were awarded by the state, and members of Los Solidos and the 20 Love gang were included in a training program in small business development. Later, they were brought to banks and city agencies, and were helped with writing applications for loans and seed money. At least three business plans were submitted to banks, but none succeeded. In one case, the loan was approved, but there were problems with zoning, and for the two other applicants, loans were denied because of either criminal records or tax problems.

When the gangs first joined with their patrons, the problems of unemployment and underemployment were the major concerns mentioned by gang spokespersons. Unfortunately, the patrons may have overpromised the degree of help that could be found, and there were many mistakes and misunderstandings in the job issue. First, a local violence reduction agency had the funds to employ members as violence reduction mediators, but many more sought jobs than the funding would allow. In the end, the mediators had bad feelings about their work, which was due to the high degree of supervision and large amount of paperwork the position involved. After about a year, most mediators left the agency. The Hartford Housing Authority hired Smurf as a violence mediator, and he too promised jobs to the members of the gang. However, he promised too many, and when jobs did not materialize, he was criticized by many and lost some of his power on the streets. Eventually, several members of Los Solidos found jobs under the auspices of the patrons, but this was the exception, not the rule.

To a certain extent, members of the community, who may have had other agendas, used the gangs—for example, two members of the business community who were angry about the hiring practices at a major construction site. They engaged the leaders of the Solids, 20 Love, and the Latin Kings to march in protest over the lack of minority jobs at the site. It turned into a riot when the protesters entered the work area against the orders of police. These two businessmen provided no support to those arrested, nor have they ever again worked with the gangs.

The Solids always linked jobs with education, so it was natural that they inquire about schooling. Based on a plan developed by Smurf, a regional educational firm, Los Solidos, and some members of 20 Love wrote a grant proposal in the summer of 1995 to create an alternative middle school/high school for gang members. The school was funded for two years, and several Solids were hired to serve as "community coaches" to recruit gang members into the schools. More than one hundred gang members eventually attended the schools, many earning the GED or a high school diploma.

From 1995 to 1997, the Solids participated in a number of events designed to educate the public about the gang's new project as a community organization—its civic project. The patrons and positive factions of Los Solidos and 20 Love organized two conferences that were attended by hundreds of professionals and received significant positive media coverage. In addition, the Capitol Region Council of Churches worked with the Solids to organize a speaker's bureau that sent gang members to press their claims at suburban churches and schools, as well as to professional organizations. Members of the African American community sponsored trips to national gang conferences for members of the Solids and the Loves to meet with nationally recognized gang activists to help develop their positive projects.

THE REORGANIZATION OF THE SOLIDS

As we observed in our fieldwork in late 1996, the arrests, convictions, and incarceration of so many key members of the gang caused a retrenchment that fragmented the gang in practice, if not in spirit—a kind of emergency decentralization tactic. This retrenchment is one of scope and awareness. The gang has moved its activities underground, but has continued drug sales. At its most fragmented state, there existed at least fourteen separate Los Solidos crews in the city. It is correct to refer to these groups as crews rather than factions, because the Los Solidos brotherhood remained strong among the members of the crews. The new leadership has only a limited relationship with the gang's former patrons, and positive projects are now more-individual initiatives of positive members, such as Smurf, G., and Big Bird, rather than the gang-initiated projects of the past.

The formation of crews was more a way of moving underground than a breakup of the gang. And although disputes among the crews occur, the leadership continues to send superiors to mediate among the parties, and they retain the authority to terminate members from the group if they do not stop fighting. Still, the incarcerations have limited the ability of the executive council to control gang activities, and younger members are taking greater risks in their drug dealing and are not seeking approval from the leadership when they want to settle a dispute with violence. Thus many of the superiors are concerned that the activities of the younger members may induce public scrutiny and result in another police crackdown.

DISCUSSION

Ball and Curry (1995) are correct in warning that defining the gang primarily on its tendency to engage in criminal behavior is a dead end because it limits theoretical innovation. The more fruitful approach understands gang members as rational actors who act on the basis of economic and personal rationality (Jankowski 1991; Padilla 1992), thereby opening lines of research that may highlight noncriminal behaviors. Los Solidos ideology is based on a reflective appreciation of this condition and it was used to legitimate the gang's organized criminal activities. The linkage of the gangster project and the family project indicates the founders of Los Solidos and its recent leaders applied a more sociological understanding of their activities than was conceded in the past. There is now a greater appreciation that gangs are more complex than in previous generations, and we now know that gangs are formed for strategic reasons beyond self-defense and criminal opportunities. However, there still remains the need to address the positive activities of certain kinds of gangs, especially in terms of how gangs change as they try to meet the needs of the membership and retain its integrity as a social unit.

Some gangs, including Los Solidos, can be viewed as both criminal organizations and as movements to address group needs and to offer to the membership a sense of social location in the community. The gang thus serves the function of a political unit, what Moore (1991) refers to as the "resistance theory" of gangs. In addition, the gang serves another function, namely, the criminal operation referred to as an "ethnic enterprise" by Padilla (1992). Analytically separating the movement from the functions it serves is helpful in explicating the idea of competing and/or complementary projects. The notion of *projects* accommodates multiple and shifting realities and alerts one to the possibilities that contradictions exist within the gang, and that progressive and positive change in gangs is neither assured nor to be unexpected. Given the data presented here, it is premature to say that gangs can become social movements of dispossessed individuals—or some other form of incipient political organization. It is clear, however, that some gang members may indeed see the gang as just that. This quality of gangs should be an important consideration for criminologists seeking to determine the place gangs can play in attempts to restructure inner-city communities to reduce crime and violence.

Keiser (1969) and Jankowski (1991) have studied the political activities of gangs, but there is otherwise very little literature on gangs as political movements, and none on how gangs structure their political agenda. Dawley's (1992) historical account of the activities of the Vice Lords in Chicago indicates the development of a political consciousness out of the context of gang beatings and poverty, but he offers only general ideas about why and how this happened. Dawley's informants explain that the gang was inspired by the civil rights movement to create a new type of gang. The Vice Lords were able to create their own institutions, secure capital to start businesses, and offer members of the gang and the community something to gain.

Returning to Los Solidos, even before events in the community and the police crackdown forced them to initiate its public relations efforts, the gang had engaged in a variety of activities that benefited the community (neighborhood cleanups, working with kids on sports teams, participating in food drives with local churches). The Puerto Rican community in Frog Hollow is characterized as having a strong sense of community and family. Los Solidos did not ignore this sense of community. Of importance, it is clear that Los Solidos sees itself as a Puerto Rican nationalist group, viewing the Los Macheteros revolutionary group as one of its models. This regard for Los Macheteros, with its mixing of crime and political activism, is instructive as to the ways in which members of Los Solidos see their relationship to the community; a relationship based on feelings of rejection and alienation, as well as concern and pride. The Solids say criminal behavior can end only if their members are welcomed back into the community and its public affairs.

For the Solids, there was a shifting of organizational structure, sometimes cohesive and other times fragmented, depending on the situation. The gang shifted from a somewhat monolithic organization to a more decentralized organization, and the latest information indicates a return to a more centralized organization. Future research should explore the ways in which such changes occur and their meaning. Research in this area may afford an opportunity to understand the interface between the notion of gangs as a form of incipient political resistance and gangs as criminal enterprises.

Los Solidos was created as a venue for the realization of the legitimate aspirations of its members—that is, its organic criminal and positive projects. Its chance to develop into a political gang similar to the New York Latin Kings and the Gangster Disciples passed without completion. Future research should explore the factors that help and hinder a gang in its political development. It is no surprise that most comments from outsiders about the activities of Los Solidos express the belief that they were nothing more than spin. This may be true, because spin has become a part of legitimate political discourse, and it should not be unexpected that gangs engage in such maneuvers. Yet to dismiss these events is to narrowly read what constitutes a social movement (Buechler 1995) and misses an opportunity to learn more about contemporary gangs as a product of the modern world.

NOTE

1. The now defunct Original Family Organization was the Baby Solids. Recruits under age 18 were placed in OFO. OFO was to avoid criminal activity, and was designed to build solidarity. OFO members were usually beefing with other gang members, however, and they sold drugs whenever possible. The Los Solidos leadership, under Pekino, was only marginally interested in controlling OFO. OFO was disbanded in 1999 and all members, regardless of age, became soldiers in Los Solidos.

REFERENCES

Alexander, Jill B. 1996. Solutions to ending gang violence. *Impact* (summer): 2–4.
Ball, Richard, and G. David Curry. 1995. The logic of definitions in criminology: Purposes and methods for defining "gangs." *Criminology*, 33 (2): 225–245.

Buechler, Steven M. 1995. New social movements theories. *Sociological Quarterly*, 36 (3): 441–464.

Chabot, Russell. 1992. Local versions: Rhode Island reggae bands as projects. Ph.D. diss., State University of New York, Buffalo.

Crachere, Vicki. 1995. Ganging up on gangs. *Tampa Tribune* 26 November, pp. 1, 17.

Dawley, David. 1992. *A Nation of Lords: The Autobiography of the Vice Lords.* Prospect Heights, Ill.: Waveland Press.

Hagedorn, John M. 1988. *People and Folks: Gangs, Crime, and the Underclass in a Rustbelt City.* Chicago: Lake View Press.

Hobsbawm, Eric. 1965. *Primitive Rebels.* New York: Norton.

Horowitz, Ruth. 1983. *Honor and the American Dream: Culture and Identity in a Chicano Community.* New Brunswick: Rutgers University Press.

———. 1990. Sociological perspectives on gangs: Conflicting definitions and concepts. In C. Ronald Huff, ed., *Gangs in America.* Newbury Park, Calif.: Sage.

Jankowski, Martin S. 1991. *Islands in the Street: Gangs and American Urban Society.* Berkeley: University of California Press.

Keiser, R. Lincoln. 1969. *The Vice Lords: Warriors of the Streets.* New York: Holt, Rinehart, and Winston.

Klein, Dorie. 1995. Crime through gender's prism: Feminist criminology in the United States. In N. H. Rafter and F. Heidenshon, eds., *International Feminist Perspectives in Criminology.* Buckingham: Open University Press.

Los Solidos Nation. No date. *Los Solidos Handbook.* Unpublished manuscript.

Moore, Joan. 1991. *Going Down to the Barrio: Homeboys and Homegirls in Change.* Philadelphia: Temple University Press.

Padilla, Felix. 1992. *The Gang as an American Enterprise.* New Brunswick, N.J.: Rutgers University Press.

Russell, Nehemiah. No date. A call for educators to accept the challenge of gang deactivation programs in our schools. Unpublished manuscript.

Snow, David A., E. Rochford Jr., S. Worden, and R. Benford. 1986. Frame alignment processes: Micromobilization and movement participation. *American Sociological Review*, 51 (4): 464–481.

Taylor, Carl S. 1990. Gang imperialism. In C. Ronald Huff, ed., *Gangs in America.* Newbury Park, Calif.: Sage Publications.

Vigil, James Diego. 1990. *Barrio Gangs: Street Life and Identity in Southern California.* Austin: University of Texas Press.

Yablonsky, Lewis. 1959. The delinquent gang as a near-group. *Social Problems*, 7: 108–117.

6

URBAN STREET ACTIVISTS: GANG AND COMMUNITY EFFORTS TO BRING PEACE AND JUSTICE TO LOS ANGELES NEIGHBORHOODS

JUAN FRANCISCO ESTEVA MARTÍNEZ

In 1998, The Street Organization Project at John Jay College of Criminal Justice[1] was involved in an ongoing research project documenting the organizational transformation of street organizations in the New York City area. Some of the street organizations include the Ñetas, Zulu Nation, and the Almighty Latin King and Queen Nation. In May 1999, the latter street organization contacted members of the Bloods in Los Angeles to mediate between them and the New York City Bloods in order to contain or stop the violence between these two groups. Bloodhound, a leading member of one of the strongest sets of the L.A. Bloods,[2] visited New York City to speak with both of these groups about different issues, including the L.A. Gang

This essay was originally published as Juan Francisco Esteva, "Urban Street Activists: Gang and Community Efforts to Bring Peace and Justice to L.A.'s Neighborhoods," in *Dispute Resolution: Alternative Perspectives on Gangs and the Community*, Working Papers Series: Research Reports, vol. 2 (New York: CUNY Dispute Resolution Consortium at John Jay College of Criminal Justice, 2001).

Truce. The team of the Street Organization Project decided that it was imperative to document this event and arranged an interview with him. During this interview, Bloodhound informed us that, to his knowledge, no similar research had ever taken place with the L.A. Bloods. Bloodhound went on to express his desire to have "the history of the Bloods documented."

> What's very interesting would be to document the transition from gangsterism to activism—which I'm in the process of—to making it a transition, and a lot of my homeboys have already made it and a lot more are in the process, and we lead through example. I mean this is like we're in the birth stage right now, so I mean, now is the best time, 'cause, I mean, you're gonna see a lot of changes within the next couple years, from people who are labeled as "gang leaders," now rising up as community leaders. I think that history, history is, people who study history are gonna wanna know, "How did that happen?" So, whoever had the courage to come forward and say, "I see what's goin' on and I wanna document this"; they are gonna be basically documenting history that's bein' made by Bloods and Crips. And these organizations have been around for a long time.
>
> *(interview, 1 May 1999)*

SOURCES AND METHODS

This study is based primarily on interviews and participant observation conducted by the author and members of the Street Organization Project. During the months of May, June, and July 1999, I interviewed forty gang members, including two recovered gang member street activists, four active gang member activists, three organic community activists, six peripheral "original gangsters" (hereafter referred to as OGs), and twenty active gang members. The sample included three female active gang members and one female OG. Special efforts were made to include as many street activists, female gang members, and OGs as possible. The sample also included an interview with a member of an Asian and a Latino set. The interviewees' ages varied: six members were from 12 to 17 years old, fifteen were 18 to 25 years old, eight were 25 to 35 years old, and six were 36 to 48 years old.

Bloodhound, a well-known member of the Bloods, gave me entrée to other gang members from different sets and geographical locations, and a street activist working in a different community organization assisted me. At the suggestion of one of my assistants, we decided to conduct interviews with members of different "sets" or " 'hoods," which included geographical locations in the city of Los Angeles such as Pueblo del Rio housing projects, Watts, Compton, Crenshaw, and Venice Beach. In addition, we included several members from the Los Angeles suburbs of Inglewood, Altadena, and Pasadena.[3] The informants were recruited at various sites including community centers, parks, political meetings, and on the streets. Given their restricted mobility, most interviews with active gang members took place in their neighborhoods and hangouts. Some of the members were kind enough to let me enter into their homes to conduct an interview. Other interviews took place wherever possible (e.g., at a cemetery, inside my rental car, and at the informants' workplace).

I used a semistructured questionnaire developed by the Street Organization Project. It included questions on family history, education, criminal experiences, economic conditions, and political participation. Specific questions regarding the origin, process, and current status of the L.A. Gang Truce were included in a separate section. Open-ended questions were added whenever the interviewee demonstrated a special knowledge in any of these areas. In most cases, the questionnaire format was followed and most were completed. The questionnaire was complemented by participant observations, as I joined street activists in several of their activities and took field notes. I was able to apply the innovative technique of "the tour" to gain access to information about geographical boundaries, local problems, and local street literacy (Conquergood 1997).[4] Through this technique, I was able to observe different forms of social interaction among a great range of social actors in these communities. Informants also allowed me to attend some of their political meetings, and to hang out with them in parks and in the streets. I was also invited to participate in leisure activities such as playing dominoes and going to the movies. Finally, I was able to obtain a variety of documents such as videos, manuals, biographies, pictures, and pamphlets, which are an invaluable source to determine the ideology, history, and range of activities of different community organizations.

THEORETICAL DISCUSSION

THE LITERATURE

A vast social science literature on street gangs focuses on the criminological aspects of these groups and its members. Academics and researchers have deployed a broad array of methodologies, models, paradigms, and theories to dissect three major issues that affect gangs and their respective communities: violence, drugs, and sex. These issues have been treated as social problems that need to be studied, understood, and controlled.[5] Three major schools of thought have studied the gang at the macro-, meso-, and microlevels of analysis, which I have called: the underclass discourse, the culture-of-poverty paradigm, and the deviant-psychopaths model. For all their insights, these treatments have created only a partial picture of the social interactions and organizational aspects of the gang. Furthermore, these studies have contributed to what Mizruchi and Fein (1999) refer to as the "social construction of organizational knowledge," in which gangs are constructed as purely socially deviant entities (Brotherton 1996) and their political dimensions are lost in the discourse of social deviance (Venkatesh, chapter 1 of this volume).

In contrast, a more humanistic, traditional approach to the study of gangs has focused on their organizational aspects (Jankowski 1991),[6] the politics of culture (Conquergood 1997), and the institutional transformation of gangs (Moore et al. 1978; Vigil 1988; Moore 1991). Although these studies have been important in creating a sociology of the gang, they have failed to identify the political agency of gangs and the political agents within gangs.[7]

Recently, studies of street organizations on the East Coast conducted by members of the Street Organization Project have developed an alternative approach to the study of gangs. These studies have focused on the structural transformations of gangs into politically and community-oriented street organizations (Brotherton 1997, chapter 8 of this volume), the spiritual and political practices of street organizations (Barrios, chapter 7 of this volume), and the empowerment and politicization of women within street organizations (Brotherton and Salazar-Atias, chapter 10 of this volume). The study in this chapter builds on this recent tradition by tracing the careers of individual members of street organizations (see Becker 1963, 1982; Hall and Jefferson 1975; and Lachmann 1988) and their transformation into political agents.[8] In addition, I trace the process in which street activists transform, and are transformed by, organizations and institutions in their environments (DiMaggio and Powell 1983; Mizruchi and Fein 1999).

In view of the vast list of literature that focuses on the negative aspects of gangs, this essay deviates from that trend by presenting an alternative perspective on gangs. This alternative perspective differs from previous studies in three ways: (1) It focuses on the gang and gang members as political actors/agents engaged in the transformation of their social milieu; (2) it identifies different types of street activists and follows their career paths; (3) it focuses on the interaction of political actors with the range of organizations that surround them. The ultimate objective of this paper is to contribute to the development of an alternative theoretical paradigm to the study of gangs.

HISTORICAL BACKGROUND

The origins of the Crips and the Bloods are ambiguous. The accounts of the origins of these gangs differ from one gang to the other, from one set to another, and from one generation of gang members to another. However, there seem to be two reemerging accounts. The first one places the origins of the Crips and the Bloods in a political context:

> The Crips street organization was formed in 1969 by Raymond Washington, and the Bloods soon followed. In a general way, both got their inspiration from the Black Panthers. The Crips name stood for Community resources for independent people. Initially it grew out of the mass arrests, jailing and killings of black youth by police who were seeking to destroy the Black Panther movement.
> *(Community in Support of the Gang Truce 1992).*

A thirty-six-year-old OG who had just been released from prison where he served sixteen years for attempted murder, gives a similar account:

> Crips was nothing but a social group, you know, trying to help the community. Because you had the Black Panthers then, so they was forming, too, like a community group. . . . It means Community Resources—I forget the name. . . . But they started pretty much as a community group, after which you had individuals that was in there who, as they suspected, was infiltrators and I don't wanna say no names on that, but then you had dudes going out in the community, identifyin' themselves by rags, names. *(interview, 16 June 1999)*

OGs and street activists who were involved in the early formation of these gangs gave similar accounts. They recount times in which the Black Panthers, the Black Stone Rangers, and other street organizations were trying to politically organize their neighborhoods and empower their communities. In fact, a Blood set still carries the name that relates it to the Black Stone Rangers and, at least rhetorically, their members adhere to the political goals of their predecessors. Some of these OGs became active members of the Black Panthers and to date they continue to work on civil/human rights issues. A second account places the origin of these street organizations in the context of racial conflict. London Carter, a forty-eight-year-old OG, describes the emergence of his particular set:

> Crips were the first ones to originate as an organization. From what I know when Crips first started, it was a group of kids that got together to go to the beach. You see, back then there wasn't that many blacks or Latinos in L.A. If we wanted to go to the beach we had to walk through all of these white neighborhoods and we would get mugged or beaten up. So these dudes would get together in a group and go through the white neighborhoods in a group. That way they wouldn't mess with them. I don't know how it happened but these kids then started messing with other blacks too and they used to do a lot of bad stuff.
>
> Well, [in 1969] the Hoover Park Family Bloods was started by a group of us who were involved in the Karate club. We used to practice Karate at the Park. There were black belts, brown belts, you name it. But to get accepted to the set you needed to know karate, that was one of our requirements. When the program ended, all of the members of the club continued to hang out together. And then there were the fights with other sets, specifically with the Crips. We decided that we were not going to allow the abuse and decided to stick together to protect the neighborhood. Yeah, all of us were members of this club and you had to know Karate that was one of our requirements. We want it to make sure that if you were part of the set that you could fight to defend yourself and the neighborhood.   *(interview, 22 July 1999)*

Although the OGs' accounts of the origins of the gangs make the connection to the civil rights movement or the Black Power movement, younger generations are less likely to make such a connection. YGs (young gangsters) show less knowledge about the political origins of the organization. Ironically, their lack of historical knowledge as well as their unhesitant use of violence to "protect" their neighborhoods has turned their neighborhoods into some of the most dangerous communities vulnerable to a number of social ills.

The Bloods and the Crips have been known to be among the largest and most violent street gangs in this nation. In fact, government documents describe them as "supergangs." These two gangs have been at war ever since their creation in the late 1960s. Regardless of the original goals of the organization, these two gangs created a rivalry that engulfed them in a vicious cycle of violence. As the above OG states, the Bloods were created to protect their communities from external violence (i.e., police and racial violence) but the violence ultimately became internal when the Bloods and the Crips used violence on one another.[9] The specific origin of the rivalry between these two groups is ambiguous, but the rivalry intensified with the introduction of drugs into these communities. In fact, according to the 1996 National Youth Gang Survey, there is a strong correlation between the increase in drugs and the increase in crime. The violence between these two groups left a great number of scars on them as their respective communities literally became war zones with groups of youths creating artificial borders and/or boundaries in the neighborhoods.[10]

For most of the sixties and the late seventies, the violence generated by these gangs was more or less directed toward each other. But during the late 1980s and the first part of the 1990s, the explosive combination of drugs as well as the unprecedented increase of high-powered weapons on the streets qualitatively and quantitatively transformed street violence. That is, violence moved from once-sporadic personal hand-to-hand combat (with the occasional use of knives and guns), to the more frequent and impersonal gang warfare where the use of automatic weapons in drive-by shootings became the standard or the norm. The target of violence moved from individual gang members to the entire group and eventually to the community that hosted the gang.

By the early 1990s, gang-related crime reached unprecedented levels. In fact, in 1992 a government report found an increase not only in gang membership but also in the number of gangs nationwide (Office of Juvenile Justice and Delinquency Prevention 1999).[11] Furthermore, in February 1998, a congressional report stated:

> In August 1994, the National Institute of Justice (NIJ) reports, "gang-related crime is above all a violent crime problem. Homicides and other violent crimes account for about half of all recorded gang-related crime incidents." In fact, the FBI reported that juvenile gang killings rose by 371% from 1980 to 1992, the fastest growing of all the homicide categories.   *(Cavanagh and Teasley 1998)*

The report also found a strong association between gang membership and carrying a gun and between gang membership and selling illicit drugs.

URBAN STREET ACTIVISTS, GANGS, AND COMMUNITY ACTIVISTS

Although much has been written about the state-sanctioned efforts to control the spread of gang-related violence, little has been written about urban street activists and community efforts to stop violence. In fact, efforts of this latter group have seldom been reported in mainstream newspapers, magazines, congressional reports, or even in academic studies. It was not until the April 1992 Los Angeles uprising that efforts of urban street activists were brought to the fore. The uprising marked a new phase in street violence between two of the nation's largest and most violent gangs, the Bloods and the Crips. One of the most unpredictable and publicized outcomes of the L.A. riots was the truce between these two gangs. The announcement of the truce temporarily caught the attention of journalists, politicians, moral entrepreneurs, and political activists who inundated the poor neighborhoods in South Central Los Angeles to report on the truce. Unfortunately, and despite the economic and social support from outside organizations and the community, the potential for a strong and lasting general truce soon crumbled.[12]

THE CHANGING GHETTO

As sociologist William Julius Wilson (1978) documented, increasing social isolation experienced in inner-city black communities during the decade of the 1970s continued in the 1980s and 1990s. Wilson shows how deindustrialization combined with black middle-class flight resulted in depleted human, social, and economic resources necessary for healthy communities (1996). Under these conditions, Wilson argues, the black ghetto experienced an increase in social pathologies including violent crime, teenage pregnancy, and out-of-wedlock births (Wilson 1987). However, the fleeing of the black middle class, who had become the backbone of the civil rights movement, did not completely exhaust the community of organic intellectuals and activists. As the more mainstream-educated black activists left the inner-city black neighborhoods, members of street organizations replaced them. Although many of these activists possessed skills to obtain jobs in mainstream America, they chose to remain in the neighborhood. They reported the love that they had for their 'hood was one of the main reasons for not leaving or moving to less violent and more affluent areas. Those who had attempted to move out and came back often recited experiences of discrimination in mainstream society as the major reason for returning to their neighborhoods (also see Bourgois 1995).

THE MAKING OF STREET ACTIVISTS

Urban street activists are individuals indigenous to their communities who are committed to change the social, political, and economic situation of their respective communities.[13] Generally speaking, street activists come from backgrounds considered by many to be deviant because they are respected members of well-organized and sophisticated gangs. This respect derives from having occupied positions of leadership within the gang. Charismatic authority within the gang and its host community is also a characteristic of the urban activist. The respected member position in gangs increases status and results in greater credibility and legitimacy. It allows street activists to freely navigate between the different levels of the gang structure and between different sets or neighborhoods and to present or disseminate their ideas.

SPECIALIZED KNOWLEDGE

Street activists' knowledge of the gang structure and cultural codes provides them with the cultural capital to survive in many depressed black communities. Their familiarity with the structure allows them to take their political message to very hermetic and secretive circles such as gangs. Their knowledge of cultural codes makes them sensitive to the gangs' cultural value system and prevents them from disrespecting (or "dissin' ") their leaders or members. This knowledge is crucial in a dangerous environment where the drug-market economy as well as other illicit ventures is widely practiced. This form of cultural capital is also important to the gang activists—especially when the political message they are proclaiming contradicts some of the values and practices of the street gang. In general, urban street activists' knowledge increases the social understanding of gangs; a type of knowledge that is, for the most part, restricted to insiders. Even with all this street literacy (Conquergood 1997) and street wisdom or understanding (Anderson 1990), street activists are still exposed to high-risk and life-threatening situations. Paradoxically, it is their socialization to the gang culture and practices that also create problems for them as they continuously expose themselves by working with rival gangs at the risk of offending other rival gang members with their speech, body language, or attire.

DEVELOPING POLITICAL CONSCIOUSNESS

The level of political consciousness varies among street activists and is contingent on their level of education, their contact with outside social movement organizations, and, more important, the amount of time involved in street activism. Although the levels of formal schooling among street activists are low, they demonstrate a vast knowledge of history and politics. Street activists acquire this knowledge from informal education that usually takes place during their frequent and sometimes extended periods of incarceration. For instance, when I asked one of the OGs about the basis of political consciousness, he responded:

> The basis of it is the Muslim help 'em, you know, the Christian, so people get influenced by different people that's already in prison, so—plus prison slows you down. You can't move around in there like you can out here, so people have a lot of time to think, you know, so they start readin' more, so they—then they start reachin' theyself and then some say. "OK, well, I'm gonna put God in my life and try to have some spiritual balance."   *(interview, 15 June 1999)*

Ironically, it is in prison where all of the interviewed street activists had their first experiences as organizers and political activists and where many of them developed their ideological basis for political action.

> Uh, the Bloods in the prison system are more militant right now. You have the United Blood Nation, which is an organization in the prison system which implements Bloods from every set, every gang, that are united under one flag, one goal, one purpose. Uh, you have the Blood Line Soldiers in the prison system, which is another organization. [These organizations] are very militant where they are organized. They learn Swahili and they learn codes. Some of them know sign language, and this is also that way the guards can't tell what is being said when they communicate with each other. The other inmates can't tell what's being said, and they do a lot of studying, they do a lot of reading. Very, very militant. You know, I gotta stress that, 'cause on the street it's not that militant.
>
> *(interview, 1 May 1999)*

It is in the prison system that street activists are incorporated into different prison political groups, which include political/religious organizations such as the Nation of Islam, Marxist/Maoist groups, and other political rights groups. Once they return to the streets, their knowledge is increased through their continuous exposure to mentors who continue their politicization.

TYPES OF POLITICAL CONSCIOUSNESS

I have identified three levels of political consciousness: parochial, national, and international. First, street activists with *parochial political consciousness* are concerned with local issues facing their communities and their neighborhoods. Sociopolitical and economic isolation—such as lack of good schooling, lack of opportunities for jobs, violence, crime, drug addiction, and police brutality within the black communities—are some of the issues dealt with by the parochial street activists. The parochial street activists' political consciousness resembles that of Black Nationalism drawn from Afrocentric thought (see Carmichael and Charles 1967; Ture and Hamilton 1972 and Collins 1990). Second, those with a more *national political consciousness* make efforts to create solidarity links with other communities facing similar issues. They do not restrict themselves to the black community and make a conscious effort to work with other racial/ethnic groups such as Latino and Asian groups. They tend to stress the similarities rather than the differences. The national-oriented street activists draw from various ideological sources including Black Nationalism, Pan-Africanism, and traditional leftist ideologies such as Marxism, Maoism, and feminism. Finally, street activists that possess an *international political consciousness* are more critical of the U.S. government and situate their struggles within an international or global framework. They stress links between global capitalism and the criminalization of youth all over the world. The outcome of this incorporation of a very diverse and broad mixture of ideologies gives this type of political consciousness a very postmodernist form. That is, they adhere to what Iris Marion Young (1994) has defined as "the politics of coalition" where the focus is on general issues rather than race, class, or gender.

The street activists' relationships to outside organizations and institutions play an important role in the determination of the level of consciousness, political goals, and strategies. Street activists with a parochial consciousness may be involved in indigenous and more local community organizations that work to resolve the immediate needs of the community. They usually have ties with local community organizations such as neighborhood associations, police brutality watch groups, as well as nationalistic organizations such as the Black Panthers, the Nation of Islam, or the Congress of Racial Equality. These types of street activists have goals that are formulated in maxims such as "the empowerment of the black race," "the self-determination of the black people," and "the liberation of black people." In contrast, national-oriented street activists see these problems not only as an outcome of American racism but also as a problem engendered by the structure of the U.S. political and economic system. Consequently, the goal is a change in the structure of the political and the economic system itself. Thus these types of street activists make use of the politics of coalition and emphasize the building of solidarity bridges with other oppressed groups. Last, the internationally conscious street activists include a more critical analysis of global capitalism and thus attempt to build bridges with young oppressed people in other nations.

STREET ACTIVIST TYPOLOGIES

I have developed three general categories[14] that describe the different types of street activists: recovered gang members, OGs, and gang members.

RECOVERED GANG MEMBER STREET ACTIVISTS

Recovered gang member street activists are those who acknowledge their history of gang involvement and deviance but, generally speaking, detach or separate themselves from the gang by describing themselves as ex-gang members. These types of street activists condemn the gang subculture, the organization, and its practices. For this type of street activist, the focus of community efforts is getting gang members off the streets by finding them jobs, raising funds to pay for school tuition, and involving them in community empowerment projects.

These street activists use an assimilationist approach to politicize gang members. Their main goal is to resocialize gang members into mainstream society through the acquisition of middle-class values. They believe that this goal is achieved by obtaining the "right" education and job training. The mission of their organizations is in total contradiction to the value systems of the gang. For instance, in its statement of purpose, a local community-based group founded by ex-gang members, Focus Youth Gang Services (FYGS), states: "Our goal is to infiltrate [*sic*] the previous negative activities of gang members into a positive behavior that will be acknowledge[d] by society." This type of approach has earned London Carter, the group's founder, the recognition, endorsement, and support of public officials such as the mayors of the cities of Compton and Inglewood, who have helped Mr. Carter and his organization improve his community.

The relationship between government agencies and FYGS is a remarkable example of institutional normative isomorphism—wherein one institution or organization is able to influence the other by means of professionals or experts. FYGS has often worked with state institutions in organizing conferences where "gang experts" (among which include the chief of police, scholars, and community economic developers) confer to develop strategies to solve the "gang problem." It is at these meetings that decisions are made about the type of adequate policies, strategies, and approaches to use in solving the issue. In their interaction, both of these institutions gain political legitimacy. On the one hand, the mayor's office and the police department obtain some form of community involvement or participation in the solution of the gang problem. This is especially helpful for government institutions that have come under heavy criticism for not including and even ignoring community participation in the solution of community problems. On the other hand, London Carter is elevated to the role of "gang expert" by the city officials. He is a resource to the community. In addition, FYGS obtains some form of legitimacy as a community organization. Perhaps it is this relationship to government institutions that impels recovered gang member street activists to adhere to middle-class values—restricting them from taking a more critical or radical stance.

OG STREET ACTIVISTS

OGs are the second type of street activists. In contrast to the recovered gang members, OG street activists still claim to have some links to the gang, which they use to recruit more gang members to work in different political activities. OGs use the strategy of co-optation as an approach to the politicization of gang members. They see the violence among the gangs as a manifestation of a misdirected and legitimate rebellion of the youths against the social conditions in which they are forced to live. OG street activists re-frain from working with government agencies, which they see as antagonis-tic to their communities. They usually work in organizations that are eco-nomically and politically independent from government institutions. This form of independence allows these organizations the flexibility to engage in a campaign critical of state institutions. As Michael Zinzun, director of the Community Against Police Brutality explains:

> We don't have a nonprofit status and that allows us to speak out, to endorse candidates who may support our attempts to get police accountability and com-munity control of the police. Our main objective is an independent civilian po-lice review board with an 11-point program that has been used by a number of cities around the country. It's probably one of the most sweeping review docu-ments in the country.   *(Stein 1997:258–259)*

Despite the antagonistic character of more-independent organizations, they still are influenced by other organizations in civil society via normative iso-morphism. Organizational structure, ideology, strategies, and so on are transferred or implemented by social movement entrepreneurs who have learned them during their participation in previous social movement organ-izations and/or during their affiliation with one of these organizations. These types of activists are more critical of state institutions. With respect to gangs, OG street activists are critical and condemn some of the gangs' practices but they justify them as a social reality. "We say that crime was here before gangs. Crime will continue as long as we have a repressive sys-tem" (Stein 1997:259).

GANG MEMBER STREET ACTIVISTS

Gang members are the third type of street activists. These types of street ac-tivists use the strategy of reconstruction or transformation—that is, they be-lieve that the gang itself can be turned around and politicized. In contrast to the recovered gang members and the OGs, gang member street activists still adhere, to a certain extent, to the gangster value system and cultural practices. Gang members foresee the potential of the gang in becoming a social movement organization. Specifically, they think that the cohesion, culture, organizational structure, and spiritual practices of the gang can be transformed into positive attributes for a social movement. When we asked

Bloodhound whether he would have to leave the gang to become an activist, he gave the following answer:

> Nah, nah. But you don't have to step out. I mean, I don't wanna step out. Right now bein' a Blood is the only thing that gives my life meaning. I'm not gonna stop being a Blood. I don't care what anyone says. My Blood ties, I'm not gonna sever 'em. You know, what I wanna do is, I wanna get the Bloods that are out there and don't know all their lessons. I want them to be able to say, "You know what? If I go and read this book, this literature, this has been approved by the United Bloods Empire, all the Bloods agree with this, this is the theology, this is our political beliefs, and this is our agenda for the year 2000." So that you can represent the 'hood in a positive way and do the things that a Blood is supposed to do. *(interview, 1 May 1999)*

To achieve this goal, gang member street activists engage in the reconstruction of the history of the gang as a political entity. They attempt to rescue the history of struggle of street organizations and build on it and they try to redirect the already existing organization. In this process of reconstruction, street activists are borrowing tactics, strategies, and structural arrangements from a broad array of organizations that range from other street organizations on the East Coast and previously existing organizations that are not necessarily political, such as the military, college fraternities, religious organizations, and so on. Mimetic isomorphism is the main tactic used by street organizations in their organizational transition.[15] In a way, they are engaged in the creation of their own selective narrative of the history and purpose of the organization.

DISCUSSION

The existence of street activists is not a new phenomenon. What is new is the relationship of street activists to outside organizations and to the gang/street organizations themselves. Throughout the history of street activism, outside political and religious organizations have attempted to assimilate or co-opt gang members into their organizations and struggles. Perhaps this is the reason why there was little evidence of political trends within the gangs, for most of the politically conscious members are drained from the organization. However, recently a higher number of gang member street activists are taking the new approach of reconstructing or transforming the gang into a political organization itself. Although there is evidence of an ideological presence of political activism, this ideology has not been able to materialize at the structural level. Street organizations and/or gangs in Los Angeles (in contrast to street organizations in New York City) have not yet fully incorporated an ideology of political struggle into their structures. However, the evidence shows a pattern of higher politicization of both members and organizations. Currently, some sets of the Bloods are going through a process of formalization that attempts to develop a political, spiritual, and structural foundation. Members of other sets have also expressed their interest in this process. This is particularly important for a gang/street organization for which, despite being one of the largest gangs nationwide, most of its affiliations are cultural rather than structural; that is, they have not yet developed an organizational structure typical of mainstream organizations.

Given the fact that some of the members and some sets are still involved in illegal activities, a more sophisticated and complex structural development of street organizations may seem an aberration for some people. Indeed, some may think that it only takes one corrupt leader to take advantage of a well-organized enterprise to use it for his or her own personal goals and benefit. But it is important to note that these changes are not occurring in a social vacuum. A network of community, political, and spiritual organizations are involved in this development. It is the involvement of these organizations that keeps the momentum of this process going and in check. I believe that the higher the participation of outside organizations in helping these street organizations in their political and spiritual structural development, the less likely it is that the street organization will deviate from its political goals into criminal activities. In fact, a full transition into a politically oriented street organization should be encouraged by a society that sees political participation as one of its most precious qualities. In effect, a politically oriented street organization may fill in the moral, social, and political vacuum left by the fleeing of the black middle class. Yet it is important to point out that as long as these depressed areas continue to be socially, economically, and politically dislocated/isolated, none of these ideologically positive changes may take place. And in fact, without support, it is more likely that these marginalized youths will continue their criminal careers. Thus government support is as crucial as community support. The inner-city youths need to have access to good educational opportunities, and more important, to employment opportunities.

NOTES

1. The research that went into the preparation of this essay was funded by the Conflict Resolution Consortium and the Street Organization Project, both of the City University of New York. I am thankful to Dr. Maria Volpe, Dr. David Brotherton, Dr. Luis Barrios, Camila Salazar-Atias, Betsy Morales, Henry Gomez, and to all the kind people that made this project possible. I would like to thank members of the Bloods and Crips for allowing me to enter into their lives and for facilitating this ethnographic study. I would also like to thank Bloodhound, StutterBox, Minister Adis X, Michael Zinzun, and London B. Carter for their kindness and hospitality. Second, I would like to thank the following organizations for allowing me to be present at their different activities and to have access to a variety of their materials: Coalition Against Police Abuse, Community in Support of the Gang Truce, Congress of Racial Equality in L.A. and Venice 2000. Finally, I would like to thank Liby Balmaceda, Helen Lara-Cea, and the Casa Joaquin Murieta's students for their hospitality and motivating discussions.

2. The term *set* was used during the 1960s and the 1970s to refer to the groups of Black youth who socialized together. Today, Black youth use the term *set* very loosely to refer to their neighborhood (or 'hood), the subgroups within the neighborhood, and/or the age-graded groups within the 'hood. Klein (1995) points out that "there is no terminological consensus" among gang members, law enforcement agents, or academics. This definitional ambiguity becomes even more confusing when the term *gang* is applied to all four of the gang's interorganizational levels. In paper, the term *gang* is used to refer to the cultural organizations with loose structure; these gangs are divided into different 'hoods, which are geographically bounded and/or territorially oriented; neighborhoods are subdivided into sets that claim certain areas controlled by the 'hood; and last, these sets are divided into age-graded groups that create what Klein (1971) and Vigil (1998) have described as "vertical lines of organization" (Klein 1971:8).

3. The Bloods are divided into independent subgroups referred to as "sets." The sets may take their name from their geographical area such as district names, official neighborhood names, parks, or housing project names. Subnames may be taken from a specific range of streets, spatial orientation, or an invented name. For instance, the name "Rolling 20s Avenues Bloods" denotes their affiliation to the gang the Bloods, the Rolling 20s set, and the Avenues subset; "Five Deuce Pueblo Bishop Bloods" denotes the affiliation to the Bloods, the Pueblo Bishop's set, and the Fifty-second Street subset.

4. Being perceived as a Mexican researcher from the East Coast was of special help to the collection of data.

5. Subsequently, researchers and academicians have suggested some form of policy (largely coercive) to ameliorate the problem. The relationship between

subject and researcher has been, for the most part, exploitative, condescending, and disrespectful.

6. Jankowski (1991) deals with the gang as an organization competing for scarce resources; yet he ignores the dynamics that involve organizational competition for political and institutional legitimacy. To analyze this dynamic, the concept of isomorphism developed by DiMaggio and Powell (1983), and further developed by Mizruchi and Fein (1999), is useful to uncover the inter- and intraorganizational influences among community organizations and their larger environments, as well as their influences, both ideological and organizational, on street activists. Finally, Mizruchi and Fein's typology of institutional isomorphism (i.e., coercive, mimetic, and normative) helps us to explain the specific mechanisms in which individuals shape community organizations and vice versa.

7. Postmodernist literature states that in the process of objectification, subjects are reduced to merely objects of study with limited agency.

8. The innovative concept of the career, developed by Lachmann (1988), is used to trace the careers of street activists. Drawing from Howard Becker (1963), Lachmann finds the career concept useful for measuring the effects of mentors, state organizations, community organizations, and audiences on the social actors' praxis and their social products. In his study, Lachmann uses this concept to trace the careers of graffiti artists, but this concept can also be used to trace the careers of street activists.

9. It seems to be a general account that the Crips was established before the Bloods. It is important to point out that although Blacks in the South use the term "blood" to greet each other, the organization itself was created sometime in the late 1960s.

10. Davis (1999) refers to this development as the creation of third borders—that is, artificial borders created to divide different neighborhoods. Davis applies this concept to describe the artificial separation of wealthy gated communities in L.A. to separate themselves from poor communities. These artificial separations consist of a great variety of physical barriers such as gates and fences. I have extended this concept to include the artificial borders created by gang members to separate their different neighborhoods. Although gang members do not use physical barriers they make use of symbolic barriers such as graffiti to delimit their territory or turf. These symbolic borders may be based on geographical boundaries created by the city, such as in the case of housing projects and district lines.

11. Nationwide, there was a sense of urgency for the control of gang-related violence. In 1996, the gang problem was defined as an important public policy issue. The response from government institutions was to implement a wide range of repressive and harsh punitive policies. The Violent Crime Control and Law Enforcement Act of 1994 (PL 103-322) and other gang-oriented acts such as S 10, S 54, and HR 3, for instance, permitted the prosecuting of

youths thirteen years of age and above as adults, amended the RICO act of 1962, and expanded it to include gangs as criminal organizations. This amendment targets particular processes, such as acts of conspiracy to violate firearms laws, and enhances penalties for firearms prohibitions. Larger sentences were issued for gang-related crimes. Gangs and their members were particularly targeted. The result was an increase in the number of incarcerations and longer sentences for gang members. In the case of California, these punitive measures include the "three strikes" law and court injunctions aimed at specific gangs and/or sets. Ironically, these punitive approaches have not deterred youths from joining gangs. Government reports document an increase in the numbers of both gang members and gangs nationwide. The violence from both state institutions and rival gangs has devastated communities. On the one hand, the inundation of drugs exacerbated a number of social and health problems such as broken households, domestic violence, drug addiction, crack babies, mental health issues, and AIDS and other venereal diseases. On the other hand, an increase in the number of incarcerations and drug-related deaths contributed to a form of internal genocide of many communities. This harsh reality prompted a mobilization of community members to find solutions to this problem (Hatch 1997:S421).

12. This statement needs qualification. The general truce is not respected by all of the different sets of the Bloods and the Crips; however, in some areas such as Watts and Compton, the Crips and the Bloods are holding to the truce.

13. These individuals resemble what Gramsci (1971) describes as organic intellectuals, but because I am dealing with gang members, I have decided to use the term *street activist*.

14. Although these three categories of street activists are neither mutually exclusive nor exhaustive, they are helpful for analytical purposes and should be treated as conceptual constructs. For instance, in real life, these categories overlap. Street activists may change their approaches and strategies to adapt to the organizational and institutional environments. Furthermore, these three types of street activists participate in, and collaborate with, different types of organizations; they are, in a sense, complementary to each other. Although they have chosen different strategies (i.e., assimilationist, co-optive, and reconstructive or transformative), the end goal seems to be the same: the politicization of gang members and/or the gang itself.

15. This form of mimetic isomorphism is unique, for the source of the information does not come from one particular type of organization or a particular population of organizations, but from an array of organizations.

REFERENCES

Anderson, Elijah. 1990. *Street Wise: Race, Class, and Change in an Urban Community*. Chicago: University of Chicago Press.

Becker, Howard. 1963. *Outsiders: Studies in Social Deviance.* New York: Free Press.
———. 1982. *Art Worlds.* Berkeley and Los Angeles: University of California Press.
Bourgois, Philippe. 1995. *In Search of Respect: Selling Crack in El Barrio.* Cambridge: Cambridge University Press.
Brotherton, David C. 1996. "The Contradictions of Suppression: Notes from a Study to Approaches to Gangs in Three Public High Schools." *Urban Review* 28 (2): 95–120.
———. 1997. "Socially Constructing the Nomads. Part One." *Humanity and Society,* vol. 21, no. 2 (May 1997): 110–129.
———. 1998. "The Evolution of New York City's Street Gangs," In A. Karmen, ed., *Crime and Justice in New York City.* New York: McGraw Hill.
Brotherton, David C., and Luis Barrios. Forthcoming. *Between Black and Gold: Street Politics in New York City.*
Carmichael, S. and Hamilton Charles. 1967. *Black Power: The Politics of Liberation in America.* New York: Random House.
Carter, London B. 1999. "Biographical Sketch." Los Angeles: Focus Youth Gang Services (in-house publication).
Cavanagh, Suzanne, and David Teasley. 1998. "Youth Gangs: Recent Developments." On-line, available: <http://www.pennyhill.com/criminaljustice/96-274gov.html>, pp. 92–491. Congressional Research Service, U.S. Library of Congress.
Collins, Patricia Hill. 1990. *Black Feminist Thought: Knowledge, Consciousness, and the Politics of Empowerment.* New York: Routledge, Chapman and Hall.
Community in Support of the Gang Truce. 1992. *No Set Tripping: All Power to the People.* Los Angeles: CSGT Press.
Conquergood, Dwight. 1997. "Street Literacy." In J. Flood, S. Bryce Heath, and D. Lapp, eds., *Handbook of Research on Teaching Literacy through the Communicative and Visual Arts,* 354–375. New York: Prentice Hall.
Davis, Mark. 1999. *City of Quartz: Excavating the Future in Los Angeles.* New York: Vintage Books.
DiMaggio, Paul J., and Walter W. Powell. 1983. "The Iron Cage Revisited: Institutional Isomorphism and Collective Rationality in Organizational Fields." *American Sociological Review,* 48: 147–160.
Gramsci, Antonio. 1971. *Prison Notebooks.* New York: International.
Hall, Stuart, and Tony Jefferson, eds. 1975. *Resistance through Ritual: Youth Subcultures in Post-war Britain.* London: Hutchinson Press.
Hatch, Orrin. 1997. Senatorial Remarks. In *Congressional Record.* Daily edition, vol. 143: S420-S421.
Jankowski, Martin Sanchez. 1991. *Islands in the Street: Gangs and American Urban Society.* Berkeley: University of California Press.
Klein, Malcom W. 1971. *Street Gangs and Street Workers.* Englewood Cliffs, N.J.: Prentice Hall.

————. 1995. *The American Street Gang: Its Nature, Prevalence, and Control*. New York: Oxford University Press.

Lachmann, Richard. 1988. "Graffiti as Career and Ideology." *American Journal of Sociology*, vol. 94, no. 2 (September 1988): 229–250.

Mizruchi, Mark S., and Lisa C. Fein. 1999. "The Social Construction of Organizational Knowledge: A Study of the Uses of Coercive, Mimetic, and Normative Isomorphism." *Administrative Science Quarterly*, 44: 653–683.

Moore, Joan W. 1991. *Going Down the Barrio: Homeboys and Homegirls in Change*. Philadelphia: Temple University Press.

Moore, Joan W., Robert Garcia, Carlos Garcia, Luis Cerda, and Frank Valencia. 1978. *Homeboys: Gangs, Drugs, and Prison in the Barrios of Los Angeles*. Philadelphia: Temple University Press.

Office of Juvenile Justice and Delinquency Prevention. 1999. *1996 National Youth Gang Survey*. Washington, D.C.: U.S. Department of Justice.

Stein, Nancy. 1997. "The Gang Truce: A Movement for Social Justice, an Interview with Michael Zinzun." *Social Justice*, 24 (4): 259–266.

Vigil, James Diego. 1988. *Barrio Gangs: Street Life and Identity in Southern California*. Texas: The University of Texas Press.

Wilson, William Julius. 1978. *The Declining Significance of Race: Blacks and Changing American Institutions*. Chicago: University of Chicago Press.

————. 1987. *The Truly Disadvantaged: The Inner City, the Underclass, and Public Policy*. Chicago: University of Chicago Press.

————. 1996. *When Work Disappears: The World of the New Urban Poor*. Chicago: University of Chicago Press.

Young, Iris Marion. 1994. "Gender as a Seriality: Thinking about Women as a Social Collective." In Linda Nicholson and Steven Seidman, eds., *Social Postmodernism: Beyond Identity Politics*, 187–215. Cambridge: Cambridge University Press.

PART 3
GANGS, AGENCY, **AND** AT-RISK YOUTH

7

THE ALMIGHTY LATIN KING AND QUEEN NATION AND THE SPIRITUALITY OF RESISTANCE: AGENCY, SOCIAL COHESION, AND LIBERATING RITUALS IN THE MAKING OF A STREET ORGANIZATION

LUIS BARRIOS

I do not believe the spiritual law works on a field of its own. On the contrary, it expresses itself only through the ordinary activities of life. It thus affects the economic, the social and the political fields.   —*Mahatma Gandhi*

Youth are joining us now not because they want to have a clique and somebody to defend them, now they got a voice to be heard and that's what we represent in New York City. A strong Latino voice that is not muzzled by these sell-out politicians that are Latinos and Black Americans that sold out the community for years. The Latin Kings wants to be something that stays in the community, for the people, by the people, with the people.   —*King Tone, Supreme Crown*

As should be clear from the choice of quotations above, my approach to the study of gangs will be somewhat different from orthodox criminological gang studies whose primary interest in gangs is to discover the origins of crime and deviance. In contrast, my foremost interest in researching these groups is to understand them as examples of collective resistance to systems of domination and as sites of spiritual practice, which extend, perpetuate, and reinforce their coherence. In other words, spirituality is presented in this paper as a strategy of resistance to dominance. This conceptual orientation is informed by my twin vocations as a social scientist and as a priest. I share these biographical details with the reader to explain not only my interest in the often neglected political arena of street youth subcultures but also why I tend to draw from sources outside the legitimated canons of sociology and criminology. Permit me to make several key points to further ground the discussion.

First, it is my view that our religious institutions have been so co-opted in the service of the dominant classes that they have misappropriated spirituality and rendered it harmless, aimless, and reactionary. The prevailing tendency is to assert that this life is but a temporary stage on our journey to an eternity with the Supreme Being. Our only responsibility in this world, they claim, is to live a "sacred life" and to "win more souls for God." Therefore, those who practice religion need only to perform personal rituals (e.g., fasting, prayers, reading the sacred books, making pilgrimage) while desisting from any collective involvement in cultural, social, or political community projects. Contrary to this interpretation, I argue that spirituality is not unique to religion nor to those who believe in God—rather, it is an intrinsic component of all human beings.

Second, spirituality as a social and political phenomenon has been, consciously or unconsciously, ignored, misread, and/or underestimated by "gang researchers." Nonetheless, spirituality may be an intrinsic aspect of gang life, and without its analysis, we cannot understand how marginalized and/or colonized members of gangs organize to preserve their personal and collective identities.

Third, following the former postulation, two central questions must be pondered if we are to take the study of gangs to a more political level: (1) To what degree do gangs represent ways for oppressed people to come together to contend with and contest subordination in their everyday lives? and (2) What is the range of roles played by spirituality in this struggle (Barrios 1998, 2000)? These two questions are especially important in relationship to groups like the Almighty Latin King/Queen Nation (ALKQN) in New York City that have taken explicitly political turns in their history (Brotherton 1999).

In the essay that follows, I will argue that: (1) the ALKQN in New York City was a Latino/Latina street political organization[1] formed by individuals in a quest for personal and collective identity; (2) the ALKQN embodied both a practice and an ideology of resistance—one example of which was a spirituality of liberation; (3) this spirituality resisted the dominant culture that constantly attempted to dehumanize, objectify, and criminalize the group and its members; and (4) as the group organized to resist the dominant class and its culture, it moved closer to the notion of a "conquest liberation" through *deideologizing spiritualism.*[2]

THE LITERATURE: FROM THE SPIRIT OF RESISTANCE TO THE RESISTANCE OF SPIRITUALITY

In a review of the gang literature dating back to the earliest systematic studies of youth street gangs, resistance to social and economic marginality has been a powerful though occluded theme in the narratives of scholars. Consequently, although many researchers have long pointed to agency and struggle as quite prominent characteristics in the subterranean worlds of street youth groups, the primary emphasis has always been on the adaptational properties of these subcultures, which has left their oppositional qualities both undertheorized and underreported.

For example, in one of the first attempts to define an urban street gang, Thrasher describes it as: "an interstitial group originally formed spontaneously and then integrated through conflict. . . . The result of this collective behavior is the development of tradition, unreflective internal structure, esprit de corps, solidarity, morale, group awareness, and attachment to a local territory"(1927:46).[3] Yet these characteristics of street youth, which would be highly prized in a social movements paradigm, are given short shrift, and we are asked to accept that such collectivist practices are produced almost without any critical mediation between the subjects and their environments.

Similarly, when gang research again gained interest and a whole host of highly skilled and reputable sociologists focused on this problem recurring in the rapidly corporatizing society of the 1950s (e.g., Cohen 1955; Miller 1958; Cloward and Ohlin 1960; Matza 1964), they made little of the cultural spaces that these groups occupied or of the meaning systems they devised other than to see in them different forms of social reproduction. And even during the 1960s, when several researchers noted the influence of the civil rights movement and the Vietnam War (Spergel 1976; Miller 1976; Jacobs 1977), revealing an encounter between gangs and radical politics, there was little attention given to the plausibility that gangs could be counterhegemonic or that subcultural agency could take many subversive forms (for an exception see Dawley 1992).

In recent years, a minority of researchers have attempted to reexplore the resistance terrain of gang development with studies of the Chicano inmate community in Los Angeles (Moore 1978), the Black "underclass" in

Milwaukee (Hagedorn and Macon 1988), the street nations (Conquergood 1993, 1997), the drug-based, community gangs of Chicago (Venkatesh 2000), and the emergence of communitarian street organizations in New York City (Brotherton 1999). Nonetheless, although all these studies indicate the existence of innovative social, political, and economic praxes employed by gangs—not only to fill glaring voids in their communities' resources but to respond to changes in the more macro dimensions of society (Hagedorn 2002)—there is a great deal still to be written about the gang and its connection to organized youth resistance beyond the foci of crime and deviance. In particular, little if anything has been written about this resistance from a spiritual perspective. Consequently, with such a limited frame of reference to guide us in the gang literature, it is time to turn to other fruitful avenues of analysis to be able to consider this chronically overlooked element of the gang phenomenon.

LIBERATION THEOLOGY AND SPIRITUALITY

With the lack of depth in the gang literature when it comes to the alternative meaning systems of gangs, how do we analytically approach a group that places so much emphasis on its spiritual practices and yet whose identity is tied to the streets? This is a central question in studying such groups as the ALKQN. The answer, in my opinion, is to invoke the theories and insights of *liberation theology*, which is both a school of thought and a practice specifically aimed at the agency of the marginalized and their spiritually based life worlds. But what is liberation theology and how does it relate to spirituality?

In liberation theology, the primary task is to set the oppressed and the marginalized free from all forms of domination—be it spiritual, material, or cultural. According to Gustavo Gutierrez (1972), the liberation theology movement started in Latin America in 1968[4] and has been described "as a faith reflection on the praxis of liberation, the theology of liberation is the thinking of the faith under the formality of a leaven of historical transformation, as the salt of the earth and the light of the world, as the theological virtue of charity exercised in the area of the social" (Boff and Boff 1986). It is important to note that liberation theology significantly departs from the theological principles of a fundamentalist faith. Whereas the latter requires that those who need salvation must accept Jesus as their personal savior, the former searches for a community faith praxis through which liberation from all kind of injustices is made possible. There are several basic tenets of liberation theology that point to the critical importance of spirituality based on the understanding that all humans are a combination of the spiritual and the material, which function together dialectically.

First, there is an interactional relationship between theology and spirituality, whereby spirituality becomes a transforming force or motivation for change with historical, political, socioeconomic, and cultural dimensions.

Second, spirituality is not a credo, a doctrine, a dogma, or a way of knowing but a way of living. In other words, spirituality is about doing, not saying.

Third, spirituality is a form of resistance praxis[5] utilized by people and/or social movements to fight back against injustice. Thus spirituality implores us to struggle for a different society despite the mundane everyday rituals of oppression and it justifies both a spirit and a spirituality of resistance and transformation.

Fourth, it is important to underscore that the primary source of spirituality is our *realidad humana* (human reality), which manifests itself in a specific time and space and never in a vacuum. Thus when we talk about our *realidad* (reality) we are talking about our social, political, and economic reality.

Finally, spirituality is a human *reencuentro* (reencounter) with the creation of God that is not limited to the practice of religion and that encourages a radical form of solidarity. This interpretation of spirituality allows people who do not believe in God to nonetheless be able to manifest their spirituality.

METHODOLOGY AND ANALYSIS

The data for this chapter derives from ethnographic research that the Street Organization Project (at John Jay College of Criminal Justice) has been conducting in New York City with the ALKQN, covering a period of four years (1996–2000). Among the data collected were eighty-five life-history interviews with members of the Almighty Latin King and Queen Nation (ALKQN), an archive of the group's internal documents, and hundreds of pages of observational field notes and photographs taken at the group's branch meetings, political rallies, and social events. Together, these data provide a detailed account of the group's transitional stages of development between a street gang and what has been termed a street organization (see above).

One of the primary questions that has emerged in the research is: How is spirituality used by the ALKQN as an empowerment weapon, or as a strategy for resistance? To address this, I will briefly discuss some of the parallels between the group and the concept of liberation theology, which will open the way for a descriptive analysis of the group's spiritual domain focusing on the primary themes of agency, social cohesion, and liberating rituals.

My approach does not aspire to be pure social science, if that term is defined as detached observation and value neutrality. Instead, it is more akin to what Stringer has called a program of "community-based action research." By this, he means, "a collaborative approach to inquiry or investigation that provides people with the means to take systematic action to resolve specific problems . . . [and] focuses on methods and techniques of inquiry that take into account people's history, culture, interactional practices, and emotional lives" (1999:15).

KINGISM/QUEENISM AND LIBERATION THEOLOGY

The philosophy and set of practices that fundamentally bind the ALKQN together are called Kingism/Queenism. At the practical level, Kingism/Queenism is constituted by the meetings of the group, the solidarity offered by members, and the discipline and commitment demanded by the organization. At the ideological level, Kingism/Queenism is an eclectic mix of principles taken from twelve-step programs—rhetorical devices borrowed from ethnic empowerment texts and a synthesis of spiritual belief systems. Out of this complex amalgam of personal ethics, social support, political doctrine, community engagement, and spiritual rituals, the twin notions of Kingism and Queenism are born, and together they offer members the possibility of an identity built on the strengths of their indigenous culture.[6] Another way of interpreting this aspect of the ALKQN is that the organization itself is the religion and Kingism/Queenism is the doctrine.

Based on this understanding of the group's theoretical and practical underpinnings, it should be clear how the set of principles and ideas embodied in liberation theology can be used to discover and interpret the deeper meaning systems of the group. In fact, we can list at least four fundamental characteristics of both praxes that make the parallels even clearer: (1) liberation is not seen as a purely religious experience; (2) those who are being oppressed should be the agents of their own liberation; (3) to become conscious of our human reality, it is necessary to reflect critically; and (4) it is possible to change our human reality through liberating all dimensions of humanity (e.g., political, social, economic, sexual, gender, cultural, religious, etc.). The task still before us, however, is to show how these systems of thought and behavior compare at the empirical level. To do this, I will focus on what constituted this group's spirituality.

SPIRITUALITY AND THE ALKQN

Similar to liberation theology, for the ALKQN spirituality is not an abstract set of inner beliefs or a pathway simply into self-reflection. It is a means to understand and support the multiple ways people can resist. Thus spirituality in the ALKQN has many different facets and interpretations—each operating on different (though connected) levels within the generalized notion of Kingism/Queenism. Below, I discuss three thematic areas that emerged from the data that help us to understand how it is that the ALKQN was engaging in liberation theology through its practice and interpretation of spirituality: agency, social cohesion, and liberating rituals.

AGENCY *Spirituality* is a critical factor in the group's ability to heighten and occasion moments of agency among its members. Though this term has long been used in sociology in juxtaposition to the notion of structure (i.e., to show the undetermined nature of human action), the definition I employ, which emerges from the field of religious activism within liberation theology, is: a process of action facilitated by a group or organization by which members change, transform, and convert injustice into justice. In the ALKQN's literature, this activist interpretation of spirituality is clear:

> The new King recognizes that the day of resurrection is here. A time for the appearance of a new manifestation of truth. The rising of the dead means the spiritual awakening of those who have been sleeping in the graveyard of ignorance. The day of the oppressor must now be judged by the oppressed."
>
> *(The Latin King Bible)*

But how do you communicate this "call to action" to the members within a spiritual framework? One of the key devices was the sermonizing of the leadership, particularly by King Tone:

And the movement took on. And I started, you know, putting in religion. I started using King's lessons and using the Bible as a concordant. So everything I learned in Kingism I would match a story from the Bible, I would preach it to the kids and break it down in knowledge and it started working on them. They started getting a sense of spirituality; they got a sense of belonging. They got a sense that I didn't want them, like the pastor, to be Jesus. I just wanted them to try and walk like he did."   *(King Tone)*

Thus, from the outset of the group's reform, a major tenet of the group's ideology and of its spirituality is the emphasis on members confronting their own reality and taking responsibility for their lives.[7] To the ALKQN, then, spirituality is critically important as a pathway into a practical, but radical, consciousness, and in many ways it is the philosophical mode through which the group develops, generates, and sustains its praxis. At the personal level, however, spirituality is used to encourage members to be reflective, disciplined, and self-critical, as evidenced in the following response from a Queen:

When it comes to my lessons and my prayers, I will die for them because that's what I live by. That's what shows that I'm proud. That's what shows that I am a Queen. In my own world I am a Queen.   *(Queen J.)*

These fundamental experiences of spirituality that Queen J. is recounting constitute a path to identity in which Kingism/Queenism, in my understanding, is a spiritual syncretism that develops and preserves the collective identity, both of the ALKQN and of the individual member, through action. What that action consists of is very important. It is the learning of one's culture, the active reciprocity of friends and comrades, and the development of self-esteem. Therefore the agency and practice of Kingism/Queenism's spirituality is very concrete and functions almost like a form of self-organized therapy for the poor and marginalized. Below, King F. repeats a refrain that many people who are familiar with the group have come to see as one of its primary appeals to nonmembers in hard-pressed communities:

I didn't need the Nation, what I needed to do—what I needed the Nation to do for me was to help me change my life. You know, to get out of this negative way of thinking and get into something more positive, you know get into my culture. And that's where I really, I learned, everything I know now was in prison, you know, just being in prison and being a King, it helped me completely. It helped me learn my culture, it helped me be a man, it helped me accept reality, you know and it also helped me get out of my drug addiction. Completely out of it. And to this day I've been home for what? About ten months now, and I gotta thank the Nation for that because if it wasn't for the Nation, I'd probably be right back in jail.   *(King F., field note, 22 March 1997)*

SOCIAL COHESION Similar to "base communities" in Latin America that are "doing" liberation theology, in the ALKQN there is enormous importance placed on the achievement of social cohesion. Thus various leaders and rank-and-file speakers at almost every meeting could be heard calling for more "unity" in the Nation and to never forget the lessons that call for the group to be "360 degrees strong and unbreakable." However, such internal solidarity was achieved in markedly different ways from so-called traditional gangs.

For the ALKQN, a major factor in reaching and maintaining a high level of internal solidarity is through practicing a form of spirituality out of which a collective identity and praxis could be constructed. In contrast, research literature on street gangs, from Thrasher to the present, argues that the key to internal cohesion is a combination of boundary maintenance, especially among territorial groups, and the threat of attack from other gangs (see Decker and Van Winkle 1996). The ALKQN's Santo (spiritual advisor) saw his group's position on this issue as follows:

Spirituality is the basic foundation that generates the energy and magnetism that binds the Kings and Queens together.

(King Héctor, interview, 30 June 2000)

Thus, in King Héctor's eyes, it is impossible to be a King or a Queen and not be in touch with one's spiritual side. To do so, he insists, not only misses the whole point about the origins of the group but also fails to understand the profundity of the organization's process of transformation. In effect, the great importance placed on members developing their spiritual sensibilities helped the group to form an effective moral consensus in Durkheim's sense (Durkheim 1912), and created what might be called a social glue.

A second aspect of solidarity through spirituality relates to the core reasons why the members have come to form such a collective in the first place. In the orthodox literature on gangs, one of the primary reasons for the formation of such collectives is the coming together of individuals who are somehow linked to societal underworlds, either through the present or future commission of crime and delinquency, and/or through kinship ties. However, with the ALKQN, a primary reason for members to join the organization is based on their need to redeem and develop their collective humanity, which has often been bruised and undermined by their membership in one of society's lowest social classes. This yen for a communal fellowship (Conquergood 1993) based on the restoration and elevation of their human dignity is a profoundly spiritual experience and makes for what I call a "sacred" collectivity (see Driver 1991). In other words, the group perceives itself as: acting in unison on behalf of God, and providing a *communitas* of individuals based on love, solidarity, and friendship. Below we see an example of this in the group's five-point behavioral code, which outlines expected performance of members if they are to remain affiliated:

Respect: Respect your brother, the crown, and the Nation. A brother's respect will show high in regard to the Nation.

Honesty: Marked by the truth your word is your crown and your crown is your Nation. A king will live by his word.

Unity: The condition of being united into a single whole "one for all and all for one." The crown symbolizes our people—Latinos. Amor de Rey (King love).

Knowledge: The knowing of your lessons and prayers gained through the experience and studies of our Nation.

Love: Love is what we carry in our hearts for our brothers, the crown, and our Nation.

The third and final aspect of the group's quest for social cohesion through its spirituality relates to the way solidarity is practiced in defiance of the fragmenting forces of the dominant culture—that is, the economic and psychosocial pressures that make people feel vulnerable and isolated from one another.

> Before, I used to define my family like discombobulated. Now, with just my mother and my sister and the Nation, I define family beautiful. It's wonderful how I could always have somebody to go to and talk to and just have so many people every day like to be there with you and hang out with you, feed you, give you money. They give you their last dollar. Anything. It's beautiful. We're always

together, we're always talking about our problems and it's like if I stay quiet for a long time they'll ask me what's wrong.   *(Queen Freckles, 19 June 1998).*[8]

Queen Freckles, in expressing her sense of belonging, emphasizes how connected she feels to a place where she receives not only social and emotional support, but also economic resources. In this example, we see a clear example of the group bringing together the spiritual with the material, which, as I argued earlier, is a key ingredient of liberation theology. Such a characteristic of the group obviously contributes enormously to the maintenance of solidarity and to the high levels of obligation demanded of the membership.

LIBERATING RITUALS This final part of the analysis focuses on the liberating rituals of the group, which are tied to its varying interpretations of spirituality. A serious concern in liberation theology is that religious rituals often serve to domesticate and disempower people instead of having the capacity to liberate them. But what do I mean by ritual?

In my interpretation, a group ritual has three basic characteristics and/or properties (see Driver 1991 and McGuire 1997): (1) It is the symbolic means used by the group to communicate meanings and bodies of knowledge to itself and thereby achieve levels of commitment from the group's members;[9] (2) It is a tool of the powerless to counteract the penetrations and hegemonic definitions of social reality by the dominant culture; and (3) It is a form of performance by which individuals and groups act on this world both morally and memorially.

In the following, I isolate four types of rituals practiced by the ALKQN that are essential elements of its liberation theological praxis: prayers, fasting, salutations, and assemblies.

Prayers: In all religions, the ritual of prayer is an important spiritual exercise for the believers. They can cover petition, entreaty, expostulation, confession, thanksgiving, recollection, praise, adoration, meditation, and interception. However, a close study of prayer rituals in different religions demonstrates significant discrepancies concerning the regulation of time, place, and posture. Similarly, an analysis of the ALKQN's prayers reveals instructions only for place and posture, without emphasizing any particular time regulation. The importance of prayer for the ALKQN is a serious matter and in the ALKQN's Bible, there are 366 prayers in the

"Kings' Gnosis" alone (this is a section of the manifesto that, roughly interpreted, means a King's way of knowing).

Fasting: The second important ritual is that of fasting. In the ALKQN's Constitution, it states: "a King will fast for two days (twenty-four times a year). The two days will be the eleventh and the twelfth of every month. The fast will start at daybreak and end at sundown." The role of fasting in the ALKQN is similar to that of other religions, including those that have been rescued by liberation theology, and is used to fortify both the individual and the group through: (1) A purification of the body that, in turn, clears the mind; (2) The process of self-sacrifice, which brings the individual closer to God; (3) The practice of self-control and self-discipline, which challenges outside society's presupposition that group members are irrational and "out of control"; and (4) The practice of petition (or *promesas* in Spanish) in which members offer part of themselves to God on behalf of their group and in return both the individual and the group receives God's blessing.

Salutations: A third ritual is that of salutations, which are public demonstrations of membership through which Kings and Queens reaffirm their identity and openly contest their class and racial invisibility (see Conqergood 1997). A central part of the symbolic makeup of the ALKQN's salutation system revolves around the concept of the crown and its omnipresence in the corporeal language of the group. In the ALKQN, there are at least three crown salutes. The first is the one used at all times when Kings and Queens greet each other and is similar to the international love sign language except that the palm of the hand is facing inwards. The second crown salute is made by pressing three fingers of both hands together to make a crown (called the royal crown), which is used when a member is speaking to a superior. The third salutation is the prayer crown, which is made by linking two hands together, making sure that the fore fingers are touching, the little fingers are crossing at the front and both thumbs are sticking out. In this salutation, the crown must make contact with the chest when the prayers are in process.

Assemblies: Finally, the fourth form of ritual is the assemblies. The most common type of assembly is called a *cipher* and is the ritual used when the group forms a circle. According to the ALKQN, the ability to have an assembly signifies that the organization is "360 degrees strong and unbreakable." The origin of this ritual is in the prison yards where Latin

King inmates first held their meetings in defiance of authorities and other inmate organizations. Within the ALKQN's numerology, this circle is broken down into five points of the almighty crown with each point representing 72 degrees of the circle, as is stated in the bible, "without the five points the circle is incomplete, so is our Nation."

CONCLUSION

From empirical data collected in a case study of the Almighty Latin King/ Queen Nation (ALKQN) in New York City, I have argued that the group can be understood through the concept of liberation theology as a religio-spiritual collectivity that has developed rituals, texts, symbols, and ideologies directly in relationship to its members' own needs. In contrast to most criminological approaches to gangs and street youth, I have focused on and analyzed this group's spiritual practices as if they were examples of "popular cultural religion."

Although the ALKQN's spirituality is not unique to Latinos/Latinas— for liberation spirituality is present in every group that takes the path of resistance in a search for identity—it is important to remember that the group nonetheless developed its own distinctive culture in a specific historical, political, and socioeconomic context. In other words, although the group's spiritual traditions herald from its earlier origins in Chicago, this aspect of the group's culture took a much more demonstrative form during the reformist years 1996–99 in New York City.

There are many, of course, who will continue to ask: What is really behind this Kingism/Queenism and the creation of the ALKQN? My answer to them is similar to that of Boff, who, when asked the same question regarding liberation theology, said: "the struggle of the people believers who make their faith a source of mobilization against oppression and for their liberation" (1991:25). In other words, I argue that what I have seen and experienced in the ALKQN is a vivid example of a spirituality of resistance where a radical praxis sought significant changes in this world's (dis)order.[10]

This radical way of organizing the streets was, in effect, a vanguard way of doing theology by providing opportunities for people, both young and middle-aged, to develop their own *religiosidad popular*,[11] as a route to power, equity, and justice by preserving both their culture and their identity. In so doing, the group effectively challenged its gang stigma by developing its notion of street spirituality and turning itself increasingly into a novel form of social movement. The dynamics and properties of this transformation, no matter how incomplete and transitional, provide rich lessons not only for the study of "gangs," as I have attempted to demonstrate, but also for grass-roots resistance in general.[12]

Finally, although I fully admit to only having scratched the surface of the group's highly complex system of signs, ideas, and practices, this analysis demonstrates the untold potential that lies in such an unorthodox focus. I conclude that without such a focus, we will continue to miss the meanings and cosmologies that inspire members like Queen J., below, leaving our work, both as researchers and as social activists, far removed from the worlds of the subjects and the hidden lives we pretentiously would like to influence:

> I love being a Queen. It gives me hope, it makes me proud to say that I've got family that I know I can always count on and no matter what happens in my life I know they'll always be there for me and they may not physically be there, but I know them spiritually and I know they will be there. You know, I've been in gangs, I've been in other nations, I've been in a lot of things, and I've never felt so at home as I have when I joined the Queens.
>
> *(Queen J., field note, 20 June 1998)*[13]

NOTES

1. A street political organization is defined as: "A group formed largely by youth and adults of a marginalized social class which aims to provide its members with a resistant identity, an opportunity to be individually and collectively empowered, a voice to speak back to the dominant culture, a refuge from the stresses and strains of barrio or ghetto life and a spiritual enclave within which its own sacred rituals can be generated and practiced" (Brotherton and Barrios, forthcoming).

2. Montero (1997:242) describes *deideologization* as follows: "Deideologization is closely linked to the notion of consciousness raising. . . . Everyone has consciousness. The purpose of this work is to create awareness about life conditions, about causes and effects, and to promote change and empowerment. The process of change begins with placing people, through their own actions and efforts, in control of their immediate environment. Action and reflection are carried out in order to transform passivity into activity, and apathy into commitment, decision making, and the transformation of everyday life." In the next section on spirituality, I argue that there are differences between spiritualism and spirituality.

3. Thrasher, rather than place an emphasis on these youths' criminal or delin-
quent-based activities, was more interested in the way poor, newly arrived
immigrants and migrants (for the most part) created a collective niche for
themselves in the bowels of an extremely underserved and somewhat inchoate
community.

4. His book, *Teología de la liberación,* was published in the English under the title, *A Liberation Theology,* in 1973.

5. I am using Dermot A. Lane's definition of praxis, which in his words is, "an
extension of the experiential base of theology; praxis is the application of the
principle of experience to the realm of transforming activity; praxis is a particular form of human experience; praxis is the experience of reflective activity" (1984:9). In addition, Otto Maduro, in his book, *Religion and Social Conflicts* (1982), elaborates on this concept of resistance.

6. This collective identity construction in Kingism/Queenism through the medium of spirituality not only changes the way they (the members) see themselves (by redefining who they are) but it reaffirms their own culture as part
of the collective identity process. For example, to be called a King or a Queen
is the antithesis of being called poor and being treated as culturally invisible.
Similarly, instead of feeling inferior because of one's designation in a white-
dominated society as a "minority," one is now feeling specially selected because in order to join the group, a member must: "Have a cultural heritage of
Latin decent. This very simply means that you must have direct blood relation to some one of Latin origin" (ALKQN Bible).

7. Spirituality, much like Marx's famous dictum on idealism, is essentially the
process of thinking about the world in order to change it and not to simply contemplate it.

8. In contrast, mainstream religion, representing mostly the interests of the dominant culture, has a way to dichotomize such religious practices. If the religious
practices do not interfere with the values, morals, and interests of the ruling
class, this sacred collectivity is usually deemed positive. On the other hand, if it
happens to challenge the status quo, the ruling class will use religion to catego-
rize and label it, describing it as a sect or as a cult. One example of this is the
liberation theology movement in Latin America, a movement inside the Roman Catholic Church, and other Protestant Churches, that has been criminal-
ized and demonized. In reality it was the creation of a sacred collectivity that
was rejected for resisting social, political, economic, and religious injustices.

9. As McGuire states: "ritual both reflects and acts on the group's meaning system" (1997:87).

10. This is what Gustavo Gutierrez, in his book, *A Theology of Liberation,* identifies as "a critical reflection on Christian praxis in the light of the Word"
(1972:80).

11. An excellent discussion of this issue of popular religiosity is in Robert J.
Schreiter's book, *Constructing Local Theologies* (1985:122–143).

12. Three important lessons for grassroots social movements I would highlight are: (1) To remain viable they have to become relevant to people's struggles; (2) They must constantly find new ways to motivate people in their quest for justice; and (3) A special emphasis must be placed on the spirituality of resistance—especially if we want to locate a transcendent driving force among the marginalized.

13. In other words, spirituality implores us to struggle for a different society despite the mundane everyday rituals of oppression, and it justifies both a spirit and a spirituality of resistance and transformation in the here and now. This is captured by Miranda when he says: "Is it more utopian to hope for the transformation of the world through justice than it is to hope for the definite elimination of sin in the world? Is it more utopian to believe in the resurrection of the flesh than in the abolition of all the injustices, enmities and cruelties in the world? In both Marx and the Bible the basis for all thought is this thesis which is the most revolutionary imaginable: Sin and evil are not inherent to humanity and history; they began one day through human work and they can therefore be eliminated" (1974:277).

REFERENCES

Barrios, L. 1998. "Santa María as a Liberating Zone: A Community Church in the Search of Restorative Justice." *Humanity and Society*, vol. 22, no. 1 (February): 55–78.

———. 2000. "Josconiando: Dimensiones sociales y políticas de la espiritualidad. República Dominicana." Editorial Aguiar, S.A.

Boff, L. 1991. "Liberation Theology: A Political Expression of Biblical Faith." In O. Maduro, ed., *Judaism, Christianity, and Liberation: An Agenda for Dialogue*, 23–32. Maryknoll, N.Y.: Orbis Books.

Boff, L., and C. Boff. 1986. *Liberation Theology: From Confrontation to Dialogue*. New York: Harper and Row.

Brotherton, D. (1999). "Old Heads Tell Their Stories: From Street Gangs to Street Organizations in New York City." *Journal of Free Inquiry in Creative Sociology*, 27 (1): 1–15.

Brotherton, D., and L. Barrios. Forthcoming. *Between Black and Gold: The Street Politics of the Almighty Latin King and Queen Nation*.

Cloward, R. A., and L. Ohlin. 1960. *Delinquency and Opportunity*. New York: Free Press.

Cohen, A. 1955. *Delinquent Boys*. New York: Free Press.

Conquergood, D. 1993. "Homeboys and Hoods: Gang Communication and Cultural Space." In L. Frey, ed., *Group Communication in Context: Studies of Natural Groups*. Hillsdale, N.J.: Lawrence Erlbaum.

———. 1997. "Street Literacy." In J. Flood, S. B. Heath, and D. Lapp, eds.,

Handbook of Research on Teaching Literacy through the Communicative and Visual Arts. New York: Simon and Schuster.

Dawley, D. 1992. *A Nation of Lords: An Autobiography of the Vice Lords*. Prospect Heights, Ill.: Waveland Press.

Decker, S., and B. Van Winkle. 1996. *Life in the Gang: Family, Friends, and Violence*. New York: Cambridge University Press.

Driver, T. F. 1991. *The Magic Ritual of: Our Need for Liberating Rites That Transform Our Lives and Our Communities*. San Francisco: Harper Colllins.

Durkheim, E. [1912] 1995. *The Elementary Forms of Religious Life*. New York: Free Press.

Gutiérrez, G. 1972. *Teología de la Liberación*. Salamanca, Spain: Ediciones Sígueme.

Hagedorn, J. M. 2002. "Gangs and the Informal Economy." In C. R. Huff, ed., *Gangs in America*. 3d ed. Thousand Oaks, Calif.: Sage Publications.

Hagedorn, J. M., and Macon, P. 1988. *People and Folks: Gangs, Crime, and the Underclass in a Rustbelt City*. Chicago: Lakeview.

Jacobs, J. B. 1977. *Stateville: The Penitentiary in Mass Society*. Chicago: University of Chicago Press.

Lane, D. A. 1984. *Foundations for a Social Theology: Praxis, Process, and Salvation*. New York: Paulist Press.

Maduro, O. 1982. *Religion and Social Conflicts*. Maryknoll, N.Y.: Orbis Books.

Matza, D. 1964. *Delinquency and Drift*. New York: Wiley.

McGuire, M. B. 1997. *Religion: The Social Context*. 4th ed. Belmont, Calif.: Wadsworth Publishing Company.

Miller, W. 1958. "Lower Class Culture as a Generating Milieu of Gang Delinquency." *Journal of Social Issues*, 14: 5–19.

———. 1976. "Youth Gangs in the Urban Crisis Era." In J. F. Short Jr., ed., *Juvenile Delinquency, Crime, and Society*, 91–128. Chicago: University of Chicago Press.

Miranda, J. P. 1974. *Marx and the Bible: A Critique of the Philosophy of Oppression*. Maryknoll, N.Y.: Orbis Books.

Montero, M. 1997. "Political Psychology: A Critical Perspective." In D. Fox and I. Prilleltensky, eds., *Critical Psychology: An Introduction*. Thousand Oaks, Calif.: Sage Publications.

Moore, J. 1978. *Homeboys, Gangs, Drugs, and Prisons in the Barrios of Los Angeles*. Philadelphia: Temple University Press.

Schreiter, R. J. 1985. *Constructing Local Theologies*. Maryknoll, N.Y.: Orbis Books.

Spergel, I. 1976. "Interactions between Community Structure, Delinquency, and Social Policy in the Inner City." In M. W. Klein, ed., *The Juvenile Justice System*, 55–99. Beverly Hills, Calif.: Sage Publications.

Stringer, E. 1999. *Action Research*. Thousand Oaks, Calif.: Sage Publications.

Thrasher, F. 1927. *The Gang*. Chicago: University of Chicago Press.

Venkatesh, S. 2000. *The American Project*. Chicago: University of Chicago Press.

8

EDUCATION IN THE REFORM OF STREET ORGANIZATIONS IN NEW YORK CITY

DAVID C. BROTHERTON

B: I seen a lot of mothers suffer. I seen a lot of people get killed. I heard a lot of things. Come on now . . . and I don't wanna get shot. I don't wanna go to jail. I don't want these guys to put me away for trying to help these kids, at the same time helping myself. I just wanna do the right thing. But you know, I learned to walk away from that. I learned to walk away because all this knowledge. . . . Remember, four years ago I couldn't read. I couldn't read [emphasis]. I didn't even know how to add. This word here [he holds a leaflet in front of him that advertises a conference on the death row inmate, Mumia]. Maybe I still drop some words . . . like this, "explosive" [he points to the word on the leaflet]. Now that word "explosive." You think four years ago I would remember that word?
D: So where did you learn it?
B: By bein' in the Nation. . . . study, culture classes. You know what I'm sayin'? 'Cause our lessons teach us that, you know. It also teaches us not only to become a man but to become a King. And when you become a King, you have responsibilities, you have self-esteem, you have self-respect, you have belief. You know?
—King B, forty-seven-year-old New York City Latin King

King B, above—honest, proud, and resilient—is discussing with the author the role of education in his "nation." In many respects, his response is typical of the ninety-eight interviews held with respondents from two "street organizations"[1] (Brotherton 1999): The Almighty Latin King and Queen Nation and the Asociación Ñeta over a period of three years (1997–2000). These empowerment claims that are so prevalent in the data are in stark contrast to the findings in most studies on gangs that presume a negative relationship between the processes and practices of formal education and gangs at the organizational and individual level (Taylor 1990; Spergel 1995; Vigil and Yun 1996).[2] Moreover, in recent years, the prevailing images of these two groups in New York City as seen through the eyes of

The research that went into the preparation of this essay was made possible by the Spencer Foundation Major Grants Program.

the corporate media and the criminal justice system have been ones of violence, crime, and mayhem. The commitment to education, therefore, or to any form of consciousness development, is a far cry from the descriptions of these groups furnished to the public. In this chapter, I will briefly discuss the literature on gangs and the educational process and then focus on the pivotal roles that both formal and informal education have played in the making and remaking of these organizations in order for them to move through their reformist phases.

THE LITERATURE

Throughout most of the twentieth century, relatively little attention has been paid to gangs and gang members regarding the complex and fluctuating attitudes they possess toward education in its various forms. From the early pioneering work of Thrasher (1927) to the more recent gang studies of the 1980s and 1990s (see the anthologies of Cummings and Monti 1993; Huff 1996; and Klein, Maxson, and Miller 2000), little empirical data have been collected regarding the role of education in the variegated meaning systems of gang members (Spergel 1995). Despite the dearth of research in this area, most of what has been written strongly asserts: (1) a negative relationship between gangs and schooling (Hutchison and Kyle 1993; Monti 1994), (2) a weak commitment by gang members to conventional goals (Hirschi and Hinderlang 1977), and (3) the tendency of gang members to produce counterinstitutions, which seals their subordination (Moore 1991).[3]

The assumption that gang members reject schooling at best and are uneducable at worst is particularly apparent in the theoretical propositions of social scientists during the 1950s.[4] For example, Cohen (1955) argued that the philosophical and ideological foundations of public schooling, which essentially replicated the idealized value system of middle-class America, was in conflict with the value system and aspirations of lower-class gang members, while Miller (1958) found that it (schooling) was virtually irrelevant to them because of other assumed focal concerns. This position, that gangs and schooling are oppositional worlds, has continued to be endorsed by most gang researchers until the present day, although the discussion has been significantly modified to account for: structural changes in the political economy (Hagedorn 1988; Taylor 1990; Jankowski 1991), the persistence of racial and ethnic segregation (Hagedorn 1988), and the contradictory influences of education on the processes of social reproduction (Willis 1977; Moore 1991; Macleod 1995).[5]

Despite this virtual consensus that gangs and schooling are a toxic mix, there are a number reasons to reexamine this issue and offer some correctives:

1. Relatively few empirical gang studies have been situated in an educational setting (a few exceptions are Brotherton 1994, 1996, 1997; Monti 1994), thus the gangs-schools nexus has not been adequately observed firsthand.

2. Most studies on gangs make education peripheral to other foci such as acts of violence, the use and distribution of drugs, and myriad forms of deviant street activities that Klein (1971) has called "cafeteria delinquency."

3. Virtually no gang studies go beyond a narrow definition of schooling— for example, considering gangs in relationship to the broader realm of knowledge and cultural production.[6]

4. Few studies have considered gangs from a social movement perspective (Brotherton 1999) with an emphasis on a gang's ability to successfully contest and even negate its "multiple-marginality" (Vigil 1988).

I will incorporate several of these issues into the overall analysis of the chapter, which will be organized as follows: First, I will begin by describing briefly the social history of the two groups and what it means to move from being a gang to a street organization. Second, I will discuss the multiple roles and functions that different types of education have had for the organization and for the individual membership in this period of transformation. Third, I will discuss the implications of these trends in street subcultures for educational and criminal justice policy.

METHODOLOGY

During the years 1996–99, a joint research venture was established with the two aforementioned street groups in New York City, focusing on the changes taking place within these organizations and the educational experiences among the respective memberships. Two key tenets of the research approach were that it should be critical and collaborative. To meet these criteria, the researchers and the researched mutually agreed on: the focus and goals of the research, the manner in which data were to be collected, and a consultative process in the interpretation of the data.

TYPES OF DATA

The data collected included: (1) both semistructured and life-history interviews of nonincarcerated rank-and-file members and leaders, (2) group-originated documents and artifacts, including manifestos, prayers, and political leaflets, and (3) systematic, written field observations of group meetings and neighborhood activities. The tables below (tables 8.1 and 8.2) provide a breakdown of the interviews.

TABLE 8.1 ALKQN

	NEW YORK CITY	DOMINICAN REPUBLIC
Street Males	44 (11 < 18 years old)	3
Street Females	29 (9 < 18 years old)	—

TABLE 8.2 ÑETA

	NEW YORK CITY
Street Males	17 (7 < 18 years old)
Street Females	5 (2 < 18 years old)

THE ANALYSIS

A content analysis of the data was carried out in which texts relevant to the experience of formal and informal education were isolated and categorized according to emergent themes. By formal education, I am largely referring to member experiences of public schooling and college, where learning takes place in an institutional setting. This is contrasted to informal education, which takes place in noninstitutional settings and includes the training and mentoring of members within the group.

FINDINGS

REFORMING THE ALKQN AND THE ÑETAS IN NEW YORK CITY: A SHORT HISTORY

The ALKQN came to New York State in 1986, founded in Collins Correctional Facility by (among others) Luis Felipe, better known as King Blood. What began as a small Latino inmate self-defense and self-help organization, based on the principles and rituals of the Latin Kings in Chicago, by the early 1990s had become an extensive street gang in New York City with perhaps two thousand or more members (New York City Police Department 1996) during its maximum growth period. It was during this period that the organization was labeled by local law enforcement as one of the most dangerous and disciplined gangs in the city and in 1994, almost its entire leadership were indicted by a grand jury for multiple counts of homicide and assault. King Blood eventually received the most severe prison sentence, other than execution, for a federal prisoner since World War II.[7]

In 1995, a new leadership emerged within the ALKQN who pledged to transform the organization into a community-based movement for the uplifting of the Latino poor in New York City. This rhetorical commitment to reform a street gang of such notoriety was met with great skepticism by law enforcement, but several years later, the new Latin Kings had effectively ended the internal bloodletting and had become a staple among the city's pantheon of radical political groups, particularly around such issues as police brutality and Puerto Rican independence.

The Asociación Ñeta have a very different history, though they too came to the streets from the prison system. Originally formed as a prisoners' rights and national independence group in Puerto Rico in 1972, the Ñetas came to the streets of New York City at the end of the 1980s via New York's city and state system of corrections. By 1993, the group had more than one thousand members throughout all five boroughs of the city and was beginning to challenge the domination of the Latin Kings while moving further away from its strict credo of being an inmate-only organization. As the membership grew, it began to incur splits among the leadership and by 1997, the more politicized wing of the organization lost out to leaders more committed to the drug trade than to any social reforms. In 1999, the more political members regrouped and the organization was again formed in accordance with its original social movement intent.

According to our observations, reforms in both groups, although they have been sporadic, significantly altered the properties of membership and the reciprocal relations between these groups and the community (Brotherton 1999). But one of the most important changes that occurred in the organizations was the emphasis placed on the achievement of education.[8]

THE MULTIPLE ROLES OF EDUCATION IN REFORMING THE ALKQN AND THE ÑETAS

GROUP ENDORSEMENT OF FORMAL AND INFORMAL EDUCATION

Because both groups were hierarchical with fluid systems of leadership development, the endorsement of education by the main decision makers of the organizations encouraged and sponsored a culture that promoted school achievement, intellectual curiosity, and strategies for self-improvement.[9]

In the following analysis, I describe the different forms that this endorsement for schooling (formal education) and needs-based self-help initiatives (informal education) took.

1. Endorsement of school

In the currently structured society, with its parsimonious funding for urban public education (*New York Times* 2001), a tidal wave of anti-affirmative-action legislation, and an increasing obsession with testing and standards, it would be unexpected that any lower-class, grassroots organization would be particularly enamored of the public school. Yet there was ample evidence that both groups have significantly emphasized the achievement of education among their members in concrete and abstract ways.

> Once a week we'll get together, make sure all the younger guys are doing good in school. That's why we actually keep it weekly and not biweekly or monthly, because we want to make sure that the guys, the younger guys especially, are doin' good in school, they're staying out of trouble, that there's no problems that are arising because anything can happen in the week.　　　*(King P.)*

Thus many ALKQN local chapters that we have been able to observe: (1) kept a strict check on the school attendance records of school-age members, (2) enforced 10:00 p.m. curfews on youth members under sixteen years of age during the week, (3) set up tutoring programs to help younger members with their homework, (4) encouraged students in trouble at school to bring their problems to the attention of senior members who would provide guidance or seek assistance from outside the organization, and (5) ensured that younger members were not engaged in needless conflicts with other groups. While all of these policies were part of a practical effort to uplift members, they were also in line with the organization's founding principles:

> You have chosen to join our Nation because of the promise you have shown in past endeavors. These are your lessons and your laws. Learn them well and engrave them in your hearts and mind. . . . Our goal is to build a strong nation within society. A Nation where our children will never experience any kind of hunger because we are there to feed them. Where they, as Latino children, will have the opportunity as the rest because we are the keys to their doors and to ensure them success because we are their guides.
>
> *(founding manifesto, ALKQN, New York City chapter)*

Similarly, there was a strong endorsement of formal and informal knowledge production among the Ñetas, but this group (with its less vertical command structure) relied less on top-down edicts and more on building peer-based support systems to get the message across.

> When I started a chapter in New York, the average of the people there was sixteen years, and these people related to me. They could speak to me what they couldn't speak with their parents 'cause I was open to them, you know? I let them do whatever they wanted in my house as long as they respected everything. . . . I gave them my heart with the Association with it, and you teach 'em and you talk to them and I don't think that you have to knock sense into people to learn. If you just sit down and talk to them one on one. *(J., a Ñeta)*

In both groups, however, a significant number of educationally motivated members were observed moving quickly up the ranks, imparting as they did so the importance of learning, achieving a credential, and even going on to college. In interviews with the leaders, they often stated that youth who were not willing to attend school or get back into school cannot become members of their organizations. King W.'s response, below, was typical of this attitude:

> We push education, actually, because, for the younger Kings, they have to bring

us their report cards, they have to be doing the right thing if they wanna be associated with the Kings now. If they're not doing anything with their life, you're not helpin' yourself. If you're not allowing us to help you then you're just what I consider dead weight.

(King W.)

2. Endorsement of self-control and self-help

Contained in numerous life-history interviews were members' descriptions of their economically marginalized backgrounds and their physically and psychologically abusive experiences continuing from childhood through their adult years. Many, therefore, described how they: had endured long periods of relentless poverty; had become addicted to alcohol or other drugs; had been physically and/or sexually assaulted as children; and were subjected to the mentally and physically punishing conditions of the prison system, with significant numbers of male respondents describing long periods of solitary confinement due to their roles in prison gangs.

Consequently, mental health problems, aggression control, domestic violence, and fluctuating states of addiction were issues that members said they were frequently confronting among both themselves and their families. In a period when the social safety net had been constantly reduced and when the provision of high standards of health care for the working and nonworking poor has failed to materialize, the ALKQN decided to create its own programs, many of which were modeled after twelve-step initiatives. Although this strategy of organized self-empowerment was less advanced in the Ñetas, they too constantly discussed how they might implement their own programs to address their members' health needs.

In the following, Latin Kings and Queens speak to these needs and how they have sought to provide their own homegrown resources.

We tried to set up NA [Narcotics Anonymous] in the Tiger tribe [Brooklyn]. . . . The brothers tried, you know, but you know how difficult that was, right? [*he laughs*] They just couldn't get people to come to a meeting without 'em smoking weed. They kept comin' stoned even though they wanted to kick the habit. So in the end they decided to end it. The AA meetings, now they still going strong and they helping a lot of brothers through some difficult times.

(King T.)

Hostility classes is a chance for the sisters to be able to have a safe setting to let their anger out, you know. That's one example, if you like, of trying to reach our goals.

(Queen S.)

I like to discuss issues about battered wives, drug abuse, homeless people. Those are things that I've always seen that have always really gotten to me and hurt me, especially within my own community.   *(Queen A.)*

THE MULTIPLE VALUES OF FORMAL EDUCATION Although, as we have seen, both groups place great emphasis on education in its various forms, there are certain contradictions that arise with this position. To better understand the complexity of this relationship, I consider the role of education from two standpoints: that of the organization and that of the individual.

At the organizational level, the pursuit of education by members signifies many positive developments for the group with only a few drawbacks. First, members who are active in education are viewed as: (1) good role models who can provide a positive external image for the group, (2) great potential for building and leading the organization in the future, (3) confirmation to the leaders that the organization has increased its appeal among youth and its influence in the community, and (4) important resources, particularly if they possess specialized skills, such as knowledge of the law and communications. The one drawback expressed by the leadership was that those members who had strong educational backgrounds were not necessarily the ones who would be on the "front lines" in street combat. This issue was of some importance, particularly during periods when internal power struggles were being fought and certain warlike stances were called for:

> King D. has gotta be a man, he's gotta stand up for himself. It's ok telling the peewees what to do and what not to do. He's good at telling 'em they gotta go to school, they gotta go to college, but he can't back down when some brother comes after him. You can't come running to the Kings to sort out your problems, we're not gonna be used that way. . . . So, when he called on the brothers to help him they stood back. Now the brother's been stripped but he'll come back, he has to learn, that's the Kings way.

At the individual level, however, the role of education was more complicated. Essentially, it was the site of a continuous tension between the promise of individual advancement and the commitment to group solidarity and class-ethnic opposition.

1. Individual social mobility and collective resistance:

> Our goal is to strive for more knowledge, more kids, more of our brothers goin' into schools without being kicked out for being a King. Becoming lawyers, doc-

tors, cops, becoming all these things that we're striving for . . . but right now it's still hard. . . . It'll eventually get there no matter how many of us get locked up, there's always gonna be more to replace.

(King D.)

Above, King D. provides his interpretation of ambition: It is not just about personal gain, but about breaking down the doors of collective exclusion, which itself is an act of political defiance. In the thinking of many members, therefore, this is precisely how individual ambition and group solidarity could coexist, for moving up from a subaltern class position is not just a victory for the individual but for everyone. Nonetheless, inevitably, some members saw education as the classic means to escape the barrio, which, although such a perspective can also be interpreted as breaking the barriers of segregation, it eventually leads to a weakening of the barrio community (Wilson 1987) and of the group itself (cf. social disorganization theory). King F. explains his position, which shows no consideration of any unintended consequences:

What we want them to do is stay in school, finish school go to college or do something good. Get out of the area, make a name for us somewhere else at a different level. And that's what we want our young guys to do. Be a lawyer be something good.

(King F.)

2. No to fatalism

A social and psychological condition that arises out of the experience of colonization is fatalism (Lewis 1966; Wolf 1969).[10] In theories about the lower classes in both advanced and less developed societies (see also Miller 1958), it is widely argued that a pathological state is ingrained into the psyche of the poor and that this supposed condition of cultural deficiency is a major factor in reproducing patterns of class, race/ethnicity, and gender subordination.[11]

Both groups in this study vehemently questioned this assumption, albeit with certain paradoxes. For example, they called for people to stay rooted in their community and resist the lure of the suburbs, but at the same time they opposed any acceptance of one's subjugated state, both at the individual and the collective levels. King B., below, articulates this position, as he links the need for an educated and purposeful membership to the basic tenets of the protestant ethic:

Well, as a whole, we want our younger members to pass, to get to have an acceptable level of reading, arithmetic, history, so that they can become productive members of society. You know, you can't be—you have to expect, if you consider yourself a King, you have to be—I feel that you can't run around with a second-grade level of education. You know, you have to have something acceptable. If you're gonna go out to work, if you don't wanna go to school any more, so be it. Don't go to school, but work. Don't be a lazy person. Do something with your life. I'm not about to sit back and watch people throw their lives away because in life there's pressure, you know?   *(King B.)*

3. Whose reality? Working, learning, and resisting

Little has been written about gangs and their relationship to the mainstream world of labor. Not least because so many gang studies have focused almost exclusively on the illicit activities of their respondents. In our sample, however, many respondents saw mainstream work as a primary activity in their everyday lives. This commitment to work was based not just on the exchange relationship of earning a paycheck but to symbolically show their worth to a society that had all too often dismissed them as failures, and to give them personal structure—especially after the devastating social and psychological effects of prison.

GROUP-BASED KNOWLEDGES THAT INCREASE THE ACQUISITION AND STANDING OF EDUCATION The ALKQN and the Asociación Ñeta make learning the groups' lessons and acquiring the knowledge(s) handed down from generation to generation a cornerstone of membership. These credos and philosophies express the seriousness with which they accord the development of ideological and intellectual frameworks to legitimize the authority of the organization. In many respects, the groups' lessons are used in a fashion similar to other radical political movements—that is, heightening the feeling of in-group solidarity, providing members with a historical identity, and helping members to understand and confront the sources of their subordinate state.

Three common themes in these lessons were for members to:

1. Transform themselves socially, spiritually, and intellectually
2. Lead productive lives whereby they will act as role models for the Latino community
3. Continuously develop the organization as a vehicle for community upliftment

All three themes are exemplified in the quotes below. The first citation, taken from the ALKQN's "bible," highlights the importance placed on the notion of reinvention and is not dissimilar from a central theme found in the doctrine of Alcoholics Anonymous or evangelical Christianity.

> We have to declare ownership of our lives with Conviction and with equal force to the law of gravity behind it. We have to say, I am in charge of me, of my thoughts and actions, and I have the power to change any negative into positive. We are limited only by our limited beliefs about our capabilities.
>
> *(From "No Limitations," ALKQN Manifesto)*

The second quote is that of a Latin King who is responding to the question: What do you say to people who think that your "lessons" only mask the true criminal nature of your organization?

> If I didn't have those lessons I wouldn't be as noble as I am right now. Those lessons teach me to be a noble human being and when it's time to react in a violent way, I use my mind. I use the mental stage. I can defeat another person with my mind, I don't have to hit him. I could just speak to him and let the person know he's wrong. That's the things that we learn.   *(King C.)*

LEADERSHIP, ROLE-DIVISION, AND EDUCATION Several gang studies have pointed to the obligations of membership and to the nature of gangs as organizations (Taylor 1990; Jankowski 1991). Most such studies, however, focus on the rational, adaptational aspect of gang membership and the members' embrace of utilitarian goals within the context of the local underground economy. Little attention, by contrast, has been given to the role of membership as a search for collective empowerment that necessarily links the individual to community traditions of resistance. Below, I discuss three essential properties in this relationship.

1. Cultural knowledge is power

In both groups, as individual members became leaders, they were expected to exhibit greater and greater mastery of the sanctioned knowledge passed down intergenerationally within the organizations.[12] This careful dissemination of in-group codes, lores, and philosophies played a very important role in the maintenance of the group's overall structure and it ensured that each snippet of textualized experience and reflection was treated with respect and even awe. At the same time, members who ascended to leading positions were not only expected to be proficient in the group's culture but also in the culture of the community. As far as both the ALKQN and the Ñetas were concerned, to learn about oneself is to learn about the community and the two are often considered indivisible. Below, King T. describes this relationship in a way that is strikingly similar to what Freire (1970) called the dialogical process in literacy development:

> Once you learn that, you become a King—learn what we about, learn your fellow man, learn your fellow person, your neighbor, learn your community, learn your culture. When I started getting into the Nation, that's when I started learning about my culture.

2. Self-value

In both groups, each member was immediately given a range of responsibilities on joining the organization. Furthermore, all recruits were expected eventually to become leaders in their own right. But the key to any development of the individual presupposed that a member would engage in a process of building and rebuilding his or her self-value. Considering the plethora of forms that self-hatred takes for colonized peoples, both organizations were fully aware that without a positive sense of self, members could not build a resistance identity. Queen S., below, explains this process through linking the humanistic themes of love and respect to the sanctity of the body:

> In order to teach, you have to practice what you preach, so to me the best way is how we all have to carry ourselves with respect that no one can reach, you know? Its just . . . sometimes little things are hard things. Like learning to love yourself, because if you don't love yourself you can't love anybody else. Learning how to help yourself . . . that's where they [the organization] stuff a lot of love and respect. Like education, and women . . . they stress women taking care of they bodies, because our bodies is really important. I mean, how we gonna reproduce and how we gonna teach our children how to live a better life if we can't do it for ourselves?

3. Containing the "seductive" (Katz 1988) pressures of street life (Anderson 1990): No distractions!

Repeatedly in leaders' speeches it is emphasized that good intentions will come to naught if members display a predilection for street fighting, turf wars, and drug sales.[13] This preoccupation of the leadership was not expressly a result of the actions of members (although some branches were definitely not toeing the "party line") but it reflected the reality that young working-class Latinos/Latinas had very few outlets other than those offered by the subcultures and cultures of the street (see Bourgois 1995); and it reflected the experience-based knowledge of leaders (many of whom had enjoyed illustrious street careers themselves) who wanted at all costs to break the cycles of socially reproduced barrio violence. Below, King Tone discusses how the ghetto has to change from the inside out and that a key to community regeneration is the new role of his organization, the ALKQN, whose members have been told to make both the streets and the schools safe for all residents.

> All you gotta do is not shoot each other, not sell drugs and walk each other's kids to school. You just make this no more ghetto. So that's where I'm at. I want to beat the ghetto. I don't want to leave the ghetto I want to transform the ghetto. And I think that the kids out of anybody is got the best chance right now.

THE IMPACT OF INTERNAL AND EXTERNAL SOCIAL NETWORKS ON EDUCATION Within the organizations there were multiple networks that attached young people to older people, connected members across race and ethnic groups, and brought diverse geographic communities into contact with one another. Additionally, there were myriad relations that the groups have developed with the broader community through their residential and kinship ties to individual community members. The impact that these internal and external networks had on members was extremely profound and affected both their social and cultural capital in ways that could not easily be predicted.

1. Mixing with the college kids

As members of both groups responded to the new alliances with outsiders, they began to be affected in myriad ways. One important group of contacts that had a big impact on the members was students. These nonthreatening, mainly middle-class contacts increasingly exposed the groups to notions of idealism and humanism that contrasted with the hard-bitten realism that was prevalent in the socialization of most of the groups' working-class members. From meetings on college campuses to marches on the street, many students from the middle- and upper-class colleges were often sympathetic to the groups, seeing in them a morally legitimate way to resist the continued oppression of the city's barrios and ghettos. In contrast, students from the more working-class colleges tended to be more empathetic, be-

cause they themselves were often from the same class and racial backgrounds and lived in the same neighborhoods as the groups' members.[14]
The following transcript is from a student-initiated ceremony at John Jay
College of Criminal Justice at which King Tone, the leader of the ALKQN,
was receiving a community award from the Black Students Union for his
contribution to the struggle for social justice in New York City:

> Our next honoree is Antonio Fernandez, a.k.a. King Tone. He's a young man
> attempting to change the image of the Latin Kings and contrary to other things
> being said about him in the media, this effort has taken a lot of practice in com-
> munity building. Without this movement that he has led these voices couldn't
> be heard. We salute King Tone for his efforts and hope that he continues ded-
> icating his life to this cause and for the community to unite with this organiza-
> tion for a better New York City.

To many members, therefore, the students' respectful curiosity was a re-
freshing departure from their dealings with other sections of the middle
class (e.g., media scribes, or the professionals of the court and public educational systems) who tended to label them as inveterate deviants and even
cast them as subhuman savages (see Conquergood 1997). Moreover, it
helped them to confirm that their struggles were important, valid, and rational. In the following, King R., an enforcer from a very humble background, spoke fondly of his student interactions:

> I notice that every time I'm in a rally or in a parade, I get college students comin'
> up to me, "would you like to go to my college?" They come up to me and what
> I do is I give them King H.'s address and it makes me feel good because they're
> interested.   *(King R.)*

2. Can the professionals help us?

A second consequence of these increasing contacts with nonmembers was
the relationship that the groups built up with educators, academics, artists,
and assorted professionals. These connections were instrumental in: (a) improving the reputation of the groups to the broader public, (b) helping the
groups to reflect and strategize on their past and future actions, (c) broadening the opportunity structure of the members, and (d) assisting the
groups in accessing institutional resources. In the following speech, King H.
considers the ways that technicians and professional intellectuals could support his group's goals:

Now we are becoming aware of being exploited. But as we grow and we evolve there are those forces that wanna keep us down. We try to fight with all the means at our disposal. But, that's the problem, and hopefully that's where the academic community can help us. We are getting into the Internet, contacting more fraternities and sororities throughout the country for speaking engagements and reaching out there. But maybe there's some technological things that could help us to continue our social movement.

(from a speech at the Annual Humanist Sociology Conference, 30 October 1996)

3. Let's get active: No justice, no peace

A third impact of these relations was the encouragement that outsiders gave to these groups in their pursuit of social justice goals. In the following statement from a Ñeta, one hears the process by which activism is stimulated. I would argue that such activism has been an invaluable factor in the proeducational policies of both groups and in the dispositional changes of the members toward schooling.

After the first year, I remember taking the initiative with a couple of other brothers and changing the administration of the Association here in New York. . . . We started making contacts with a lot of powerful people in the community as far as activism is concerned and we were being invited to all types of events. We were being invited to be part of different things, whether it be security for the event or just being there for the event and having our voice heard. We started introducing these events into the pueblo through the people of the Association and then the meetings started changing. *(J. B., a Ñeta)*

4. Reaching out to the community

As the groups spread out into the community, they began to see more clearly their potential roles as problem solvers. This new role began to be taken very seriously, particularly as they realized that their access to certain strata of the most alienated youth in the barrios increased their level of responsibility. In many respects, the groups began to function as street-level social workers and counselors in a situation where local, state, and federal governments were increasingly limiting their funding and decimating any form of social safety net under the aegis of welfare "reform."

See this kid here *(King H. puts his arm around a little boy)* he's running wild, wild in the streets. He ain't got nobody looking out for him but us. So he wants to join the Kings, he's desperate to join the Kings, but he can't 'cos he's too young.

He's only fourteen years old but we gotta take care of him. We can't let him be just another dope dealer out there, 'cos you know that's how its gonna end. So, we're trying to give him somebody to look up to, someone who's gonna take an interest in him, give him love. But I can't be around all the time so Queen R. here *(he points to a young woman)* is gonna make sure his teachers are teaching him, making sure he's going to school and do all the things his family should be doing. *(King H.)*

In the above analysis, I have highlighted the central importance that both street organizations placed on the meanings, roles, and functions of education during certain stages of reform in their evolutionary development. Despite this fairly consistent position by a substantial portion of the membership, and by most of the leadership, few members of the city's social control establishments have made any efforts to formally contact these groups other than through police raids, grand jury indictments,[15] and special school investigations.[16] It would seem that any number of agencies could see the benefits of engaging these groups in a multipronged approach to community and youth problems, particularly as they relate to education and training.

In a more humane and reasonable world, we would have an enormous amount to learn from these groups' efforts to organize the disenfranchised and underserved populations (see also Curtis 1998) of the barrios and the ghettos. Public schools, for example, could take note of the system by which these groups build self-esteem among members who are riddled with self-doubt and negative self-images. Similarly, schools could study the ways such groups develop leadership skills and bonds of loyalty among youth who were once certain to be high school dropouts. Further, schools could learn a great deal from the curriculum that these groups develop, much of which is based on revisionist interpretations of imperial and colonial history and an eclectic politics of spiritual liberation.[17] A leader of the Ñetas put it this way:

Education? That's supposed to be about understanding the life of a young person and they really don't, you know? One of the things that I see, and I remember myself vividly in my teenage years when I see the teenagers that I work with, is that once you put up an opposition to something that the young person does, that's even more of a challenge and more of a reason to rebel against you and just go ahead with it, you know? And I can see the Board of Education actually being a help to young people if they would just accept the fact that this Association does exist. That this Association does have its positive aspects, and that . . . instead of shunning it or trying to criminalize it, if it would just sit down with the leaders and just sit down with the members and try and learn about it first and foremost . . . and then facilitate, you know . . . workshops, offer space in the schools for the young people to come in, facilitate activities that the Association, itself, could be a part of, to help out, to have the leaders mediate amongst the young people that are taking it to a violent level in the high schools or whatever. Just include us in the institution.

Nonetheless, the dominant view among the city's current political and educational administrations is that the more "gang-related" youths who are arrested and processed the closer we come to the elusive victory over crime.[18] In the face of such logic, much of which is based on simplistic law-enforcement reasoning, enlightened strategies that treat all citizens as resources are unlikely to materialize. In fact, quite the opposite will happen as we continue to "amplify deviance" (Young 1971) through criminalizing processes that come in the form of "curfews," "zero tolerance" policies, and anticombination acts. All of which are sure to push poor, working-class minority youth increasingly toward gangs and street organizations in order to have their social, cultural, physical, and material needs met.

NOTES

1. By the term *street organization*, I am referring to: "a group formed largely by youth and adults of a marginalized social class which aims to provide its members with a resistant identity, an opportunity to be individually and collectively empowered, a voice to speak back to and challenge the dominant culture, a refuge from the stresses and strains of barrio or ghetto life and a spiritual enclave within which its own sacred rituals can be generated and practiced" (Brotherton and Barrios, forthcoming).
2. Certainly, New York City's leading social control establishments—which include the criminal justice system, the correctional system, law enforcement, the Board of Education, and the tabloid media industry—all hold that these two groups are nothing more than street gangs running organized criminal enterprises throughout New York State.
3. Moore states: "The gang becomes good socialization for lower-level working jobs. At worst it becomes effective socialization for prison and the prison aftermath of labor-market marginality. . . . The thing that has changed now,

however, is that many of those lower-level jobs that young gang members used to obtain in the 1950s are gone" (1991:79).

4. Who, for the most part, did little primary data collection themselves.

5. In other words, although certain working-class youth saw through the reified relationship between schooling and social mobility—what Willis (1977) calls "penetrations"—they used this knowledge to reinforce their own subordinate class position rather than to overcome it.

6. Doing so would allow consideration of gangs themselves as active agents in the learning process. See, for example, Conquergood's (1997) notion of street literacy as it pertains to the production of gang culture.

7. King Blood received 145 years, the first 45 to be spent in solitary confinement.

8. Despite these changes, however, membership can still have serious negative consequences whether they are due to societal labeling, legal persecution/prosecution, or the continued involvement of group members in criminal relationships.

9. This active encouragement of learning in the broadest sense, of course, met with some resistance by those who preferred the validation of street knowledge over book knowledge. This conflict between high culture and low culture was a constant issue in both groups and was often described as a struggle between good and evil, or between positive and negative elements within the organization. For example, the ALKQN's leadership would often refer to those who wanted to take the group back to a gang footing as working for the forces of "darkness." Similarly, the Ñetas would refer to such elements as *"negativos."*

10. In many respects, fatalism resembles the social-psychological concept of "learned helplessness."

11. This interpretation of the lower classes' pathological properties remains, of course, very controversial, and there are many who have contested this position (Valentine 1968). Nonetheless, there has to be some validity to theories of social reproduction, otherwise capitalist states would have to rely much more on the apparatuses of coercion than they in fact do.

12. In fact, it is only when members reach a certain standing within the organization that they can actually have access to specific forms of group knowledge.

13. In the Chicago manifesto of the Latin Kings, members who identify with gang-banging are referred to as "primitive," which is the lowest level of development that a member can attain.

14. Of course, there were some students who were also highly skeptical, especially if they had come from neighborhoods where the groups had negative reputations based on previous antisocial actions and activities.

15. Such police attention might seem to contradict the thrust of my essay, but it is important to note that a great deal of evidence presented against group members comes from informers who are paid well and who are eager to make a deal to save their own skins. For example, at the trial of a leading Latin King I attended in January 1999, the main evidence behind the charge of "conspiracy to

kill" was provided by three informers. According to a detective under oath, the lead informer was paid $55,000 and the other two were paid $21,000 a piece. These are extraordinary sums, given the poverty of most members.

16. In 1997, the Special Commissioner of Investigation for the New York City School District launched an inquiry into the influence of the "Latin Kings" on the city's public schools. Although the six-month investigation produced mostly anecdotal and dated evidence, one of the conclusions was: "Schools are in fact critical to the Latin King's success. The Kings use graffiti and gang 'colors' to intimidate students who want to stay out of trouble. They actively seek out children from troubled homes, offering a perverted sense of family. Once brought into the gang, the students, now recognized as peewees, start making their way through the organization. Peewees are often utilized to hold weapons or drugs for older members, because they are less likely to face serious jail time if apprehended. Many peewees ultimately find their way to prison nonetheless. Schools and school playgrounds are often used as meeting grounds and as places where 'beefs' are settled, sometimes with violence" (New York City School District 1997:53).

17. Social workers could certainly learn from the family structures of these organizations and the exact role that they play in shoring up frayed communities. Finally, criminal justice professionals could get some tips on diversion and rehabilitation and take heed that building more prisons and creating more laws only has the effect of expanding the reach of these groups for generations to come.

18. This denial that such groups could be of any assistance in attacking social problems is in strict contrast with official strategies some thirty years earlier. During the 1960s and 1970s, such entities as the Youth Board and the Roundtable for Youth (Collins 1979) were set up to coordinate antidelinquent policies in alliance with the poorest youth in the city and their respective street organizations. Even when the gang problem was at its height in the mid-1970s, and it was estimated that fifty thousand youths were involved in the street-gang subcultures (Collins 1979), these forums, think-tanks, and advisory bodies still met with the blessing of the Mayor and the rest of the political establishment, and no one thought to question the rationale. Today, such talk of intervention is greeted by adults in power as tantamount to "consorting with the enemy"—such is the warlike footing of a society weaned on crusades against the children of the "dangerous classes"(Males 1996).

REFERENCES

Anderson, E. 1990. *Streetwise: Race, Class, and Change in an Urban Community.* Chicago: University of Chicago Press.

Bourgois, P. 1995. *In Search of Respect: Selling Crack in El Barrio.* New York: Cambridge University Press.

Brotherton, D. 1994. "Who Do You Claim? Gang Formations and Rivalry in an Inner City High School." In J. Holstein and G. Miller, eds., *Perspectives on Social Problems*. Vol. 5, pp. 147–171. Greenwich, Conn.: JAI Press.

———. 1996. "The Contradictions of Suppression: Notes from a Study of Approaches to Gangs in Three Public High Schools." *Urban Review*, 28 (2): 95–120.

———. 1997. "Socially Constructing the Nomads: Part One." *Humanity and Society* (June): 1–21.

———. 1999. "The Old Heads Tell Their Stories." *Free Inquiry in Creative Sociology*, 2 (1): 1–15.

Brotherton, D., and L. Barrios. Forthcoming. *Between Black and Gold: The Street Politics of the Almighty Latin King and Queen Nation.*

Cohen, A. 1955. *Delinquent Boys*. New York: Free Press.

Collins, H. 1979. *Street Gangs: Profiles for Police*. New York: New York City Police Department.

Conquergood, D. 1997. "Street Literacy." In *Handbook of Research on Teaching Literacy through the Communicative and Visual Arts*. New York: Simon and Schuster Macmillan.

Cummings, S., and D. Monti, eds. 1993. *Gangs: The Origins and Impact of Contemporary Youth Gangs in the United States.*

Curtis, R. 1998. "The Improbable Transformation of Inner-City Neighborhoods: Crime, Violence, Drugs, and Youth in the 1990s." *Journal of Criminal Law and Criminology* vol. 88, no. 4 (summer): 1233–1276.

Freire, P. 1970. *Pedagogy of the Oppressed*. New York: Seabury Press.

Hagedorn, J. 1988. *People and Folks*. Chicago: Lake View Press.

Hirschi, T., and M. Hinderlang. 1977. "Intelligence and Delinquency: A Revisionist Review." *American Sociological Review*, 42: 471–486.

Huff, C. R., ed. 1996. *Gangs in America*. Thousand Oaks, Calif.: Sage Publications.

Hutchison, R., and C. Kyle. 1993. "Hispanic Street Gangs in Chicago's Public Schools." In S. Cummings and D. Monti, eds., *Gangs: The Origins and Impact of Contemporary Youth Gangs in the United States.*

Jankowski, M. S. 1991. *Islands in the Street: Gangs in American Urban Society*. Berkeley: University of California Press.

Katz, J. 1988. *Seductions of Crime: Moral and Sensual Attractions in Doing Evil*. New York: Metropolitan Books.

Klein, M. 1971. *Street Gangs and Street Workers*. Englewood Cliffs, N.J.: Prentice Hall.

Klein, M., C. Maxson, and J. Miller. 2000. *The Modern Gang Reader*. 2d ed. Los Angeles: Roxbury.

Lewis, O. 1966. "The Culture of Poverty." *Scientific American*, 215 (4): 19–25.

Macleod, J. 1995. *Ain't No Makin' It*. Boulder: Westview Press.

Males, M. 1996. *The Scapegoat Generation: America's War on Adolescents*. Monroe, Maine: Common Courage Press.

Miller, W. 1958. "Lower Class Culture as a Generating Milieu of Gang Delinquency." *Journal of Social Issues*, 14: 5–19.

Monti, D. 1994. *Wannabe: Gangs in Suburbs and Schools.* Cambridge, Mass.: Blackwell.

Moore, J. 1991. *Going Down to the Barrio: Homeboys and Home Girls in Change.* Philadelphia: Temple University Press.

New York City Police Department. 1996. *A Handbook on New York Gangs.* New York: Gang Intelligence Unit.

New York City School District. 1997. "An Investigation into the Latin Kings: No Tolerance for Gangs in Public Schools." The Special Commissioner of Investigation for the New York School District, New York City Board of Education.

New York Times. 2001. "Judge Rules that New York City Schools are Short Changed." 11 January, p. A1.

Spergel, I. 1995. *The Youth Gang Problem: A Community Approach.* New York: Oxford University Press.

Taylor, C. S. 1990. *Dangerous Society.* East Lansing: Michigan State University Press.

Thrasher, F. 1927. *The Gang: A Study of 1,313 Gangs in Chicago.* Chicago: University of Chicago Press.

Valentine, C. 1968. *Culture of Poverty: Critique and Counter-Proposals.* Chicago: University of Chicago Press.

Vigil, J. D. 1988. *Barrio Gangs: Street Life and Identity in Southern California.* Austin: University of Texas Press.

Vigil, J. D., and S. C. Yun. 1996. "Southern California Gangs: Comparative Ethnicity and Social Control." In C. R. Huff, ed., *Gangs in America.* Thousand Oaks, Calif.: Sage.

Willis, P. 1977. *Learning to Labor: How Working Class Kids Get Working Class Jobs.* Westmead, UK: Saxon House.

Wilson, W. J. 1987. *The Truly Disadvantaged.* Chicago: University of Chicago Press.

Wolf, E. 1969. *Peasant Wars of the Twentieth Century.* New York: Harper and Row.

Young, J. 1971. *The Drugtakers: The Social Meaning of Drug Use.* London: MacGibbon and Kee.

PART 4
WOMEN AND
GANGS

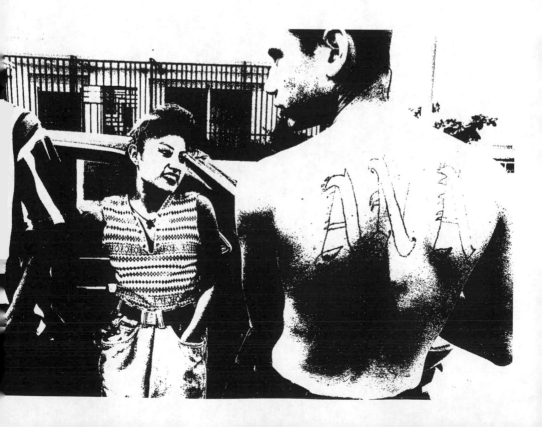

9

LIBERATING YET LIMITING: THE PARADOX OF FEMALE GANG MEMBERSHIP

DANA NURGE

Throughout the 1990s and continuing into the new millennium, the public has been bombarded with dramatic headlines, sound bytes, and images depicting female gang members (e.g., Ford 1998). Stories about female violence are always a hot topic, but recent increases in female delinquency arrest rates have fueled the media fire (Chesney-Lind 1993, 1999). Although it could be argued that increased attention to the existence of female gangs is warranted and, in fact, long overdue, the sensational nature of the media's portrayal of "girl gangsters" as ruthless, amoral predators has generated public fear and outrage, while providing minimal understanding of the context of their lives or the dynamics of their groups. The media attention has also contributed to a renewed academic interest in female gangs, however, and recent studies in several cities have begun to shed further light on female gangs' structure, activities, gender dynamics, and delinquency/violence (Lauderback, Hansen, and Waldorf 1992; Brotherton 1996; Venkatesh 1998; Hagedorn and

Devitt 1999; Joe and Chesney-Lind 1999; Portillos 1999; Hunt, MacKenzie, and Laidler 2000; Miller 2001; Nurge, forthcoming).

Despite the variety of accounts that have emerged, two major strains of thought regarding females' participation and roles in the gang have received the most attention in the female gang literature. The "liberation hypothesis" (see Taylor 1993; Curry 1998), essentially a modern rendition of the 1970s liberation theories (Adler 1975; Simon 1975), emphasizes shifting gender roles and suggests that females are taking advantage of increasing opportunities to participate in gangs, violence, drug sales, and/or other activities traditionally conceived to be "male/masculine."[1] Attributing increases in female crime to "women's liberation" is certainly not a new idea, but this notion received renewed attention and interest in the early to mid-1990s when media hype about shifts in the nature and extent of female gang membership was substantiated by a couple of studies suggesting that female gang members were becoming more involved in drugs, guns, and violence (e.g., Lauderback, Hansen, and Waldorf 1992; Taylor 1993). Although less explicitly discussed in the gang literature, liberation could also be conceived in microlevel terms; in other words, individual females may achieve a sense of freedom, empowerment, or liberation in their gang membership (which may or may not have any connection to macrolevel changes affecting women's positions in society or the streets) (Curry 1998; Nurge, forthcoming).

The other theme running through much of the female gang literature is referred to as the "social injury hypothesis." This approach posits that gang involvement is more harmful and damaging for females than for males (Moore 1991; Curry 1998). Given females' heightened potential to be exploited, victimized (by gang males or through gang-related activities), and stigmatized (due to breaking gender role expectations), their gang membership tends to further marginalize them (economically and socially) and weaken their future prospects (Curry 1998; also see Moore, 1991; Joe and Chesney-Lind 1995; Hagedorn and Devitt 1999). Although often presented as competing paradigms, the liberation and social injury perspectives need not be considered mutually exclusive (Curry 1999); female gang membership may be a product of increasing opportunities, and/or be individually liberating for females, while also exposing them to situations and behaviors that may harm them.

Using data from a recent qualitative study of female gangs and cliques in Boston (Nurge, forthcoming), this chapter examines the applicability of each of these hypotheses. Findings from this study suggest that female gang membership is not likely to be a result of women's liberation but is, in fact, a liberating experience for many young women. Despite the liberating benefits, gang participation typically exposes young women to risky and harmful situations and additional problems. Although the former gang members interviewed were acutely aware of the gangs' drawbacks, they themselves appear to have experienced minimal long-term social injury from their involvement. After reviewing the prior literature on female gangs and current trends in girls' delinquency and gang membership, I provide a general description of the findings that emerged from a qualitative study of female gangs and cliques in Boston, and subsequently highlight and discuss specific findings pertaining to the "social injury" and "liberation" hypotheses.

PRIOR RESEARCH ON FEMALE GANGS

Although girls' involvement in gangs has been documented since the 1800s (Asbury 1927), much of the traditional literature on gangs, beginning with Thrasher (1927), either ignored females completely or made a mere passing reference to them (Campbell 1991). When early researchers did discuss female gang members, the focus was typically on their psychological dysfunctions and social maladjustment (e.g., Cohen 1955; Short and Strodtbeck 1965). Because most of the traditional gang studies were undertaken by male researchers who interviewed male gang members, the older literature represents male gang members' views of female members, rather than firsthand explanations of females' gang experiences (Campbell 1990, 1991; Chesney-Lind 1993). As such, these early accounts produced stereotypical images of gang girls. They were generally described as either "tomboys" or "sex objects" whose primary function was to serve male members in the following capacities: as girlfriends; providers of sexual services; to carry weapons and/or drugs; to lure rival male gang members to fighting locations; and to spy on rival gangs (Swart 1991; Campbell 1991; Chesney-Lind 1993).

These stereotypes prevailed until the late 1970s and early 1980s, when researchers began to directly examine female gangs. Although some of the functions outlined above were corroborated in these later accounts, females' roles were revealed to be much more complex and meaningful than previous studies had documented. A new body of qualitative research emerged, which situated females' gang involvement in relation to the broader context of their lives—examining how their families, ethnicity/race and cultural heritage, gender, communities, and the urban economy influenced their gang membership (e.g., Miller 1973; Quicker 1974; Brown 1977; Harris 1988; Horowitz 1990; Campbell 1991; Moore 1991).

In contrast to the earlier depictions of female gang members as completely subservient to male members, this newer body of research revealed that females' gang activity was neither wholly dependent upon—nor solely focused around satisfying—gang males (Miller 1973; Quicker 1974; Brown 1977; Harris 1988; Campbell 1991). The most in-depth account of female gang involvement to date comes from Campbell. Consistent with the other research from this time period, she noted that the females sought asylum in the gang to escape the current limitations of their poverty and the problems and difficulties they expected to face in the future. The gang represented a temporary refuge from the harshness and drudgery of their lives; Campbell noted five problems that may drive young females to seek asylum in a gang: (1) a future of meaningless domestic labor with little possibility of educational or occupational escape, (2) subordination to the man in the house, (3) responsibility for children, (4) the social isolation of the housewife, and (5) the powerlessness of underclass membership (1991). Although the gang would not provide a permanent escape from their poverty and marginalization, it could provide a refuge in which the females could collectively escape their fate, at least temporarily.

On the basis of her research, Campbell (1991) acknowledged that the male gang still paved the way and opened doors for the female affiliates, but she also noted that once formed, the female gang developed its own individual solidarity and that sisterhood had values and ways to attain status that did not revolve around male members. Campbell's work, along with the other research undertaken during this time period, demonstrated that previous stereotypes of gang girls inadequately explained their gang involvement (Quicker 1974; Harris 1988; Horowitz 1990; Campbell 1991; Moore 1991; Fishman 1995). Female gangs were neither completely at the mercy of male gang members, nor completely free of their influence. Fishman's research on the Vice Queens (1995), an African American female auxiliary gang present in Chicago in the late 1960s, exemplified the duality of female gang membership revealed (to varying degrees) in most of these contemporary accounts. On the one hand, gang girls exhibited some independence in their decision making, leadership, and activities. Yet at the same time they were closely linked to the male gang and had certain obligations and expectations that came with their auxiliary status. Although the Vice Queens' major activities revolved around male members, with sexual availability being expected (they even worked as prostitutes for male members' profit), they also acted independently of the male gang at times, engaging in property crime and fighting with other female gangs without the participation of their male counterpart (Fishman 1995).

Moore's research (1991) on former Mexican American male and female gang members in Los Angeles barrios also revealed some autonomy for females within their cliques but, consistent with Fishman's study, did not find sexism to be completely lacking. In comparing the male and female gang experience, Moore noted that female gang members were more likely to: come from extremely troubled home environments—families with alcoholic, drug-addicted, or criminally involved members—and suffer more long-term harm from their gang membership (1991, 1994).

RECENT TRENDS IN FEMALE DELINQUENCY AND GANGS

Given that males have continuously constituted the vast majority of the offending population, and that our society generally admonishes females who defy gender-role expectations through deviant or aggressive behavior, it is unsurprising that stories about female criminality, especially violence, pique the public's interest. Aside from being a perennial topic of interest, the recent upsurge in media coverage of female delinquency and gangs can be attributed to both an increase in girls' arrest rates, and increased *recognition* of girls' gang membership. Despite the general trend of declining crime and youth violence in the United States, official statistics (e.g., arrest rates), popular accounts (media/journalistic portrayals), and some scholarly research (both qualitative and quantitative studies) dealing with female delinquency and gang membership suggest *increases* in girls' involvement. Although girls account for only 26 percent of the total juvenile arrest population, law enforcement and juvenile court records indicate that their involvement in delinquency and violence has risen in the past decade (Poe-Yamagata and Butts 1996; Budnick and Shields-Fletcher 1998; Snyder and Sickmund 1999); these statistics also reveal that girls are engaging in delinquent behavior at a younger age (Community Research Associates 1998). Between 1981 and 1997, the Violent Crime Index arrest rate rose 103 percent for girls, compared to a 27 percent increase for boys (Uniform Crime Reports 1998; Acoca 1999). Female arrest rates for weapons law violations tripled between 1981 and 1997 while the male rate doubled; and, although juvenile property crime rates declined 17 percent for males between 1981 and 1997, female rates rose 39 percent (Snyder and Sickmund 1999).

Alarming as these increases appear, it is important to recognize that they may look more dramatic than they actually are; given the low base rate of female offending, any percentage increases appear relatively large. Furthermore, at least some of this increase may be attributable to shifts in the responses of the police and public, whereby incidents that may not have previously resulted in an arrest of a female now do. For example, some cities have just recently begun to include females in their official definition of, and response to, gangs, thereby increasing the likelihood of a female being arrested for a "gang-related" offense (Curry 1999). Moreover, female aggression and fighting that may have once been ignored or dealt with informally may currently be subject to more formal sanctions (for a further discussion of these issues, see Chesney-Lind and Shelden 1998).

Although it is difficult to definitively ascertain the driving force behind girls' arrest increases, there is widespread speculation—and some scholarly support for the claim—that gangs are playing a key role (Taylor 1993). A lack of comparative data (from previous eras and across jurisdictions) precludes a complete understanding of whether female gang involvement has truly increased or changed, but recent studies in several cities suggest that girls *are* involved in gangs (Fagan 1990; Esbensen and Huizinga 1993; Bjerregaard and Smith 1993) and that they *may* be playing a more central role in gang activity (including violence and drugs) than in the past (Lauderback, Hansen, and Waldorf 1992; Taylor 1993; Moore and Hagedorn 1999). Most journalists' accounts (and some researchers') have explained such increases as indicative of females' increasing liberation—essentially, that such shifts are a result of urban females demanding and achieving equal involvement and status in the traditionally "masculine" arenas of urban gangs, drug markets, and violence. Many researchers disagree, arguing that females' positions and opportunities within urban gangs and drug markets have not changed markedly. They contend that the "streets"—a microcosm of the larger society—remain marked by gender discrimination and that increases in female criminality are better explained through females' increasing economic marginalization, rather than liberation (Maher and Daly 1996; Maher 1997; Chesney-Lind 1999).

Whether there have been shifts in females' roles in gangs, drug markets, or other domains traditionally conceived of as masculine remains debatable. It may be true for some females in some cities or neighborhoods and not others, and it may be largely a product of media hype or shifts in police behavior. Although researchers debate whether (and why) female delinquency/criminality and gang membership have changed, there is much empirical evidence to demonstrate that girls (and boys) who *are* involved in gangs are more involved in delinquency, violence, and drug use than their nongang peers (Bjerregaard and Smith 1993; Esbensen and Huizinga 1993; Deschenes and Esbensen 1999). Longitudinal and cross-sectional studies comparing gang and nongang youths consistently find that the prevalence and incidence of offending is significantly higher among female gang members than among females unaffiliated with gangs[2] (Fagan 1990; Bjerregaard and Smith 1993; Deschenes and Esbensen 1999) and ethnographic research on female gangs reveals high rates of both victimization and offending among members (Miller 1998; Moore and Hagedorn 1999; Nurge, forthcoming).

Recent qualitative studies undertaken in various cities have produced multiple (sometimes contrasting) images of female gang members (Lauderback, Hansen, and Waldorf 1992; Taylor 1993; Joe and Chesney-Lind 1995; Brotherton 1996; Miller 1998; Venkatesh 1998; Hagedorn and Devitt 1999; Hunt, Mackenzie, and Joe-Laidler 2000), confirming that females' gang involvement is as varied, dynamic, and complex as males.' Whereas some of this research has lent support to media claims about increasingly violent gang girls (e.g., Lauderback, Hansen, and Waldorf 1992; Taylor 1993), other research has disclosed minimal female gang delinquency and violence (Joe and Chesney-Lind 1999). Overall, however, while revealing variation in female gang structure, activities, and involvement in crime/delinquency, these recent studies emphasize the importance of examining the context within which females become involved with gangs and the societal and community-level factors that influence such decisions.

A DESCRIPTIVE OVERVIEW OF FEMALE GANGS AND CLIQUES IN BOSTON

Between 1997 and 2000, I conducted interviews with a community sample of young females (ages 13–24) who considered themselves to be members of either a gang or a clique in the city of Boston. Fieldwork was also undertaken among a subgroup of fifteen "at-risk" urban adolescent girls (ages 11–18; approximately one-half of whom were gang/clique members) involved in a recreational basketball league during this same time period. With the assistance of local youth outreach workers (most of whom were former gang members themselves and/or currently worked closely with gang-involved youth), a targeted snowball sample of young women from various gangs across the city was eventually drawn (Watters and Biernacki 1989). The final sample included fifty-eight females (thirty gang members and twenty-eight clique members) representing twenty-five different groups from fifteen different neighborhoods. Of the thirty gang members interviewed, ten were former members who had been out of their group for varying lengths of time (between six months and six years). The average age of current gang/clique females interviewed was sixteen (the average age of former members was nineteen), and 60 percent of the young women were African American, 32 percent were Latina, and 8 percent were of mixed racial/ethnic heritage.

Although cliques and gangs are different types of groups, the girls who belonged to each came from largely similar backgrounds, in terms of family life, communities, school experiences, and related issues. Two-thirds of the female gang/clique members lived in public housing in economically depressed neighborhoods. Although technically living above the poverty line (most of their mothers were employed in at least one full-time job and were not receiving welfare benefits aside from subsidized housing), many of the females' families were struggling to make ends meet. The majority of the girls interviewed were living with their mother and siblings (and sometimes a stepfather or mother's boyfriend), and typically had no relationship with their father. A large proportion of the interviewees' family members had been arrested and incarcerated; for example, 73 percent of the clique members' fathers and/or brothers had been imprisoned. Although not all of the female gang/clique members interviewed had come from troubled home environments, it was a common theme. According to the self-report survey administered, about 50 percent of the gang and clique-involved females had run away from home in the past year, and several of the older females had permanently left home at a young age. Most of the girls who had run away from home cited abuse as the motivating factor in their decision to leave.

Approximately one-third of all clique and gang members interviewed (29 percent of current and former gang members and 36 percent of clique members) admitted they had experienced sexual and/or physical abuse at the hands of a family member or boyfriend. Most of the females that discussed their victimization also noted that other girls in their groups had similar experiences. In several cases, girls described a therapeutic function of their group; it was a context that allowed them to share traumatic experiences of abuse/neglect with empathetic others. As ZZ explained:

> Half the girls in my clique were abused by somebody . . . we all talk about it together. It's sad sometimes but after we talk about it we're able to laugh and say that it's in the past and behind us.

The labels of—and distinctions between—cliques and gangs emerged from both the females' self-definitions (when questioned about what they labeled their group and why) and their descriptions of the group's characteristics (including the organization/structure, initiation, leadership, rules, commitment/loyalty, amount and nature of time spent together/activities, and group/individual involvement in delinquency, violence, and drugs), which were subsequently uncovered through the interview questions (Nurge, forthcoming). With few exceptions, the females' labels and definitions of their groups (as cliques or gangs) were consistent with the subsequent descriptions they offered about their group's characteristics, although it was clear that some groups were trickier to define and characterize than others. For example, one group was difficult to classify because members offered contrasting definitions and depictions of its structure and nature, largely due to differences in their roles and status within the group, and what the group meant to them. There were also a few groups that had demonstrated fluidity over time, changing from a clique to a gang or vice versa (depending on leadership, membership, conflicts with other groups, and so forth). (A more thorough discussion of these issues is beyond the scope of the current chapter, but see Nurge, forthcoming for further elaboration on the distinctions between cliques and gangs and the difficulties inherent in defining such groups.)

Gangs and cliques fulfilled similar functions for their members (providing protection, sisterhood, and opportunities to achieve status; table 9.1) and the females who joined each type of group were similar in terms of age, socioeconomic status, family backgrounds, neighborhoods, and school experiences, yet there were notable distinctions between the two types of groups. Whereas cliques were typically small groups of friends (averaging about five members) that displayed minimal or no group structure, most gangs were larger, more organized (although usually rather loosely), had a leader and rules (whether formal or informal), initiation requirements, and stronger loyalty expectations. Self-defined clique members described their group as an informal group of friends who gave themselves a name in order to "be known" and/or protect themselves from other groups' provocations. Clique members asserted that they "don't look for trouble" but are "down for each other," and "have each others' backs" if trouble should come their way. They differentiated themselves from a "regular" group of friends by noting their willingness to fight and stick together, and sometimes get in trouble, yet they also distinguished themselves from gangs, which they considered to be larger and more organized groups that regularly engaged in serious delinquency and crime.

TABLE 9.1

TYPOLOGY OF GROUP FUNCTIONS/ACTIVITIES

PRIMARY FUNCTIONS/ACTIVITIES OF THE GROUPS: [COMPUTATIONS REFLECT THE PERCENTAGE OF GROUPS IN WHICH THIS WAS THE PRIMARY GROUP FUNCTION]	% OVERALL SAMPLE (25 CLIQUES AND GANGS)	% GANGS (14 GANGS)	% CLIQUES (11 CLIQUES)
1. Entrepreneurial (makin' money/survival)	24%	43%	0
2. Fighting	40%	36%	45%
3. Fun and belonging (hang out/ be known)	32%	14%	55%
4. Cultural pride and unity	4%	7%	0

Gangs were, in fact, involved in more serious types of crime than cliques (and committed such acts more frequently), but the prevalence of clique and gang members' arrests was similar. About 50 percent of all clique and gang members had been arrested at least once. Whereas the majority of clique members' arrests (91 percent) were for fighting (typical charges for fighting were simple assault or assault and battery), gang members' arrests were more varied and included: shoplifting, armed robbery, disorderly conduct, drug sales, attempted murder, and assault and battery. Overall, there was great variation in the extent to which gangs (collectively) and gang members (individually) engaged in crime and delinquency. Some gangs regularly sold drugs, engaged in ongoing fights with other gangs, or engaged in other types of crime (e.g., one coed gang specialized in car theft; another frequently shoplifted/boosted), while other groups were seldom involved in any type of delinquent or criminal activity.

Almost all of the gang and clique members were frequently involved in fights (both alone and with their group). Although protection was touted as a major reason for joining their group, ironically, girls were even more vulnerable to threats and attacks from other individuals and groups after joining, and ended up fighting more frequently (to represent/defend their group name and to back up their fellow group members). Most fights arose over issues of "disrespect" (perceived or actual). Whether directed at the group or an individual, acts of disrespect most often included some form of name calling ("talkin' shit") or a combination of name calling and dirty looks. Such slights might be direct and blatant or fairly subtle—a quietly muttered insult, a nasty look, or a rude gesture (e.g., a teeth-clicking or lip-smacking type of sound) were frequently cited as acts of disrespect. Although they fought very frequently, most cliques and gangs rarely used weapons in their individual and group fights. Females' weapons of choice were knives, razors, and shanks; the majority of young women interviewed had never carried or used guns (although gang members were much more likely than clique members to have access to firearms).[3]

Boston's female gangs and cliques assumed many shapes and styles: 24 percent of the groups were all female/independent (with no links or ties to males or male groups), 32 percent of them were affiliates or subgroups of male gangs (these female gangs typically had separate leaders and varying levels of attachment to the male group) 16 percent were coed groups (with shared leadership and activities), and 28 percent of the female groups (primarily cliques) had some form of loose connection to a group of males (without being their official affiliate/subgroup). Like most male gangs in Boston, the majority of female gangs and cliques studied (64 percent) were territorial in nature; they attached great importance to a local turf (typically a housing project, street, and/or park) and violations or disrespect of turf were a frequent source of conflict. For the mixed-gender groups, there was great variation in the extent to which males exerted control over the females. Whereas some groups appeared to be quite egalitarian, others demonstrated more traditional gender roles. Some girls and groups were fully independent of males, others had relationships that reflected at least some degree of subordination to males, but most fell somewhere in between the two extremes.

Aside from their varying structures, the groups studied were also characterized by different functions and activities. Based on discussions with females about (1) what their group did together (on a daily basis; in an average week), (2) what they perceived the group's function(s) and goal(s) to be, and (3) what they, as individuals, gained from membership, I categorized the primary functions and activities of the groups studied (see table 9.1). Whereas gangs emerged as primarily entrepreneurial and/or fighting groups, the typical function and activity of cliques was hanging out together, having fun (which typically included frequent marijuana use), and "being known." Although some groups were involved in a variety of activities and fulfilled multiple functions, most groups were readily classified into this general framework (see Nurge, forthcoming for a more detailed typology and analysis of group function/activity and a discussion of the limitations of such typologies).

LIBERATING AND LIMITING: THE BENEFITS AND DRAWBACKS OF GANG MEMBERSHIP

This section focuses on female gang members and draws on former members' perceptions about their gang experiences. Most of the current and former gang females interviewed expressed mixed feelings about their membership. They viewed their gang involvement as beneficial to their lives (typically through the emotional or economic support it provided), yet recognized the risks it presented and would not want their loved ones (brothers, sisters, and children) to become members. The majority of former members expressed both gratitude and regret about their gang experience. The contradictions apparent in their responses emerge from the context within which they joined and left the gang. Consistent with Campbell's (1991) assessment of the gang as a temporary asylum within which to escape or defer reality, the gang was able to meet these young women's immediate needs but was not a long-term solution to their problems. For some of the girls who were displaced (due to family problems, abuse, early pregnancy, and so forth) and in need of shelter, food, and support, it was the most practical and attractive option available to them at the time. For example, Zena and her three small children were kicked out of her parents' home when she was sixteen. Rather than living with her abusive boyfriend (her children's father) she decided to join and live with a coed gang that specialized in car theft. For her, the gang ensured economic survival—the ability to house and feed her children. When asked why she wanted to be part of it, she explained:

> To survive. That was the way for me to survive and see my kids. Even though it was the wrong way, it was the only way I could've done it. . . . They were doing their own little thing—kinda stealing here and there and ya know, I started doing the same thing 'cause it was hard for me to get things for my kids, ya know. And I was struggling, my mom wasn't helping me. I never got to see my father. I was by myself, so I was doing things by myself, ya know, and with the guys and stuff like that.

Although Zena eventually left the gang after a few years "to set a better example for my kids and do things the right way . . . the hard way," she remains grateful that her gang membership enabled her family to survive a difficult period:

> Me doing the things that I did helped me get the things my kids needed. It helped me get their food, 'cause nobody was giving me money, nobody was paying my rent, nobody was giving me clothes for my kids, nobody was paying my hospital bills from when my son was in the hospital when he was six months old. Their food, their toys, their beds, my house was hooked up. Nobody was doing that for me if I wasn't doing it on my own. The other guys helped me— they bought some things.

Similarly, Adalisse also expressed mixed emotions about her gang experience, wishing that what she gained from the gang had been available through other outlets. She joined her large, coed gang for various reasons, including an attraction to the cultural pride and unity they displayed.

> [I joined] to get away from an abusive relationship and so I'd get a family, security, stuff like that. . . . What it meant to me was a whole lifestyle. It wasn't just who I hung out with. At the time I was really just enwrapped with the whole philosophy and Puerto Rican pride.

When asked what being in a gang meant to her, she explained:

When I was younger I was always like the odd one out at one school. I was the only Hispanic, then when I went to another school that was full of Hispanics, I was the only Dominican—stuff like that. I was always left out in some way and then when I met them (this was before I even graduated high school) I was more than part of the family. . . . They had this need for me. Everyone wants to feel needed and I felt really at home with them. The other thing was I wasn't alone, anytime day or night, I could just pick up the phone and call someone. Financial-wise, also, I remember a couple times, like my first time moving out, I remember a couple times being worried about making rent and all the responsibilities. Guys would just come by with the groceries. . . . They helped me be able to go to college. . . . I couldn't have done it without them.

After a few years of membership, during which she rose to a high-ranking position in the gang and helped to advance the role of women therein, she left the group after growing dissatisfied with the leadership and the group's increasing use of violence. Like many of the other former members interviewed, Adalisse expressed mixed feelings about the experience—gratitude, as explained in the quote above, and regret, as evidenced below:

Oh yeah. If there was any way I could've known about the things they taught me. . . . my Latino heritage and the strength within me, without actually being a member. There's a lot of things that I can't take back that I've done that I'll just have to live with for the rest of my life. Hurting people, losing a lot of friendships in order to do what the organization requires sometimes, you know . . . and a lot of these things, well people say you're forgiven. It's not so much forgiveness from other people, it's forgiving myself. But one of the big things was . . . if I could've found the good in other places, I wouldn't have joined at all. That's about it.

Adalisse's closing response was echoed by almost all of the former gang members interviewed—they wished they could have gained the benefits that the gang provided without having to experience the negative ramifications of gang life. This goes to the heart of the issue regarding "liberation" and "social injury." Although females' gang involvement does not appear to have benefited from women's *liberation* per se, it does indeed appear to be a *liberating* experience for many of them.[4] The former members talked about gaining strength and self-esteem through their gang involvement and many explained that they needed to join the gang in order to "survive"—it provided them with physical, social, and economic security that they deemed necessary and otherwise unavailable at the time of joining. Many of the young women joined their group to empower themselves (for some it was an escape from an abusive boyfriend or family member; for others it was an opportunity to make money; for others it was a chance to be part of a family and play a role in it) and succeeded in doing so. Despite these benefits, however, the majority of the former members interviewed also acknowledged that the overall gang experience was harmful and negative, and noted that they would not want their children and brothers and sisters to be involved in such a group. Thus gang membership can sometimes empower and liberate young women while causing them harm.

A couple of the other former members—for whom the gang experience was not deemed necessary to survive but was an opportunity to socialize, have fun, and be part of something—also felt they had gained something from their membership. For instance, Emma was exposed to, and involved in, drive-by shootings and assaults during her gang membership and eventually left the gang to spend more time with her two children. Now living Campbell's (1991) life of domestic drudgery and single motherhood, she reminisced about the fun and excitement of her former lifestyle, and expressed minimal regret about the experience.

Dana: What do you miss about being in it?

E: Hangin' with them, chillin' with them, having fun. Now my days are boring.

Dana: What don't you miss about it?

E: Nothing.

Dana: There's nothing you *don't* miss? No? Do you regret leaving?

E: Yeah, I regret leaving.

Dana: Do you see it as having been a good thing in your life (or a bad thing or neutral)?

E: It was a good thing because we was all part of chilling, getting drunk and that's about it . . . if it comes down to fighting then we'll do it.

In contrast to Emma, many females pointed out membership drawbacks—some of them expressing frustration with the violence associated with it, and a couple noting that the promise of sisterhood was stronger than the reality of it. As one young woman explained:

It ain't worth it. At the time, you think that you have a family and all this support, but when it come down to it, they're not your family and you can't count on 'em. They didn't come see me when I got locked up. Nobody called, nobody wrote, nobody sent a dime.

Another member, Jade, couched her decision to join a female affiliate gang in terms of survival—she was able to escape an abusive situation in her household (she had experienced nine years of sexual abuse at the hands of siblings and cousins). She subsequently lived with, and engaged in robberies, shoplifting, and drug sales with a female affiliate gang. Although Jade was able to escape a dangerous environment at home, she faced new challenges to her safety and well-being. At the time, however, she preferred the risks associated with her new lifestyle to those she had encountered in her home. Eventually though, Jade decided to leave her gang because "it's not fun being out in the streets, it's not fun being alone, selling drugs; you have to walk by yourself at night, you ain't got no protection, guys pulling over, it's not fun." She was currently attempting to dissuade her younger sisters from involvement in the streets and gangs (despite the benefits she gained from it):

I've talked to them before—sat them down or whatever. . . . I tell 'em "look, it's not fun being out there, it's not fun starving, it's not fun selling drugs, being cold, you ain't got a coat or whatever, being cold out there. It's hard to get what you need out there . . . you just have your friends, nothing else."

Dana: Do you think that being in the gang has helped you more than it's hurt you? Has it been more positive or negative for you?

Jade: It helped me. It helped me get what I needed in life. They've been there for me more than anybody has. It helped me have my own self-esteem.

Dana: But you wouldn't want your sister to do it?

Jade: No. If my sister ever needed anything and it's the last money I have I would give it to her instead of her going to a gang. Instead of her going out there, doing what I did.

Similarly, another former member who joined after running away from a troubled household looked back on her gang experience (several years after a prison term ended her involvement), and recognized that it delayed her life and damaged relationships with family members, but at the time it meant a place to live, a supportive environment, and a means of making money.

Mary: Yeah, I mean I don't like my past. . . . I mean I'm not proud of it—what I was doing back then. But now that I did it, I wouldn't want to go back to that. I mean it's just a waste of time. If you think about all that, what I'm doing now I could have been doing back then, instead of doing. . . . Because it took a lot of time to get where I'm at now.

Dana: So do you regret the stuff that you did?

Mary: Yeah. I mean for one thing I should have been better to my mother 'cause I never was too close at first but then she just recently passed away so I got close the last two years—that's when I started like talking to my mother. I mean I regret doing that because I was like hurting her at the time. And now I know, 'cause I'd feel the same thing if my daughter do that to me. Now I know why she was feeling hurt 'cause I wouldn't want that to happen to me either.

Although most members readily admitted that they were exposed to (or involved in) negative and harmful situations during their gang tenure, it is difficult to conclude from this study that the gang experience caused them ongoing "social injury."[5] Unlike Moore's former female gang members (1991, 1994) who had suffered extensive long-term harm from their gang involvement, these former members appeared to be faring relatively well. Even those members who were involved in the most serious forms of gang violence appeared to have successfully put their negative gang experiences behind them. They were all employed or in school—some of them had taken college courses or received advanced training in various fields, some of them were raising children (while working), and overall, they seemed to be fairly happy, healthy, and well-adjusted. Some of these women spoke of fellow female members who did not fare as well as them, however, and were now deceased, incarcerated, working as prostitutes, or addicted to drugs.[6]

This study of female cliques and gangs uncovered notable variation in their structures and functions. Although there were common reasons for joining, gangs (and to a lesser extent, cliques) played a variety of roles in the lives of these young women. Many females joined a gang to empower themselves— whether to escape an abusive situation, protect oneself in other ways, or make money—and were successful in doing so, at least temporarily. For others, the clique or gang played a less central role in their lives but was an available source of friendship and recreation. There was no dominant image of a "gangster girl"—the gang served multiple functions and girls played myriad roles within their group. Although on the surface some of the gang members interviewed might appear to fit the media portrayal of a "dangerous gangsta girl," a closer examination revealed girls and young women struggling with the challenges confronting all adolescents—making the transition from child to adult, negotiating friendships, discovering and exploring one's sexuality, developing an identity, and so forth—while shouldering the additional burdens imposed by virtue of their gender, race/ethnicity, and socioeconomic status.

Interviews with former female gang members revealed the paradoxical nature of their gang experiences. Virtually all of them reflected upon their membership as a largely positive experience, yet most acknowledged the drawbacks and wished there had been other ways to gain the gang's benefits. Although it appeared that these particular members may have, in fact, reaped more benefits than drawbacks from their gang experience, they would not recommend gang membership to others or condone a loved one's involvement. Their experiences within, and perceptions about, their gangs suggest that the liberation hypothesis is applicable—if considered in terms of females achieving a sense of *individual* liberation through their membership—but there was no evidence to suggest that their membership was influenced by "women's liberation" or increasing opportunities to engage in traditionally "male" behavior. And, although cognizant of membership drawbacks, former members interviewed for this study had not suffered obvious long-term harm in terms of severely limited opportunities or problems stemming from (or related to) their gang involvement—thereby failing to provide strong support for the "social injury" hypothesis.

By framing girls' gang involvement simply in terms of "female liberation" or "social injury," researchers (and journalists, policymakers, etc.) may fail to capture the reasons girls decide to be part of such groups, the nature of their groups, and the variety of membership roles they play therein. Most of the females (both current and former members) saw the gang or clique as a logical place to turn for protection, love, income, and status—however fleeting those rewards might be in actuality. Some of them viewed the gang as an opportunity for empowerment and personal liberation. When appropriately contextualized, young women's choices to join gangs often appear to be practical (albeit temporary and limited) solutions to the multiple problems and limitations they face in their homes, schools, and communities. The fact that such groups are more readily available and able to meet urban youths' needs than other institutions calls attention to the impact of existing social policies (regarding the labor market, education, housing, child care, health care, and welfare) on inner-city communities. Serious efforts to reduce the violence associated with youth gangs must therefore begin with an understanding of the lives and circumstances of their members.

NOTES

1. Freda Adler and Rita Simon both published books on female offending in 1975, which collectively became known as the basis for the "liberation" theory. Each author linked increases in female crime to the emergence of the women's movement and increasing female liberation. Adler's findings, coined as the "masculinity thesis," suggested that a shift was occurring in the female self-image, resulting in women acting more like men (competitive, aggressive, etc.) as they are put in traditionally male positions of power and influence. Simon's work became known as the "opportunity thesis" and focused on women's increasing opportunities to commit crimes due to their entry into traditionally male professions. These early "liberation" findings have since been extensively critiqued on a number of grounds (e.g., see Steffensmeier 1993).
2. How gangs facilitate criminality has been the subject of much of the early gang research (Thrasher 1927; Short and Strodtbeck 1965), but the issue of group process remains poorly understood and understudied. Analysis of longitudinal youth survey data indicates that gang members have levels of delinquency and crime roughly comparable to nongang members prior to joining, and members' rates decline upon leaving the gang, leading researchers to conclude that the gang itself somehow influences individual delinquency/criminality—in support of a social learning model, rather than a control theory model (Elliott and Menard 1992; Thornberry et al. 1993).
3. For a more thorough examination of girls' fighting behavior and the "code of the street" see Nurge (1999, forthcoming).
4. This study did not trace female gang roles and activity over time, however, and therefore can draw no definitive conclusions on the plausibility of claims about increasing opportunities and roles for gang-involved females.
5. Why some of their fellow members experienced more long-term social injury from the gang experience than these young women did remains an open question.
6. Given that this study did not provide a comparative analysis of male and female gang experiences (or postgang experiences), the issue of whether females were more harmed by their gang membership than males remains unaddressed.

REFERENCES

Acoca, Leslie. 1999. "Investing in Girls: A Twenty-first Century Strategy." In OJJDP report, *Juvenile Justice*, vol. 6, no. 1. Washington DC: Office of Juvenile Justice and Delinquency Prevention.

Adler, Freda. 1975. *Sisters in Crime: The Rise of the New Female Criminal*. New York: McGraw-Hill.

Asbury, Herbert. 1927. *The Gangs of New York: An Informal History of the Underworld*. Garden City, N.Y.: Garden City Publishing Company.

Bjerregaard, Beth, and Carolyn Smith. 1993. "Gender Differences in Gang Participation, Delinquency, and Substance Use." *Journal of Quantitative Criminology*, 9 (4): 329–355.

Brotherton, David C. 1996. "'Smartness,' 'Toughness,' and 'Autonomy': Drug Use in the Context of Gang Female Delinquency." *Journal of Drug Issues*, 26 (1): 261–277.

Brown, Waln. 1977. "Black Female Gangs in Philadelphia." *International Journal of Offender Therapy and Comparative Criminology*, 21: 221–228.

Budnick, Kimberly J., and Ellen Shields-Fletcher. 1998. "What About Girls?" OJJDP Fact Sheet no. 84. Washington, D.C.: U.S. Department of Justice, Office of Justice Programs.

Campbell, Anne. 1990. "Female Participation in Gangs." In C. Ronald Huff, ed., *Gangs in America*. Newbury Park, Calif.: Sage.

——. 1991. *The Girls in the Gang*. 2d ed. Cambridge, Mass.: Basil Blackwell.

Chesney-Lind, Meda. 1993. "Girls, Gangs, and Violence: Anatomy of a Backlash." *Humanity and Society*, 17 (3): 321–344.

——. 1999. "Girls, Gangs, and Violence: Reinventing the Liberated Female Crook." In Meda Chesney-Lind and John M. Hagedorn, eds., *Female Gangs in America: Essays on Girls, Gangs, and Gender*. Chicago: Lake View Press

Chesney-Lind, Meda, and Randall G. Shelden. 1998. *Girls, Delinquency, and Juvenile Justice*. Pacific Grove, Calif.: Brooks/Cole Publishing Company.

Cohen, Albert K. 1955. *Delinquent Boys: The Culture of the Gang*. New York: Free Press.

Community Research Associates. 1998. "Juvenile Female Offenders: A Status of the States Report for the Office of Juvenile Justice and Delinquency Prevention." Champaign, Ill.: Community Research Associates.

Curry, G. David. 1998. "Female Gang Involvement." *Journal of Research in Crime and Delinquency*, 35 (1): 100–118.

——. 1999. "Responding to Female Gang Involvement." In Meda Chesney-Lind and John M. Hagedorn, eds., *Female Gangs in America: Essays on Girls, Gangs, and Gender*. Chicago: Lake View Press.

Deschenes, Elizabeth Piper, and Finn-Aage Esbensen. 1999. "Violence Among Girls: Does Gender Make a Difference?" In Meda Chesney-Lind and John M. Hagedorn, eds., *Female Gangs in America: Essays on Girls, Gangs, and Gender*. Chicago: Lake View Press.

Elliott, Delbert, and S. Menard. (1992). "Delinquent Friends and Delinquent Behavior: Temporal and Developmental Patterns." In J. David Hawkins, ed., *Some Current Theories of Crime and Deviance*. New York: Springer-Verlag.

Esbensen, Finn-Aage, and David Huizinga. 1993. "Gangs, Drugs, and Delinquency in a Survey of Urban Youth." *Criminology*, 31 (4): 565–587.

Fagan, Jeffrey. 1990. "Social Processes of Delinquency and Drug Use among Urban Gangs." In C. Ronald Huff, ed., *Gangs in America*. Newbury Park, Calif.: Sage.

Fishman, Laura T. 1995. "The Vice Queens: An Ethnographic Study of Black Female Gang Behavior." In Malcolm Klein, Cheryl L. Maxson, and Jody Miller, eds., *The Modern Gang Reader*. Los Angeles: Roxbury Publishing Company.

Ford, Royal. 1998. "Razor's Edge." *Boston Globe Magazine* (24 May): 12, 22–28.

Hagedorn, John M., and Mary L. Devitt. 1999. "Fighting Female: The Social Construction of Female Gangs." In Meda Chesney-Lind and John M. Hagedorn, eds., *Female Gangs in America: Essays on Girls, Gangs, and Gender*. Chicago: Lake View Press.

Harris, Mary. 1988. *Cholas: Latina Girls and Gangs*. New York: AMS Press.

Horowitz, Ruth. 1990. "Sociological Perspectives on Gangs: Conflicting Definitions and Concepts." In C. Ronald Huff, ed., *Gangs in America*. Newbury Park, Calif.: Sage.

Hunt, Geoffrey, Kathleen MacKenzie, and Karen Joe-Laidler. 2000. " 'I'm Calling My Mom': The Meaning of Family and Kinship Among Homegirls." *Justice Quarterly*, 17 (1): 1–31.

Joe, Karen A., and Meda Chesney-Lind. 1999. "Just Every Mother's Angel: An Analysis of Gender and Ethnic Variations in Youth Gang Membership." In Meda Chesney-Lind and John Hagedorn, eds., *Female Gangs in America*. Chicago: Lake View Press.

Lauderback, David, Joy Hansen, and Dan Waldorf. 1992. "Sisters Are Doin' It for Themselves: A Black Female Gang in San Francisco." *Gang Journal*, 1 (1): 57–72.

Maher, Lisa. 1997. *Sexed Work: Gender, Race, and Resistance in a Brooklyn Drug Market*. New York: Oxford University Press.

Maher, Lisa, and Kathleen Daly. 1996. "Women in the Street-Level Drug Economy: Continuity or Change?" *Criminology*, 34 (4): 465–492.

Miller, Jody. 1998. "Gender and Victimization Risk among Young Women in Gangs." *Journal of Research in Crime and Delinquency*, 35 (4): 429–453.

———. 2001. *One of the Guys: Girls, Gangs, and Gender*. New York: Oxford University Press.

Miller, Walter B. 1973. "The Molls." *Society*, 11: 32–35.

Moore, Joan. 1991. *Going Down to the Barrio: Homeboys and Homegirls in Change*. Philadelphia: Temple University Press.

———. 1994. "The *Chola* Life Course: Chicana Heroin Users and the Barrio Gang." *International Journal of the Addictions*, 29 (9): 1115–1126.

Moore, Joan, and John Hagedorn. 1999. "What Happens to Girls in the Gang?"

In Meda Chesney-Lind and John M. Hagedorn, eds., *Female Gangs in America: Essays on Girls, Gangs, and Gender*. Chicago: Lake View Press.

Nurge, Dana M. 1999. "R-E-S-P-E-C-T—Find Out What It Means to Me: Female Gang Members and the Code of the Street." Paper presented at the American Society of Criminology meetings, Toronto, November.

——. Forthcoming. Book on female gangs and cliques in Boston. Northeastern University Press.

Office of Juvenile Justice and Delinquency Prevention. 1998. "Guiding Principles for Promising Female Programming: An Inventory of Best Practices." OJJDP report. Washington, D.C.: Office of Justice Programs.

Poe-Yamagata, Eileen, and Jeffrey A. Butts. 1996. "Female Offenders in the Juvenile Justice System: Statistics Summary." OJJDP report. Washington, D.C.: Office of Juvenile Justice and Delinquency Prevention.

Portillos, Edwardo Luis. 1999. "Women, Men, and Gangs: The Social Construction of Gender in the Barrio." In Meda Chesney-Lind and John M. Hagedorn, eds., *Female Gangs in America: Essays on Girls, Gangs, and Gender*. Chicago: Lake View Press.

Quicker, John C. 1974. *Homegirls: Characterizing Chicano Gangs*. San Pedro, Calif.: International University Press.

Short, James F., and Fred L. Strodtbeck. 1965. *Group Process and Gang Delinquency*. Chicago: University of Chicago Press.

Simon, Rita. 1975. *Women and Crime*. Lexington, Mass.: Lexington Press.

Snyder, Howard N., and Melissa Sickmund. 1999. "Juvenile Offenders and Victims: 1999 National Report (September)." OJJDP report. Washington, D.C.: National Center for Juvenile Justice, Office of Juvenile Justice and Delinquency Prevention.

Steffensmeir, Darrell. 1993. "National Trends in Female Arrests, 1960–1990: Assessment and Recommendations for Research. *Journal of Quantitative Criminology*, 9 (4): 411–441.

Swart, William J. 1991. "Female Gang Delinquency: A Search for Acceptably Deviant Behavior." *Mid-American Review of Sociology*, 15 (1): 43–52.

Taylor, Carl S. 1993. *Girls, Gangs, Women, and Drugs*. East Lansing: Michigan State University Press.

Thornberry, Terence P., Marvin D. Krohn, Alan J. Lizotte, and Deborah Chard-Wierschem. 1993. "The Role of Juvenile Gangs in Facilitating Delinquent Behavior." *Journal of Research in Crime and Delinquency*, 30 (1): 55–87.

Thrasher, Frederick M. 1927. *The Gang: A Study of 1,313 Gangs in Chicago*. Chicago: University of Chicago Press.

Uniform Crime Reports. 1998. *Crime in the United States*. Clarksburg, W. Va.: Federal Bureau of Investigation.

Venkatesh, Sudhir. 1998. "Gender and Outlaw Capitalism: A Historical Account of the Black Sisters United 'Girl Gang.' " *Signs* (spring): 683–709.

Watters, John K., and Patrick Biernacki. 1989. "Targeted Sampling: Options for the Study of Hidden Populations." *Social Problems*, 36 (4): 416–430.

10

AMOR DE REINA! THE PUSHES AND PULLS OF GROUP MEMBERSHIP AMONG THE LATIN QUEENS

DAVID BROTHERTON AND CAMILA SALAZAR-ATIAS

Oh, my God . . . they always say we're the gang. They never give us an opportunity because we're a gang. And a gang, a gang, a gang, we're into criminal activities. I'm not a gang member. I'm in an organization. I will not put my kids into a gang, 'cause I got raised right. How am I gonna put my kids into a gang? So that's the main problem we always have, "we're a gang," "we're killers," "we're murderers," we're this, we're that. I'm not a murderer. I'm not a killer. I'm a mother with two kids and I'm tryin' to raise my kids right and tryin' to help others so when time comes and I die I know that I did the best thing I could as a human being.

—Queen H., author interview

During the years 1997–99, the Street Organization Project at John Jay College of Criminal Justice carried out an ethnographic study of the Almighty Latin King and Queen Nation (ALKQN) in New York City, which included a substudy of the female members and their role in the transformation of the group into a "street organization" (Brotherton and Barrios, forthcoming).[1] On the basis of interviews with female members and observations of the group's formal and informal practices over time, we will provide an analysis of: the self-reported motives behind membership in the Latin Queens, and the multiple ways that the Latin Queens meet their members' needs and aspirations. The article makes a contribution to the gang female literature by extending the discussion on gang female agency that has been developing in recent years (Moore 1991; Taylor 1993; Hagedorn 1998; Miller 2001).

FROM INVISIBILITY TO AGENCY AND PATHOLOGY: THE PUSHES AND PULLS OF GANG FEMALE MEMBERSHIP

Research on group behavior among adolescent inner-city youths for most of the last century has: (1) mainly been concerned with questions of male criminality (Pfohl 1985), (2) mostly been written by male criminologists, and (3) generally been resistant to discussions on the role of gender either in the commission of deviance or in its representation. This tendency toward female exclusion at the conceptual, empirical, and analytical levels has been particularly pronounced in studies of gangs. In a recent literature review by two prominent researchers, the authors concluded:

> Much of the research on gangs has ignored females or trivialized female gangs. Influential early studies of gangs, which for years shaped the research agenda, concentrated almost exclusively on males. The implicit message of these studies was that female gangs were unimportant. *(Moore and Hagedorn 2001:2)*[2]

Although it is evident that the roles of gender in general and of females in particular have long been neglected, obscured, or miscast in gang research, more recently—starting with two pioneering studies by Quicker (1983) and Campbell (1984)—a number of works have appeared that contest the terrain. In this newer literature, influenced by feminist critiques of the discourse, gang females are viewed: (1) as multidimensional; (2) in an interactional relationship with gender, race, and class structures; and (3) as purposive social agents (see, for example, Harris 1988; Moore 1991; Lauderback, Hansen, and Waldorf 1993; Joe and Chesney-Lind 1995; Fishman 1995; Brotherton 1996; Miller 2001; Nurge, chapter 9 of this volume). Thus the days when the "gendered habits" (Joe and Chesney-Lind 1995) of white, middle-class, male researchers could represent gang females as little more than "bad girl" caricatures (e.g., tomboys, sex objects, vamps, etc.) when perceived as "active," or as appendages of male gangs when perceived as "passive" (Campbell 1984) are, for the most part, behind us.[3]

Nonetheless, although gang females have certainly merited and have begun to receive much more studied attention as subjects in themselves, their treatment within criminology has not been without its tensions. David Curry has found that most of the recent gang female research has been conducted within one of two conceptual tropes: the "liberation hypothesis," whose adherents argue that there is a new, independent gang female who is as criminally deviant as her male counterpart (see Taylor 1993), and the "social injury hypothesis," which "holds that any benefit in personal liberation that girls may gain from gang involvement is outweighed by the social costs of such affiliation" (Curry 1998:128). As hypotheses in and of themselves, both represent a correction to earlier stereotypes by helping to locate gang females as active players in the urban drama of social and economic dislocation brought about by deindustrializing capitalism. However, when each construct is used to describe a pure, ideal type (Weber 1946) of offender/victim, the resulting analyses tend to simplify and pathologize the subject, as context, agency, and history are all sacrificed for the sake of proclaiming the novelty of the discovery (see Joe and Chesney-Lind 1995; Miller 2001).

Despite these theoretical/empirical shortcomings, our knowledge of gang females has increased considerably, particularly in the factors behind their emergence and regeneration. It is our aim in this chapter to advance our understanding a little more and look at the variations in this process by showing the changing nature of both gang female participation and organization over time.

WHY DO GIRLS JOIN GANGS?

As mentioned above, one of the most important contributions of the recent research into gang females has been the depth of the debate surrounding the conditions influencing the mutual and reciprocal relationship between girls and gangs. In the parlance of mainstream criminology, this is sometimes referred to as push/pull factors of gang membership (Decker and Van Winkle 1996).

To summarize from the literature, we might describe the "push" factors that influence females to join gangs as a combination of the socioeconomic, political, psychological, and cultural determinants that structure and constitute the daily lives of inner-city females such that the membership in gangs is a viable option among their life choices. This rather broad, all-encompassing appreciation of the macro- and micro-ecological context in which a gang female orientation is developed is in contrast to the narrow, highly functionalist conception of "pull" factors that is omnipresent in much of the research—particularly on males—an example of which is the following:

The neighborhood gang provides both instrumental and social benefits to its members. The instrumental advantages include . . . money from drug sales, robbery, or property crime, as well as protection. . . . The social benefits . . . include power, prestige, or thrills associated with gang membership. In addition, the gang provides a place to "hang out" with friends, something to do.

(Decker and Van Winkle 1996:27)[4]

Integrating and delineating these "push/pull"factors into conceptual themes, we have arrived at five interrelated, though distinct, areas that were prominent in the literature: (1) issues of identity, (2) family pressures, (3) economic survival, (4) community networks, and (5) class experiences.

ISSUES OF IDENTITY

Two critical factors influencing females' pathways into gangs are the twin issues of gender and ethnic identity. In Campbell's early work, she found that females who joined gangs were engaged in a struggle to resolve the nature of their femininity that could be traced to the prescribed womanhood practiced by their mothers. She argues that females moving toward gang life were rejecting such traditional female traits as stoicism, passivity, and loyalty—all of which are key tenets of the culture of *Marianismo* (relating to the life of the Virgin Mary)—and embraced the idealized values of the assimilated American woman: independence, the freedom to consume, and the notion of the suburban middle-class family. This struggle to construct a female self (i.e., one that is willed by the individual rather than culturally conditioned and socially reproduced) is also present to some degree in numerous other studies across a range of ethnicities (see Fishman 1995; Hunt, McKenzie, and Laidler-Joe 2000; Nurge, chapter 9 of this volume).

It is not surprising that certain females gravitate toward gangs because the females in such organizations send powerful signals of togetherness and collective empowerment to outsiders. Similarly, gang females, who are mostly minorities, have been found to strongly identify with their own ethnic affiliations (Harris 1988) and utilize their gang membership to symbolically subvert and/or invert their marginalized sociocultural status (Quicker 1983; Brake 1985; Moore 1991; Brotherton 1996). Thus we know that many gangs that are known by their ethnicity-based monikers produce a range of race-

and ethnicity-related ideologies, which contain such sentiments as upholding their race, fighting the conspiracies of white-supremacist culture, and developing their imagined "nation" (Conquergood 1997; Brotherton 1998; Esteva, chapter 6 of this volume).

FAMILY PRESSURES

In a number of studies, gang females are shown to be seeking companionship, love, trust, and security. With many girls coming from unstable, chaotic, and highly dysfunctional family backgrounds, they have found it difficult, if not impossible, to develop enduring friendships in school, in the community, or even in the family (Campbell 1984; Miller 2001). This sense of isolation and vulnerability is compounded in families where sexual violence is all too commonplace (Moore 1991; Joe and Chesney-Lind 1995). Thus many girls are understandably seeking groups that can promise a sense of refuge, a feeling of protection, and social relationships that are more permeable (Brotherton 1996). Further, gendered constraints on the female can be unbearable in very traditional family cultures and such expectations are thrown into stark relief when set against the more individualistic and liberal family norms for middle-class girls of the United States. Likewise, the gang can present itself very attractively as an alternative extended family with fictive kinship, "respected" older mentors, and youth sections as staples of the organization (Moore 1991; Conquergood 1997; Brotherton and Barrios, forthcoming).

ECONOMIC SURVIVAL

With the majority of gang females drawn from the most economically marginalized strata of the population, it makes sense that a number would be looking to improve their opportunity structure. In certain neighborhoods, the only obvious men of means are the drug dealers (Bourgois 1995) and the only sources for income generation are the drug and associated trades—such as prostitution (Maher 2000). For some females, associating with gang members and becoming members themselves assures them a certain economic status not available to them under the punitive conditions of welfare/workfare or the segmented labor structures of the legitimate marketplace.

WORKING-CLASS/UNDERCLASS EXPERIENCE

The multiple factors that constitute the oppressive day-to-day conditions of members of the urban working- and underclass are legion. Little social mobility; high levels of criminalization and morbidity; poor standards of health and health care; unsafe, low-tier schools; noisy, disruptive neighborhoods; and inadequate or no political clout are the rule. Not surprisingly, many females from such backgrounds are looking for excitement, opportunity, responsibility, and status, anything to ameliorate the futility, boredom, and predictability of a life on the "mean streets" (Thomas 1967) of the ghettos and the barrios of both our large and small cities (Venkatesh 2000). Gangs, meanwhile, are known for spending a lot of time indulging in self-initiated "leisure activities." Drug use of various sorts is common, sexual activity is promoted, and the groups boast ready-made friendship networks for anybody who is "down" (Vigil 1988). Furthermore, gang female self-representation can be seen as an audacious act of self- and collective defiance on behalf of highly marginalized, stigmatized, and colonized populations (Mendoza-Denton 1995).

As can be seen, the above literature is a welcome antidote to the years of "invisibility" for gang females (Chesney-Lind and Hagedorn 1999). In the following section, we will extend the analysis of the motives behind group membership for females and set them against the provisions offered by the group. Our aim is to take this aspect of the literature a step further toward a fuller elucidation of the contemporary gang female experience.

METHODOLOGY

The research literature is very explicit about the problems of gaining access to gang females who are considered a "hard-to-reach" population (Morgan and Joe 1996). Among the challenges researchers have typically confronted are: respondents who are guarded toward outsiders, finding a trusted informant, and myriad external and internal developments that can have a negative impact on the research climate—for example, police harassment campaigns, arrest and imprisonment of key members, threats from other groups, high turnover in leadership personnel, and sensationalistic media stories (Hagedorn 1998). To counter these difficulties, we developed a collaborative relationship with the ALKQN under the aegis of the Street Organization Project, in which we agreed on: (1) the details of the research design (i.e., life history interviews with a cross-section of the membership over three years and field observations of meetings, social gatherings, and political events), (2) compensation for interviews ($25.00 was paid for each interview into the group's general fund), (3) the confidentiality of all data and the anonymity of all subjects, (4) the payment of a consultation fee to anyone who functioned as a project liaison and recruiter of respondents, and (5) the mode of publication of the data (i.e., that journal articles and a book on the reform history of the ALKQN would appear). As part of this research relationship, we negotiated with the leadership of both the Kings and Queens to carry out a substudy of the Latin Queens, from which the data for this paper are derived.

With this agreement in hand, formal access to the membership was not a major impediment and the leadership of the ALKQN used general meetings to explain to the members that we, the researchers, were looking for subjects to interview and that such interviews were endorsed by the group. In time, a number of women came forward and through different liaisons in the Queens, a selective sample of female members offered to be part of the study. In the first year of the project, two female interviewers carried out thirteen life history interviews primarily at large meetings of the entire group. These interviews yielded a great deal of descriptive data but it was clear that a lot of background information was missing and that the respondents were not being as self-reflective as they could be. Over the next two years, we decided to change the approach and carry out more of the interviews in the respondents' neighborhoods. During this period (1997–99), a third interviewer (Salazar), visited members' homes, attended both formal and informal meetings of the group, and developed a mutually trusting relationship with a range of key female informants. These contacts and interactions yielded a further fifteen interviews, with several members being interviewed on repeat occasions for follow-up information and clarification purposes.

The interview guide consisted of open-ended questions that focused on identity formation, experiences with the U.S. education system, family history, motives for joining the group, political consciousness, group relations with mainstream society, internal group dynamics, criminal and job histories, drug experiences, and both individual and group aspirations.

THE HISTORY OF THE LATIN QUEENS

The New York State Queens were founded in 1991 after a manifesto for the Queens was penned by King Blood (a.k.a. Luis Felipe), the First President of the New York State Latin Kings, from his prison cell in Attica State Penitentiary. Until that time, there had been no organized group for women who wanted to join the Latin Kings, although it was evident that a number of women were drawn to the organization, primarily through boyfriends and husbands. From 1991 to 1996, the Queens expanded and grew to approximately sixty members. They were called the Naia Tribe of New York State and they would meet separately from the Latin Kings, although they would all come together for their monthly general meetings. Toward the end of this period, the group changed its name from the Almighty Latin Kings to the Almighty Latin King and Queen Nation and the role of the Queens began to grow, especially with the prominence of one Queen in particular, Queen Zulma, who married King Blood through the Nation and became one of the most powerful figures in the overall organization of the group.

After 1996, the role of the Queens began to expand even more with the ascension of King Tone to the Inca position (First President) of the New York State ALKQN. Under King Tone's leadership, the rules of the Queens were amended and for the first time the Queens began to put forward their own demands, which challenged some of the discriminatory rules and male privileges of the group (e.g., the right of Latin Kings to have mistresses while Latin Queens can be expelled for the same practice). By 1998, the Queens had grown to more than two hundred members throughout New York State and they had split into female-only adult branches in all five boroughs, each with their own leadership structure. In addition, there was a large number of younger females active in the Pee Wee or youth section of the ALKQN. These were male and female members under eighteen years of age organized in the only coeducational branch of the group, called the Cacique Tribe. In late 1998, the first female was elected to the Supreme Team of the organization, which was the highest decision-making body in New York State. The Queens throughout this period were referred to as the "backbone"of the organization and were highly regarded for their loyalty and support of their Kings and their ability to literally reproduce the Nation. By the time the reform period of the ALKQN ended, contradictions between the Kings and Queens were increasingly apparent as the formal roles of the females as esteemed symbols of motherhood in a traditional Latino family conflicted with their greater self-confidence and knowledge about their rights as women and as Latinas.

CHARACTERISTICS OF THE SAMPLE

Twenty-eight Latin Queens were given life history interviews during 1997–99. The ages ranged from fourteen to forty-five, with six of the respondents under eighteen years of age and therefore members of the Pee Wees (i.e., the coeducational youth section of the group). The length of membership in the organization varied greatly, with some of the younger members having joined six months prior to the interview and three of the oldest females having been members for more than five years.

In terms of ethnicity, only three respondents were born outside the mainland United States, in Puerto Rico, whereas of the fifty-six parents, only nine were born in the United States (i.e., thirty-seven were born in Puerto Rico and ten in the Dominican Republic). With most of the sample coming from second-generation families, it is perhaps surprising that only four stated they did not speak Spanish and only two self-identified as "American," with the rest identifying themselves as Nuyorican, Puerto Rican, or Dominican. Nearly all the respondents reported growing up in one of the barrios or ghettos of New York City, with nine describing particularly high rates of residential mobility. In other descriptions of their immediate environment, eighteen said that they lived in areas with high rates of both violence and drug use, while only five felt that their neighborhoods were relatively safe.

The class background of the sample was almost entirely working class, with only six of the parents reported to be employed in low-status white-collar occupations, such as secretaries or dental assistants and three had fathers in the armed forces. The rest of the fathers were or had been in blue-collar jobs such as construction workers, janitors, merchant seamen, and city employees, and two reported that their fathers were or had been full-time criminals. Five respondents described the economic conditions in which they were raised as "comfortable" or "well off," twelve described them as "poor" or "very poor," and the rest said that they felt they were neither poorer nor richer than others in their community.

The family structures within which the respondents grew up were quite varied. Ten members reported that they were raised in two-parent families, thirteen were mostly raised by their mothers, and five by their grandparents, their uncles and aunts, or foster parents. The size of the families for most respondents was modest with most reporting one or two siblings; only six respondents said they came from large families with four or more children. Within many of the families however, there was a strikingly high level of abuse. Ten respondents openly talked about physical beatings by fathers, mothers, spouses, boyfriends, and guardians, and of these, four described various levels of sexual abuse by different members of the family including incest.[5] Eleven respondents said that they had become pregnant as teenagers (i.e., under seventeen years of age), with two reporting having had children when they were as young as thirteen years old and one reported having been married at age twelve.

In terms of their education, most of the sample attended public schools in the city (twenty-five) and five had experienced some form of college, with one member attaining a Bachelor's degree from Fordham University. Eleven reported that they had not finished high school, and of these, seven had dropped out of the system entirely without attaining a General Education Diploma. Four were still attending a secondary education institution. As for criminal histories, eleven reported that they had arrest records and seven more talked about "selling drugs" in the past and engaging in different forms of low-level delinquency including assault, graffiti, shoplifting, and status offenses such as running away from home. Five respondents reported having spent some time in prison or in a juvenile detention center, with the maximum sentence of the sample being three and one-half years for a drug offense.

Finally, entry into the ALKQN for the majority (eighteen) came via other male members who were their fathers, husbands, brothers, or uncles. In all, fifteen respondents stated they had multiple family members in the organization.

MOTIVES FOR JOINING AND THE PROVISION OF NEEDS

The respondents described their motives for joining either directly or indirectly under a multitude of different themes that spoke to the effects of systematic physical abuse, economic deprivation, health problems, emotional trauma, cultural denial and family disintegration. We will analyze these in greater depth by breaking them down and contrasting the findings to the five themes identified in the literature.

IDENTITY

In certain aspects, the respondents' discussion of feminine identity was similar to the findings and interpretations of Campbell (1984), and in other aspects it was not. We found, for example, that respondents spoke of their femininity in terms of: motherhood and being able to school, care for, and raise their children with some security in their own community; and standing behind their man/men and being the "backbone" of the Nation. We encountered few aspirations of becoming individualistic, middle-class women or of pursuing the American Dream by moving to the suburbs.[6] On the other hand, all the respondents rejected their roles as stoic sufferers of male privilege and freedom and they all wanted a level of autonomy that, as Latinas, would assure them and their community some political, economic, and social ascent. In the following, two local leaders of the Queens talk about what motivates them as women to be agents of social change:

C: Can you talk about Queenism?

Queen T: Queenism? To me being a Queen and Queenism is like being strong, being independent, on your own, having the right to speak your mind, being a woman 'cos not many women could speak their mind. There's a lot of men who always shut them up and stuff like that and being a Queen . . . Queenism means power . . . having power on your own, being independent.

C: We want to get an idea of the people you admire. Who are your heroes/heroines?

Queen F: I like Gloria Steinem because I think that she, you know. . . . I don't know about now, but I know back in the days she . . . was all into equality and pro, pro, pro all this [i.e., groups like the Latin Queens], you know? She was just like the ultimate role model for someone to look up to when they wanted to learn what bein' a woman was all about. She was one of my role models. I don't know who else is my role model. Mostly all my role models are women, I don't have any male role models.

Part of this construction of the Queens' collective feminine identity is based on a basic tenet of the Nation's ideology that there should be no divisions between males and females and that both genders must subscribe to Nation unity at all times. However, because the Nation allows the women to organize separately, there is an implicit recognition that female members have their own concerns and require their own spatial autonomy to better empower themselves. The Nation, therefore, offers two possibilities of womanhood that merge both old and new traditions: (1) a form of membership that might be described as unity in diversity, and (2) the acceptance of certain tenets of *Marianismo* (i.e., commitment to children, child rearing, and loyalty to one's partner), while rejecting a third tenet, docility and stoicism.

The second aspect of identity that was powerfully present in most of the respondents' accounts was identification with their racial and ethnic heritage. For most respondents, whether they were fully or only half Puerto Rican or Dominican, they unambiguously claimed their Latino roots and bristled at the notion that they might be considered "American."

C: OK. Do you feel that you are Americanized now?

Queen H: That I'm American what?

C: Americanized. That you're more American, that you are more heavily influenced by the American culture?

Queen H: I'm always gonna be Boricua no matter what. American or no American, that's my heritage. That's where I was born at. If they think 'cos we, that Puerto Rico is a part of the States, that they control some of that . . . but I'm still one hundred percent Boricua. I would never say, "I'm American." No, 'cos I know where I come from.

For some, however, this unambiguous declaration of ethnic selfhood, in the context of a highly racialized society, was much more complex and it spoke to the contradictoriness of race/ethnicity within the ALKQN (see also Conquergood 1997).

I said to mom, "Why you told me don't go out with a black guy?" My father is more black than the blacks. I'm gonna show you a picture of my father. He's really, really black. I said to her, "What kind of mistake am I?" I never loved my mother because of that. In her family, they look at my father, they don't wanna talk to my father, you know what I'm sayin'? It bothers me 'cos that's in my

blood, that's my father, I'm willing to die for him. . . . Recently, I decided to go
to college. When I was doing the application, you know, they say, "What you
are? Spanish, Black, Indian, American?" . . . all that crazy stuff. And I say, "I
don't have to put none of that shit. I'm everything. I mark everything, because
I'm like everything. I'm American, I'm African, I'm everything. Puerto Rico's
got everything from everybody. We Africanos, we Americans, we Indian, we're
Spanish, we're from everywhere. *(Queen D.)*

The Nation claims that it is an organization dedicated to uphold the Latino
community and that, in its original New York manifesto, no "morenos"
(blacks) would be allowed into the organization. However, in the reformed
Nation there was a struggle to rid the organization of its antiblack past and
to accept a much wider race- and ethnicity-based membership. Moreover,
there was a greater acceptance of both the Puerto Rican and the Dominican members' African heritage, which hitherto had only been tangentially
acknowledged in the Nation's ideology. For many females who had grown
up in mixed-race families or who had dated males from other racial categories, and for their "sins" had faced prejudice and/or discrimination, the
new Nation's racial openness was a welcome port in the storm.

FAMILY PRESSURES

In concurrence with some of the literature: many of the respondents joined
the ALKQN looking for a symbolic family to replace the one they had experienced, and nearly all these women came from traumatic social backgrounds, suffering high rates of violence in their homes, which often forced
them to move out or run away at a very early age, some as young as nine years
old. However, contrary to almost all the literature, most of the respondents
found they could not get out of the violence cycle (Widom 1998) until they
encountered the Nation, which became the only viable mechanism for escape
from the rituals of daily abuse. Once in the Nation, respondents reported
that their true family life began as they learned to trust and rely on older men
and women, perhaps for the first time. They also spoke of the Nation not
simply as a surrogate family but as a supplement to the family they already
had. In a number of cases, the Nation functioned as a kind of weigh station,
a social support system that helped the respondents heal from their previous
wounds until they were strong enough to repair the bonds with their true

blood relations, if they so desired. There were four central subthemes that ran through the motives; they are categorized as follows:

1. In search of security, safety, and support

Many of the respondents spoke of suffering violence from either one or both parents, uncles, brothers, foster parents, guardians, spouses, or boyfriends. A number of the parents who beat their children were drug and/or alcohol addicted, and the beatings would mostly come when the parent was "high." Sometimes the beatings from the men would be part of a pattern of sexual abuse. The women reported that they had few options to stop these assaults, unless a state agency intervened, and at least six of the respondents talked of being removed from their parent(s)' home as a child or as an adolescent. In the following excerpt, Queen F. describes being physically abused by both her guardians:

> c: OK. How about your uncle? You don't have any conflicts with him any more?
>
> Queen F: No, because, see, my little sister ran away. She's a runaway. They're lookin' for her. We don't have contact 'cause the last time I seen him he tried to hit me 'cause he was running after my sister tryin' to get my sister and the reason why we don't have contact with each other is because I went and I told the social worker that he used to hit me, his boyfriend used to hit me, and the boyfriend used to try to get fresh with me, so I told her and that's why we don't have contact with each other.
>
> In many cases, the beatings only stopped when the subject encountered members of the Nation who assured her that the organization could be relied upon for support in the form of a refuge and sometimes physical intervention. Below, Queen I. remembers how she first crossed paths with the Latin Kings in California:
>
> c: I want to talk to you about the organization that you're currently a member of. How did you learn about it?
>
> Queen I: The Nation? I didn't really learn about it, the Nation saved my life . . . almost twelve years ago. I was married at the age of twelve, OK? And my husband was chosen for me so it wasn't the right choice. For ten years I took abuse, beatings, insults and I had four kids. One day on the beach, my husband came back because his mistress had left him and that's the only time I was ever happy, when he

had a mistress, he wouldn't hit me. He came by, he took an aluminum baseball bat, broke all my ribs, both my legs, my arm, and he was ready to strike on my head when a Latin King stepped in and said, "You hit her again and we're gonna give it to you to see how you like it." You know? A while after that, my husband passed away. He had a truck accident and uh, I was a mass of nothing. I don't even consider myself at that time a human, you know? 'Cause if you would speak a little loud to me, I was already ducking and covering myself 'cause I thought you were gonna hit me. You know? They made me what I am today. I could withstand everything and anything God dishes up to me today. That was when I came to my Nation.

2. Seeking independence

All the females wanted some form of increased autonomy in their lives, as noted in the literature (Joe and Chesney-Lind 1995; Brotherton 1996). They wanted to be rid of their family's restrictive ties on their social lives and on their sexuality; they wanted to be free of abusive relationships and of disrespectful men in general; and they wanted the freedom to be "somebody" through continuing their education and eventually choosing a career beyond the options normally reserved for children of the barrio. Queen A. and Queen F., below, respond to questions on their home life and leave no doubt about the clash between parents who tried to enforce the old gendered family traditions of the "island" and the more liberal approaches to the urban family in New York:

> Queen A: I was always home. Always home. I guess, the way my mother brought me up, it was the women who have to stay in the house. . . . Most of the time always home, home, home, helping my mom . . . I didn't have many friends, girlfriends no. . . . Then I met the Nation I got involved by my ex-husband, he mainly got me involved first.
>
> Queen F: I had a lot of rules and regulations. I could never go outside, I could never have a boyfriend, I could never be with my friends, or nothin.' I would just have to come home, do my homework, eat, take a shower, and then go to bed and then go to school the next day.

3. The surrogate family

The literature notes that in certain cases, females—particularly at the beginning of their gang tenure—can view the group as a replacement family.

Certainly, the Nation in its manifesto and prayers constantly refers to itself as a greater Latino family that provides unconditional love and acceptance to those who are privileged to become members, and this same sentiment was reflected in many of the respondents' retorts:

C: What does family mean to you?

S: All my Latin King/Queen Nation.

C: And how do you define that?

S: Beautiful. Love, respect, I'm treated like gold, you know, like I should've been treated, you know? That's my life. You know, if I fall they're there to pick me up. They raised me, you know? I grew up in it.

There are few reports in the literature of cases where older members of a group such as the Nation both formally and informally adopt young females who have been victimized or abandoned by their rightful kin. Yet this practice was not at all uncommon in the ALKQN (we should also add that some older females also adopted younger males).

C: OK. Are you closer to your mother or your father?

Queen B: Um, see, I'm a daddy's little girl 'cos I have so much hate for my mom. Not hate, but she put me through so much shit it's like everybody want me to swallow it and I just can't. I've been swallowin' it for too many years, and I'm a daddy's little girl, but I never had a daddy. That's where King Step comes in. Now I'm a daddy's little girl 'cos that's my daddy.

Queen S: I have a father through the Nation, you know? He adopted me through the court system. That's when I first joined the Nation and I was in trouble with the law and they helped me out big time, you know? . . . They would always help me when I had a problem with my boyfriend. They was always there for me. It was just a family to me before I came in.

4.   The complementary family

Much of the gang intervention literature paints the gang-family connection in highly simplistic and alarmist terms, portraying persons who join gangs as virtually bereft of past family ties. This was not at all the case with most of the respondents, however, who emphasized repeatedly that the Nation-family nexus was complex, flexible, and subject to change over time. Certainly, as we have noted, when the member came from a particularly destructive family background, the Nation played a surrogate family role, but for those members who came into the Nation from high-functioning and cohesive family backgrounds it was a different picture.

C: What does family mean to you?

F: Now? I mean, since I've been in the Nation family means a lot to me, but my mother and my sisters they mean the world. They mean the world. My mother and my sister, but the Nation, they mean the world to me, too. I mean, I love the Nation to death.

In other words, often the family-Nation relationship was quite complementary for female members, and several leaders reported working diligently with parents to get their children back into school and/or to bring more discipline and social control into their lives (e.g., imposing 10:00 p.m. curfews on young female members during weekdays). Because Nation members under eighteen years old have to get their parents' permission to join the group, it can be understood why the organization can have a much more open, reciprocal, and supportive relationship with a member's family than is supposed by many outside the group.

ECONOMIC SURVIVAL

In a number of studies, some of which fall within the "liberation hypothesis," researchers have found females participating as gang members in the illicit marketplace driven by blocked opportunities. Among the Queens, respondents spoke of many different types of support related to improving their economic standing, but none of it was related to the illegal, informal economy.

The respondents referred to the following kinds of aid that the group offered: (1) help during pregnancy such as the holding of baby showers to provide clothes and furniture for the new baby; (2) babysitting for single mothers to help them navigate the welfare system and attend job interviews; (3) employment contacts in the legitimate economy, especially in the nonprofit sector; (4) referrals to job training services, particularly women facing new welfare/workfare regulations; (5) help with housing (e.g., keeping a list of friendly landlords and when necessary, providing temporary housing for homeless Queens); (6) educational support for Queens attending school or GED classes, including in-house tutoring and peer pressure to succeed; and

(7) short-term loans from a Queens welfare fund (set up in 1999 with female members contributing five dollars per month). Below, a member explains the Queens' attitude to mutual aid:

C: Tell me about how you resolve some of your conflicts?

Queen H: There's always problems as for the school. . . . The girls sometimes they have kids and it's hard so they need somebody to listen to
them . . . we always do, no matter what. We are always there in good
and bad situations. We are always there and always there to help
them. It's hard, 'cos, you know, with bein' a mother goin' to work
and goin' to school. . . . We're there. Day or night. If it's in the
meeting or it's not in the meeting, we'll call each other and we'll
speak upon it and they'll feel relief. They always tell me, "Thank you,
my sister. I needed that." There's times I always need someone to
talk to and they're always there. I can never say they're never there for
me. They are always there. Always.

C: So what kind of conflicts most frequently occur within the group?

Queen H: You know, the babies and schooling . . . when they need Pam-
pers or they need this . . . we're there. You know, it's little things but
we always got each other and we be strong and we support them and
the conflict goes away real quick and they'll go right away and do
what they gotta do. Yeah.

C: So the conflicts get resolved by talkin' or . . . ?

Queen H: Yeah, or if they need an economic way with money we always
there. . . . It comes out of our pockets. They ain't nothing to it. If
somebody needs something, there you go. There's always a helping
hand. There's never nobody that tells us no. It's always somebody
there to help us.

COMMUNITY/FAMILY NETWORKS

A number of females reported joining the group because, for them, it was a natural thing to do (Thrasher 1927). In essence, it was harder to stay "neutral" than to inquire about membership and, if accepted, enter the first stage of induction (called "Five Alive"). Respondents who reported membership via these channels spoke of encountering Kings and Queens in their immediate families or as part of their friendship networks "hanging out" at the local park, at handball courts, on the stoop, or outside of their apartment buildings. Girls who joined mainly because of their peers were usually brought into the organization through contacts with male family members or boyfriends and only a small minority joined through their female friends. Toward the end of the research, however, as the Queens section grew, we noticed that a number of new Pee Wee recruits were being brought to meetings via female contacts.

> Queen T.: I have family in it. I have cousins . . . probably three . . . and
> people I grew up with, everybody in it, and then my family was in it
> so wherever I would go there was Kings—always Kings, anywhere I
> would go there was always Kings, and so I started hanging out with
> them.

> Queen P.: I was just always around them, regardless . . . it just became a
> way of life, naturally. . . . I would look at the Kings and stuff like that
> and my cousin, he was in it since he was real young, um, my mother
> was into jail. She's become a Queen, too. It just happened. It just
> started. You know, I was always with them.

WORKING CLASS/UNDERCLASS EXPERIENCE

The literature is full of accounts of lower-class, urban youth seeking self-respect in schools, on the streets in their neighborhoods, and in the criminal justice system (Sullivan 1989; Bortner and Williams 1998; Anderson 1999). This struggle for self-recognition and subjectivity (McDonald 2000) by such youths is in response to the fragmentation of whole communities brought about by intergenerational social and economic disinvestment (Wilson 1987). However, although there is a great deal of discussion about males, there has been relatively little attention paid to working-class females who are also in search of equal treatment, recognition, opportunities for leadership, and increased self-value (Brown 1998). We have divided this final part of the analysis into three aspects of life that are integral to the working-class and subproletarian experience: dignity, self-control, and politics.

1. The struggle for dignity and respect
Most of the literature, when referring to the tangible benefits of gang membership, often mention the real or illusory increase in power, prestige, and status that members feel as they become part of the street aristocracy (Katz

1988). In such accounts, it is argued that the source of such power among gang members resides in their leverage over others and, in particular, in their ability to issue and make good on threats (Decker and Van Winkle 1996) vis à vis other gang and nongang members. The role of power in gaining dignity and respect in the ALKQN, according to the respondents, was seen quite differently.

In the lessons of the Nation (that all members have to learn) there are innumerable passages that encourage and require members to reach a level of inner strength as part of becoming a new man or a new woman. As members gain knowledge of their own individual and collective potential, they are obliged to demonstrate this increased mastery of their environment as living examples of the Kings' and Queens' doctrine. This release of the inner power of the individual as well as the collective power of the organization is in direct contrast to most members' objectively low power status within the mainstream society. A Queen, below, discusses what attracted her to the ALKQN and the importance she places on others' appearance and physical aura, and on their ability to exude self-control, dignity, and pride:

> c: I want to talk to you about the organization that you are currently a member of. How did you learn about it?
>
> f: My friend, well, first of all, she was going out with a King. He would be with us every day. I seen how they carried themselves, I seen how they showed each other so much love. They like were so proud of themselves. I was like really I would really like to get to know more about them, and that's how I joined the organization.

2. Regaining self-control

As noted earlier, some of the literature refers to females seeking out gangs to experiment and escape from the rigors of lower-class existence (Fleischer 1998). However, a rather different picture emerges from many of the respondents when asked about their previous lifestyles.

At least half of the females reported problems with drugs in the past, especially crack and to a lesser extent heroin. Some of them had engaged in selling and simultaneously using while others were just abusers. In a number of cases, their pathway into drugs began with the modeling effect of their parent(s) who had made drugs a normative aspect of domestic life. But the onset of addiction often came with running away from home and surviving on the streets. Under such conditions of extreme vulnerability and insecurity, drugs were used to mask depression and/or gain acceptance into other marginal peer groups. The Nation usually entered their lives at the stage when they were deciding to go "straight," providing them with a holistic, almost therapeutic milieu, complete with structure, ideology, and a social support system that fostered high levels of self-esteem and self-efficacy, helping them to regain a level of self-control they had not known in many years, if ever. Below, Queen G. describes her pathway back to a drug-free life style:

C: So you told me about the drugs. Did that affect your neighborhood or any family?

G: It didn't affect my family, it affected me, you know, because I wanted to be known, I wanted to be popular, I wanted to have money, I wanted to be . . . you know? The best. You know? Have the best dressing, so I started selling drugs but not using and after a while I started smoking marijuana and then I went into heroin and then I met my husband after a while and then he stopped me from it— which his name is King James, he stopped me and everything. That's when I started coming to the Nation. I read about it, you know, no drugs, no nothin', and I said, "well I like it, I have to come into it," and I stopped, and they helped me. Well, the old people that used to be here, the old Kings and the old Queens, they helped me kick my drug habit because I had a really bad drug habit. I didn't go into methadone programs or nothin' like that, I did it by myself with the Nation. Yeah, they became my sisters while I kicked the drugs, and from then I've been clean, just cigarettes.

3. Looking for politics

There is very little literature that addresses the political orientations of young working-class females, especially females involved in gangs. Respondents in this study often referred to engaging in political thinking prior to joining the ALKQN but feeling frustrated at the absence of movements in which to become involved. In contrast, all the respondents reported that on entering the Nation, they were immediately involved in a program of activism and community solidarity. Queen H. explains below how she felt about joining:

C: I want to talk to you about the organization of which you are a current member. How did you learn about it?

H: By my ex husband, he mainly got involved first. Don't ask me how, but he just did it. He came home and said, "This is great! They have so many things about the people, that we could help each other and help the poor," and, you know, all this and all that, so I was like, "Hmmm." I'm not gonna lie, at first, I thought it was a gang, yeah. I did, 'cos I wasn't familiar with any activities of gang members, but, you know, out here, you know how it is in the street. But as I go along he kept bringin' me the papers and kept tellin' me, you know . . . things to do and activities and rallies and I was like, "That sound great. That sound great. I think I should join. Why not? Why not help our people? Nobody else is gonna do it for us, right?"

For many new members, part of their initiation into the group was to help out at homeless shelters and soup kitchens around the city. Usually, within a few weeks, they would get their first taste of street politics, finding themselves marching on issues related to police brutality, Puerto Rican political prisoners, public education, and AIDS funding, attending weekly culture classes organized by the group, and listening to discussions of local and national political importance in their monthly "universals" meetings. Below, Queen S. and Queen J., both leading members of a youth section in Manhattan, respond to questions about the nature of their political consciousness:

C: Can you describe your heroes or heroines?:

Queen S.: Lolita LeBron. I love her, I swear I do. . . . She was part like of an organization that used to go around to all of the Latin countries and fight for independence for Puerto Rico . . . she went around everywhere by herself with no money. . . . This is why I know it can be done, if one person can set their mind and heart and everything to do it, it can be done.

C: What are the main goals of the organization?

Queen J.: To show our people that we don't have to take what society says that we have to. We don't have to be second-class citizens in America, you know, that we can achieve the American dream. You know, we don't have to say, "Oh, well, they're arresting such and such number of Hispanics every day. Oh, well." No. "Why are they arresting that many? What's going on in the community that they've chosen this way of life that gets them arrested?" . . . In the community that we come from everyone's searching for hope, everyone's searching for a way to make a difference and when it comes down to the Kings and Queens they see that opportunity to make a difference.

As we have stated, most Queens come from backgrounds where racism, sexism, poverty, and limited opportunities are prevalent. They joined the Nation in search of empowerment, identity, and support to compensate for a life in which they have often been left to fend for themselves as children and then left with minimal support to take care of their own children. For most of these women, social institutions have failed them or they have been largely absent, the schools they attended did a better job of alienating them than educating them, the families they emerged from were often riven with inner conflict and turmoil, the male relationships they were exposed to fell short of their needs and sometimes were purely based on abuse. Ironically, for many Queens the only time they received any guidance and help was if they had served time in prison. There they received anger management classes, conflict resolution techniques, and psychiatric help, and on their release they used this knowledge to tutor their fellow sisters on what they had learned.

This focus on the situated agency of the Queens is not to say that the Nation was without its limitations and contradictions. While it incorporated these women into a male-dominated organization and gave them the tools to empower themselves and to once again take control of their lives, it did so without fully engaging its own sexist rules, established hierarchies, and culture(s), even though the reform period was the first time that such a process had been attempted within the group. Thus there were lots of double standards still being applied to the Queens by the Kings and it was not accidental that during the three years of our study, more than five leaders of the Queens came and went, due to conflicts over: (1) demands by females for more power in the organization; (2) sexual transgressions for which females were punished and not the males; (3) male leadership double standards demoralizing the females; and (4) divisions within the Queens between factions upholding traditional models of womanhood and those who wanted a more radical agenda.

Nonetheless, the ALKQN functioned for these women as the only grassroots movement that: was sufficiently indigenous that it could be trusted by the most marginalized of urban females; could or would address their multiple needs at critical junctures in their life course; and offered the opportunities for emotional, spiritual, social, and political growth that few other organizations have dared to imagine. Although the layered motives that caused these women to seek out such a group have been reported in other studies, among the Queens we have found that the degree of purposive action, utopian imagination, and sociocultural resilience that are all part of the motivation process (Touraine 1988) was higher than with any other cohort found in the literature. Further, the characteristics of the organization they joined, the ALKQN, were also very different to almost all other gang groups reported in gang female studies, further justifying the need to embrace noncriminological theories and definitions to account for the range of street female collective practices. Finally, the group's emphases on politics, structure, self-renewal, sisterhood, male-female solidarity, cultural affirmation, and spirituality not only make the mix of "lures" for troubled, victimized, and simply curious lower-class females more understandable but they explain why so many other "mainstream" interventions fail to attract such respondents.

NOTES

1. By *street organization* we mean: "a group formed largely by youth and adults of a marginalized social class which aims to provide its members with a resistant identity, an opportunity to be individually and collectively empowered, a voice to speak back to and challenge the dominant culture, a refuge from the stresses and strains of barrio or ghetto life and a spiritual enclave within which its own sacred rituals can be generated and practiced" (Brotherton and Barrios, forthcoming).

2. Among the reasons cited in the literature behind this male centrism are: the male dominance and male positionality of social scientists (Harding 1987), the mutually reinforcing effects of "cognitive purification" and urban male stereotyping (Moore 1991), and the tautological reasoning that because males do most of the crime, they should receive most of the attention (as if males emerged from a gendered vacuum).

3. At least in nonjournalistic, social scientific accounts.

4. However, based on the more recent literature on gang females (and males), we might conclude that the instrumental aspect of gang membership has been more associated with male gang members and that females are more drawn by a gang's "social benefits."

5. Eleven refused to answer the question, which probably indicates that the rate of abuse was much higher.

6. The respondents saw the source of their own identity as women contingent on the broader notion of community uplifting and empowerment—the achievement of which would bring with it a level of resources from which they, as Latinas, could demand both individual and collective respect.

REFERENCES

Anderson, Elijah. 1999. *Code of the Street : Decency, Violence, and the Moral Life of the Inner City.* New York: Norton.

Bortner, M. A., and Linda M. Williams. 1998. *Youth in Prison.* New York: Routledge.

Bourgois, Philippe. 1995. *In Search of Respect: Selling Crack in El Barrio.* Cambridge: Cambridge University Press.

Brake, Mike. 1985. *Comparative Youth Cultures: The Sociology of Youth Culture and Youth Subcultures in America, Britain, and Canada.* London: Routledge and Kegan Paul.

Brotherton, David C. 1996. " 'Smartness,' 'Toughness,' and 'Autonomy': Drug Use in the Context of Gang Female Delinquency." *Journal of Drug Issues,* 26: 261–277.

———. 1998. "The Old Heads Tell Their Stories." *Free Inquiry in Creative Sociology,* 27 (1): 1–15.

Brotherton, David C., and Luis Barrios. Forthcoming. *Between Black and Gold: The Street Politics of the Almighty Latin King and Queen Nation.*

Brown, Lyn Mikel. 1998. *Raising Their Voices: The Politics of Girls' Anger.* Cambridge: Harvard University Press.

Campbell, Anne. 1984. *The Girls in the Gang.* New York: Basil Blackwell.

Chesney-Lind, Meda, and John M. Hagedorn. 1999. *Female Gangs in America: Essays on Girls, Gangs, and Gender.* Chicago: Lake View Press.

Conquergood, Dwight. 1997. "Street Literacy" In James Flood, Shirley Brice Heath, and Diane Lapp, eds., *Handbook of Research on Teaching Literacy through the Communicative and Visual Arts.* New York: Simon and Schuster/Macmillan.

Curry, G. David. 1998. "Female Gang Involvement." *Journal of Research in Crime and Delinquency,* 35: 100–118.

Decker, Scott H., and Van Winkle, Barrik. 1996. *Life in the Gang.* Cambridge: Cambridge University Press.

Fishman, Laura T. 1995. "The Vice Queens: An Ethnographic Study of Black Female Gang Behavior." In Malcolm W. Klein, Cheryl L. Maxson, and Jody Miller, eds., *The Modern Gang Reader,* 83–92. Los Angeles: Roxbury Publishing Company.

Hagedorn, John M. 1998. *People and Folks: Gangs, Crime, and the Underclass in a Rustbelt City.* 2d ed. Chicago: Lakeview Press.

Harding, Sandra, ed. 1987. *Feminism and Methodology.* Bloomington: Indiana University Press.

Harris, Mary G. 1988. *Cholas: Latino Girls and Gangs.* New York: AMS.

Hunt, Geoffrey, Kathleeen McKenzie, and Karen A. Laidler-Joe. 2000. " 'I'm

Calling My Mom': The Meaning of Family and Kinship among Homegirls." *Justice Quarterly*, 17 (1): 1–31.

Joe, Karen A., and Chesney-Lind, Meda. 1995. " 'Just Every Mother's Angel': An Analysis of Gender and Ethnic Variations in Youth Gang Membership." *Gender and Society*, 9: 408–430.

Katz, Jack. 1988. *Seductions of Crime: Moral and Sensual Attractions in Doing Evil.* New York: Basic Books.

Lauderback, David, Joy Hansen, and Dan Waldorf. 1992. "'Sisters are Doin' it for Themselves': A Black Female Gang in San Francisco." *The Gang Journal*, 1: 57–70.

Maher, Lisa. 2000. *Sexed Work: Gender, Race, and Resistance in a Brooklyn Drug Market.* New York: Oxford University Press.

McDonald, Kevin. 2000. *Struggles for Subjectivity.* Cambridge: University of Cambridge Press.

Mendoza-Denton. 1995. " 'Muy Macha': Gender and Ideology in Gang Girls' Discourse about Makeup." *Ethnos*, 61 (1–2): 47–63.

Miller, Jody. 2001. *One of the Guys: Girls, Gangs, and Gender.* New York : Oxford University Press.

Moore, Joan. 1991. *Going Down to the Barrio: Homeboys and Homegirls in Change.* Philadelphia: Temple University Press.

Moore, Joan, and John M. Hagedorn. 2001. "Female Gangs: A Focus on Research." OJJDP report. Washington, D.C.: U.S. Department of Justice, Office of Justice Programs, Office of Juvenile Justice and Delinquency Prevention.

Morgan, Patricia, and Karen Joe. 1996. "Citizens and Outlaws: The Private Lives and Public Lifestyles of Women in the Illicit Drug Economy." *Journal of Drug Issues*, vol. 26, no. 1 (winter): 125–142.

Pfohl, Stephen. 1985. *Images of Deviance and Social Control: A Sociological History.* New York: McGraw Hill.

Quicker, John C. 1983. *Homegirls: Characterizing Chicana Gangs.* San Pedro, Calif.: International University Press.

Sullivan, Mercer. 1989. *"Getting Paid": Youth Crime and Work in the Inner City.* Ithaca, N.Y.: Cornell University Press.

Taylor, Carl. 1993. *Girls, Gangs, Women, and Drugs.* East Lansing: Michigan State University Press.

Thomas, Piri. 1967. Down These Mean Streets. New York: Knopf.

Thrasher, Frederick M. 1927. *The Gang.* Chicago: University of Chicago Press.

Touraine, Alain. 1988. *Return of the Actor.* Minneapolis: University of Minneapolis Press.

Venkatesh, Sudhir Alladi. 2000. *American Project: The Rise and Fall of an American Ghetto.* Cambridge: Harvard University Press.

Vigil, James Diego. 1988. *Barrio Gangs.* Austin: University of Texas Press.

Weber, M. 1946. *The Methodology of the Social Sciences.* New York: Free Press.

Widom, Cathy Spatz. 1998. "Childhood Victimization: Early Adversity and Subsequent Psychopathology." In B. P. Dohrenwend, ed., *Adversity, Stress, and Psychopathology*, 81–95. New York: Oxford University Press.

Wilson, William Julius. 1987. *The Truly Disadvantaged: The Inner City, the Underclass, and Public Policy*. Chicago: University of Chicago Press.

PART 5

GANGS AND
SOCIAL CONTROL

11

GANGS AND THE LAW

LOREN SIEGEL

A recurring theme in American legal history is the targeting of pariah groups whose members serve as scapegoats for a whole range of social, political, and economic problems. Members of these groups—whether they are political radicals, immigrants, or welfare mothers—are invariably denied basic civil liberties that are guaranteed to others. Often, particularly during periods of social, political, or economic stress, the courts go along with majoritarian prejudices, rather than protecting minority rights.

This happened during the time of World War I, and again in the 1950s, when "red scares" brought intense assaults on First Amendment rights to freedom of speech, press, and association. The "threat of international communism" and political subversion were used to justify police infiltration of political groups, ideological jailings, loyalty oaths, mass deportations, and congressional inquisitions. Similarly, during World War II, a potent combination of racism and war hysteria led to the internment of 110,000 Japanese American citizens and the confiscation of their property by the U.S. government. Although no interned Japanese American was ever charged or even suspected of treason or espionage, this crude deprivation of liberty and property withstood constitutional challenge: "Pressing public necessity," said the Supreme Court, "may sometimes justify the existence of such restrictions."

Gangs and suspected gang members are today one of American society's pariah groups, and their basic rights have been under sustained attack for some time. According to the National Youth Gang Center, a research arm of the federal government's Office of Juvenile Justice and Delinquency Prevention (OJJDP), more than 70 percent of all states have enacted some form of legislation relating to gangs.[1] Although some of these laws address legitimate law enforcement problems like drive-by shootings and car jackings, many involve constitutionally questionable tactics. This chapter will describe three current antigang legal tactics, each of which raises grave constitutional concerns: gang loitering laws, antigang injunctions, and gang databases.

GANG LOITERING LAWS

Loitering laws and their first cousins, vagrancy laws, have a long history in this country and have always been used to remove "undesirable" people from public places before they had the chance to engage in criminal activity. They differ from traditional criminal laws in that they make it a crime simply to be a person of a certain status or condition. In the nineteenth century, the U.S. Supreme Court ruled that vagrancy laws were a "necessity":

> We think it as competent and as necessary for a state to provide precautionary measures against this moral pestilence of paupers, vagabonds, and possible conflicts; as it is to guard against the physical pestilence.[2]

But in 1972, a more civil libertarian Court issued its landmark decision in *Papachristou v. City of Jacksonville,* striking down a loitering law that prohibited "wandering or strolling around from place to place without any lawful purpose or object."[3] The Court ruled that the law was void for vagueness, meaning that it "fails to give a person of ordinary intelligence fair notice that his contemplated conduct is forbidden" and thus violated the right to due process of the law. Following *Papachristou,* most vagrancy and loitering laws were found to be unconstitutional by state and federal courts.

Nonetheless, municipalities continue to experiment with this inherently unconstitutional legal tactic.

In June 1992, just prior to a dramatic decline in national crime rates, but under growing pressure to "do something" about the gang problem, the Chicago City Council held public hearings. More than thirty citizens testified about troubling illegal gang activities occurring in their neighborhoods. They also described their efforts to obtain adequate police services and their growing frustration with the Chicago Police Department. Those who testified did not so much seek passage of new laws as they did better and more consistent enforcement of already existing laws. Witnesses from inner-city neighborhoods complained that the police took too long to respond to calls for help or simply did not show up at all. Alderman Steele testified that the City of Chicago already had a curfew law, a safe school law, and other laws on the books, and suggested they were being inadequately enforced. And Alderman Jones expressed concern that a loitering-type ordinance would bring back the days of street sweeps in the early 1980s.

Chicago Police Deputy Superintendent Gerald Cooper was the only police representative to testify at the hearings. Although he acknowledged that the ordinance could provide "another tool" for law enforcement, he also expressed concern that the police had "been down this road before" and predicted that "innocent or lawful people" would be arrested under the ordinance. Deputy Superintendent Cooper also noted that in about 90 percent of the examples of gang conduct given at the hearing, gang members would be subject to arrest under existing laws.

In spite of this less-than-ringing endorsement, the Chicago City Council enacted the Gang Congregation Ordinance.[4] Supporters of the law justified its passage on the grounds that:

> The very presence of a large collection of obviously brazen, insistent, and lawless gang members and hangers-on on the public ways intimidates residents, who become afraid even to leave their homes and go about their business. That, in turn, imperils community residents' sense of safety and security, detracts from property values, and can ultimately destabilize entire neighborhoods.[5]

The ordinance prohibited "criminal street gang members" from "loitering" and provided that "whenever a police officer observes a person whom he reasonably believes to be a criminal street-gang member loitering in any public place with one or more persons, he shall order all persons to disperse and remove themselves from the area." Loitering was defined by the law as "to remain in any one place with no apparent purpose." Failing to obey the order to disperse was a criminal offense punishable by a fine of up to $500, imprisonment for not more than six months, and 120 hours of community service.

Soon after its enactment, the ACLU of Illinois challenged the law, but it remained in effect for three years while the lawsuit was pending. During that time, the Chicago police issued more than 89,000 dispersal orders and arrested more than 42,000 people for violating the ordinance.[6] The ordinance was enforced on the streets, in parks, at schools, and in housing projects. Most of those targeted by the police were African American and Latino residents, many of whom were not gang members.

Loitering ordinances are inherently vague (and have been invalidated by the U.S. Supreme Court on "void for vagueness" grounds), but Chicago's Gang Congregation Ordinance possessed an almost surreal quality. What does "no apparent purpose" mean? How was a police officer to know, without actually listening in on private conversations, whether or not people had gathered for a purpose? The impossibility of rationally applying such a standardless law was highlighted during the trial when the ACLU lawyer offered the following hypothetical situations. In each case, the City's witness conceded that it could reasonably be interpreted by a police officer as having "no apparent purpose," thereby justifying an order to disperse under threat of arrest:

- Two people debating the constitutionality of the ordinance.
- A minister arguing with gang members.
- A community outreach employee actively seeking out gang members to assist them in breaking free of the gang.
- A street corner seminar with gang members on the merits of President Clinton's economic program.

In October 1997, the Illinois Supreme Court found that the Gang Congregation Ordinance was void for vagueness because it (a) provided the police no guidelines for determining when persons have apparent purposes, (b) amounted to a grant of unfettered discretion to police officers, and (c) failed to notify persons of ordinary intelligence what formerly innocent (or lawful) conduct it was criminalizing. Undaunted, the City of Chicago appealed to the U.S. Supreme Court.

In its legal brief to the Court, the ACLU presented five constitutional arguments upon which the Court could strike down the loitering ordinance:

THE ORDINANCE WAS "VOID FOR VAGUENESS"

The Supreme Court's void-for-vagueness doctrine requires that a criminal law define the offense with enough definiteness so that ordinary people can understand what conduct is prohibited. This is a fundamental aspect of due process of law protected by the Fifth and Fourteenth Amendments. But a law prohibiting a person from remaining in one place "without an apparent purpose" is not one to which people can easily conform their conduct. People almost always have a purpose for whatever it is they are doing, but they don't always display their purpose. Would two people harmlessly waiting on a corner for a third person have an "apparent purpose," or would they be subjected to a dispersal order from the police? In its opinion striking the ordinance down, the Illinois Supreme Court agreed:

> People with entirely legitimate and lawful purposes will not always be able to make their purposes apparent to an observing police officer. For example, a person waiting to hail a taxi, resting on a corner during a jog, or stepping into a doorway to evade a rain shower has a perfectly legitimate purpose in all these scenarios; however, that purpose will rarely be apparent to an observer.

The void-for-vagueness doctrine also requires that criminal statutes "establish minimal guidelines to govern law enforcement." Without guidelines, police are apt to substitute their own discretion—and prejudices—for the rule of law. In the *Papachristou* decision invalidating vague loitering laws, the Court warned that such laws furnished a convenient tool for "harsh and discriminatory enforcement by local prosecuting officials against particular groups deemed to merit their displeasure." Given the prevalence of racial profiling by law enforcement agencies in this country, we know that racially discriminatory enforcement is an inevitable consequence of vague criminal laws.

THE ORDINANCE VIOLATED THE RIGHT OF FREE MOVEMENT

The ability to move freely in public places—to take a walk, to jog through a park, to stroll with friends on a warm summer evening—is so basic that most of us don't even think of it as a legal right. It was, however, identified as such in the English Common Law adopted by the American legal system. William Blackstone, the British legal philosopher whose thinking greatly influenced the framers of our Constitution, wrote that: "Personal liberty consists of the power of loco-motion, of changing situation, or removing one's person to whatsoever place one's own inclination may direct."[7] Blackstone's formulation has been echoed in numerous court decisions since. For example, in a landmark 1958 decision in which the Supreme Court ruled that the government could not deny passports to Americans because they were affiliated with the Communist Party, the Court said:

> The right to travel is a part of the "liberty" of which the citizen cannot be deprived without due process of law. . . . Freedom of movement across frontiers in either direction, and inside frontiers as well, was a part of our heritage. . . . Freedom of movement is basic in our scheme of values.[8]

By subjecting to dispersal or arrest anyone who appeared idle in public with another person anytime a police officer suspected one of them was a gang member, the Chicago ordinance violated this fundamental right.

THE ORDINANCE VIOLATED FREE SPEECH

Laws that interfere with citizens' peaceful enjoyment of public streets, sidewalks, and parks directly implicate the First Amendment rights of speech, assembly, and association. The ACLU argued that the Chicago law was "overbroad" because it swept in individuals who were not suspected of being gang members. Its overbreadth was neither speculative nor marginal: Among the documents submitted to the state court by the ACLU was an affidavit from Julio Matias, an antigang counselor, who expressed fear of being arrested if he continued holding meetings with troubled youth in public places. Even a mother talking with her teenage child on a street corner was likely to be ordered to move on and possibly arrested by a police officer who thought her child belonged to a gang. The magnitude of the dispersal orders issued during the three years the ordinance was in effect—89,000 in all—attests to the fact that thousands of innocent people were penalized for thousands of innocent acts.

The ordinance was also overbroad because it swept in the activities of gang members that were not only lawful, but that were constitutionally protected. In increasing numbers of communities, gangs themselves have become engaged in community-based political activities. In Washington, D.C., gangs have formulated a "peace plan" for Latino community development.[9] In Chicago, gangs have been involved in activities around health care, education, voter registration, and the support of candidates for office.[10] In Los Angeles, gangs have organized around issues of employment.[11] These are classic free speech activities that are entitled to the highest level of constitutional protection. The Chicago ordinance was unconstitutional because it placed substantial burdens on the exercise of those rights.

THE ORDINANCE VIOLATED THE EIGHTH AMENDMENT

The Eighth Amendment to the U.S. Constitution protects individuals from the infliction of cruel and unusual punishment by the government. In an important case decided in 1962, the Supreme Court held that the criminalization of status alone amounted to cruel and unusual punishment. In that case, *Robinson v. California*, a state statute making it a crime to "be addicted to the use of narcotics" was struck down. In a 1968 case, *Powell v. Texas*, the Court further explained that although the state could not criminalize alcoholism, it could penalize the conduct of public drunkenness. Together, *Robinson* and *Powell* prohibit the use of the penal power of the state against people, when defined by their status (e.g., drug addict, alcoholic, homeless person, gang member, friend of a gang member), solely upon the belief that they are more prone to criminal behavior than others.

As expected, the City of Chicago argued that the ordinance did not violate the *Robinson-Powell* principle because "loitering" is conduct. But in many communities, including Chicago's lower income neighborhoods, such public behavior (i.e., hanging out) is virtually involuntary: school might be out; jobs might be scarce; home might be without air conditioning; home might even be dangerous. The ordinance violated the Eighth Amendment precisely because it banished from public space a group of individuals defined by their status, and not their actions.

THE ORDINANCE VIOLATED THE FOURTH AMENDMENT

The Fourth Amendment protects each of us against unreasonable searches and seizures and requires that the police obtain a warrant based upon probable cause before they can conduct a search or make an arrest. The Chicago ordinance basically does an end run around the Fourth Amendment, or, as the Appellate Court of Illinois wrote, it is "a transparent attempt to avoid the probable cause requirement." It allows the police to arrest gang members, and anyone with a gang member, upon mere suspicion of future criminal activity.

On 10 June 1999, the Supreme Court issued its long-awaited decision in *City of Chicago v. Morales*. Justice Stevens, writing for the majority, held that the gang loitering ordinance was unconstitutional on void for vagueness grounds because it did not give the public fair notice of what conduct was prohibited:

> It is difficult to imagine how any citizen of the city of Chicago standing in a public place with a group of people would know if he or she had an "apparent purpose." If she were talking to another person, would she have an apparent purpose? If she were frequently checking her watch and looking expectantly down the street, would she have an apparent purpose?

Justice Stevens found that the ordinance also violated the void-for-vagueness doctrine because it failed to establish minimal guidelines to govern law enforcement:

> The mandatory language in the enactment directs the police to issue an order without first making any inquiry about their possible purposes. It matters not whether the reason that a gang member and his father, for example, might loiter near Wrigley Field is to rob an unsuspecting fan or just to get a glimpse of Sammy Sosa leaving the ballpark; in either event, if their purpose is not apparent to a nearby police officer, she may—indeed, she "shall"—order them to disperse.

The decision was a victory for all Americans, but it was an especially meaningful victory for young men of color in Chicago and across the nation.

ANTIGANG INJUNCTIONS

In 1987, when fear of gangs had reached a fever pitch, the Los Angeles City Attorney's Office announced it was going to use a new weapon in the fight against gang violence. This weapon was a court injunction issued against specific members of the Playboy Gangster Crips gang operating in the Cadillac-Corning neighborhood of West Los Angeles. The injunction barred named individuals alleged to be gang members from congregating together, talking on the street, littering, or remaining in public for more than five minutes.

The injunction is a powerful legal remedy that is not really new at all. We inherited it from English Common Law. By issuing an injunction, a court can order a specific person to either perform or cease to perform some action or activity. If the injunction is disobeyed, the violator is subject to contempt penalties, including imprisonment and fines. Injunctions can serve the cause of justice; indeed they were potent weapons in the hands of civil rights advocates who used them to compel southern public schools to desegregate in the 1960s and 1970s. But they can also be an instrument of repression. For example, in the 1930s, before the National Labor Relations Act was passed, companies routinely obtained injunctions against workers and union leaders to prevent them from striking, picketing, or otherwise protesting against unfair labor practices.

California, as is so often the case, was a trendsetter in this instance. State prosecutors hailed the injunction, based on the state's power to abate public nuisances, as a quick and reliable way to save neighborhoods from the grip of violent street gangs. By 1996, gang injunctions had proved to be so popular in California that Governor Pete Wilson included in his proposed budget a $2.5 million "Gang Civil Injunction Fund" which would "provide grants to local prosecutors and underwrite the costs of obtaining and enforcing additional injunctions against threatening or intimidating gang activities.[12] By 1997, injunctions had been issued or were being sought in close to a dozen California cities, including San Jose, Burbank, Los Angeles, Westminster, Pasadena, and Redondo Beach. Perhaps the most far-reaching antigang injunction to date was obtained by the Los Angeles City Attorney's Office in 1993 against the Blythe Street Gang, a Latino gang. The injunction named five hundred members, giving the police enormous powers to suppress any and all activity, both legal and illegal.

The San Jose antigang injunction, obtained in 1993 and upheld by the Supreme Court of California in 1997, named thirty-eight young Latinos who were alleged to be members of two street gangs: the Varrio Sureno Locos, and the Varrio Sureno Treces. It prohibited these alleged gang members from "standing, sitting, walking, driving, gathering, or appearing anywhere in public view" with any other suspected gang member. Those named were barred from carrying "glass bottles, rocks, bricks, chains, tire irons, screwdrivers, hammers, crowbars, bumper jacks, razor blades, razors, sling shots, marbles and ball bearings." They were enjoined from "approaching vehicles, engaging in conversation or otherwise communicating with the occupants of any vehicle," as well as "making, causing, or encouraging others to make loud noises of any kind." *None of these activities are, per se, illegal.* But if performed by a gang member, they could trigger arrest, a six-month jail sentence, and a $1,000 fine.

The ACLU brought a constitutional challenge to the San Jose injunction on behalf of eleven of the young Latino men and women named in the injunction. The ACLU argued that the standards used by the San Jose police to identify individual gang members were extremely broad and subjective. The police conceded at trial, for example, that a person could be labeled a gang member if he or she were seen on just one occasion wearing clothing indicative of gang membership, such as a blue jean jacket, cut-off sweat pants, any clothing associated with the Los Angeles Raiders, or white, blue, gray, black, khaki, or any other "neutral" colored item. As one of the plaintiffs, Miguel Moreno, testified:

> I was stopped by a policeman when I was walking down the street. I was wearing a shirt and cap with Raiders on them and the police officer told me that Raiders clothes were gang clothes. I was only wearing these clothes because I am a Raiders fan and that is what I told the officer. The policeman took my picture without asking me and said it was for his collection.

On the basis of this photo, Miguel Moreno became a suspected gang member, was named in the injunction, and was stripped of his constitutional rights.

In January 1997, the California Supreme Court ruled that cities could constitutionally obtain injunctions against suspected gang members who were otherwise engaging in legal activities, and the ACLU petitioned for review by the U.S. Supreme Court. In its petition for review, the ACLU complained that "the California Supreme Court has expanded the use of the injunctive power beyond precedent and beyond recognition":

> By labeling personal conduct to be a public nuisance, and sweeping within its reach lawful and protected conduct by individuals who have committed nothing wrong, it has permitted local judges to devise local penal codes that allow the police to make arrests on city streets and sidewalks when persons congregate together or "annoy" other persons. In effect, the California Supreme Court has

approved a regime in which a judge may banish persons from joining together in public view in certain neighborhoods by, in essence, imposing conditions of parole prophylactically *before* a crime is committed.[13]

The U.S. Supreme Court was unmoved and refused to review the California court's decision. Although the Court's inaction was not tantamount to an endorsement, for all intents and purposes it gave the green light to other municipalities who were considering the antigang injunction tactic. It is all but certain that the Supreme Court will have to confront the constitutionality of this use of the injunction in the very near future.

GANG DATABASES

Local law enforcement agencies throughout the country are, to an increasing extent, building complex computer databases in order to monitor suspected gang members within their jurisdiction. According to a survey of newspaper accounts by the ACLU, there are plans to develop statewide databases in Florida, Illinois, Ohio, Tennessee, and Wisconsin, as well as plans to create local gang databases in numerous cities, from Albuquerque to Wichita. The federal government is also actively monitoring gangs through its National Gang Tracking Network.

Once again, California has advanced the furthest down this road. Its statewide database program, called CalGang, contains the names of more than two hundred thousand suspected gang members, and it is used primarily for investigative purposes by law enforcement agencies from around the state. CalGang tracks an incredible two hundred data fields on gang members, including personal information such as name, address, physical description, gang moniker, social security number, and associates or acquaintances, as well as information about the gang to which the individual allegedly belongs. The system also includes photographs.

The proliferation of gang-tracking lists and databases raises profound civil liberties problems. They potentially subject individuals who have not committed any unlawful acts to an extremely high level of government scrutiny and surveillance. And because law enforcement agencies are under no legal obligation to notify an individual that he or she has been entered into a gang database, those mistakenly entered have no way to contest their inclusion. This offends the most basic notions of due process of law and the right to privacy. The database issue has not yet been fully litigated, and at the present time, the government's ability to collect and track gang members is more or less unfettered.

It is important to understand that gang membership is not, in and of itself, against the law. The First Amendment's guarantees of freedom of assembly and association have long been interpreted by the Supreme Court to mean that an individual cannot be penalized solely for membership in a group, even if that group advocates illegal acts. Rather, it must be shown that the group has unlawful aims *and* the individual specifically intends to further those aims.[14]

Nonetheless, under current practice, not only "suspected gang members," but also "gang associates," may be included, so that young people who have done nothing more than hang around with gang members at parties or on a street corner can find themselves enmeshed in a nationwide web of linked gang databases. The criteria for inclusion can be frighteningly broad. Officials in Burbank and Westminster, California, for example, were allowing identification of a gang member for database purposes if *just one* of the following criteria were satisfied: self admission; tattoos indicating gang membership; clothing indicating gang membership; the statement of a reliable informer within the gang; or association with other gang members along with commission of gang-related crimes. And because decisions about gang affiliations are usually left entirely to the discretion of police officers, abuses inevitably follow.

Several years ago, three Vietnamese American girls, Minh Tram, Quyen Pham, and Annie Lee were waiting to use a pay phone in downtown Garden Grove, California. An unmarked car drove up and two men got out and identified themselves as police officers. One of the girls later testified:

> They detained us and said we looked like gangbangers. We told them we were waiting for my brother to pick us up, and we said we were going to page him. They made some comment about how we were probably paging someone to get drugs. One officer sat us down and gave us a whole talk about how if you walk like a duck and talk like a duck . . . and then he said we're nothing more than street kids. This had never happened to us before, so we all started crying. Then they lined us up against a wall and took our pictures.

All three girls were honor students at their high school. Their only "crime" was wearing baggy pants.

The FBI also has a database, the Violent Gang and Terrorist Organization File, which local police agencies are encouraged to dump their data into. It is not an exaggeration to say that federal and state law enforcement agencies are labeling huge numbers of young people as suspected gangsters in massive databases without their knowledge, without due process or clear confirmation that the information is accurate, and without clear controls over how the information can be used.

Inclusion in a gang database significantly increases the likelihood of police harassment and detention, because the police refer to it in the course of criminal investigations. In a lawsuit challenging the San Jose Police Department's use of an "Asian mugbook," for example, Ted Nguyen, a young Vietnamese man who had never been arrested for a crime, was falsely identified as the perpetrator of a robbery by a witness looking at the mugbook. Although eventually acquitted, Nguyen spent three months in jail, and he was stigmatized in his own community merely for appearing in the mugbook.

There is also real concern that the police are disclosing this information to schools, landlords, and employers. A letter recently received by the ACLU of Georgia suggests that this is happening in some states. The letter was from a high school student who used to be a member of a gang. He wrote that he had been in foster care for two years and was trying to make a clean start by staying out of trouble and maintaining a B average. But when he tried to attend a school dance, he was refused admittance because he was on the school's "Gang List."

As is the case in so many other areas of the criminal justice system, the gang databases disproportionately target people of color. Reverend Oscar Tillman, a senior official with the Denver NAACP, upon learning that two out of three young black men in Denver were on a gang suspect list, complained, "They ought to call it the blacklist. This is harassment. It's not a crackdown on gangs; it's a crackdown on blacks."[15] The overinclusion of African Americans on Denver's gang list is particularly shocking because blacks are only 5 percent of that city's population (but 47 percent of the gang database).

Other cities' databases suffer from the same racial bias. According to a report by the Los Angeles District Attorney's Office, 46.8 percent of the African American men between the ages of twenty-one and twenty-four in L.A. County have been entered into the police gang-tracking database. In contrast, less than one-half of one percent of white men in the same age group have been entered into the system. San Jose's database is 95 percent nonwhite; 69 percent Latino. For young people of color, the United States is coming more and more to resemble the kind of police state that existed in the former Soviet Union and the countries of Eastern Europe. Relative anonymity is one of the hallmarks of a free society, but for tens of thousands of Blacks, Latinos, and Asian Americans, including many who have never committed an illegal act, anonymity is no longer possible. Their names, addresses, and telephone numbers, and other personal information, are easily accessible to the police and other law enforcement agencies.

It is impossible to avoid the similarities between antigang legal tactics today, and those that were in play against communists and other left-wing individuals during the McCarthy period. Then, as now, there were blacklists. Then, as now, people were labeled based on who they associated with, rather than on any unlawful acts they may have committed. Then as now, once you were on the list, there was no way to get off it, assuming that you knew you were on the list in the first place. Then, as now, the rights to privacy, freedom of association, due process, and equality were under severe assault.

One piece of good news is that the 1997 California Supreme Court decision upholding the San Jose antigang injunction as constitutional was not unanimous. One lone justice, Judge Stanley Mosk, wrote an eloquent dissent from the majority's opinion that was true to constitutional principles:

> The majority would permit our cities to close off entire neighborhoods to Latino youths who have done nothing more than dress in blue or black clothing or associate with others who do so; they would authorize criminal penalties for ordinary, nondisruptive acts of walking or driving through a residential neighborhood with a relative or friend. In my view, such a blunderbuss approach amounts to both bad law and bad policy. There are some who think that the way to save freedom in this country is to adopt the techniques of tyranny. The majority here appear to embrace that misguided belief. Accordingly, I dissent.[16]

Often, powerful dissents, though lonely when written, eventually come to be adopted by court majorities. One day, it is hoped, Justice Mosk's interpretation of the law will prove to be one of those prematurely correct opinions.

NOTES

1. On-line, available: <http://www.iir.com/nygc/gang-legis/analysis.htm>.
2. *Mayor of New York v. Miln*, U.S. Supreme Court (1837).
3. *Papachristou v. City of Jacksonville*, 405 U.S. 156 (1972).
4. Chicago Municipal Code 8-4-015 (added 17 June 1992).
5. From the City of Chicago's brief to the U.S. Supreme Court, *City of Chicago v. Morales*.
6. *City of Chicago v. Morales*, U.S. Supreme Court (June 1999).
7. William Blackstone, commentaries 134 (1765).
8. *Kent v. Dulles*, U.S. Supreme Court (1958).
9. Pamela Constable, " 'Peace Summit' Aims to Steer Young Latinos from Gang Violence," *Washington Post*, 4 April 1996, p. B5.
10. Don Terry, "Chicago Gangs, Extending Turf, Turn to Politics," *New York Times*, 25 October 1993, p. A12.
11. "Gang Summit Ends with Call for Jobs," *Los Angeles Times*, 3 May 1993, p. A13.
12. Office of the Governor, Governor's Budget Summary, 10 January 1996, "State and Local Alliance for Public Safety," p. 2.
13. ACLU Petition for a Writ of Certiorari in *Gonzalez v. Gallo*, dated 30 April 1997, p. 15.
14. *Healy v. James*, 408 U.S. 169, 186 (1972).
15. Dirk Johnson, "2 Out of 3 Young Black Men in Denver Are on Gang Suspect List," *New York Times*, 11 December 1993, p. A8.
16. Dissent in *Gallo v. Acuna*, 1997, U.S. LEXIS 4093.

12

THE GANG CRACKDOWN IN THE PRISONS OF MASSACHUSETTS: ARBITRARY AND HARSH TREATMENT CAN ONLY MAKE MATTERS WORSE

PHILLIP KASSEL

A version of this paper was originally published in the *New England Journal of Civil and Criminal Confinement* (winter 1998). Some of the details of the administration of the Massachusetts Department of Correction's policy toward alleged prison gangs have changed since then. The policy as of August 2002, however, operates essentially as described herein, and any minor changes do not affect the analysis set forth.

Both the media and law enforcement officials often attribute more coherence and organization to street gangs and prison gangs than really exists.[1]

> Prison gangs present a unique and different problem for correctional administrators. . . . [Their] activities pose a substantial threat to the orderly operations of individual institutions and the total operation of the Department. Operating through force, intimidation, secrecy, extreme loyalty to fellow gang members and dedication to their individual gang by-laws, charters, manifesto's, etc., gangs' potential for destructive activity is well recognized nationwide by corrections officials.[2]

In April 1995, citing the security threat posed by incarcerated street gang members, Commissioner Larry E. DuBois ordered the transfer of approximately 135 prisoners[3] so identified to Massachusetts Correctional Institution-Cedar Junction (MCI-CJ),[4] the state's maximum security prison. DuBois announced that certain members of gangs, referred to as "security threat groups," (STGs)[5] would thereafter be subject to "restrictive housing" at MCI-CJ and be prohibited from transferring to an institution less restrictive than medium security.

Approximately 90 percent of the prisoners confined to the MCI-CJ housing units reserved for alleged gang members are Latinos.[6] These prisoners are locked in their cells virtually all of the time and are otherwise maintained in extremely harsh conditions. They may reasonably have anticipated that during the period of their incarceration they would move from medium to minimum security and then prerelease facilities prior to consideration of parole and their ultimate discharge.[7]

The legality of the DOC gang policy is more than open to question,[8] but this chapter will focus on public policy considerations. A description of the policy and how it is applied will be followed by an analysis of its likely ramifications in light of research on gang structure and behavior.

The conclusion set forth is that the DOC gang policy is not merely unfair, or even cruel, it is counterproductive. Labeling and mistreatment actually encourage prisoner self-identification as gang members. Practices that reinforce gang member commitment to the group enhance gang cohesiveness and criminal capacity, undermining both prison security and public safety. Fair disciplinary policies, focusing on prisoner conduct, staff training, and educational opportunities that offer an alternative identity to that of gang member, are more effective strategies for preventing prison disturbances and promoting safer communities.

THE GANG POLICY IN OPERATION

The ostensible purpose of the DOC gang policy[9] is to avoid prison disturbances fomented by gangs. Despite this, no coherent statement of how the gang policy is designed to accomplish this end exists. Nevertheless, it is clear that the policy has the effect of incapacitating significant numbers of prisoners maintained in segregation. Further, the policy justifies the secure confinement of nearly two thousand prisoners considered to have gang ties.[10] Presumably, DOC officials believe that limiting prisoners' access to general population and minimum-security settings, in combination with gang deprogramming efforts described below, will dampen gang influence in DOC prisons.

Incapacitation in the MCI-CJ gang blocks is reserved, according to DOC policy, for gang "leaders" or participants in STG incidents.[11] The DOC has not defined these terms. The DOC staff person who supervises the gang cell blocks has said that "maybe twenty-five" of the 152 prisoners then confined could be considered leaders. Further, there are no formal criteria distinguishing "security threat group incidents" from routine prison occurrences. Essentially, the gang unit manager stated that gang-related incidents are those that involve perceived gang members.[12]

Alleged gang members are locked up with alleged cronies. Separate cell blocks are largely devoted to each of the three Latino gangs primarily targeted by the policy—La Familia, the Latin Kings, and the Asociación Ñeta.

Conditions of confinement in the gang units are severe.[13] Prisoners are released from their cell merely one hour per day during four days of every five-day cycle. On the fifth day, they do not leave their cells at all.[14] Out-of-cell activities—showers, personal and legal telephone calls, medical care, and two brief noncontact visitation periods per week—are invariably scheduled during prisoners' one-hour release time. Library access, institutional canteen purchases, and outside property receipts are extremely restricted. Education, treatment, and work opportunities are virtually nonexistent.[15] Prisoners state that they are frequently physically abused and subjected to racial slurs and insipid ethnic barbs.

Many prisoners have remained in the gang blocks at MCI-CJ since the DOC gang policy was initiated in Spring 1995. The average incarceration in these blocks is nearly one year.[16] A significant number of prisoners report that confinement in the gang blocks brought on mental health problems for the first time, or exacerbated existing conditions. Prisoners often complain about insomnia, depression, nightmares, violent mood swings, anxiety attacks, claustrophobia, paranoia, hallucinations, and generalized feelings of nervousness, irritability, and anger. One prisoner stated that, "shortly after being housed in lockdown conditions I began hearing imaginary voices. I also now suffer from hallucinations."[17] Such reports are consistent with clinical studies attributing severe psychiatric consequences to prolonged solitary confinement.[18]

The DOC has "certified" twenty-three alleged prison gangs as STGs.[19] Prisoners are labeled "gang-affiliated" by prison intelligence officers who employ a worksheet that lists seventeen criteria for determining gang involvement, each of which is assigned a point value. Prisoners may be labeled as "suspect/associates" or "members."[20]

A qualifying score is not difficult to achieve: Prisoners bearing tattoos thought to signify gang membership and who socialize with "confirmed" members may be regarded as members themselves. Prisoners identified by outside law enforcement, who have contact with friends or relatives of alleged gang members, or pictured in "Group Related Photos," also score points.[21] Misconduct is not a prerequisite to being labeled as a gang member.

Completed worksheets are forwarded to a DOC central office staff person who reviews the worksheet, confirms that relevant documentation is attached, and "validates" the identification. Those who wish to contest membership determinations may request an informal interview with the DOC central office.[22] Prisoners receive no notice of the evidence against them prior to the interview and have no right of representation.[23] Of 110 prisoners who requested interviews prior to February 1997, 105 were thereafter confirmed as gang members.[24]

Prisoners are also given an opportunity to sign a form "renouncing" their gang membership. As of February 1997, 239 of 681 prisoners identified as gang members indicated a willingness to renounce. The DOC does not automatically accept renunciations. The policy calls for prisoners to be monitored for a period of time, depending upon the length of their sentence. Only seventeen renunciations were accepted by February 1997. Prisoners whose renunciations are "verified," but are later "observed associating with any STG members or involved in any STG activities" are thereafter considered STG members for the duration of their incarceration and irrevocably subject to gang policy deprivations.[25]

It should not be surprising that many prisoners identified as gang members and confined to MCI-CJ or other segregation blocks are profoundly embittered. Many report that they were not informed as to why the DOC considered them gang members, or were told simply that they were labeled by confidential informants or observed "associating" with "known gang members" by assisting with language translation or litigation. Some prisoners claim they were informed that a tattoo or possession of some insignia, such as a Black Panther Party poster, was the basis for their identification. Some state that their transfer to MCI-CJ was precipitated by misconduct, such as fighting, but deny that the incident was gang related.[26]

Certain prisoners' claims of unfair labeling are supported by the official DOC record.[27] David St. Onge, a white prisoner from Springfield, Massachusetts, who speaks Spanish and has Latino friends, attributes his confinement at MCI-CJ to the fact that he engaged in what the prison staff considered a "ritual handshake." His prison file indicates he was cited for a disciplinary infraction for this reason, and was punished with a suspended sentence of two weeks loss of canteen privileges. St. Onge claims that he was never apprised of any other "evidence" supporting the DOC claim that he was a "leader" of the group La Familia.[28] His formal record discloses no basis for this conclusion. Such a story is typical.[29]

There are only two routes out of the MCI-CJ gang blocks. A prisoner may choose to participate in antigang programming provided to a limited number of prisoners at MCI-CJ. The MCI-CJ program is called the "Criminal Sentiments Program" and can accept a maximum of eighteen prisoners. According to the DOC's description, this program "targets those beliefs (cognitions) that support criminal behavior" and seeks to shift the thinking that supports these beliefs. Prisoners who complete this program are transferred to Old Colony Correctional Center, the second most secure DOC prison, for an additional fifteen-week course that "employs the same theoretical basis as the Criminal Sentiments program, reinforcing the skills initially obtained along with emphasis on anger management and relapse prevention." In order to graduate from the Old Colony program, prisoners must renounce gang membership.[30] Many prisoners have refused to participate because they are unwilling to commit themselves to a course of treatment that ultimately requires that they renounce an affiliation they claim does not exist.

The other way to get out of the MCI-CJ gang blocks is to complete a prison sentence and be discharged from custody.[31] Of the 194 prisoners released from restrictive confinement at MCI-CJ directly to the streets between April 1995 and January 1997, at least forty-eight were alleged gang members.[32]

POLICY IMPLICATIONS

According to surveys of prison officials, the above-described approach to prison gang management is commonplace. "Special" housing for gang members under lockdown conditions is in widespread use nationwide.[33] There has, however, "been absolutely no evaluation research whatsoever reported on the efficacy of any of these techniques or strategies" typically used by correctional administrators for dealing with prison gangs.[34] In the absence of valid studies of effectiveness, there seems to be no choice but to construct policy on the basis of what is known about gang structure, behavior, and the apparent impact of intervention strategies in use by law enforcement and correctional authorities.

Gang researchers and commentators seem to agree that, "the formulation of effective policy responses to gangs depends upon a reliable and valid foundation of knowledge of the 'gang problem.' "[35] Thoughtful and deliberate policy making in this area, however, is not typical. "Traditional strategies and techniques for dealing with prison gangs appear to represent a 'shoot from the hip' approach to *ad hoc* correctional management and decision making." Such strategies are often counterproductive.[36]

According to gang literature, three related tendencies embedded in law enforcement and correctional approaches to gang intervention contribute to counterproductive results. These are: (1) policies that proceed from an inaccurate view of what gangs are; (2) intervention strategies that enhance gang cohesiveness; and (3) misidentification of gang members. A fourth related factor, racial and cultural stereotyping, affects disciplinary and classification policies generally. There are abundant reasons to believe that these phenomena characterize the DOC gang policy and will produce unfortunate results both inside and outside of prison.

GANG MYTHOLOGY

"Without a precise and parsimonious understanding of what constitutes a gang and gang behavior, it is often difficult to separate fact from mythology."[37] The statement of Commissioner DuBois quoted near the beginning of the chapter evokes imagery of tightly knit, clandestine organizations. "Soldiers" move quickly to effect leaders' plans to disrupt prison security. If the literature is any guide, it is more than likely that this imagery lacks foundation.

According to leading gang researcher Malcolm W. Klein, law enforcement claims regarding gangs are typically overblown, projecting a "conspiracy-oriented mentality" that is "well beyond the capacity" of the gangs to which they refer. Meritless assertions are often parroted uncritically by the press and even by gang researchers. Exaggerated accounts of street gang control of drug trafficking, for example, have failed to withstand close scrutiny.[38]

Prison authorities are not immune to this tendency. Commissioner DuBois, in the sworn affidavit quoted near the beginning of this essay, labeled three prison disturbances as "gang-related" in the absence of any definition of this term or any apparent evidence.[39] The *Boston Globe* reported, evidently in reliance on DOC sources, that fifteen hundred "members" of

120 prison gangs were identified.[40] In formal responses to litigation discovery requests in *Haverty v. DuBois*,[41] however, the DOC stated that it notified or validated only 681 members of twenty-three "certified" gangs.[42]

The weight of literature on gang structure indicates that gangs do not meet the image of rigidly organized and hierarchal groups that Commissioner DuBois describes.[43] Although there may be local variation,[44] in general: "There tends to be a rather low focus on group goals as such. Gangs are not committees, ball teams, task forces, production teams, or research teams. The members are drawn to one another to fulfill individual needs, many shared and some conflicting; they do not gather to achieve a common, agreed upon end. Thus, gang cohesiveness is rather tentative."[45]

Individual gang member commitment to the group varies significantly between "core" and "fringe" members, constituting "a rather amorphous collection of sub-groups, cliques, pairs, and loners."[46] The National Institute for Corrections (NIC) states that 75–85 percent of the total membership of a prison gang may be composed of "marginal members," and that "a gang may not be as closely controlled by its leadership or as cohesive as it seems."[47] "It is an almost impossible task . . . to determine who the 'gang leaders' are, because leadership tends to be diffused over a number of members, even within each age level."[48] Prison administrators, asked to respond frankly to a survey, described prison gangs as more disorganized than organized.[49]

It appears unlikely that the street gangs that are now in DOC prisons, merely by virtue of their incarceration, have become more cohesive. Imprisoned street gang members are drawn from communities throughout the state of Massachusetts and are confined in any of ten maximum- or medium-security institutions.[50] The DOC has almost complete authority to classify prisoners to these institutions in order to avoid concentrations of fellow street gang members.[51] Further, even when placed in the same prison, gang members may have little contact with each other due to internal housing assignments and institutional restrictions on prisoner movement.[52] The natural effect of incarceration, therefore, is to *weaken* street ties, which were not strong to begin with.

Gang literature demonstrates that an inaccurate "conspiracy"-dominated view of gangs can generate ironic consequences. Exaggerated views of gang cohesiveness and capacity motivate suppression measures that can convert myth into reality.

SUPPRESSION AND COHESIVENESS

Malcolm Klein details numerous gang suppression programs and seriously questions their utility and effect, concluding that most can be shown to cause an increase in gang cohesiveness.[53] Heavy-handed antigang measures solidify targeted individuals' self-identification as gang members. As gang expert C. Ronald Huff has stated, gang suppression:

> often backfires when marginal gang members and "wanna-bes" (those who may be considering gang membership or may just be "groupies" who hang around with the gang) are lumped together with leaders and hard-core followers . . . because these marginal members often react by saying, "Well, the police believe I'm in this gang and treat me as if I am, so I might as well be in it."[54]

Gangs "staffed" with more highly committed members are obviously more dangerous. Thus, as Steve Daniels points out, prison authorities' "specific steps to alleviate disruptive group activities [may] only foster these groups, making them more powerful and adding credence to their cause."[55]

The literature supports what intuition suggests about the effect of the DOC's policy on gang cohesiveness. By imposing harsh, even tortuous, conditions, the DOC only heightens the need for a "sense of belonging," which is what causes gang members to gravitate toward one another in the first place. Prisoners labeled as gang members and locked in cell blocks with alleged peers will thus tend to band together.[56] Although opportunities for interaction are limited, gang-labeled prisoners commiserate during out-of-cell periods and communicate to some extent between cells while they are locked up. They are forced to rely on each other for human contact and support, because there is no other source. By putting alleged gang members in this position, the DOC encourages the gang identities of marginal, aspiring, and entirely misidentified prisoners alike.

MISIDENTIFICATION

Correct identification of gang members is extremely difficult. In a case challenging the administrative segregation of alleged gang members, a federal court monitor reported that it "is inherently virtually impossible to ascertain or discover [the gang members' identity] with precision. The gang's only tangible existence is in the minds of prisoners and prison officials. It is quite unlikely that any two individuals would independently list the same set of persons as members of the group."[57]

The identification problem, as well as the distortion in perception described earlier, contributes to a nationwide "misidentification" pattern.[58] Law enforcement data is generally mistrusted by gang researchers. Different definitions of the term "gang related" can account for variances of as much as 100 percent in the labeling of crimes, and thus criminals.[59] The increased use of interagency computerized databases for gang identification purposes only compounds the unfairness by broadly disseminating often inaccurate information.[60]

Given these problems, gang and correctional researchers George M. Camp and Camille Graham Camp recommend that gang identification for intelligence gathering purposes be "based on sound demonstrative criteria."[61] Additionally, a number of commentators and correctional authorities have stressed the importance of staff training in the area of gang member identification.[62]

DOC criteria for identification of gang members are not "sound." Listed indicators may "demonstrate" marginal or past gang affiliation (a tattoo, for example, may indicate only prior involvement or "wanna-be" status) or fail to suggest a reliable basis for the formulation of *any* conclusion about gang involvement.[63] In the insular prison society, some contact with prisoners considered gang members may be impossible to avoid. Further, the DOC places heavy reliance on what may be entirely inaccurate information from law enforcement sources.[64] Moreover, DOC staff responsible for initial gang identifications have received no formal training.[65]

Additionally, as noted above, prisoners accused of gang membership have little opportunity to defend themselves. The lack of procedural safeguards, key terms that remain undefined, policy implementation by untrained staff, and murky identification criteria, which mostly have nothing to do with actual misconduct, inevitably result in arbitrariness in the designation of gang members and the imposition of punitive consequences.

STEREOTYPING

It is not surprising that more than 90 percent of those prisoners who have borne the most severe consequence of the DOC's gang policy—solitary confinement—are Latinos, and nearly all are prisoners of color.[66] "Racial bias and other manifestations of the abuse of discretionary power are made possible when decision making occurs behind closed doors."[67]

There is substantial evidence that cultural stereotyping plays a significant role in harsh treatment of prisoners of color. According to several studies, labeling of prisoners occurs due to racial bias in the enforcement of disciplinary rules and pervasive cultural stereotypes, which often affect the perceptions of correctional officers. Additionally, "racial biases built into the official classification system reinforce these perceptions . . . leading to additional biases in the way in which rules are enforced." Discriminatory treatment, in turn, effects a self-fulfilling prophecy, as prisoners tend to conform their conduct to the negative expectations of prison authorities.[68]

Even assuming there is some basis for targeting Latin American street gangs, it seems likely that cultural stereotyping, unchecked by procedural safeguards, contributes significantly to the disproportionate targeting of Latinos. This tendency is most likely exacerbated by many Latinos' need or ability to communicate in a language understood by few correctional officers, engendering what may be wholly unwarranted suspicion.[69]

Latinos, as members of the ethnic group that the DOC apparently considers most disruptive, are thus also the prisoners most likely to be misidentified. Unfairness toward them will tend to swell the ranks and enhance the cohesiveness of the gangs the DOC most fears.

PRISON SECURITY AND PUBLIC SAFETY RAMIFICATIONS

Motivated by an inaccurate perception of gangs and how they operate, the DOC has adopted a suppression policy that will enhance group cohesiveness and the identities of gang-affiliated prisoners. The policy will also promote new gang connections for prisoners who, due to the difficulties inherent in gang identification, inadequate procedures, and racial stereotyping, are misidentified.

The DOC policy raises obvious moral and ethical questions. Our present focus, however, is on whether the gang policy makes sense from a law enforcement and correctional perspective. Even if the DOC is creating or enhancing gang identities, why does it matter? Alleged gang members maintained in solitary confinement, after all, are effectively disabled from committing acts of misconduct when locked in their cells.

Increased gang cohesiveness in medium-security prisons, where most prisoners are not locked up constantly, has serious implications for prison security. The great majority of the population of accused gang members are maintained in these facilities under the threat of transfer to solitary confinement upon the whim of administrators. They are also forbidden from minimum-security and prerelease facilities as well as, effectively, from parole.[70] These prisoners may rally in response to the perceived injustice of their circumstances or to the transfer of fellow Latinos into lockdown conditions.[71] To the extent that genuine "leaders" are correctly identified and transferred, other prisoners will move to the fore.[72]

The psychology of gangs is "oppositional." A gang members' sense of worth and group status is tied to repudiation of authority. Prisoners labeled as gang members and denied access to minimum-security institutions thus may not be deterred by the threat of transfer to restrictive confinement from gang involvement and the concerted behavior the DOC so fears. "The operation of deterrence is greatly complicated when group pressures may not only inhibit the expression of the fear of sanctions but also in some instances convert stigmata into status symbols."[73] Further, because only seventeen gang renunciations have been accepted,[74] and these prisoners can be restored to the gang rolls at any time, gang-affiliated prisoners in medium security have little positive incentive to refrain from gang involvement.

Aside from prison concerns, the impact of reliance on long-term solitary confinement will be felt most profoundly on the streets and in the communities to which prisoners return. By February 1997, the DOC discharged 194 prisoners, many of them alleged gang members, directly from MCI-CJ segregation blocks to the streets.[75] In general, 96 percent of all prisoners return to society. Although there are no recidivism studies focusing on gang-affiliated prison releasees,[76] there is evidence that gang members may retain their gang identity upon release.[77]

Gang cohesiveness is definitively linked to criminality. "Most social science literature indicates that increasing group cohesiveness also increases group morale and productivity. One of the products of gangs is crime."[78] To the extent that prisoners are released with enhanced gang identities from either MCI-CJ or medium-security prisons, it is likely that they will commit crimes at higher rates than otherwise, and may even contribute to the "productivity" of the street gangs with which they associate upon their release.

Thus the DOC gang policy not only fails to enhance prison security, it also undermines public safety.

ALTERNATIVES

Whether or not DOC claims regarding the security threat posed by gangs are credible,[79] it is worth considering a more effective approach to defusing gangs and preventing prison disturbances. There are actions the DOC can take that will enhance prison security and public safety.

First, the DOC must consider its own role in creating the conditions that precipitate prison disturbances. The National Institute for Corrections (NIC)—in a publication on management strategies for dealing with gangs and prison disturbances derived from a seminar involving prison administrators and security personnel—stated that ineffective management, inmate inactivity, inadequate inmate services, and facility problems were the primary causes of prison unrest.[80] Additionally, official commissions of review that have studied major prison conflagrations have blamed trends in correctional practices chillingly similar to those long underway in Massachusetts.[81] For present purposes, it is appropriate to focus on two areas. The DOC interest in prison security and the public interest in safety would be well served if any gang problem were addressed by encouraging fair treatment and introducing meaningful programming options to suspected gang members.

FAIR TREATMENT

It should be clear from the foregoing that the DOC has hardly made the creation of safeguards against unfair treatment a policy priority. Commentators on effective gang measures, however, emphasize: "policies that specify distinctions between gang and nongang behavior must be fair. They should meet legal requirements for nondiscriminatory and humane treatment of inmates."[82] Implementation of this mandate could mean incorporating three principles.

First, punish prisoners' conduct, not their status. The Camps, whose work relies entirely upon reporting by correctional authorities, concluded that "criminal behavior" should be the touchstone of antigang measures.[83] Another correctional expert, Sergeant William Riley, the disruptive groups information analyst at the Washington State Penitentiary in Walla Walla,

Washington (home of the first documented prison gang), recommends that no action be taken against a prisoner for gang membership alone.[84] Punishing status, particularly because accurate gang identifications are so difficult, can give rise to the justified perception of arbitrariness in prison management, contributing to instability.[85]

Second, comply with existing regulations. As noted above, the DOC has, thus far, successfully eluded compliance with court-mandated regulations requiring that prisoners only be placed in segregation if a hearing tribunal determines that they are "a substantial threat" to institutional security.[86] According to the NIC, the cost of retaining complete discretion to treat prisoners brutally is high.[87] A genuine commitment to more secure prisons means establishing checks against abuses of authority. "Inmates must have a legitimate grievance mechanism that provides a fair review and redress of their complaints."[88]

Third, treat alleged gang members with respect. As noted above, segregated prisoners claim to be the persistent targets of racial epithets and abuse. Unnecessary humiliation of alleged members is counterproductive. Police departments staffed by officers who consciously attempt to avoid demeaning gang members are more effective.[89] As one commentator characterized the advice of experienced police officers, "you cannot be heavy handed, and you must not destroy face, or try to make object lessons of gang members. You must treat them like men."[90]

The DOC should send a message to staff that racism is unacceptable. Further, "staff need to become knowledgeable of and sensitive to the variety of cultural differences among gang inmates. Recruitment of a racially and ethnically diverse staff is essential."[91]

PROGRAMMING/IDENTITY ALTERNATIVES

Education, training, and work opportunities have steadily diminished in DOC prisons in recent years. The DOC reduced programming expenditures between 1990 and 1996 from $585 to $350 per inmate, and spends only 1.2 percent of its budget on prisoner education.[92] Almost half the prisoners in DOC custody are functionally illiterate, yet the DOC has "made no noticeable effort to upgrade the accessibility of books and other tools for learning."[93] The decline in prison programming is particularly pronounced at MCI-CJ, where most of the population has no access to education, vocational programs, or work opportunities. In a recently completed study that focused on the public safety impact of Massachusetts criminal justice practices, a public policy "think tank" concluded that Massachusetts should restore and expand the prison-based rehabilitation efforts that have established a proven track record of reducing future crime rates.[94]

Rehabilitation efforts also enhance prison security.[95] A former California prison official believes that, because gangs provide relief from the boredom that characterizes prison life, effective gang control requires that prisoners be occupied more productively. "Without full and genuine work and activity it is inconceivable that the gangs will attenuate in influence, numbers and violence."[96]

Further, it appears from the literature that enrolling gang members (who typically suffer from a low sense of self-esteem[97]) in education and training programs is a particularly effective means of inspiring fundamental personal transformations while enhancing prison security. "To provide identity alternatives to the gang is to provide an additional source of social control. . . . At the heart of gang affiliation is the deeper cluster of motives and experiences generally spelling out alienation. Alienation, anger and conflict tend to feed and reinforce gang membership." Reducing these feelings is "a logical method of countering" prison gangs.[98] Education and training addresses alienation by increasing a prisoner's ability to "control his or her own fate." This reduces prison violence.[99]

The gang deprogramming provided by the DOC to some prisoners, even if greatly expanded in scope, cannot substitute for education and training. Some prisoners may not ultimately be coerced into shedding gang identities. Even those who appear to make progress in unlearning criminal tendencies[100] will need further assistance in order to complete any transformation. These prisoners will need an identity with which to *replace* the self-concept tied to gangs and crime. According to the research, such an identity can emerge from meaningful education and training. Without an "identity alternative," behavioral changes accomplished by virtue of increased self-awareness realized by gang deprogramming are likely to be short-lived, particularly when prisoners return to medium-security prisons that lack educational or training opportunities or return, unskilled, to the streets.

The analysis set forth in this chapter does not rely on doubt cast on the commissioner of correction's characterization of the operation of gangs in

Massachusetts prisons. The greater the security threat posed by these groups, the more important it is that correctional authorities adopt effective approaches to dealing with them. Enhancing gang cohesiveness cannot serve any useful end under any interpretation of the facts.

Unfortunately, effective approaches to gang control and to the prevention of prison disturbances involve the very policies the DOC has abandoned in favor of more punitive measures. The only purpose clearly served by the gang policy is to justify maintaining nearly two thousand prisoners in secure settings.

The DOC policy highlights just how badly the agency needs a strong dose of enlightened self-interest. As a prison warden with successful experience in dealing with prison gangs concluded, "good security cannot be established without good treatment and good treatment cannot be maintained without good security."[101] Conversely, it is the lesson of history that bad treatment can work out badly.[102]

In law enforcement, the notion that police need to be more responsive to our communities is gaining acceptance.[103] Correctional authorities, however, are not typically charged with the duty to consider the ramifications of their decisions beyond prison walls. As long as the general public remains ignorant of its stake in how prisons are run, officials will continue to pursue policies without regard for the public interest.

NOTES

1. Matthew Silberman, *A World of Violence*, in Harry E. Allen and Clifford E. Simonsen, eds., *Corrections in America*, 45 (Prentice Hall, 7th ed. 1995).

2. Affidavit of Larry E. DuBois, Commissioner, Massachusetts Department of Correction, at 2, *Haverty v. DuBois*, no. 95-3634 (Mass. Sup. Ct. Suffolk County 1995) [hereinafter Affidavit of DuBois]. This affidavit was submitted in response to prisoners' request for an order ending the lockdown of MCI-CJ that lasted from April through August 1995.

3. The number of cells devoted to these prisoners swelled to 180, or four 45-cell blocks, and later returned to the number of initial transferees, 135, or three 45-cell blocks. See Affidavit of DuBois, supra n. 1, at 5–6, *Haverty v. DuBois*; Deposition of Mark J. Powers, at 17, idem.; Defendant Ronald Duval's Supplemental Answers to Plaintiffs' First Set of Interrogatories, at 7, idem.; Deposition of Christopher Crown, at 25, idem. [hereinafter Deposition of Crown]; MCI Walpole, Inmate/Block Room Listing (23 Jan. 1997) (on file with author).

4. The transfer of these prisoners occurred during a "lockdown" of MCI-CJ, which began on 3 April 1995, when, in an incident deemed "gang related," a group of prisoners maintained in segregation attacked a prison guard with a sharpened broom handle (interviews with prisoners at MCI-CJ, spring 1995). Prisoners throughout the institution were maintained in virtual around-the-clock cell confinement for approximately four months. The lockdown ended only after prisoners filed suit. See Memorandum and Rulings, at 1, *Haverty v. Dubois*, supra n. 1.

5. See Commonwealth of Massachusetts, Department of Correction, *Security Threat Group Management Procedural Statement*, F-1 (n.d., on file with author) [hereinafter Security Threat Group Management]. This term is not entirely coextensive with "gang." Certain groups not typically referred to as gangs are deemed "security threat groups," such as white-supremacist groups. See idem. In general, however, the term STG is euphemistic. Because the DOC policy particularly targets Latinos alleged to be affiliated with well-known street gangs, the term *gang* will be used in this article.

6. Based on documents obtained in formal discovery in *Haverty v. DuBois*, supra n. 1 (on file with author).

7. Four such prisoners submitted affidavits in the related case of *Gilchrist v. DuBois*, no. 93-6300 (Mass. Sup. Ct. Suffolk County 1995), claiming that nothing about their conduct in the prison system merited the harsh treatment afforded them at Cedar Junction after their transfer due to alleged gang involvement. See idem. (on file with author): Affidavit of David St. Onge, at 1; Affidavit of David Cosme, at 1; Affidavit of José Abel Lopez, at 1; Affidavit of Francis Melendez, at 1–2[hereinafter Affidavit of St. Onge; Affidavit of Cosme; Affidavit of Lopez; Affidavit of Melendez].

8. In *Haverty v. DuBois*, the Massachusetts Superior Court determined that prisoners in the Cedar Junction East Wing, including the gang blocks, were confined in violation of their federal due process rights as well as their rights under state regulation to be free from long-term segregation confinement unless they pose a "substantial threat" to prison security. This decision has been stayed pending review by the Massachusetts Supreme Judicial Court, which, as of September 2002, has not issued a decision as of August 2002. The claim of Latino members of the plaintiff class in *Haverty* that they are victims of illegal racial discrimination was tried in the superior court in April–June 2001 and is also pending decision.

9. Descriptions of how the DOC policy works in practice are taken from official documents and sworn testimony elicited during the *Haverty* litigation, unless otherwise indicated. Except for representations attributed to prisoners, there is no dispute between the parties to the *Haverty* case about the description of the gang policy set out in this section, including the description of conditions in the STG housing blocks at MCI-CJ. See Affidavit of DuBois, supra n. 2, at 2–3; see also Zachary R. Dowdy, *Prisons Target Gang Violence*,

Boston Globe, B-1 (20 March 1997); Security Threat Group Management, supra n. 5, at F-1.

10. See Gangs and Members Basic List (9 Jan. 1997), obtained from the DOC in formal discovery in *Haverty v. DuBois*, supra n. 1 (on file with author).

11. See Security Threat Group Management, supra n. 5, at 4.

12. Deposition of Crown, supra n. 3, at 21–23, 25. There was the following colloquy:

> Q: How would you distinguish a disruptive incident generally from a security threat group disruptive incident?
>
> A: I think—are you asking if there was a fight involving six inmates at one place and a fight involving six inmates in another and one could be security threat and one not?
>
> Q: Right.
>
> A: The one that could is the one involved with inmates that have already been identified as security threat group inmates most likely of the same group.

13. See Security Threat Group Management, supra n. 5, at 5–6.

14. See Deposition of Crown, supra n. 3, at 31.

15. See the Commonwealth of Massachusetts, *MCI-Cedar Junction Inmate Orientation Handbook*, 34 (1995) [hereinafter Handbook]; see also Deposition of Crown, supra n. 3, at 41, 43–44. Only three "runners" are employed in each cell block.

16. See MCI Walpole, Inmate Block/Room Listing (23 Jan. 1997) (on file with author).

17. Affidavit of Cosme, supra n. 7.

18. See Stuart Grassian, *Psychopathological Effects of Solitary Confinement*, 140 Am J Psychiatry, 1450 (1983). Dr. Grassian studied prisoners at MCI-CJ in the early 1980s (see idem. at 1451). His work confirmed the identification of a "solitary confinement syndrome" in previous extensive research by nineteenth-century German clinicians (see idem. at 1453). Grassian reported that the symptoms observed in the subjects of his study diminished rapidly upon the subjects' release from solitary confinement. More recently, in testimony on behalf of prisoners challenging conditions at California's prison at Pelican Bay, Grassian stated that solitary confinement "exacerbated . . . previously existing mental condition[s,]" or caused prisoners to develop symptoms of mental illness not previously apparent. See Amended Declaration of Dr. Stuart Grassian at 4, *Madrid v. Gomez*, no. C-90-3094 (N.D. Cal. 1990) (on file with author); see also Holly J. Burkhalter, *Barbarism Behind Bars: Torture in U.S. Prisons*, The Nation, 17 (3 July 1995).

19. See Memorandum from Donna M. Driscoll, Captain, Massachusetts Department of Corrections, to Mark W. Reilly, Deputy Chief (15 Jan. 1997) (on file with author). The DOC has, thus far, refused to divulge the bases for

these determinations. Among the twenty-three gangs is the Black Panthers, a group most would consider of historical significance.

20. See Security Threat Group Management, supra n. 5, at 2, A-1.

21. Ibid.

22. Ibid., 2–3.

23. See Deposition of Mark W. Reilly, at 62–66, *Haverty v. DuBois*, supra n. 1 [hereinafter Deposition of Reilly]; see also Security Threat Group Management, supra n. 5, at 3–4.

24. See Defendants' Answers to Plaintiffs' Third Set of Interrogatories, at 10, *Haverty v. DuBois*, supra n. 1 (on file with author).

25. See Security Threat Group Management, supra n. 5, at 7–8; Defendants' Answers to Plaintiffs' Third Set of Interrogatories, at 10, *Haverty v. DuBois*, supra n. 1 (on file with author).

26. The description of the prisoners' side of the story is based on an analysis of correspondence received by Massachusetts Correctional Legal Services (MCLS) since the April 1995 lockdown at MCI-CJ and the initiation of the gang policy. Broad-based verification of prisoner claims, or the claims of the DOC about these prisoners, will not be possible until documentation supporting individual decisions to "certify" particular groups as STGs and to label particular prisoners as gang members is closely analyzed. This has not been possible to date due to the DOC's unwillingness to provide the documentation, despite a court order to the contrary in *Haverty v. DuBois*.

27. Four prisoners filed affidavits in support of plaintiff Lonnie Gilchrist's petition for contempt in *Gilchrist v. DuBois* (supra n. 7). See Affidavit of St. Onge, Affidavit of Cosme, Affidavit of Lopez, and Affidavit of Melendez, supra n. 7. Each claimed that he was subject to the same conditions and entitled to the same due process protections as plaintiff Gilchrist. The court agreed, stating that the order previously issued on Gilchrist's behalf pertained to all persons similarly situated.

28. See Affidavit of St. Onge, supra n. 7.

29. Francis Melendez was transferred to MCI-CJ and locked in a gang block after he was identified as a "leader" of the Latin Kings, based on information received from a "confidential informant." See Affidavit of Melendez, supra n. 7. He testified: "I am not a leader or even a member of the Latin Kings. The crime for which I am sentenced is not gang related. I have never received a disciplinary ticket for gang related activity. I have never been in a gang. I have friends who are in various gangs, but I made a decision not to join a gang." Classification reports issued prior to his transfer made no mention of any alleged gang involvement. In fact, a majority of the classification board panel recommended his transfer to minimum security, but the superintendent rejected this recommendation (see idem.).

30. ee Security Threat Group Management, supra n. 5, at 5–7; see also Deposition of Crown, supra n. 3, at 51. The DOC claims to have "graduated" 129

prisoners from their program as of February 1997, though at least 5 of these were returned to MCI-CJ. This figure is based on lists of graduates and returnees submitted by the DOC in response to formal discovery on 21 February 1997 in the case of *Haverty v. DuBois*, supra n. 1 (on file with author). Evaluation of the quality of this programming is beyond the scope of this article. There is nothing in DOC literature about their gang policy, however, that establishes any necessary link between long-term solitary confinement and antigang programming. In other words, DOC does not claim that segregation in the MCI-CJ gang blocks is "treatment." Indeed, if the conclusions expressed in this essay are correct, segregation in the MCI-CJ gang blocks *creates* the need for gang deprogramming in many prisoners.

31. See Deposition of Crown, supra n. 3, at 55. According to the testimony of Christopher Crown, it is conceivable that a prisoner could be classified out of MCI-CJ due to a so-called "enemy situation." Because prisoners are rarely out of their cells, it seems unlikely that any difficulty in protecting a prisoner would necessitate transfer.

32. This is based on lists of prisoners released from MCI-CJ between 21 April 1995 and 8 January 1997, submitted by the DOC in response to formal discovery on 4 February 1997 in the case of *Haverty v. DuBois*, supra n. 1 (on file with author). These prisoners were released from the cell blocks specifically reserved for gang members. Some unknown number of other gang-labeled prisoners may have been maintained in other restrictive blocks in which conditions are marginally less austere.

33. See American Correctional Association, *Gangs in Correctional Facilities: A National Assessment*, at 17–20 (1993) [hereinafter Am. Correctional Assessment]; see also National Institute for Corrections Information Center, *Management Strategies in Disturbances and with Gangs/Disruptive Groups*, at 9–12 (1991) [hereinafter NIC Study] (on file with author).

34. George W. Knox, *Introduction to Gangs*, 284 (Vande Vere, 2d ed. 1993). Work subsequent to this 1993 appraisal has not filled this void. See Irving A. Spergel, *The Youth Gang Problem, a Community Approach*, 235–243 (Oxford University Press, 1995).

35. See Scott Decker and Kimberly Kempf-Leonard, *Constructing Gangs: The Social Definition of Youth Activities*, 5 Crim Justice Policy Rev, 271 (1991), reprinted in Malcolm W. Klein et al., eds., *The Modern Gang Reader*, 14 (Roxbury, 1995).

36. Knox, *Introduction to Gangs*, supra n. 34, at 292.

37. Robert J. Bursik, Jr. and Harold G. Grasmick, *Defining Gangs and Gang Behavior*, in *Modern Gang Reader*, supra n. 35, at 8, 9.

38. See Malcolm W. Klein, *The American Street Gang: Its Nature, Prevalence, and Control*, 86–135 (Oxford University Press, 1995). Klein characterizes the alleged gang/crack connection as half "pure hype." He also criticizes the logic of some law enforcement authorities in attributing drug traffic to gangs as "quite astounding, twisted, and termed to guarantee by definition an intimate

connection between gangs and drug sales" (40). See also ibid., 40–43 and chap. 4; Cheryl L. Maxson, *Research in Brief: Street Gangs and Drug Sales in Two Suburban Cities*, in *Modern Gang Reader*, supra n. 35, at 228 (disputing claimed connections between gangs and drugs); Patrick J. Meehan and Patrick W. O'Carroll, *Gangs, Drugs, and Homicide in Los Angeles*, in *Modern Gang Reader*, at 236 (disputing the theory that a substantial proportion of homicides are related to gang involvement in drug dealing).

39. See Affidavit of DuBois, supra n. 1, at 2. The author reviewed a significant volume of disciplinary records, issued as a result of one of these incidents, that make no reference to gang involvement. The DOC has not divulged any evidence of gang involvement in the other two incidents that purportedly played a role in motivating the DOC's gang policy. See Defendants' Answers to Plaintiffs' Third Set of Interrogatories, supra n. 25 (on file with author).

40. See Dowdy, *Prisons Target Gang Violence*, supra n. 9.

41. See *Haverty v. DuBois*, supra n. 1.

42. See Defendants Answers to Plaintiffs' Third Set of Interrogatories, *Haverty v. DuBois*, supra n. 1 (on file with author).

43. See text accompanying supra n. 1.

44. For example, Texas prison gangs are portrayed as having a high degree of organization and discipline by certain correctional authorities and researchers. See Robert S. Fong et al., *Prison Gang Dynamics: A Look Inside the Texas Department of Correction*, in Peter J. Benekos and Alida V. Merlo, eds., *Corrections: Dilemmas and Directions*, 57 (Anderson Publishing, 1992). The credibility of this work is open to question. Certain claims rely entirely on correctional surveys—namely, the assertion that prison gangs "are responsible for 50% or more of all prison violence and problems" (idem., 71, citation omitted). Fong fails to even discuss important definitional questions, such as how incidents of prison violence are deemed "gang related," and his central thesis—that prison violence and the proliferation of gangs may be attributed to judicial intervention and prison reform—seems fundamentally at odds with the analysis of other correctional authorities. See NIC Study, supra n. 33, at 15. Furthermore, the description of prison gang rules is undermined by the author's own subsequent research. See Robert S. Fong et al., *Blood In, Blood Out: The Rationale Behind Defecting from Prison Gangs*, J Gang Res, 45–51 (summer 1995). This subsequent work describes how gang members leave the gang without apparent concern about negative consequences for such reasons as "loss of interest" (48). Even if the Texas prison gang portrayal is accurate, it may not reveal much about what prison gangs are like in Massachusetts prisons. Texas gangs, according to the authors, are formed "indigenously." See Salvador Buentello et al., *Prison Gang Development: A Theoretical Model*, Prison J, 3,5 (fall–winter 1991). There is no question that the Massachusetts gangs upon which the DOC has focused are street gangs "imported" into Massachusetts prisons. See Dowdy, *Prisons Target Gang Violence*, supra n. 9. Further, Texas prison gangs

are clearly more entrenched and thus perhaps more cohesive. See George M. Camp and Camille Graham Camp, *Prison Gangs: Their Extent, Nature, and Impact on Prisons*, 19–20 (U.S. Department of Justice, 1985). Texas reported 322 members of six gangs that began formation in 1975. Massachusetts authorities reported three members of one gang and could not say when that gang began (19). "Prison gangs were once considered weak or non-existent in the Massachusetts corrections system" (Dowdy, supra n. 9). The present, therefore, is likely a propitious time to consider policies that will not cause gangs in Massachusetts prisons to follow the course of Texas gangs.

45. Klein, *American Street Gang*, supra n. 38, at 80–81. But see Martin Sanchez Jankowski, *Islands in the Street: Gangs and American Urban Society* (University of California Press 1991) (attributing greater cohesiveness to gangs than most researchers). Klein criticizes Jankowski's methodology and conclusions. See Klein, supra n. 38, at 134–35.

46. Klein, *American Street Gang*, supra n. 38, at 61.

47. NIC Study, supra n. 33, at 9.

48. Klein, *American Street Gang*, supra n. 38, at 62.

49. See Camp and Camp, *Prison Gangs*, supra n. 44, at viii.

50. See Memorandum from Larry E. DuBois, Commissioner, Department of Correction, to Superintendents/Unit Directors, 1 (18 April 1995), stating correctional institutions/security levels (on file with author). Cf. James B. Jacobs, *Stateville*, 2 (University of Chicago Press, 1977). The author states that the great majority of Stateville prisoners are drawn from the streets of Chicago.

51. See *Hastings v. Commissioner of Correction*, 424 Mass. 46, 49–50 (1997).

52. The DOC recently imposed a rule at the medium-security prison at Gardner requiring that all movements within the prison occur during a limited number of fifteen-minute periods during the course of the day (telephone interview with unnamed prisoner, NCCI Gardner, 24 June 1997).

53. See Klein, *American Street Gang*, supra n. 38, at 159–186, and at 7.

54. C. Ronald Huff, *Denial, Overreaction, and Misidentification: A Postscript on Public Policy*, in C. Ronald Huff, ed., *Gangs in America*, 310, 313 (Sage, 1990).

55. Steve Daniels, *Prison Gangs: Confronting the Threat*, Corrections Today, 66, 126 (April 1987).

56. See, e.g., Marilyn D. McShane and Frank P. Williams III, eds., *Encyclopedia of American Prisons*, 218 (Garland Publishing, 1996). Deprivations make confinement so difficult as to require a group rather than an individual adaptation (359–360).

57. See *Toussaint v. Rowland*, 711 F. Supp. 536 (N.D. Cal. 1989). Quoting from: Scott N. Tachiki, comment, *Indeterminate Sentences in Supermax Prisons Based upon Alleged Gang Affiliations: A Re-examination of Procedural Protection and a Proposal for Greater Procedural Requirements*, 83 Cal L Rev, 1115, 1142 (1995) (quoting 3d Special Report of the Monitor, at 22, *Toussaint v. Rowland*).

58. See Huff, *Denial, Overreaction, and Misidentification*, supra n. 54, at 313.

59. See Cheryl L. Maxson and Malcolm W. Klein, *Street Gang Violence: Twice as Great, or Half as Great?* in *Modern Gang Reader*, supra n. 35, at 24, 31.
60. See Klein, *American Street Gang.* supra n. 38, at 190–191. Klein proffers a critique of the Gang Reporting, Evaluating, and Tracking (GREAT) system.
61. Camille Graham Camp and George M. Camp, *Management Strategies for Combating Prison Gang Violence*, 19 (Sept. 1988) (unpublished case study, on file with author).
62. See Knox, *Introduction to Gangs*, supra n. 34, at 292; see also Victor E. Casillas, *Identifying and Supervising Offenders Affiliated with Community Threat Groups*, Fed Probation, 11, 18–19 (June 1994); Am. Correctional Assessment, supra n. 33, at 55.
63. Criteria such as "observed association," or "contact with known associates," for example, at most indicate that the prisoner knows a prisoner who may be a gang member or knows "associates" of suspected gang members (see Security Threat Group Management, supra n. 5, at A-2). Compare the selection criteria utilized by Randall G. Shelden, an associate professor in the department of criminal justice at the University of Nevada, Las Vegas, in a study of the behavior of gang members in a prison setting; see Randall G. Shelden, *A Comparison of Gang Members and Non-Gang Members in a Prison Setting*, Prison J, 50 (fall–winter 1991). Shelden would not consider a prisoner a gang member for purposes of his study unless three or more of the following criteria were satisfied: (1) in a court case it was proven or admitted by the offender that he was a gang member; (2) gang membership was admitted by the offender and noted in the presentence report; (3) gang membership was confirmed through police reports; (4) the inmate has confirmed gang tattoos; (5) in the prison classification report, gang membership was admitted by the offender; (6) an informal confidential file (based in part upon an informal snitch network) of gang members, suspected gang members, associates and "wanna-be's" [sic] is kept (51).
64. See Security Threat Group Management, supra n. 5, at A-1.
65. Based on responses to formal discovery in *Haverty v. DuBois* (supra n. 1).
66. See Massachusetts Department of Correction, *A Statistical Description of the Sentenced Population of Massachusetts Correctional Institutions on January 1, 1995*, 17 (1996). For example, 20.1 percent of prisoners in DOC custody are considered Hispanic (see idem. at 17, table16) and 50.4 percent are members of minority groups. Discovery responses in the *Haverty* case reflect that Latinos are disproportionately placed in the gang blocks at MCI-CJ, where they number approximately 90 percent of the total prisoners confined. Estimates of the percentage of Latinos among all prisoners labeled as gang members— and thus a comparison of Latino prisoners deemed gang-affiliated maintained in segregation relative to all gang-labeled prisoners—are difficult due to the uncertain ethnicity of particular groups alleged to contribute members to the prison population—for example, "Always Packing Boys" and "Dog Pound." Nevertheless, it appears certain that a substantially higher percent-

age of Latinos are maintained in the gang blocks at MCI-CJ than gang-labeled prisoners of other ethnicities.

67. Silberman, *World of Violence*, supra n. 2, at 47.
68. See ibid., at 93–95, 98; quote appears at 94.
69. The DOC has not responded to the plaintiffs' request in *Haverty v. DuBois* for statistical information on the racial composition of correctional staff. Latino prison guards, however, are rarely noted by visitors and, according to prisoners, are not placed in Latino gang cell blocks.
70. According to Massachusetts Parole Board data, prisoners are paroled far less often from medium- (32%) and maximum-security (3%) than from minimum-security (51%) or prerelease (67%). See Massachusetts Parole Board, *1994 Annual Report*, 17 (1994). Being designated as a gang member cannot help a prisoner's chances of being paroled. See Mass. Regs. Code title 120, 300.05(1)(i), (2) (1993).
71. See Knox, *Introduction to Gangs*, supra n. 34, at 285–286.
72. See Am. Correctional Assessment, supra n. 33, at 2: "Locking up gang leaders or security threat group members in segregation units creates a void for new leaders to emerge and can lead to continuing disruption within the facility."
73. See Klein, *American Street Gang*, supra n. 38, at 186, quoting Franklin E. Zimring and Gordon J. Hawkins, *Deterrence: The Legal Threat in Crime Control* 217 (University of Chicago Press, 1973).
74. See supra text accompanying n. 25.
75. The number of prisoners who have spent time in solitary confinement and who, prior to release, moved on to engage in DOC gang deprogramming efforts directly from medium security, is unknown.
76. See Knox, *Introduction to Gangs*, supra n. 34, at 279.
77. See, e.g., Camp and Camp, supra n. 61, at viii, ix; Salvador Buentello et al., *Prison Gang Development: A Theoretical Model*, Prison J, 3, 8 (fall–winter 1991).
78. Klein, *American Street Gang*, supra n. 38, at 7. Klein reports on the link between cohesiveness and criminal activity.
79. See supra n. 26.
80. See NIC Study, supra n. 33, at 13–14. Causes and subcauses identified are:

- Ineffective Management:
  - Vague lines of responsibility
  - Lack of visibility and accessibility of administrator
  - Practices or policies seen as unfair or based on favoritism
  - Staff perceived as not in control
  - Inconsistency in application of rules and guidelines
- Inmate Inactivity:
  - Lack of programs
  - Lack of work opportunities
  - Idleness

- Inadequate Inmate Services:
  - Poor or insufficient medical care
  - Poor food service
  - Overly restrictive visiting opportunities
- Facility Problems:
  - Unsafe, unsanitary conditions
  - Crowded conditions
  - Outdated or poorly maintained facilities

81. In two infamous examples—the New York State Prison at Attica in 1971 and the New Mexico State Penitentiary in 1980—riots were attributed in large part to correctional policies emphasizing segregation, deprivation, and inactivity. The McKay Commission stated that before the Attica riot, educational and recreational programs were nonexistent or in such short supply that the principle occupation of prisoners was idleness. See Attica, *The Official Report of the New York State Special Commission on Attica*, 16–45 (1972) [hereinafter Attica]. "If inmates were rehabilitated, it was not because of Attica but in spite of it." (21).

    The New Mexico Attorney General concluded that conditions leading to a serious prison riot in 1980 were created by the replacement of positive incentive controls with harsher treatment, citing a reduction in prison and community-based programs, the arbitrary and excessive use of segregation, tighter restrictions on inmates, and sharp limits on contact with persons outside the prison. See State of New Mexico Office of the Attorney General, *Report of the Attorney General on the February 2 and 3, 1980 Riot at the Penitentiary of New Mexico, Part II, the Last Ten Years, Conditions Leading to the Riot, Conclusions, and Recommendations*, 26–27 (1980) [hereinafter New Mexico]. When these policies were instituted, the level of violence in prison increased almost immediately (28–29). Thus "prison programs cannot be viewed as mere window dressing" (34).

82. Office of Juvenile Justice and Delinquency Prevention, *Gang Suppression and Intervention: Community Models*, 14 (1994) (on file with author) [hereinafter Gang Suppression].

83. See Camp and Camp, *Management Strategies*, supra n. 61, at 53.

84. See William Riley, *Taking a Two-pronged Approach to Managing Washington's Gangs*, Corrections Today, 68 (July 1992); see also Julie Gannon Shoop, *Image of Fear: Minority Teens Allege Bias in "Gang Profiling,"* Trial, 12, 16 (Oct. 1994).

85. See generally, NIC Study, supra n. 33. According to the NIC, policies that create the perception of unfairness contribute to ineffective management (5–6).

86. See supra n. 8.

87. See NIC Study, supra n. 33, at 43–46; see also John P. Conrad, *Who's in Charge? The Control of Gang Violence in California Prisons*, paper presented to The American Justice Institute (3–4 Nov. 1977) (on file with author). Conrad,

a former California correctional administrator, reported: "I have welcomed the tardy recognition that due process of law is necessary, desirable, and possible in our prisons" (210).

88. Michael P. Lane, *Inmate Gangs*, Corrections Today, 98, 128 (July 1989).

89. See David Freed, *Policing Gangs: Case of Contrasting Styles*, L.A. Times, pt. 2, at 1 (19 Jan. 1986) (reprinted in *Modern Gang Reader*, supra n. 35, at 288). Freed contrasts the gang suppression styles of the Los Angeles Police Department and Los Angeles Sheriff's Department. The latter agency is credited with a far more effective and productive approach to law enforcement vis à vis gangs. See also Klein, *American Street Gang*, supra n. 38, at 159–186 (concurring with this opinion).

90. Edwin J. Delattre, *Character and Cops: Ethics in Policing*, 263 (AEI Press, 2d ed. 1994).

91. See Gang Suppression, supra n. 82, at 15.

92. See Zachary R. Dowdy, *Volunteers Teach, Preach within Mass. Prison Walls*, Boston Globe, A1 (19 Nov. 1996).

93. See Massachusetts Institute for a New Commonwealth, *Criminal Justice in Massachusetts: Putting Crime Control First*, 7 (1996), quote appears at 30. The DOC, by contrast, has been "aggressive about down-grading athletic facilities."

94. See ibid., at 33. Studies show that completion of adult basic education and G.E.D. programs by prisoners is positively correlated with lower rates of recidivism. For example, in a Wisconsin study, 38 percent of all released prisoners returned to prison within four years. See Anne Morrison Piehl, *Learning while Doing Time*, 14 (Apr. 1994) (unpublished manuscript, on file with author). Prisoners who complete education programs are 5.5 percent less likely to return to prison and have higher rates of employment (20).

95. See Attica, supra n. 81; New Mexico, supra n. 81.

96. Conrad, *Who's in Charge?* supra n. 87, at 208.

97. See supra n. 56 and accompanying text. Gang membership is often motivated by the need to gain a sense of belonging. See Daniels, *Prison Gangs* supra n. 55, at 126.

98. Knox, *An Introduction to Gangs*, supra n. 34, at 282.

99. See generally, Matthew Silberman, *Resource Mobilization and the Reduction of Prison Violence*, paper presented at the Annual Meetings of the American Sociological Association (Aug. 1994) (on file with author).

100. See Dowdy, *Prisons Target Gang Violence*, supra n. 9.

101. Spergel, *Youth Gang Problem*, supra n. 34, at 240 (citation omitted).

102. See supra n. 81 and accompanying text.

103. See, e.g., Patricia Smith, *It's the Kid Who Decides*, Boston Globe, B1 (21 Feb. 1997); Charles A. Radin, *Tough Talk on Penalties Irks Some; President Says Little About Prevention, Groups Say*, Boston Globe, A12 (20 Feb. 1997). See generally, Robert Trojanowicz and Bonnie Bucqueroux, *Community Policing: A Contemporary Perspective* (Anderson Publishing, 1990).

PART 6
GANGS AND
PHOTOGRAPHY

13

ON THE SUBJECT OF GANG PHOTOGRAPHY

RICHARD T. RODRÍGUEZ

In his essay "The Work of Art in the Age of Mechanical Reproduction," Walter Benjamin argues, "The enlargement of a snapshot does not simply render more precise what in any case was visible, though unclear: it reveals entirely new structural formations of the subject" (1968:236). Metaphorically bending Benjamin's claim, the "enlargement" or enhancement of the mere snapshot to an item for (legal) documentation also shifts the subject of gang photography—photography that focuses on Chicanos affiliated with street gangs in greater Los Angeles—from a mere photographic image to a rendering of that subject as a suspect of gang activity by means of "new structural formations of the subject." In other words, the subject's appearance on film necessarily casts his/her image in a completely different light when placed in the hands of others. For what may be believed to stand as a personal, political, or artistic photograph inevitably produces ulterior meanings in other contexts. With this in mind, I will show that although certain photographic practices may be compelling, they cannot be simply understood by way of their author's personal stakes, political intentions, and aesthetic interests.

I will examine the politics and functions of three approaches to the gang photography phenomenon. The first, exemplified by the intriguing work of British documentary photographer Robert Yager, can be characterized as *ethnographic*. Yager's photographs are best understood as products that stem from recourse to what I will call the "negotiated pose." This categorization of Yager's work resonates with contemporary ethnographic notions about dialogic impulses informing ethnographic practices. Such impulses produce competing accounts of a peculiar ambition to represent and be represented. Yager's photographic ethnography, however, poses a set of problems bearing upon the relationship between those participating in the "photographing of culture" and the potential viewers of these photos. How, for example, are the dialogic impulses of photographic texts read strategically by disparate interpretive communities? What are the ideological stakes of the interpretations and uses of the photos?

The second approach identifies particular *autoethnographic* modes of gang photography as they function to produce "gang" self-representation. Similar to the stakes of "family" portraiture, this kind of photography relates individual selves to a communal self by establishing a specific pictorial scene. Autoethnographic photos are not produced on behalf of "professional" interests, nor are they intended for museum display; rather, their purposes are somewhat more intimate. As an example of autoethnographic gang photography, I have chosen one of my relative's photos to be read alongside the cover of Miguel Durán's 1992 novel *Don't Spit On My Corner*, and selected photographs in *Teen Angel's Magazine*, a publication that circulates within Chicano youth subculture communities. These photographs provide the material for a detailed analysis of the ways in which photography has functioned for Chicano youths in the past and present, especially for those associated with "gang" cultures. Such photographs prevail in circles that receive them as familiar, or "familial," on the grounds of sustaining a group memory. I ask, how do these photos challenge the dominant media's images of Chicano youths as "gang members?" In what contexts are these photos to be read, and how are the photos altered to underscore a self-inscriptive impulse?

As the historical use of photography in law enforcement is quite complex and extensive, the third approach I investigate focuses on dominant media

and law enforcement agencies. These social entities use both their own photographs and those ethnographic and authoethnographic gang photographs
in "official" catalogs to identify and eventually apprehend gang members.
Often arranged alongside ethnographic and autoethnographic gang photos,
these police photographs are primary documents stored in police archives
and compiled in file cabinets and "mug books," serving as visual documentation to reference (possible) culprits. But routine photographing of gangs
is a law enforcement strategy that frequently violates the rights of youth
(who are marked by racial and class differences) that the police purport to
defend. It should be no surprise, then, that these photos inevitably produce
images of gang members stereotyped as prone to violence and delinquency.

The three approaches outlined above also raise three questions. First,
how do we read the photographer as ethnographer and interpret photography as ethnography? Second, how do we relate autoethnographic photography to the task of imaging a communal self? Third, how might police photography as a genre be held accountable for pictorially reproducing a specific
subculture that serves to criminalize members of that subculture? I argue
that textual productions such as photographs offer many interpretive possibilities for how Chicano gangs are represented. Furthermore, the discours-
es of aesthetic interest, personal retrospection, and law enforcement must be
read vis-à-vis the social contexts and tensions that frame the subjects of
gang photography.

TRACKING THE NATIVES OF EAST L.A.

I see Yager as an ethnographer (and not simply as a documentary photographer) and I read his photos as ethnography. In no way do I argue, as John
Collier Jr. and Malcolm Collier have, that photographing, instead of writing, culture gives even the "novice fieldworker" claims to authority, because
"photographic orientation" produces the kinds of "control and authenticity"
that writing does not (1986:21–23). Such claims render the photographer an
all-seeing participant-observer whose work stands as objective and an authority figure who matches silhouettes with the old-school anthropologist
who writes only what is true (Clifford 1988). I recast the idea of participant
observation in which the authority to represent, once seemingly delegated
to the ethnographer, *demands* an approach in which those "being studied"
necessarily participate in the process of (their) cultural inscription. This ap-

proach maps the interrelations between actors whose performances enable the production of cultural texts.

These interrelations, emphasized by what I call negotiated poses, are pivotal in photographic accounts of ethnography. The act of posing helps us understand the angles of (self-) perception that Yager's photos intend to convey. An awareness of the presence and aim of the camera on the part of the photographer, as well as the gangsters, allows one to recognize poses as performative moments of concession between Yager and his subjects. To argue that Yager commands all authority as photographer of Chicano gangs and that the gangs fall victim to whatever intentions Yager has in mind is to foreclose debate on the interactive procedures at work in a collaborative endeavor. As Pierre Bourdieu writes in *Photography: A Middle-brow Art*, "Striking a pose means respecting oneself and demanding respect" (1990:80). For the subjects of Yager's photography, their poses convey this demand for respect; those appearing in his photos stake claims to how he or she is represented, given how the negotiated pose hinges on the agency of those configured in the visual realm.

To be sure, posing should not be regarded as a passive stance; rather, it is an instance in which conversation (even debate and dispute) is taking place, a dialogic "contact zone" as Mary Louise Pratt would put it (1992:6–7). But more than that, the conventionally understood notion of the pose as a passive stance is transfigured into an act of establishing the subject's claim to self-perception. As Jimmie Durham writes regarding a photograph of Apache Indian Geronimo:

> Geronimo, as an Indian "photographic subject," blew out the windows. On his own, he reinvented the concept of photographs of American Indians. At least he did so far as he could, concerning pictures of himself, which are so ubiquitous that he must have sought "photo opportunities" as eagerly as the photographers. Yet even when he was "posed" by the man behind the camera, he looks through the camera at the viewer, seriously, intently, with a specific message. Geronimo uses the photograph to "get at" those people who imagine themselves as the "audience" of his struggles. He seems to be trying to see us. He is demanding to be seen, on his own terms. *(1992:56)*

Thus the ethnographic photo is an instance wherein parties on both sides of the camera are partaking in the production of visual imaging. Take, for example, the photo "Playboy 'Muerto' Puts a Gun in His Mouth" (figure 13.1).

FIGURE 13.1

In side profile, we see a young man with a bent arm and wrist aiming a hand-gun in his mouth. His lips appear secure in covering the tip of the gun's bar-rel while his forehead, eyebrows, and the area around his nose and mouth go sour. His face is wrought with tension. An index finger with a tattooed "Y" wraps around the trigger. Behind Muerto there is a portion of a mural-like, spray-painted gun aimed over and past his head. By juxtaposing an "artistic" reverie with the very "real," Yager and Muerto undoubtedly wish to provide the viewer with a commentary on the persistence of violence in urban L.A. However, the photograph most forcefully addresses the psychic life of gang subcultures that makes meaning of Muerto's name. For he need not worry about death when he is literally and figuratively already "dead."

How does this image of a young Chicano gripping a gun aimed in his mouth exemplify Yager's photographic ambition, which—paraphrasing an *LA Weekly* writer—aims to depict gangsters with a "hint of humanity" (*LA Weekly* 1995:28)? These hints of humanity, I would argue, are constructed by the pose. The "artistic" gun is not aimed at Muerto. Obviously it cannot kill him. But what about the "real" gun in Muerto's mouth? Yager and Muerto are suggesting that unlike the gun aimed above Muerto's head, there are higher stakes involved regarding the gun in his hand, given its potential use for murder/suicide. Furthermore, the pose fuels the desire to engender masculinist threads that tie and bind gang formation and existence by challenging the hard and fast power of the gun. After all, *la vida loca* is living life on the edge, a motto some affiliated with gangs adopt as a rule of thumb. In a sense, the photo suggests that gang life is suicidal, while it highlights Muerto's name. These interpretations of Muerto's reading of himself in the photo suggest that "he is trying to photograph himself, but from within," if indeed "he is taking a photograph of his thoughts" (Durham 1992:58).

In spite of the dialogic relationship I have described above, it is imperative to expose the problems of Yager's project to establish an undercurrent of ambivalence when discussing the personal intentions behind his photographs—as well as when considering the photos' prospective interpretive communities. Identifiable as representation struggles within relations of power—struggles embedded in most ethnographic endeavors—the production of photographic signification always produces contentious rationale like any courtroom trial involving conflictual testimony and evidence. Yager's testimony is that his photographs attempt "to document a relatively unexamined subculture that has a major impact on society," an attempt to humanize the too-often-vilified gangster. After all, he informs us that these photos were produced "for a grant in humanistic photography for which [he] was a finalist" (Yager 1993:32). If the evidence is in his photos, what exactly connects his testimony with his visible evidence? Could we call some witnesses to the stand, perhaps those who were photographed? Aside from their appearance on film, precisely how are they positioned in photographic signification? Although the gangsters may be possible witnesses, we cannot say they would necessarily affirm Yager's efforts to "humanize" them; their participation may in fact hinge on the promise of their photo taken, money given, or favors offered. And who is to say that they care at all about Yager's justification for taking their picture?

Regardless, Yager and his subjects are allies in the eyes of the law. In this courtroom drama, which indeed takes place, the LAPD serves as prosecutor and Yager (and his company of gangs not present) as defendant. But before we align Yager and the gangsters, I will examine how Yager's role as photographer lays claims to an uneasy, self-conscious authority.

FIGURE 13.2

Printed in column-layout next to a photo of a young man from The Playboys, who " 'mad-dogs' the camera" (figure 13.2), the descriptive text written by an unidentified author reads:

Robert Yager began photographing gangs three years ago because he felt they were not being adequately explored by most media. Coverage focused more on the effect of gangs—graffiti, carjackings, murders—than on gang members themselves. Almost never were they allowed any hint of humanity. As an immigrant himself (from England) and having lived in Mexico, Yager was interested in exploring the culture of Latino gangs and in documenting the daily lives of their members. The photographs that follow were culled from among nearly 6,000 frames he has shot so far.   *(LA Weekly 1995:28)*

A license for ethnographic authority is issued to Yager in this text. Although Yager is an "immigrant," there is no telling whether his ethnographic subjects are too. Also, the fact that Yager lived in Mexico would seem to grant him sweeping cultural authority for photographing Chicano gangs in Los Angeles. Yager's immigrant status and his living in Mexico do not excuse his possible generalizations or errors. Most of all, in no way can these supposedly shared factors insert Yager in the photographic and sociocultural realm his work envisions. If ethnographic practices shifted, how might the young Playboy envision himself? Would his photos look anything like Yager's?

In his essay, "Camera Man: A Photographer Reflects on How His Work with Gangs Got Him Arrested," Yager tells of how an invitation to take pictures at a West Side Playboys party led up to his arrest:

> Soon after the party got going, a police helicopter began circling above, its spotlight illuminating the courtyard like a disco. I was well into my second roll of film when roughly a dozen police in full riot gear burst through the gate. I took a quick shot from midcourtyard. The party guests rushed to leave as the police ordered them to disperse.
>
> In the chaos, I noticed at least two officers whacking at kids with their batons. "Take pictures, Camera Man! They're beating us up," one of the gang members shouted.
>
> I took two more photographs, possibly capturing a baton being swung.
>
>   *(Yager 1993:32)*

It is not known for sure if a swung baton was captured on film because the roll in his camera was soon destroyed by police. What followed was some harsh police treatment toward Yager despite his attempt to certify his attendance with an LAPD press pass. Grabbed by the throat by an officer, he was shoved up against a gate; his camera equipment lambasted—" 'Get his film!' another officer shouted. Police in riot helmets closed in. Hands snatched my equipment. The flash snapped off and fell to the ground. In a wrenching yank to my neck, my camera was taken." Of course, he was arrested, "They threw me to the ground, handcuffing my hands tightly behind my back. I put up no resistance and they placed me in the back of a squad car." In the midst of the turmoil, Yager meets up with "Martinez," an officer from the Rampart Division's CRASH Unit (Community Resources Against Street Hoodlums), who revokes Yager's press pass and commands his arrest. It turns out this is not Yager's and Martinez's first confrontation:

> I had encountered Martinez before. In August, while taking photographs for a grant in humanistic photography for which I was a finalist, I'd been hanging out with some gang members on a street near Pico and Vermont. No one was doing anything illegal. The police came and began searching the kids and asking them questions. Martinez ordered me not to take pictures, threatening to arrest me if I did.
>
> I have always tried to show respect for the officers who police the often violent streets of Los Angeles. I realize they have a difficult job. In August, I tried to explain to Martinez why I take pictures of gang members, how I am attempting to document a relatively unexamined subculture that has a major impact on society.
>
> He insisted that I was glorifying gangs with my photographs. He even suggested that gang members wrote graffiti and broke bottles in the street *just because of my presence.* I took no more pictures that day, as Martinez requested.
>
> *(Yager 1993:32, emphasis mine)*

Martinez's observations—whether or not correct—offer compelling information about the photographic subject's negotiated "gangster" poses and actions that are part of Yager's work. For Martinez, these poses also create threats to law enforcement codes of proper conduct.

Martinez's response to the photographer unfolds a more complex situation when he reveals that he collects Yager's photos because they help police identify suspects of gang activity:

> At the police station, Martinez brought out a copy of *Camera and Darkroom* that featured a twelve-page spread of my photos and an interview with me. He asked me which kid was in a photograph of mine that had run as a *Newsweek* cover. I was surprised he was so up on my work. *(1993:32)*

For law enforcement units, such as CRASH, photographs are necessary to identify criminals, which is no surprise once Yager's photos are published. Yager's investments in his photos—his attempts to humanize his subjects and his humanities grant—cannot stop the competing interpretations that are bound to surface. For intstance, the cover of the 2 August 1993 issue of *Newsweek* shows a sketchy, suggestively violent photograph of a young man's side profile manipulated with the stipple effect (figure 13.3). William J. Mitchell identifies the stipple effect as "posterization" and states that through the act of digital posterization, "A digital artist . . . must adjust the dynamic range and distribution appropriately to the content and occasion" (1992:99). One reader interprets this image as "a young Latino running through the streets with a rifle" (Senft 1995:40). Yet the only information *Newsweek* gives about the photograph is that it was taken by Robert Yager, and the caption reads, "Teen Violence in the Streets." Given the stipple effect of the photo, this is a stock image, and one of those competing interpretations is that a vague image associated with a prominent photographer is going to be read in a very specific way, as the reader's interpretation and the manipulation of the image suggests. The digital artist's manipulation of Yager's photograph, therefore, fits the content of *Newsweek*'s cover story.

The concentration of white tinting contrasted with the purple/black/gray shading in the photo appears to highlight particular features of the *Newsweek* cover. For example, the subject's clenched hand and, more salient, index finger that lines nearly half the length of the gun's body offer a provocative gesture. Illuminated by this "light" and "dark" juxtaposition, his hand and index finger are highlighted and etched in the form of a gun in contrast to the darkness of the gun he is holding. Given the eye-catching white void that contours his hand and index finger, he emphasizes the gun as the object embodying the dangers of "teen violence" announced on the cover. A similar assessment could be made regarding the shading of the figure's semimuscular arm accentuated by his white undershirt. The white (under)shirt often signifies gangster attire that also issues "rhetorical challenges to the law" (Hebdige 1988:18)—particularly for Chicano youths. Moreover, the white shirt accentuates the urgency of violence that the *Newsweek* cover circulates. To depict someone or something wild in the streets, there should be some motion that connotes the wildness at work, hence the overall manipulation of the photo.

This cover photo's "dynamic range and distribution" of tonal refinements are greatly accentuated when we compare the *Newsweek* image with the cover of Malcolm W. Klein's book, *The American Street Gang: Its Nature, Prevalence, and Control* (1995), which features a replication closer to Yager's

FIGURE 13.3

original photo. Although the image is not readily attributable to Yager, the image on the dust jacket of Klein's book is much more photographically clear. There is less of an ominous tinge; however, the gray and white (originally black and white) photo no doubt holds similar meanings. It is possible to consider the image of the man as in the process of either fading away or coming into view. The space in between appearing and disappearing is part of the control Klein's book yearns for—wildness transfixed.

Furthermore, the unidentifiable man aiming a gun at some unknown target supports mass media conceptions of violence and "The American Street Gang." This photo correlates with images heavily circulated by the media around the time of the upheaval propagated by the Rodney King verdict. Given the racially ambiguous figure of the photo, the pan-ethnic composition of Klein's gangs of study, and *Newsweek*'s sweeping coverage of what counts as "Teen Violence," the photographic subject could be anyone or anything identified with the "L.A. riots," "gangs," or "violators." This specific image assists in the visualization of particular ideologies, but it is vague enough to produce manifold meanings for a variety of contexts. Paraphrasing Roland Barthes, "the more technology develops the diffusion of information (notably images)"—perhaps through posterization—"the more it provides the means of masking the constructed meaning under the appearance of the given meaning" (1985:201). The constructed meaning is the pose and the given meaning is the wildness of Latino youth gangs.

The photograph, "the gang member shooting heroin" (figure 13.4), raises several issues regarding the pose of the subject compared to the "young Latino in motion." The negotiation process between Yager and his photographic subject explicitly and implicitly produce a multilayered relationship that invokes the subject positions of ethnographer and ethnographed, photographer and photographed. In other words, if indeed the "gang member shooting heroin" is informed of Yager's status as a professional photographer, he may be aware that the photograph for which he posed may be published in a magazine spread, which in turn may also be documented into a police archive. If Yager enables humanistic representations of such "gang members," this photo must serve a purpose, but, with the information offered vis-à-vis the photographic realm, that purpose remains obscure at best.

In the "gang member shooting heroin" photo, the man posing for the photo is facing down while tugging with his teeth the strand of a belt tied around his arm while he "shoots up." This specific pose may have been negotiated; perhaps promises were made during the negotiation. Such examples and countless others stand as possible hypotheses regarding the negotiation process between Yager and his photographic subjects. The traffic of shooting—shooting heroin, shooting gangs—leaves the readers/viewers of these texts with nothing more than questions about the nature of the negotiation between Yager and his subjects. For, although Yager may be attempting to humanize these subjects, there is so much more at stake in the readings of his photos.

Building upon the notion of photography as inherently dialogic, ethnographer and visual arts theorist Eric Michaels also details the multivalent

FIGURE 13.4

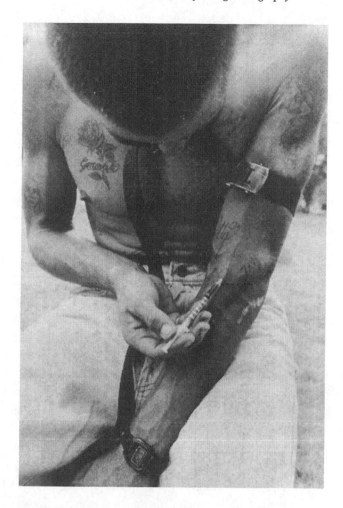

problems of perception. Arguing for a "cooperative photography," an ethnographic practice similar to the dialogism of the negotiated pose I have
discussed above, he too is aware of the meanings conveyed by and to the
photograph's "exterior" communities of readers. As he notes:

> There are certain kinds of images, camera positions, cropping and composi-
> tion, which suggest, perhaps subconsciously, certain attitudes toward the sub-
> ject in the "grammar" of photography. For example, the direction of the sub-
> ject's gaze toward the lens may convey much meaning. But . . . they guarantee

little in terms of a viewer's evaluation, and could hardly serve as a defense in any disputation.   *(1994:14)*

Michaels pointedly articulates my suspicion of ethnographic photography. Keeping this tension in place, I will now shift to another instance of ethnographic expression in gang photography that emphasizes the stakes of self-representation. I would like to engage a variety of texts (including autoethnographic narrative), to provoke dialogue about promising possibilities, but possibilities that are fraught with tensions emerging from autoethnographic photography.

THE AUTOETHNOGRAPHIC IMPULSE: "WHAT WE WERE REALLY LIKE"

Picture, if you will, one hot August day in 1994 in a southern California city. I caught a bus headed downtown to the library but decided to stop off at an aunt's house on impulse. After some customary warm greetings, we discussed my project on gang photography. She brought from a dresser drawer a photograph her husband, my uncle, received a few years back from some neighborhood friends. The full-color photo shows around twenty-five Latino men who belong(ed) to the L.A. "neighborhood" and with whom my uncle once associated. The members of the group assume various poses: Some squat with dangling hands between their knees, while others stand at soldierlike attention. A paired-off few engage in a handshake while staring toward the camera, four or five are "throwing their set" (the hand gestures symbolic of their distinct neighborhood). They range in age from thirteen to thirty years old. And there is a mural in the background. Emblazoned with the neighborhood's name etched in black ink, the back of the photograph accentuates as the title a familiar oldie tune, McKinley Mitchell's "The Town I Live In." From left to right, the nicknames of everyone represented correspond with their photographic placement.

Miguel Durán's semiautobiographical novel, *Don't Spit on My Corner* (1992), a narrative rich with details described from the eye of a young Chicano male in the World War II era of East Los Angeles, came to mind. The novel comments on the historical accounts of the media and law enforcement propagation of the 1940s Zoot Suit Riots. "Zoot Suiters," or pachucos, are often regarded as the forefathers of contemporary Chicano gang subcultures, and Durán's narrative proves effective for elucidating that family resemblance and its historical relationship with law enforcement and other communities or social institutions. The cover of the book shows a photograph of a group of young men. Juxtaposing this photo with my uncle's enables an amazing comparison. It is not just the photographic family resemblance that is striking, but also the genealogical threads of "poverty, stressed families, unemployment, underemployment, undereducation, racism, and the breakdown of sociocultural institutions" (Hutson et al. 1995:1031), spanning half a century and connecting these autoethnographic photos. Durán's narrative helps make those ties stronger.

Mary Louise Pratt uses the terms *autoethnography* and *autoethnographic expression* "to refer to instances in which colonized subjects undertake to represent themselves in ways that engage with the colonizer's own terms . . . in response to or in dialogue with those metropolitan representations" (1992:7–9). Echoing Pratt, bell hooks writes "Unlike photographs constructed so that black images would appear as the embodiment of colonizing fantasies, snapshots gave us a way to see ourselves, a sense of how we looked when we were not 'wearing the mask,' when we were not attempting to perfect the image for the white-supremacist gaze" (1995:62). Extrapolating from Pratt and hooks, I understand autoethnography as a practice in which colonized subjects turn the gaze inward.

In Durán's book, "Little Mike" describes a scene in which he feels the need to take up the camera:

> I had a camera, so I lined them up and took their picture. They were all young and good-looking, just like the song that Jesse Pinetop sang about our barrio. Eddie was in his sailor uniform. Butcher was home on furlough and wearing Levis instead of his sailor suit. The others in the picture were Chapa, Ballena, Joe, Rudy, Pope, Jesse, Pato and Chueco. They were just a small part of what made up the barrio of Tortilla Flats. . . . We were attracted to one another. There was a bond between us that was very strong. There probably would be several adventures with this group. Some things to laugh about and some to hang our collective heads over.
>
> *(1992:108–109)*

Little Mike's description works well as a reading of my uncle's photo precisely because both photographs comprise a particular genealogy of visual autoethnography. On the whole, *Don't Spit on My Corner* broaches the historical predicaments of self-fashioning in the face of legal retribution. In particular, several issues regarding Chicano youth gang representation float to the surface when these two photographic texts are juxtaposed.

In *Mi Vida Loca/My Crazy Life*, the 1993 film about girl gang members in Echo Park directed by Allison Anders, *Teen Angel's* magazine makes a cameo appearance when Sad Girl (Angel Aviles) introduces the magazine to her "school girl" sister La Blue Eyes (Magali Alvarado). While holding it in her hands, La Blue Eyes names the magazine that she swipes from Sad Girl: *Teen Angel's*. The voice-over, which is Sad Girl in the role of narrator, declares: "There was this magazine that shows us how we were really like." Her statement is one example of many a teen angel's claims to self-representation and is evidence for autoethnographic imaging. In color and black and white, there they were—those youths whose photos paraphrased a line from that classic song "Teen Angel": "Teen angel/Can you hear me?" becomes "Teen angel/Can you see me?"

This scene in *Mi Vida Loca* represents the autoethnographic stakes in *Teen Angel's* for a Chicano/Chicana youth in "real" life. (In fact, the film reveals why the magazine is always in demand because obtaining copies is difficult.) One distributor informed me that he was one of two people in San Francisco who stocked the magazine. Another distributor in Los Angeles told me it was risky business carrying *Teen Angel's* because the magazine acts as a mug book for police gang units. It should come as no surprise that recent issues of the magazine print a rider, "*Teen Angel's Magazine* supports the A.C.L.U. and the Bill of Rights." Although the publisher of the magazine is unknown through the information offered within its covers, the readers, who are often the contributors, make the magazine what it is. It is important to note that not all photos featured in *Teen Angel's* are "gang" photos; there are indeed photos that do not bear any noticeable trace of gang/neighborhood affiliation. But those that unabashedly declare allegiances to particular neighborhoods, cities, and/or state locations (e.g., Northern or Southern California) are the photos that—read in specific ways—carry the burden of representation.

Take a look at a familylike photo from South Side Los Angeles or SO.SI.LOS. Closer examination reveals the specific south side barrio those subjects in the photo claims, "Rooks Towne." "Ruketeros," their barrio moniker, is written above their images with what appears to be a permanent marker. At the bottom of the photo, the written text emblazoned on the pants of those in the picture was probably made possible with the etching of a pin. The etched text in the photo bears the markers X3, XIII, RTX3, and BRTX3R, all references to the number 13, and used as a metonym for Southern California. Sylent, whose name appears on its own in the bottom left-hand corner, probably took the picture, but other names are also marked on the photo, totaling eleven. There are also four women visually represented whose names are not present on the photo. Although the women are clearly participating in the production of RT13's image, with some even gesturing with hands and fingers Rooks Towne's "set," it is obvious that they are not fully partaking in the communal imaging of this photo.

Another photograph in the same issue shows a Chicano squatting before the camera, his back facing a mirror with the mirror facing the viewer of the photo. His arms, chest, and back are completely covered with tattoos. White shoes peek out from under the baggy pants he is wearing. There is a chain around his neck, and sunglasses (also known as "maddoggers") cover his eyes. He is tightlipped, offering a stern look to the viewer and photographer. Again, writing on the photo informs the visual text revealing the subject's name, "Mr. Woody," and his allegiance is to SURX3. Above his head looms the "LA" insignia of the Los Angeles Dodgers baseball team. East Los Angeles, or "ELA" as it is written, is "1#," meaning, of course, number one. (A misreading of the picture itself would presume complete attention to the image of Mr. Woody.) The text, however, offers another example of autoethnographic gang photography staking claims for the sake of collective memory. Twice in the photograph the writer of the text, most likely Mr. Woody, pays homage to a lost homeboy, "Teaser Valdo," to rest in peace or "R.I.P." Although not visually represented, Teaser interrupts the photographic realm through his friend's remembering him in writing on the photo.

In her discussion of Chicano narrative photography, Jennifer A. González notes, "Many contemporary photographers . . . have made use of the anchoring possibilities of text in their work, some to create political or metaphorical juxtapositions with an image, others to produce a narrative context" (1995:19). Autoethnophotographers, such as those described above, do employ such narrative strategies. As a means of "anchoring" the personal stakes of the photo, the photo becomes a twofold inscriptive text—either to allow a contextualization of details not visually evident or to elucidate the figures pictorially present. The photo thus becomes an illustration of multifold signification in that the visually graphic meets up with another version of graphic communication: writing.

Autoethnographic photos function as writerly texts as opposed to ethnographic photos. Barthes notes that "a writerly text is one I read with difficulty, unless I completely transform my reading regime" (1977:118). Although I attempt to read them, as exemplified above, I am certain there are details that go unaccounted for in my text. There are undeciphered symbols, names that cannot be connected to faces, acronyms impossible to decode, and moments and lived experiences that I cannot claim to have known. My readings, therefore, are untrustworthy. Following Barthes's suggestion, I deem these photos as "receivable" texts. As such, I am held accountable "to the following response: I can neither read nor write what you produce, but I receive it, like a fire, a drug, an enigmatic disorganization" (118). The importance of autoethnographic photos, nonetheless, should not rely on my readings alone but among the communities that produce and read them, such photos execute the vital, personal stakes always embedded in the process of imaging.

Yet as I have read these photos, others do, too—namely, the police, who read these photos not for their meaning but for their reference. The police, with their familiar interpellative gestures, depend upon the potential of photographic signification and are also compelled to take up the camera to produce that essential gangster image.

THE (RACED) BODY AND THE (POLICE) ARCHIVE

Allan Sekula and Sandra S. Phillips note how the necessity of criminals and the photographic figure of the criminal help maintain boundaries between good and bad, right and wrong, and self and other. In her essay "Identifying the Criminal," Phillips writes:

> We need criminals because they are not us. Crimes are transgressive acts, committed not by "normal" people but by those we define as outside the norm. It would appear that the systematic reaffirmation of this distinction is fundamental to our society. Our ability to distinguish right from wrong enables us, as responsible citizens, to identify, prosecute, and punish outlaws—individuals who flaunt social values. Paradoxically, the status of criminals as outsiders has made them heroes in our culture: The guilt, the "otherness," ensures freedom from society's strictures in a way that simultaneously attracts and frightens us.
>
> *(Phillips 1997:11)*

On the one hand, Phillips accurately points out that "our ability to distinguish right from wrong enables us to identify, prosecute, and punish outlaws." On the other hand, she insightfully highlights how "criminals as outsiders" are rendered "heroes in our culture." Because the criminal functions *as a fetishized object*—a point Phillips implicitly makes when she writes that the criminal "simultaneously attracts and frightens us"—we are able to distinguish right from wrong. For fetishism, Stuart Hall reminds us, "involves disavowal." And because "disavowal is the strategy by means of which a powerful fascination or desire is both indulged at the same time denied" (Hall 1997:267), the strange allure of the criminal is ultimately denied in order to maintain a "proper" split between self and other. Nevertheless, Phillips emphasizes photography as "a nineteenth-century technological invention seen to embody the new authority of empiricism" (1997:12):

> Photographs, used as evidence of fact, readily partook of and circulated within [a] larger scientific atmosphere, where the new study of criminology was emerging as a parallel cultural phenomenon. Many of the important scientific projects of the era exploited the photograph's perceived impartiality—as well as its speed, accuracy, and fidelity—to record or constitute their findings. Such forensic use continues to the present day. *(12)*

Indeed, the importance of photography for the police continues to rely precisely on the "perceived impartiality" of the image. This is evident in *Sansone's Police Photography*, where Larry L. Miller writes:

> Even though photography may develop into an electronic medium with most pictures recorded and stored on video tape, the basic principles of photography will not change. We still have the basic laws of perspective, correct tone reproduction, and so forth. Photographic processes are but a means to an end, and police are primarily concerned with whether the final photographic exhibit is a fair and accurate representation of a subject, rather than how it was reproduced. *(1993:4–5)*

Certainly, how police distinguish a "final photographic exhibit" that is "a fair and accurate representation of a subject" from one that is an unfair and inaccurate represenation of a subject is not always contingent upon the photograph's (or the visual text's) assumed objectivity. The Rodney King beating caught on video serves as a good illustration. Despite the video's visible evidence that Rodney King was severely beaten by four LAPD officers, the "evidence" read by the Simi Valley jurors, when they acquitted them of charges, was that the police were acting in self-defense. Lynne Kirby rightly notes, "even the camcorder's claim to objectivity as successor to the photographic camera has been thrown into doubt by the Rodney King verdict, leaving the question of technology as open as ever" (Kirby 1995:75). With the question of technology as open as ever, the visual text can be (mis)read for alternative interpretations when certain readings conflict with state hegemony. The visual image never only produces objective meaning in and of itself. But police interpretations of photos (or videos) are always concomitant with the ideological forces of the state that also maintain a tight grip on interpretations of the visual field. For example, as Judith Butler argues, "The visual field is not neutral to the question of race; it is itself a racial formation, and episteme, hegemonic and forceful" (1993:17).

In his insightful essay, "The Body and the Archive," Allan Sekula details how photographs have been utilized to detail what the criminal body looks like and how it should look in the process of "quite literally . . . facilitat[ing] the arrest of their referent" (1986:3). Key to Sekula's project is tracing the "biotype," a biologically determined criminal, and his/her impact on "the science of criminology" created in the photography he examines. Moreover, Sekula draws from the interpretive paradigms established in the nineteenth century by Alphonse Bertillon and Francis Galton. Although "the first rigorous system of archival cataloguing and retrival of photographs was invented by Bertillon," Galton established an "essentialist system of typology to . . . regulate social deviance by means of photography" and to "regulate the semantic traffic in photographs" (55). "Unfortunately," writes Sekula, "Bertillon and Galton are still with us":

> "Bertillon" survives in the operations of the national security state, in the condition of intensive and extensive surveillance that characterizes both everyday life and the geopolitical sphere. "Galton" lives in the renewed authority of biological determinism, founded in the increased hegemony of the political Right in the Western democracies.   *(62)*

"Bertillon" and "Galton" have especially affected minoritized subjects. As captured on the cover of Miguel Durán's book (1992), World War II coincides with the U.S. government's attempts to vilify Chicano youths. By

FIGURE 13.5

way of what Mauricio Mazón calls "symbolically annihilating" moves, the psychodynamics of general perception collapsed the views of Mexican Americans into a "condensed imagery" of them as "gangs, pachucos, and zoot-suiters" (1984:xi). The media-fueled "zoot suit" craze served as a catalyst to single out Mexican American youths based on a shared stance, "distinctive speech, body movement, and body adornment" (Luckenbill 1990:1). Although this stance was also adopted by white, black, and Filipino youths, it was the Sleepy Lagoon case of 1942 and the Zoot Suit Riots in 1943 that put Chicano Zoot Suiters on the most-wanted lists. Although my summary of the "Zoot Suit moment" is admittedly brief and broad, my intention is to focus more specifically on how law enforcement and media of this era produced photographs that were necessary for the invention of racialized deviants, and for their archival importance in police filing cabinets, mug books, and on corkboards.

The numerous photos appearing on the covers of Los Angeles newspapers during that time were often taken by and provided to the police. For example, in the exhibition catalog *The Pachuco Era*, Dan Luckenbill examines a photograph published in 1942 in the *Los Angeles Daily News* (figure 13.5):

> A report to a 1942 Los Angeles Grand Jury implied that Mexicans were like "wildcats." This supported the assumption that if a pachuco were detained, it would be "useless to turn him loose without having served a sentence." The wildcat "must be caged to be kept in captivity." This photograph shows one technique of labeling pachucos as "hoodlums." The bars of jail imply guilt. Actually, the pachucos show a sense of style in their resistant stance. *(1990:viii)*

The resistant stance detected by Luckenbill works in a similar fashion as the poses in ethnographic gang photography; however, the collaborative efforts between the media and law enforcement are evident in the photos. Also, like Yager's photo on *Newsweek*'s cover, the racialized bodies of these Mexican "wildcats" ultimately signify the exact opposite of civility and accentuate a presumption of wildness.

Another photo from the *Daily News* shows a mug shot of a well-known individual, Henry Leyvas, the key suspect of the Sleepy Lagoon case who was charged with conspiracy to commit murder (figure 13.6). Luckenbill writes, "Harsh photographs of the Sleepy Lagoon defendants taken under jail circumstances contributed to the effect of their being guilty before the trial" (4). This photograph illustrates how Mexican Americans were cast as uncivilized and criminal through the photo, especially the mug shot. Such photographs provide viewers with details, images, and evidence that may have convicted defendants based on biological features and clothing.In *Race, Police, and the Making of a Political Identity: Mexican Americans and the Los Angeles Police Department, 1900–1945*, Edward J. Escobar discusses how traditional interpretations of the zoot suit hysteria blame newpapers like the *Los Angeles Daily News*, the *Los Angeles Herald and Express*, and the *Los Angeles Examiner* (the latter two owned by William Randolph Hearst) "for fomenting fears about Mexican American youths" (Escobar 1999:198). But the press was not solely to blame for igniting the flames of these fears, Escobar explains:

FIGURE 13.6

The press may indeed have incited the public to hysteria, but the newspapers generally did not fabricate the stories they printed. Rather, reporters wrote their stories with the active assistance, support, and encouragement of law-enforcement and political officials. As Nick Williams, the night news editor for the *[Los Angeles] Times* during the hysteria, noted, reporters could not have written their stories without information from police sources. Williams's recollections are supported by the many news stories that specifically acknowledged that the information they contained came from police. Thus, the press could claim, as Williams later did, that while the coverage "may have been inflammatory, . . . at the time, we thought we were objectively covering the news."   *(198)*

This information sheds light on the significance of these newspaper photographs. Because the photos, like the information for articles, came from police sources, the objectivity of the images along with the news accompanying them is questionable. Indeed, the rhetorical force of these photos also "promot[ed] the idea that Mexican Americans, and especially Mexican American youths, presented a serious crime problem or, even worse, that they were biologically inclined toward crime and violence" (198).

Daniel C. Tsang writes about instances of branding Asian American youths as gang members in Orange County, California: "police have detained and photographed Asian youths merely on suspicion that they belong to gangs or are 'gang associates,' " all the while aided by the "police department's alleged practice of keeping a 'mug book' on Asian American youths who have never been arrested" (1993:B5). The same story holds as true for Chicano youths as it does for other youths of color. As the mug book photos document, they are guilty until proven innocent given their supposed biological inclination toward crime and violence. One scene in Anders's *Mi Vida Loca* depicts the police taking photographs of suspected gang members. Giggles (Marlo Marron), recently released from prison and up on her knowledge of legal protocol, attempts to prevent the cops from taking snapshots of "gang-bangers" with a Polaroid camera. Giggles is well aware that this practice is in violation of their legal rights because some girls being photographed are minors. Yet photographing minors suspected of gang member affiliation is not uncommon in police circles, and collapsing innocence with guilt is even more common for those who are (mis)read as a threat to society. The recent dismantling of Los Angeles CRASH units over proven allegations of police misconduct serves as a fitting reminder. Although Giggles is unsuccessful in her attempt to interrupt the photographic gaze of the police, Robert Yager has shot back by capturing these police photographic practices in his own work (figure 13.7).

PERCEPTION OVER REPRESENTATION

The historical presence of Chicano gangs firmly anchors both baiting and fascination; therefore the image of the gangster probably will not fade away any time soon. Moreover, the evils of gangs is a topic taken up by a range of influential people, from Los Angeles board supervisor Gloria Molina to the president of the United States. At the same time, there is a strong in-

FIGURE 13.7

trigue with or appeal to street gangs within a number of arenas. Also, ethnographic photography is by no means limited to Robert Yager. Photographers José Galvez, Graciela Iturbide (1996), and Joseph Rodríguez (1998) have expanded the field of gang photography and its vision. But what about the material conditions of their existence from which gangs are often abstracted?

The frameworks of conservative and liberal politics, the media, the trafficking of drugs and guns that leads to violence are continually detached from their interlocking relations to how such political-economic institutions thrive on maintaining antagonistic oppositions between rich/poor, white/of color, and male/female. What conditions—social and otherwise—circumscribe some communities, provoking them to kill with little remorse? This is a question U.S. society and our leaders need to be asking, particularly those who shy away from fully comprehending the notion of "youth in crisis." Larger questions and discussions need to be engaged by those whose evaluations derive from representations of "hoodlums," "thugs," "scum," and—according to one Los Angeles news anchor—"the vilest of the vile." Extrapolating from the classic study on the ideological creation of the "moral panic" around a "mugging problem" in 1970s England (Hall et al. 1978), Marjorie S. Zatz notes that the creation of a moral panic around Chicano gangs is more often than not propagated by "the social imagery of Chicano youth gangs, rather than their actual behavior, that lay at the root of the gang problem" (1987:153). Zatz is critical of this misleading, racialized, and class-biased discourse in which youth gangs are "defined as a serious social problem—a problem to which the media and law enforcement agencies respond vociferously and vigorously" (153). Moreover, because quick-fix solutions to prevent gang formation have yet to be uncovered, attempts to stop violence are too frequently masked by the desire to "control" gang members. These means of control are often coded in military-style terminology and practices that endorse tactics that are comparable to (talk about) wiping out undesirable populations and that ignore the socioeconomic conditions and conditioning particular to those populations. The goal is to seize the criminal in an attempt to control his or her purportedly inherent defiant nature.

Not surprisingly, photographs have been used to identify the criminal and to pin down the alleged suspect/subject of gang activity. Photographs give credence to identifying a suspected gang member on the basis of a shaved head, baggy pants, white T-shirt, body posture, and other signifiers of the gangster stance. Victor Burgin rightly notes, "a photograph is not to be reduced to 'pure form,' nor 'window on the world,' nor is it a gangway to the presence of the author." Rather, "Photography is one signifying system among others in society which produces the ideological subject in the same movement in which they 'communicate' their ostensible 'contents' " (Burgin 1982:153). In turn, the subject of gang photography must ultimately pose a set of questions and problems for the ideological forces through which imaging is necessary in the name of (self-) representation but is never an innocent practice.

REFERENCES

Barthes, Roland. 1977. *Roland Barthes by Roland Barthes*. Translated by Richard Howard. New York: Hill and Wang.

————. 1985. "The Rhetoric of the Image." In Robert Innis, ed., *Semiotics: An Introductory Anthology*, 192–205. Translated by Stephen Heath. Bloomington: Indiana University Press.

Benjamin, Walter. 1968. "The Work of Art in the Mechanical Age of Reproduction." In Hannah Arendt, ed., *Illuminations: Essays and Reflections*, 217–251. Translated by Harry Zohn. New York: Shocken Books.

Bourdieu, Pierre. 1990. *Photography: A Middle-brow Art.* Translated by Shaun Whiteside. Standford: Standford Universtiy Press.

Burgin, Victor. 1982. "Looking at Photographs." In Victor Burgin, ed., *Thinking Photography*, 142–53. London: Macmillan.

Butler, Judith. 1993. "Endangered/Endangering: Schematic Racism and White Paranoia." In Robert Gooding-Williams, ed., *Reading Rodney King/Reading Urban Uprising*, 15–22. New York: Routledge.

Clifford, James. 1988. *The Predicament of Culture: Twentieth-Century Ethnography, Literature, and Art.* Cambridge: Harvard University Press.

Collier, John Jr., and Malcolm Collier. 1986. *Visual Anthropology: Photography as a Research Method.* Albuquerque: University of New Mexico Press.

Durán, Miguel. 1992. *Don't Spit on My Corner.* Houston: Arte Publico Press.

Durham, Jimmie. 1992. "Geronimo!" In Lucy R. Lippard, ed., *Partial Recall: Photographs of Native North Americans*, 55–58. New York: The New Press.

Escobar, Edward J. 1999. *Race, Police, and the Making of a Political Identity: Mexican Americans and the Los Angeles Police Department, 1900–1945.* Berkeley: University of California Press.

Gonzáles, Jennifer A. 1995. "Negotiated Frontiers: Contemporary Chicano Photography." In Chon A Noriega, ed., *From the West: Chicano Narrative Photography*, 17–22. Exhibition book. San Francisco: Mexican Museum.

Hall, Stuart. 1997. *Representation: Cultural Representations and Signifying Practices.* London: Sage.

Hall, Stuart, Chas Critcher, Tony Jefferson, John Clarke, and Brian Roberts. 1978. *Policing the Crisis: Mugging, the State, and Law and Order.* London: Macmillan Press.

Hebdige, Dick. 1988. "Hiding in the Light: Youth Surveillance and Display." In *Hiding in the Light*, 17–41. New York: Routledge.

hooks, bell. 1995. "In Our Glory: Photography and Black Life." In *Art on My Mind: Visual Politics*, 54–64. New York: New Press.

Hutson, H. Range, Deirdre Anglin, Demetrios N. Kyriacou, Joel Hart, and Kelvin Spears. 1995. "The Epidemic of Gang-Related Homicides in Los Angeles County from 1979 to 1994." *JAMA: Journal of the American Medical Association* 274, no. 13 (4 October): 1031–1036.

Iturbide, Graciela. 1996. *Images of the Spirit.* New York: Aperture Foundation.

Kirby, Lynne. 1995. "Death and the Photographic Body." In Patrice Petro, *Fugitive Images: From Photography to Video*, 72–84. Bloomington: Indiana University Press.

Klein, Malcolm W. 1995. *The American Street Gang: Its Nature, Prevalence, and Control.* New York: Oxford University Press.

LA Weekly. 1995. "A Troubled Eye: Robert Yager's Photographs of Life in the Gangs." *LA Weekly*, 26 May–1 June, p. 28.

Luckenbill, Dan. 1990. *The Pachuco Era.* Exhibition book. Los Angeles: UCLA University Research Library.

Mazón, Mauricio. 1984. *The Zoot-Suit Riots: The Psychology of Symbolic Annihilation.* Austin: University Research Library.

Michaels, Eric. 1994. *Bad Aboriginal Art: Tradition, Media, and Technological Horizons.* Minneapolis: University of Minnesota Press.

Miller, Larry L. 1993. *Sansone's Police Photography.* 3d ed. Cincinnati: Anderson Publishing.

Mitchell, William J. 1992. *The Reconfigured Eye: Visual Truth in the Post Photographic Era.* Cambridge: MIT Press.

Phillips, Sandra S. 1997. "Identifying the Criminal." In Sandra S. Phillips, Mark Haworth-Boot, and Carol Squiers, eds., *Police Pictures: The Photograph as Evidence*, 11–31. San Francisco: Chronicle Books.

Pratt, Mary Louise. 1992. *Imperial Eyes: Travel Writing and Transculturation.* New York: Routledge.

Rodríguez, Joseph. 1998. *East Side Stories: Gang Life in East L.A.* New York: Powerhouse Books.

Sekula, Allan. 1986. "The Body and the Archive." *October* 39: 3–64.

Senft, Bret. 1995. "Yager Arrested while Covering L.A. Gangs." *PDN: Photo District News* (August): 40–45.

Tsang, Daniel C. 1993. "Is 'Innocent until Proven Guilty' a Lost Principle?" *Los Angeles Times*, 30 August, p. B5

Yager, Robert. 1993. "Camera Man: A Photographer Reflects on How His Work with Gangs Got Him Arrested." *LA Weekly*, 26 May–1 June, p. 32.

Zatz, Marjorie S. 1987. "Chicano Youth Gangs and Crime: The Creation of a Moral Panic." *Contemporary Crises*, 11: 129–158.

14

FROM CIVIL WAR TO GANG WAR: THE TRAGEDY OF EDGAR BOLANOS

DONNA DECESARE

For more than a decade, U.S. street gangs have been spreading to Central America and the Caribbean. It is a trend exacerbated by the policies of the U.S. Immigration and Naturalization Service (INS). At first glance, one might ask: Why not send immigrants who have broken American laws home—especially if they belong to gangs? But sweeping the gang problem across U.S. borders has proven to be neither a tidy nor a fair solution.

The emergence of youth gangs in El Salvador with ties to Los Angeles gangs is emblematic of a problem that affects not only El Salvador but all of Central America and the Caribbean. But in the case of El Salvador, it is also tragically linked to the trauma of an earlier decade of war in which the United States played a pivotal role. El Salvador's twelve-year-long civil war drove more than one million refugees from that country, a majority of them making their way illegally to southern California.

U.S. citizens in the 1980s were divided over a Cold War foreign policy that—in the name of defeating "communism"—provided billions of U.S.

tax dollars to a Salvadoran military regime responsible for terrible human rights violations. Salvadoran refugees were shunned by some Americans, but were welcomed and defended by church groups and citizens opposed to U.S. involvement in the war. However, as domestic concern over crime and illegal immigration rose in the late 1980s and early 1990s, the U.S. Congress pressed the INS to improve its record of deporting illegal aliens.

1992 was a fateful year for El Salvador. The signing of the Salvadoran Peace Accords ended civil war, but did not solve the economic inequities that inspired it. Salvadorans in El Salvador and refugees in the United States faced the 1990s task of rebuilding their traumatized country and family life with diminished interest and support from the U.S. church and human rights workers who redirected their triage efforts to Bosnia and elsewhere. In the riots that followed the Rodney King verdict in 1992, the *Los Angeles Times* reported that thousands of Latinos were detained, and the INS deported almost eight hundred of them, many to El Salvador. That year, the INS launched its Violent Gang Task Force amid a new wave of anti-immigrant sentiment. Then, in 1996, new laws took effect that aimed at deporting illegal and legal immigrants who have fallen afoul of U.S. laws.

In 1997, nearly fifteen hundred Salvadorans with criminal records were deported from U.S. streets and prisons, according to INS statistics.[1] In 1998 and 1999, the numbers have increased. And these figures do not reflect the many more expulsions that occur as "voluntary departures" rather than formal deportations. Many among the criminal deportees to El Salvador belong to two rival L.A. gangs: Eighteenth Street or Mara Salvatrucha (MS). The result for El Salvador has been a decade of gang warfare, crack houses, renewed death squad activity, and a homicide rate higher than the death toll during the war years.

THE STORY OF EDGAR BOLANOS

Edgar Bolanos, also known as "Shy Boy," trudges to the edge of a soccer field with his friend "Scrappy" a few steps behind. They are searching for the "original" Shy Boy. Even the walls of this remote village in rural Sonsonate, El Salvador are marked with gang symbols. But Shy Boy passes the graffiti disinterestedly. He's not looking for a local homeboy. He changes direction several times, finally spotting what he is after—his brother José's grave.

Edgar tells the same story I have heard from his mother Ana and his brother Hugo. He is haunted by a three-year-old's memory of soldiers torturing and killing his uncles and other villagers in a soccer field a few miles from this one near his brother's tomb. He remembers the bravery of his grandmother withstanding soldiers' punches for refusing to tell where his father, a guerrilla fighter, was hiding. The fierce bond of loyalty and code of silence that saved their father is emulated by the surviving Bolanos sons.

The boys were raised by their peasant grandparents until their mother Ana, who had fled El Salvador in 1983 fearing her husband's guerrilla involvement and the consequent army threats on her life, could send for her sons to join her in Los Angeles. The reunion, which had taken six years, was difficult.

The boys clashed, first with their new stepfather and then with Chicano gang members in school. It was not long before Hugo and José joined the Mara Salvatrucha gang. Edgar was only thirteen when, to his mother's dismay, he followed in his big brothers' footsteps. "My mom brought me back here to El Salvador, because José told her some Eighteenth Street gang members were going to kill me in Los Angeles," Edgar says in a low voice. "The bullet meant for me got him instead."

Ana Bolanos remembers events differently. She says she thought that bringing her youngest son to live with her mother would keep Edgar in school and safe from the life in and out of U.S. prisons that her eldest son Hugo seemed destined to live. But shortly after she brought Edgar to El Salvador, Hugo was deported. Within a few months, José, her son who remained in L.A., was murdered in a drive-by shooting. "They killed my son because he was in love with a girl from the Eighteenth Street gang," Ana recalls tearfully. "They found them together in a parked car. José was dead, but the girl survived."

Edgar reacted by taking his dead brother's gang name—Shy Boy. Shortly after José's body was brought from L.A. for burial in El Salvador, Edgar tattooed his mother's name Ana above a tombstone with the name "Shy Boy" on his back. Then he left his grandmother's house and began hanging out in the gang crash pads of San Salvador where he continues to live.

During predusk hours when school children in crumpled uniforms race home, past the *maquila* factory workers wearily descending from buses, Shy Boy and his friends emerge alert and ready for business. They scatter in clusters around their cul-de-sac. Several move toward a grocery store, displaying their crop of gold chains and other "hot" items for interested buyers.

A middle-aged woman, with stern Indian features, balances a basket of fruit on her head as she glides past graffiti-sprayed walls. Three not-so-muscular youths in tight muscle shirts wave their tattooed arms wildly, throwing gang hand signs and flirting to grab her attention. Finally she cracks a smile. Wiping her hands on her stained ruffled apron, she lowers her basket. The boys laugh as mango juice escapes from their lips. She laughs with them.

Shy Boy, aloof and elusive, takes in the scene. "People here think I'm the gang leader because I used to live in Los Angeles," he says almost wistfully. "But we don't have leaders. I have respect from the homeboys, but I don't tell other people what to do."

This corner and the surrounding streets of this working-class enclave are Big Gangsta Locos territory. About thirty youths belong to BGLS, a subgroup or clique of the infamous Mara Salvatrucha or MS gang of Los Angeles. Apart from Shy Boy, all of the mostly fifteen- and sixteen-year-old "gangstas" in this enclave have never lived outside El Salvador. Shy Boy, who will soon turn nineteen, is the oldest member of the group. Although he may not be the leader, it is clear from the way the others approach and quietly confer with him that his opinions are valued highly.

As darkness falls, the homeboys begin to make their rounds, setting off in groups of twos or threes, to check out who is on their turf. "We protect the people here from enemy gangs and thieves that would rob them," Shy Boy says proudly. "We never steal from our own barrio. That is why we get along with people here."

It is true that many people stop to chat or joke with the youths, as they saunter along. But just as many tense up or clutch their children tighter, not daring to look at the tattooed faces they hurry past. And the resentful stares of a small group of men—among them an off-duty police officer and the owner of the local bus route—follow the youths as they progress down a lane.

Two blocks over, a foot patrol of the National Civilian police stop and briskly frisk Shy Boy, Flash, and Scrappy. They sternly demand identification papers, which none of the youths have. Finding neither drugs nor weapons, they let the boys go with an angry warning to go home and stay out of trouble. "They're not doing anything right now," the cop remarks to no one in particular. "But when they get drunk and drugged they are a plague on these streets."

Shy Boy admits that many of the homeboys get into street fights when they are drunk or stoned. He himself recently suffered permanent loss of feeling and movement in three fingers, after a neighborhood drunk (not a gang member) severed the nerves in his right hand with a machete. The same man attacked Scrappy with several dangerously deep gashes to the head. "We were really high so we didn't even understand what was happening." Shy Boy recalls. "No one came to help us. I guess it's a miracle that we are still alive."

Indeed it is no small miracle. According to the Pan-American Health Organization (PAHO), El Salvador's homicide rate of 150 per 100,000 people is the highest in the hemisphere, surpassing even Colombia.[2] Moreover, the PAHO figures would indicate that violence—if defined by the annual homicide rate, the most commonly cited proxy for crime and violence in general—is greater in El Salvador now than during the 1980s, when civil war grabbed international headlines and hundreds of thousands of peasant refugees escaping mayhem and economic collapse sought sanctuary in the crowded slums of Los Angeles.[3]

Shy Boy lists the names of homeboys killed in shoot-outs with rival gangs. There are five he knew well. As he continues his honor roll of MS dead, he mentions a homeboy the author first met in Los Angeles. After his deportation to El Salvador, "Chino" was executed with a bullet to the head and found with his thumbs tied behind his back. La Sombra Negra (the Black Shadow), a paramilitary-style death squad that targets gang members in El Salvador, claimed responsibility for his murder.

Chino was executed in the spring of 1995 just before the *Washington Post* reported a spate of death-squad-style killings that left more than thirty youths dead in less than two months. At the time, the Roman Catholic Church's Legal Aid Office—Tutela Legal—charged that the vigilante groups included active members of the newly formed civilian police force. Created under the 1992 Peace Accords, the National Civilian Police (PNC) replaced the security forces associated with the repressive military regimes of the preceding years. Their raison d'etre is to provide democratic nonpartisan law enforcement. By 1995, several Black Shadow vigilantes—police agents with ties to the old terror networks of the 1970s and 1980s—had been arrested for the 1994 extrajudicial killings of three Mara Salvatrucha members in the eastern city of San Miguel.[4] Since then, the rate of murders by death squads has been less dramatic. But they continue: sometimes unnoticed except by grieving family members, sometimes acknowledged in the Salvadoran press or in human rights statistics.

The criminal violence of vigilantes acting against youth gang members is seldom vigorously investigated in El Salvador. And many Salvadoran citizens don't care. They are fearful and angered by the rising assault and homicide rates they read about as they sip their morning coffee. Newspaper reports mentioning youth are, with few exceptions, stories about crime or the menace of *maras*, the Salvadoran term for gangs. Most callers responding to a call-in poll conducted by YSU, one of El Salvador's most popular radio stations, supported the Black Shadow and some even invited the group to come clean up their neighborhoods.[5] Several Salvadoran newspapers have published poll results with nearly half of respondents supporting the "social cleansing" activities of death squads that target those perceived as criminals.[6]

The Salvadoran government's response to youth violence is gang suppression: emergency crime legislation suspending rights of habeas corpus and the formation of special antigang police units trained by experts from the Los Angeles Police Department. Reform of the juvenile justice code and modest improvement in prison conditions followed a spate of violent prison uprisings in which inmates were hacked to death by other prisoners wielding knives.

But the antiquated judicial system is rife with corruption. At the time of the initial research for this report (1999), the United Nations Latin American Institute for the Prevention of Crime (ILANUD) reported that Salvadoran prisons were filled to more than double their capacity and that more than 70 percent of those incarcerated were unconvicted prisoners awaiting trial. Despite some improvement, the system is still in need of reform. According to a report issued by the Salvadoran Government department of corrections in July 2002, prisons are now operating at approximately 45 percent beyond their capacity. Slightly more than half of those incarcerated have been sentenced, with around 48 percent being unconvicted prisoners awaiting sentencing.[7]

Bribes buy murderers instant freedom while innocent indigents languish in unsanitary and overcrowded cells for up to two years before their cases are heard and dismissed.

It is disturbing to contemplate where Salvadoran demographics and economics seem headed. Nearly half the country's population is under eighteen years old and three-quarters of Salvadoran children live in poverty.[8] What is changing is perception—the fact, for example, that Salvadorans now experience their poverty and define themselves through the window of television.[9] Even if most impoverished Salvadoran youths could aspire to a *maquila* factory job—the fastest growing sector of the Salvadoran economy—they would earn the Salvadoran minimum wage of four dollars a day. With the price of a pound of beans—the Salvadoran staple food—the same as it is in the United States, such wages barely ensure subsistence. But slick television advertising and the aggressive marketing of American youth culture have whetted consumer desires in a generation that largely will be unable to satisfy those desires or even their most basic needs through work. What will happen when they begin to swell the ranks of the "lost generation"—glue-addicted children, crack-addled teenagers, and tattooed "gangstas" who have been orphaned by war and emigration or deportation?

Of the 800,000 adolescents thirteen to eighteen years of age, constituting 14 percent of the total El Salvador population, UNICEF estimates that only 40 percent attend school and 29 percent work.[10] How the remaining 31 percent, roughly 249,000 youths, occupy their time is unknown. But youth gang membership is growing at an alarming pace, and some studies suggest that as many as 30,000 youths may belong to street gangs nationwide. Salvadoran gang members once aped the "look" seen in popular Hollywood "gangsta" movies like *Colors* or *American Me* with homegrown versions of *cholo* style. Now Dickies and Ben Davis pants and Pendleton shirts are being marketed in the shopping malls of San Salvador. Rappers Snoop Doggie Dog, Control Machete, and Doctor Dre blare from barrio radios. And kids desperate for "real" Nike kicks will spend a family's whole remittance check, sell crack, or steal to buy them. Acquiring style is costly and requires effort of some kind. Clearly poverty isn't the only thing drawing Salvadoran youths into gangs.

Miguel Cruz, who teaches at the Jesuit-run Central American University, seems an unlikely expert on the attractions of gang life. It would be hard to imagine this mild intellectual, who conducts political campaign polls and public opinion surveys, approaching gang members, much less training them. But that is exactly what Professor Cruz has done. "We trained gang members to be investigators for our public opinion survey of the gangs," he explains, "because we realized that if a bunch of university professors and students could even get gang members to talk to us, the responses would have been much different."

Cruz's survey of more than one thousand gang members from Mara Salvatrucha and Eighteenth Street gangs in San Salvador offers evidence that most gang members are seeking respect and friendship, as well as an identity and a replacement family. Twice as many respondents considered drug addiction their biggest problem as compared with the next-highest-ranked problem, unemployment. When asked about their future dreams, jobs topped the list, followed by a stable family. More than 80 percent of the youths interviewed said that violence is a negative aspect of gang life that they desperately wish would end. Nearly 70 percent had experienced the murder of a close friend or family member, and half had themselves been injured badly enough to require hospitalization. The vast majority are fatalistic about change and skeptical of politics.

At the top of the cul-de-sac where Shy Boy's clique gathers, Luis Polanco owns a small grocery store. Looking around his working-class enclave, Polanco says there is a feeling in the air that reminds him of the early war years when things began to fall apart. He knows of at least four vigilante groups, backed by small businesses in his neighborhood, who are arming themselves to eradicate the local youth gangs.

"They are waiting, but they are serious and one of the cops agrees with them," Polanco says in hushed tones. He understands his neighbors' resentment and frustration, though he doesn't condone their actions. "You ask yourself, 'Why should I work sweating like a slave all day to sell Coca-Colas, and have these vagabonds constantly begging for money to pay for their drugs and shiftless life?'" He shakes his head sadly and continues, "This war here did terrible things to people. And what was it all in the end except poor people killing other poor people?"

Across the street, Shy Boy sits lost in thought. He is wondering if there is some way he can remove his tattoos—at least the ones on his face and arms. He says he wants to get a job so he can have kids. But there is another reason too. Shy Boy no longer wants to die. Edgar is beginning to realize that his brother José's fate was neither his fault nor his responsibility to avenge. He is at a turning point, struggling urgently with questions about who he is, the meaning of family and loyalty, and the kind of future he wants for his children.

Edgar Bolanos is the new El Salvador, caught between a peasant past and the dislocations of the present, caught between the generation of romanticized rebel fighters and that of vilified young "gangstas." His search for identity parallels El Salvador's search for a shared definition of justice, respect, and participation.

EPILOGUE

Edgar Bolanos now lies in Sonsonate in the same grave as his brother José: the fragile light of his dawning hopes extinguished by an assassin's bullet. Edgar was killed on 9 January 1999, during the two-month period of December 1998 to January 1999 when Tutela Legal, the Human Rights Office of the Catholic Church in San Salvador reported a pattern of increased death squad and vigilante activity and extrajudicial killings of youth gang members.

Who killed Edgar Bolanos? His death remains an unsolved mystery shrouded in rumor. The police investigation has been inconclusive. His mother Ana spoke with several witnesses who allege that the drive-by shooting that occurred at ten10:00 in the morning outside his in-laws' home was done by local vigilantes.

NOTES

1. INS, 1997 year-end report.
2. "Assessing Personal Security in Latin America," *Latin America Special Report*, Departamento de Registro y Control Penitenciarías, de la Dirección de Centros Penales, dependiente del Ministerio de Gobernación [Salvadoran Ministry of Government, Bureau of Penal Centers, Department of Control and Registration in the Penitentiaries], April 1997. This report cites statistics prepared by the Pan-American Health Organization (PAHO) Health Situation Analysis Program, 1997, and the World Bank publication "Crime and Violence as Development Issues in Latin America and the Caribbean," 1997.
3. With a population of 5.8 million people and a homicide rate of 150 per 100,000 people, El Salvador would have about 8,700 murders each year. Salvadoran police statistics place the homicide figure even higher than PAHO, at roughly 11,000 per year. It is estimated that about 70,000 lost their lives in the twelve-year-long Salvadoran civil war—approximately 5,833 per year.
4. A total of twelve civilians and four policemen were arrested for the 1994 slayings. During the April 1997 trial of three of these Sombra Negra members, the mayor of San Miguel praised them and they were acquitted. Reported in the *New York Times*, 10 August 1997.
5. *Washington Post*, 27 May 1995.
6. Ibid.

7. *Latin America Special Report*, April 1997; statistics from ILANUD (Instituto Latinamericano de las Naciones Unidas para la prevención del Delito. [United Nations Latin American institute for the prevention of crime.]).

8. UNICEF, *State of the World's Children* (New York: UNICEF, 1999).

9. Ibid. UNICEF estimates that one out of every ten Salvadorans owns a television and 48 percent own radios. The figures for household ownership would be much higher.

10. Internal UNICEF document footnote: UNICEF estimates based on the 1995 household survey.

FIGURE 14.1

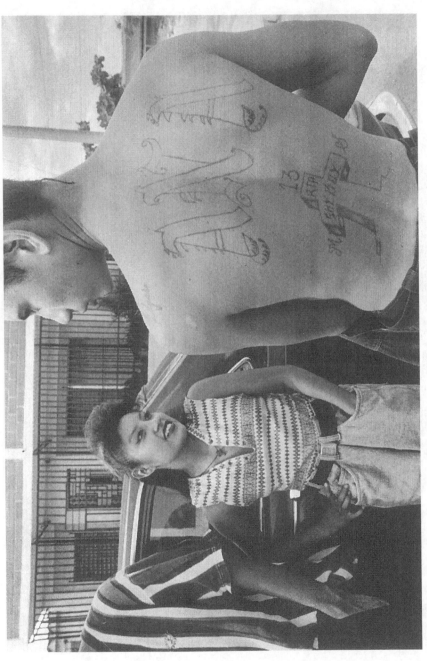

FIGURE 14.2

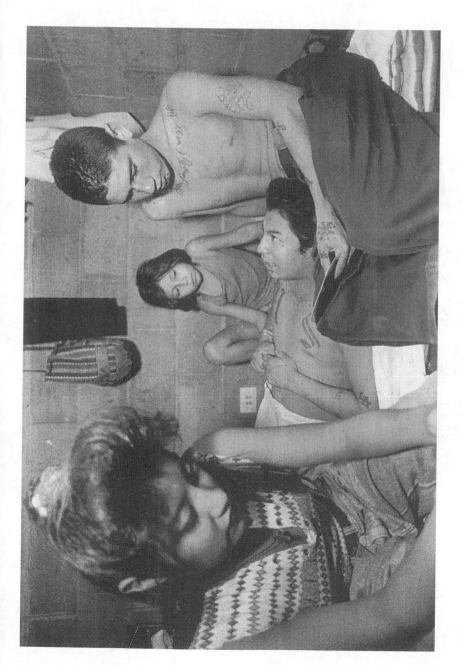

FIGURE 14.3

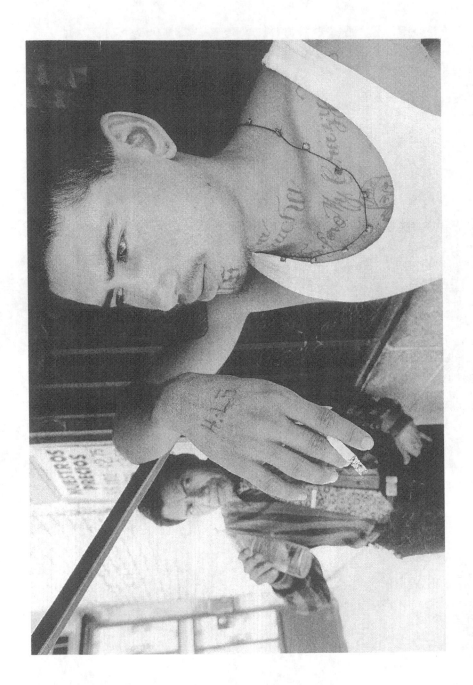

FIGURE 14.4

FIGURE 14.5

FIGURE 14.6

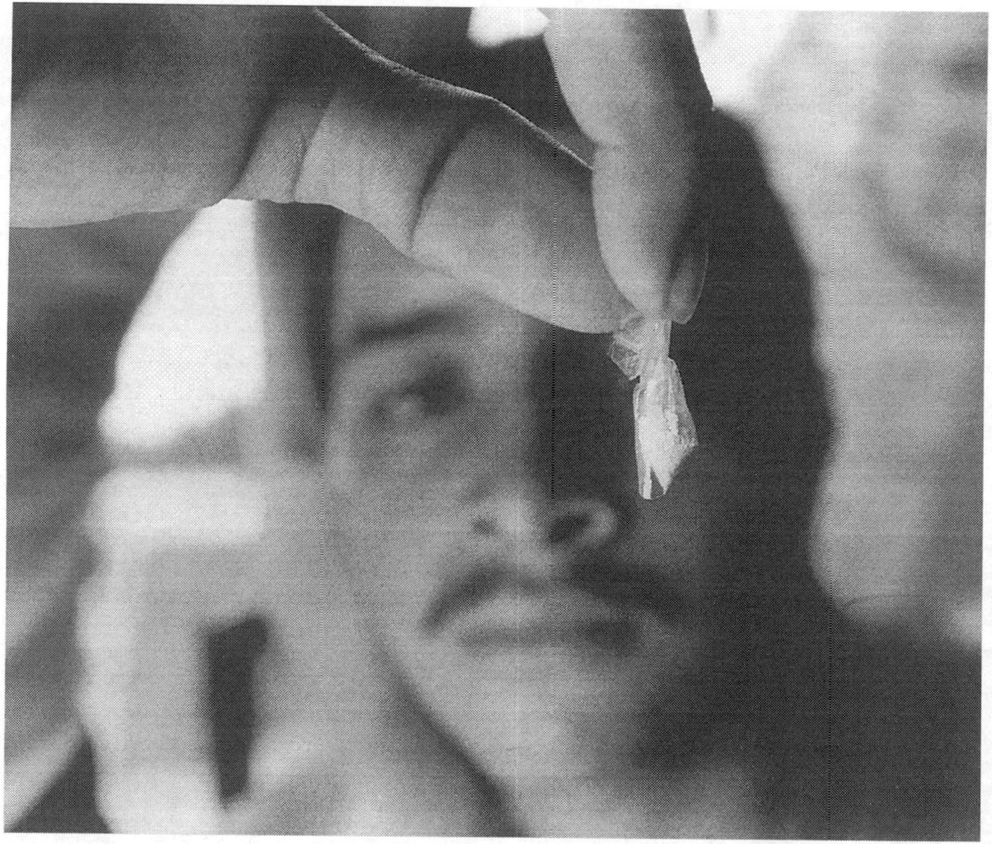

FIGURE 14.7

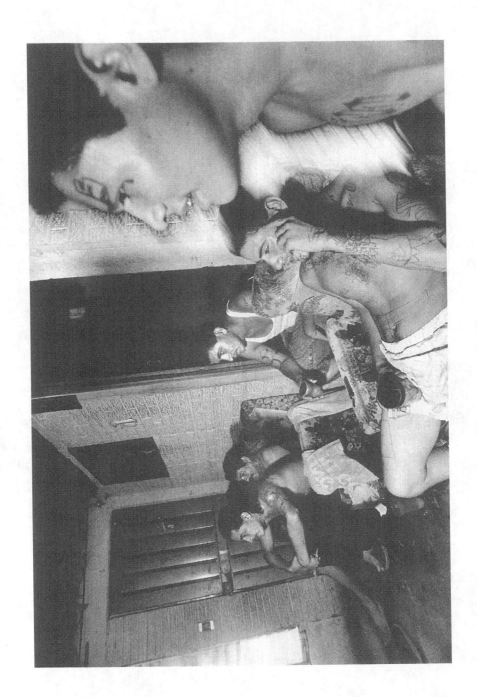

FIGURE 14.8

FIGURE 14.9

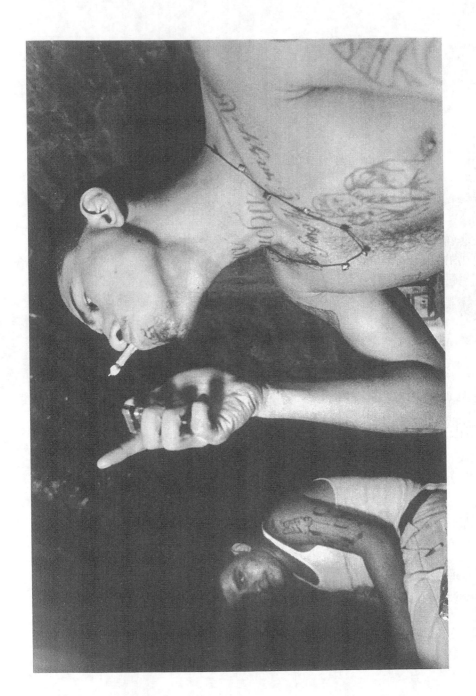

FIGURE 14.10

FIGURE 14.11

FIGURE 14.12

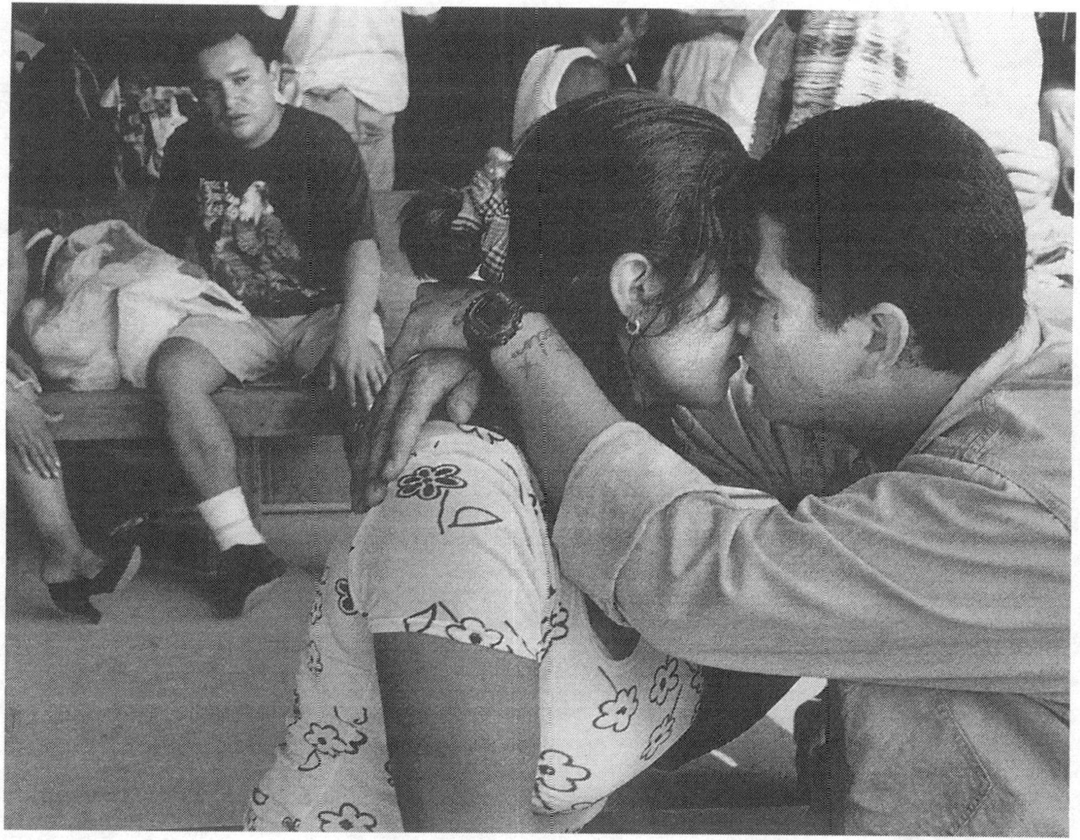

FIGURE 14.13

FIGURE 14.14

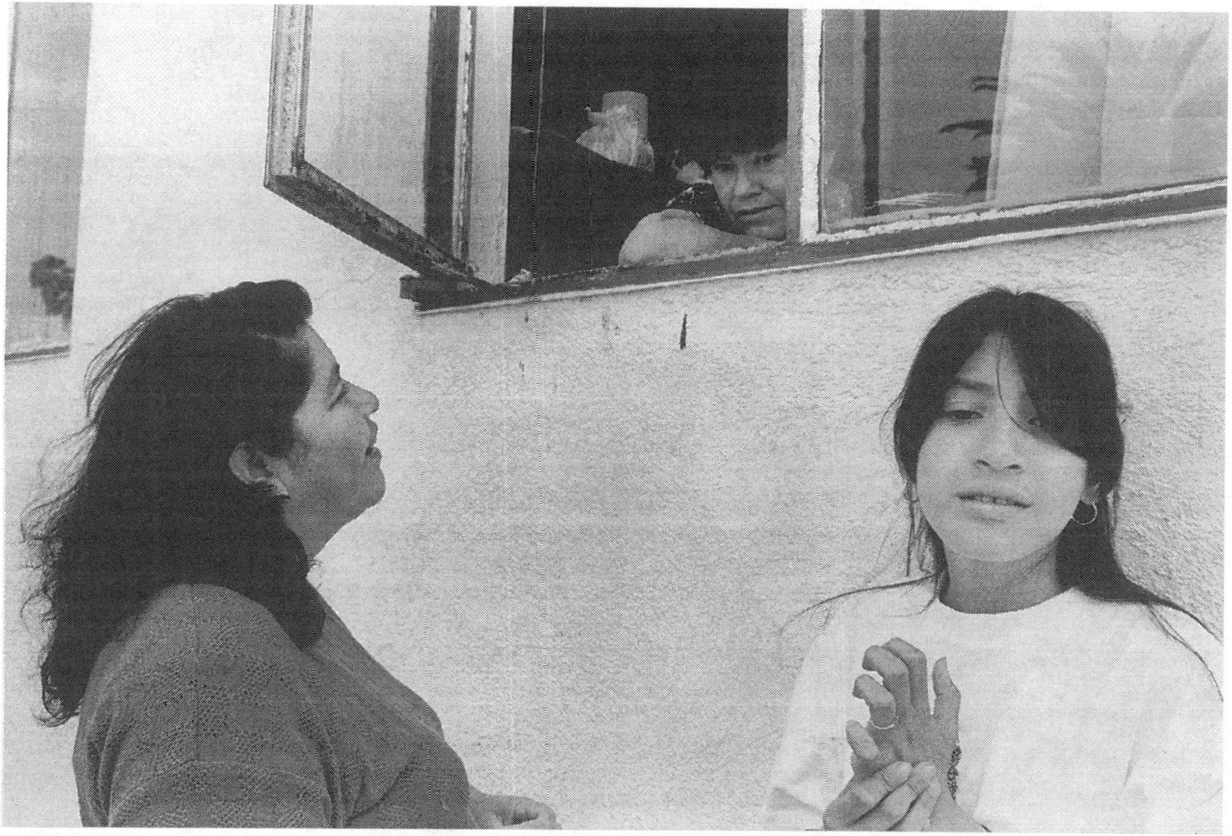

FIGURE 14.15

FIGURE 14.16

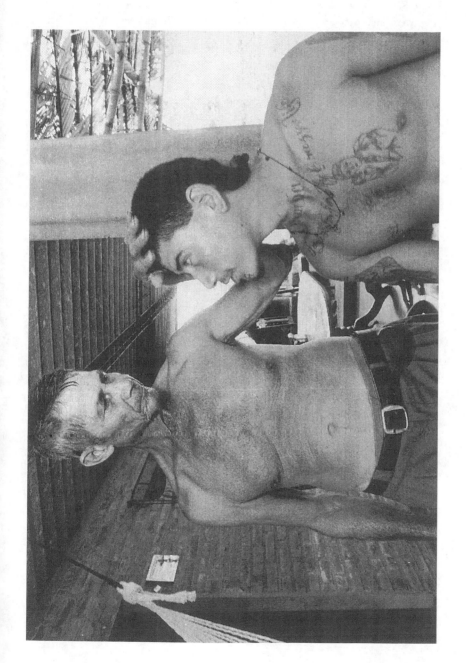

FIGURE 14.17

FIGURE 14.1 José's Grave

Edgar Bolanos, known as Shy Boy, trudges to the edge of a soccer field with his friend Scrappy a few steps behind. He changes direction several times, finally spotting what he is after. His brother José's grave. "My mom brought me back here to El Salvador, because José told her some Eighteenth Street gang members were going to kill me in Los Angeles," Edgar says in a low voice. "The bullet meant for me got him instead."

In hushed tones, Edgar tells about other murders. He is haunted by a three-year-old's memory of soldiers torturing and killing his uncles and other villagers in another soccer field a few miles from here. He remembers the bravery of his grandmother withstanding soldiers' punches and refusing to tell where his father, a guerrilla fighter, was hiding. That his father was saved by this fierce bond of loyalty and silence is a lesson learned well by the surviving Bolanos brothers.

FIGURE 14.2 Shy Boy Tattoos

Although according to Edgar's mother, her son José was killed because he was in love with a girl from the rival Eighteenth Street gang, Edgar reacted by taking his dead brother's gang name: Shy Boy. Shortly after José's burial, Edgar tattooed a tombstone with the name "Shy Boy" on his back and began hanging out in the San Salvador gang crash pads that have become his home.

FIGURE 14.3 Gang Crash Pad

"La Loquita," "Cashy," and "Shy Boy" once lived in Los Angeles. At first, they thought only of getting back to the United States. Survival is difficult without close relatives in a country one barely remembers. They find fellow "homeboys" on the streets of San Salvador. The gang is their family and means of support.

FIGURE 14.4 Man Watching

At age eighteen, Edgar Bolanos, known as Shy Boy, lives in fear of death. "There are lots of people who want to kill me." he says. "I don't mean homeboys. I mean the really bad people from the organized crime rings and other people who just hate us." Shy Boy, aloof and elusive, takes in the scene. "People here think I'm the gang leader because I used to live in Los Angeles," he says almost wistfully. "But we don't have leaders. I have respect from the homeboys, but I don't tell other people what to do."

FIGURE 14.5 Homies

This corner and the surrounding streets of this working-class enclave are Big Gangsta Locos territory. About thirty youths belong to BGLS, a subgroup or clique of the infamous Mara Salvatrucha (or MS) gang of Los Angeles. Apart from Shy Boy, all of the mostly fifteen- and sixteen-year-old "gangstas" in this enclave have never lived outside El Salvador. Shy Boy, who will soon turn nineteen, is the oldest member of the group. Although he may not be the leader, it is clear from the way the others approach and quietly confer with him that his opinions are valued highly.

FIGURE 14.6 Punishment Beating

A homeboy being "disciplined" during a gang meeting. Shy Boy explains that the meetings, known in both the United States and in El Salvador as "giving court," are how the homeboys from the Mara Salvatrucha gang in both countries keep loyal and united. "The vato molested the homeboy's wife." Shy Boy explains, "If she'd been a woman from another neighborhood, maybe we'd laugh about it over a few beers," he shrugs. "It's not right, I know," he says somewhat ruefully. "But that's street justice L.A. style and that's how we are here too."

FIGURE 14.7 Spider with Cocaine

"Spider" triumphantly displays a bag of cocaine. An amount this size costs 50 colones, or $5.75. That is nearly a day and a half's wages at the Salvadoran minimum wage of $4.00 per day. Cocaine addiction, once limited to the Salvadoran upper class, has become a commonplace of street-gang life. Gang members often resort to begging, stealing , or selling drugs in order to support their drug habits.

FIGURE 14.8 Another Gang Crash Pad

Shy Boy, Scrappy, Spider, and Spike settling in with a bottle of vodka to watch El Salvador battle Jamaica for a soccer championship. The house belongs to Spider's and Spike's dad. Shy Boy has lived here for much of the last year.

FIGURE 14.9 Coke Mirror

Spider watches as Shy Boy prepares to mix cocaine with marijuana. "When I go to my grandparents in the countryside, it's really hard at first not smoking," Shy Boy confides, his hands trembling. "But after I'm there awhile these nervous feelings slow down."

FIGURE 14.10 Shy Boy Smoking

Spider waits for Shy Boy to pass the joint. As he gets high, Shy Boy begins to confide his feelings. Recently, a drunk wielding a machete severed the nerves of his left hand, causing permanent loss of movement in three of his fingers. "I had to get away from here. I was afraid someone would kill me. I went to my grandfather's for a month," he explains quietly. "But my girlfriend won't talk to me now because I went away," he sighs. "She says her parents don't want her to see me. But I think maybe another homeboy from a different clique is trying to take her away from me. Some people are saying she's going with another vato [Chicano slang for "guy," "gangster"]. I feel angry at her, but I love her. So now I don't care about anything."

FIGURE 14.11 Shy Boy with Baby

Shy Boy hugs the daughter of one of his homeboys. He has no children. "I want a family of my own," he says. "But It's not right to spread babies everywhere. First I need a job, a house. I need a future."

FIGURE 14.12 Hugo in Prison

Edgar's brother Hugo is in Apanteos prison. When this photograph was taken (1997), he had been in jail for five months, waiting for his case to be heard. His trial was expected to take another six months. According to Hugo, a drunken gunfight broke out between a cop and Hugo's friend who is an ex-cop. Hugo's friend was wounded, but the cop was killed. "The way I see it they both were at fault," Hugo says, shaking his head. "But if I say I saw what happened, my friend would get life, because the guy who died was a cop. What would you do?" he asks rhetorically. "I know I should pick better friends. But I can't be a snitch. The guy has kids."

FIGURE 14.13 Leslie Goodbye
Hugo has just learned that he will be transferred to prison eighteen hours away. He says goodbye to Leslie at the end of their visit knowing that she will seldom be able to visit with their two daughters in the future. (As of December 1999, Hugo had been in prison for almost three years. His case still had not been tried—nor will his time spent in jail waiting for trial count toward his sentence, whatever it turns out to be.)

FIGURE 14.14 Letter from Mom
Edgar reading a letter from his mother in Los Angeles. "My Dear Edgar," she writes, "All I want is for you to have a decent life, to find peace and happiness. I don't think you will find those things the way you are living now. Why don't you stay with my father and help him. He is old and could use your help." When Edgar finishes the letter, there are tears in his eyes.

FIGURE 14.15 Ana in L.A.
In Los Angeles, Ana Bolanos and her sister-in-law fret about fresh uncertainties the new U.S. immigration law brings. In the past, Ana could sneak back over the border if she felt she needed to make a visit to counsel and console her sons Edgar and Hugo in El Salvador. But what if she got stuck in El Salvador? Her preteen American-born daughter Rocio, who lives surrounded by gangs in Los Angeles, would be left without her mother, at an age when a girl really needs guidance. Both women fear losing their work permits early next year. The hardship will be felt not only in Los Angeles, but by Ana's parents and sons back in El Salvador. And Rocio, who always listens intently to adult conversations, fears that uniformed men from the immigration service might come in the night and take her mother away from her.

FIGURE 14.16 Shy Boy Ironing
Tomorrow, Edgar plans to go to Metalio to get a copy of his birth certificate so that he can get his *cedula* or identity card. With the tattoos that show on his face and arms, he knows it will be very hard to find work. But getting his papers is a first step.

FIGURE 14.17 Shy Boy's Grandpa
Edgar visiting his peasant grandfather. He migrates between gang crash pads in the city and his grandparents' small parcel of land in rural Santa Ana. He always

visits at the planting time and harvest to help with the work. But he grows restless easily and can't sit still in one place. He says the back-breaking work the peasants do is too hard for his grandfather and he wants a better kind of job for himself.

"I am proud that we are peasants. Peasants are humble, they have generous hearts. But I could never settle in the country. I miss the action of the city; then I grow bored of that too. Wherever I go, I want to be someplace else."

Edgar now lies in Sonsonate in the same grave with his brother José—the fragile light of his dawning hopes extinguished by an assassin's bullet.

Who killed Edgar Bolanos? His death remains an unsolved mystery shrouded in rumor. The police investigation has been inconclusive. His mother Ana spoke with several witnesses who allege that the drive-by shooting that occurred at 10:00 in the morning outside his in-laws' home was done by local vigilantes.

15

SNAPSHOTS OF A MOVEMENT: THE NEW YORK LATIN KINGS AND QUEENS 1996–99

STEVE HART AND DAVID BROTHERTON

In September 1998, a journalist from the London daily newspaper, the *Guardian,* called me at the Street Organization Project in New York City and asked if I would introduce him to leaders of the Almighty Latin King and Queen Nation (ALKQN). He had heard about the group and wanted to be the first to produce a story for the British public on this self-described gang-turned-social movement. After discussing his plans with several of the group's leading members, the journalist came to New York a couple of months later and the newspaper hired a local photographer to provide the images to accompany the story. It was during a large monthly meeting of the Nation in Washington Heights that I first met that photographer, Steve Hart, carrying out his assignment. Since that time, Steve has become an essential part of the Street Organization Project, accompanying its team of researchers into many different settings. The following images were selected by me to reflect the different facets of the ALKQN over time. I want to take this opportunity to thank the many men, women, and children of this organization and their supporters for opening their doors to us "outsiders," for their generosity of spirit, and for their sincerity in struggling for a better future.

DAVE BROTHERTON

REFERENCES:

Brotherton, D., and L. Barrios. Forthcoming. *Between Black and Gold: The Street Politics of the Almighty Latin King and Queen Nation.*
Parenti, C. 1999. *Lockdown America.* New York: Verso Press. .

FIGURE 15.1

FIGURE 15.2

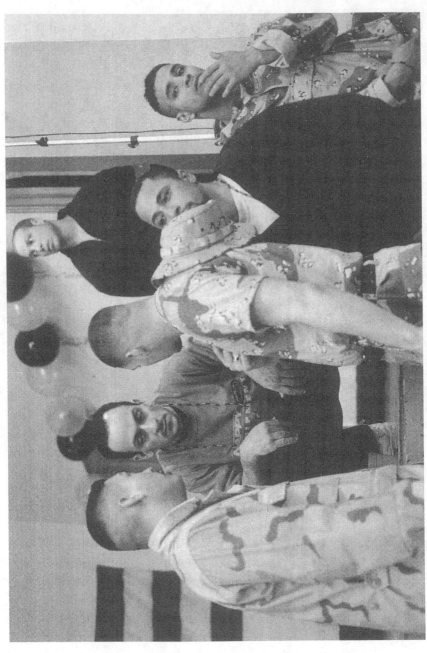

FIGURE 15.3

FIGURE 15.4

FIGURE 15.5

FIGURE 15.6

FIGURE 15.7

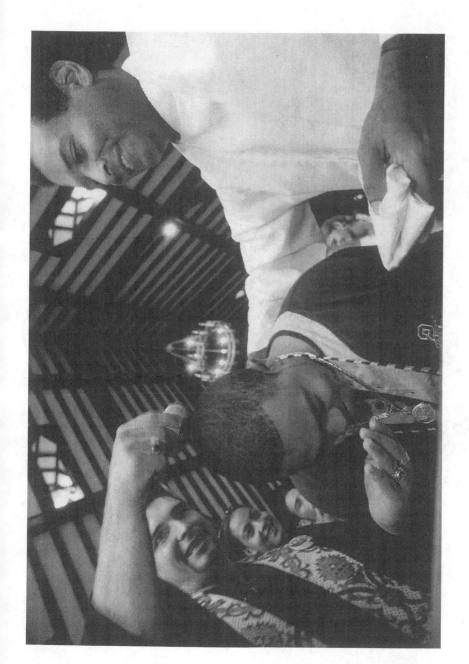

FIGURE 15.8

FIGURE 15.9

FIGURE 15.10

FIGURE 15.11

FIGURE 15.12

FIGURE 15.13

FIGURE 15.14

FIGURE 15.1

The first chapter of the New York Latin Kings (which had been originally formed in Chicago in the late 1940s) was founded in Collins Correctional facility on 6 January 1986. The first Inca, or president, of the group was Luis Felipe, better known as King Blood. Within a couple years, the New York Latin Kings had grown throughout the New York State correctional system to become a well-disciplined force on the streets of New York City with several hundred members. By 1995, however, the Almighty Latin King and Queen Nation, as it was then known, was in disarray, as many leading members were brought to trial under the RICO (Racketeering Influence and Corrupt Organizations) statute of 1970, an act that ostensibly was passed to fight organized crime but has mostly been used against leftists and radicals (Parenti 1999) and contemporary street gangs. In late 1996, Antonio Fernandez, also known as King Tone, became the new Inca of the organization and began an effort to transform the "gang" into a "street organization"(Brotherton and Barrios, forthcoming).

FIGURE 15.2

One of the key organizing and cultural events of the ALKQN is its monthly general meetings, called "universals." At such events, the leadership structure takes turns in reporting on the progress of the group while exhorting the members to become more deeply committed to the organization and its ideals. In the above photograph, we see an example of the physical and verbal displays of solidarity that typically characterize such occasions. A universal usually lasts several hours and is often followed by a relaxed social gathering where members can mix and network over food and nonalcoholic drinks offered by the Queens, while groups of young Latin Kings perform or play their own self-styled rap creations. These high-energy, collective dramas bound by rituals and protocols of the group comprise a mix of meeting styles: a pep rally, a revival, and a form of political theater all in one. It is no wonder that members often describe them as the high point in their social calendars. Before King Tone took over the organization, such meetings would have been off-limits to outsiders; but with the shift to a more conscious engagement in politics, the emphasis changed to openness and inclusivity. Hence, during this period of reform, many community leaders and radical organizers could be observed as "guests" at such events, including members from the Nation of Islam, the Congress for Puerto Rican Rights, Mothers Against Police Brutality, the Asociación Neta, the National Action Network, the Workers World Party, and the Union Theological Seminary.

FIGURE 15.3

The "universals" are carefully scripted events in which the leaders constantly confer on the dynamics of the day. A great emphasis is placed on security, not least because the group is always under some form of surveillance by the police and there is no shortage of internal factions or external enemies who could pose a threat to the organization at various times. Above, we see some of the security team in their customary military-style clothing. Hector Torres, the second figure from the left, was the Santo of the group (see Barrios, chapter 7 of this volume) or the "spiritual advisor" to the Inca.

FIGURE 15.4

Sometimes the universals had to be held in the open air. A favorite place for these to take place was in Highland Park, Brooklyn. Above, we see the group creating what is called a 360, which is a circle formed by members who stand with their feet splayed slightly apart, gently touching the next person's foot. A member of the security team meanwhile patrols the inside of the circle, staring into each member's eyes, which is a military-type drill strategy that ensures everybody is concentrating on the business at hand and that nobody is daring to speak or move out of turn. The practical and symbolic importance of this meeting to the Nation cannot be overestimated. Not only did it represent the membership's commitment to solidarity and unity but it functioned as an excellent setting for increasing the level of communication, especially between the leaders and the rank and file. It should be noted that no one outside of the organization was allowed to enter the "circle." The only time that this was reported to have happened during our three years of research with the group was when Father Barrios (coeditor of this book) was once brought into the circle by King Tone to bless the membership and issue a call for unity. In fact, the photograph above was taken on this unique occasion.

FIGURE 15.5

On 25 November 1998, the Almighty Latin King and Queen Nation held their monthly universal at a church hall in Washington Heights, New York City. The area houses the city's largest Dominican population and is located in the northern reaches of Harlem. This was the first time that the group held its meeting at this location. It had lost its regular space the previous month after the resident priest at the church decided that the congregation was becoming too Latino in a historically African American neighborhood. The group had been the subject of an enormous sweep only several months before, code-named Operation Crown. Out of a total of ninety-eight arrests, more than fifty members were picked up in a series of coordinated arrests at 4:00 a.m. on a weekday. Both the mayor of New York City and the commissioner of police had vowed to break the organization and they were both prepared to put all necessary resources into the job. The ostensible reason for this focus on one group was to stem the tide of organized street crime before it could begin. But the ALKQN had long renounced its involvement in the illegal aspects of street life.

FIGURE 15.6

The young group of members above were part of the youth section of the ALKQN called the Pee Wees. These are young members under the age of eighteen. The young woman on the right was one of the leaders of this group. The Pee Wees were one of the more radical elements of the ALKQN and could be relied upon to be at the forefront of the many political demonstrations that the group attended. Despite the stereotypes surrounding the behavior of young males in so-called gangs, it was rare to see the young Latin Kings acting offensively or antisocially. On the contrary, a high premium was placed on discipline in the Pee Wees and there was tremendous internal solidarity and camaraderie. Although the social and economic backgrounds of the youths varied (most were from poor, working-class families), all the Pee Wees who were interviewed considered themselves members of a resistance organization committed to uplifting the Latin community and to the positive reinforcement of their own cultural identity. A seventeen-year-old male member of the Pee Wees gives a typical response when asked about the organization's view of education and his reasons for joining:

> **P.W.:** The way I see it, if you don't go to school you don't work or you don't do nothin' they don't give you love. Love is when you throw the sign up and you throw the crown up. . . . I'm a Pee Wee but in the future I'm gonna be somebody. As a King I'm gonna be somebody. Now if I don't wanna be somebody why would I wanna be a Latin King?
>
> **I:** What are your reasons for joining?
>
> **P.W.:** My reason was I wanted to be part of a Nation, part of a Latin Nation, you know what I'm sayin'? A Latino, everybody Latino. We all Latinos. I came in too for brown wisdom. . . . I love that word, brown wisdom. Brown wisdom is knowledge of Latinos, knowledge of the past and of the present. That's the reason why.

FIGURE 15.7

The Latin Queens are a crucial part of the ALKQN and they are often described by male members as the backbone of the group. The Queens have their own manifesto, which was originally written by King Blood (Luis Felipe) in 1993. In many ways, the original Queen manifesto was a replica of the males', with some added points on being loyal to a King, to reproduce for the good of the Nation and other "rules" that were clearly written for the benefit of the male hierarchy. In 1996, however, the Queens began to change, and a new leadership of women came to the fore. These new Queens wanted to have more autonomy and wanted to see the Nation develop along the lines of gender equality. This caused some tension within the ranks and there were constant debates about how far the Queens could go in their pursuit of independence without risking disunity. The debate was very healthy, however, and it seemed that the more the Queens were present in the day-to-day organization of the group, the more rapid and deep seated the reform process became. The two quotes below are quite typical of reasons the Queens gave for joining the Nation:

> I joined to show our people that we don't have to take what society says that we have to. We don't have to be second-class citizens in America, you know, that we can achieve the American dream.   *(Queen J.)*

I want to bring people together as one so that the government, the city, the state, the world, could hear our voice. . . . I want the Puerto Ricans to know they did something for themselves. . . . Education has to get much better . . . the tax money, what are they doing to it, a lot of it is being used for jails—less on schools, less on after-school programs. . . . A lot of young females don't know how it is to be respected because they don't know how to respect themselves. A lot of money is used on the rich neighborhoods, why can't they use them in the poor neighborhoods? *(Queen S.)*

FIGURE 15.8

One of the many rituals of the group was the baptism of new and old members and of members' children. During the organization's heyday (1997–99), there were a number of occasions when multiple baptisms were carried out. Sometimes these would be held in a church and sometimes, in summer months, at a New York City beach, but they were always events at which members expressed high levels of optimism, self-sacrifice, and group solidarity. On such occasions, it seemed that there were few urban social problems that the organization was loath to tackle. Ironically, in the photograph above, King Tone is performing the baptismal rites while he was still under one year's house arrest. Not long after this shot was taken, the organization lost some of its key leaders to the criminal justice system and consequently entered an era of disunity, factionalism, and parochial leadership. Nonetheless, memories of such occasions still leave me with a glimpse of what the organization is capable of being. It demonstrated that it could mobilize hundreds if not thousands of highly marginalized Latinos and Latinas, giving them a sense of political and spiritual purpose and a way to culturally affirm their subordinate identities. In a colonialist (or even postcolonialist) society that is given to deny the present and the past of so many citizens, this was no small feat.

FIGURE 15.9

As children are born to Latin Kings and Queens, they automatically become Kings and Queens by birthright. The young boy above is wearing his beads, which are an adornment that is derived from the traditions of the rosary and signifies that he has been blessed by the Nation. At all group events, irrespective of the occasion, children were present in large numbers. Thus at large monthly universals, local branch meetings, demonstrations, social gatherings, and baptisms, there were always babies and toddlers with their parent(s). This emphasis on the family is a major characteristic of the group and is a theme that runs throughout the ALKQN's ideological texts and myriad cultural practices. With the bulk of ALKQN members drawn from a range of Latin American ethnic populations (primarily Puerto Rican but with a strong representation of Dominicans and, more recently, Mexicans), all of which are extremely family centered, it would seem natural that the organization would also place a high priority on family traditions and kinship networks. Members of the ALKQN often repeated a dictum, "we don't die we multiply," which was an acknowledgment that societal racism and economic marginalization ensured that the group would remain attractive to those seeking self-affirmation, and that the group would grow naturally due to expanding bloodlines.

FIGURE 15.10

At ALKQN events, entire families would attend, spanning a range of generations. Not everybody who attended the meetings were members, and above we see a good example of the support networks that were always in evidence at the big events. The involvement of so many nonmembers demonstrated that the Nation had deep links in the Latino community and that this community base prevented it from being easily marginalized, even during times when the group was being demonized in the media or excoriated by the political establishment. During the reform period of the ALKQN (roughly 1996–99), an increasing emphasis was placed on developing the organization's openness in an effort to show that the group was not the secret, conspiratorial, and violent gang that members of law enforcement were fond of describing.

FIGURE 15.11

The ALKQN met regularly at St. Mary's Episcopal Church in West Harlem. The church was located opposite the twenty-fifth police precinct, one of the largest precinct houses in New York City. This extraordinary spatial confluence of seemingly oppositional social actors was somewhat indicative of the way that cultures and subcultures are so complexly interwoven in the daily life of the great metropolis. In this highly organized and layered locale, individual citizens and their group affiliations have to interact and negotiate with each other, and sometimes the distances that groups try to keep from one another fail to materialize. In the above photograph, we see another example of the ALKQN crossing the kinds of social and cultural boundaries that both media and law enforcement constructions of the group would find difficult to explain. Nonetheless, in the symbolic gestures and performances of the parishioners and those of the ALKQN's members there are a great many shared meanings—not least of which is the individual and collective performance of prayer, which is signified by the hands held aloft by the lay members of the congregation and by the crossing of hands and fingers by the members of the ALKQN.

FIGURE 15.12

Tattoos have long been a popular expression of symbolic affinity in youth subcultures. Many of the bodily adornments that can be seen among members of gang subcultures originally derive from the prison inmate culture. One such design that often appears on male inmates' and ex-inmates' faces is that of the teardrop. The meaning of this symbol varies according to the individual but usually it means that the member has fought on behalf of the organization and has either shed his own blood or that of someone else. With the increasing amount of urban working-class

Latino/Latina and African American youths and adults entering the criminal justice system over the last ten years, the influence of prison subcultural styles on the streets is obvious. This meshing of the two subcultures is not, however, about the heightened levels of street crime and the more efficient responses of the police as some claim; rather, it reflects the obscene consequences of discriminatory sentencing, draconian drug laws, selective law enforcement, and the lack of competent legal representation for the poor. The result, arguably, was the most extensive criminalization of lower class youth of the twentieth century. In a shameful statistic provided by New York City's Department of Juvenile Justice, 95 percent of youth in detention in 1999 were African American and Latino (64 and 31 percent, respectively), although both groups only accounted for 67 percent of the city's total youth population. Sometimes, a facial tattoo can signify much more than the wearer intended.

FIGURE 15.13

King Skibee, above, is a Royal Lion. He was given this title by King Blood while they were both in solitary confinement in Attica Prison, New York State. During an interview, I asked Skibee to explain the significance and meaning of his organizational title:

> A royal lion is like, to me a royal lion is like this, I'll break it down to you. "R" stands for Righteousness. The "Y" stands for Yahve. The "A" stands for Almighty. The "L" stands for Latino. Lion . . . Love, right, Obedience, Independent Nation, that's Royal Lion. It's my breakdown significance of Royal Lion. I'm all that. I've proven that to Tone, I've proven that to King Blood, and I've proven it to my crown. That's what a Royal Lion is.

FIGURE 15.14

On 15 January 1999, King Tone gave himself up to the federal authorities in downtown Brooklyn. He was later to enter a plea of guilty to "Conspiracy to Distribute and Possess with Intent to Distribute heroin, a Class C Felony" (Eastern District Court of New York Presentence Investigation Report, 10 May 1999). Tone had been implicated by a tape recording made by an undercover narcotics officer and by a Latin Kings informer who had been a long-time player in the illicit drugs economy. Tone decided not to fight the charges because he had accumulated ten criminal history points over the previous ten years, which meant that if he failed to prove himself innocent he faced a mandatory twenty-five years in prison. He said he wanted to see his three children while they were still young and at least, with the thirteen-year sentence he received after "copping a plea," his children would still be in their teens when he returned to the outside world. In his final interview (20 July 1999) from the Manhattan House of Detention ("the Tombs") before being sent to the maximum-security prison at Leavenworth, Kansas, Tone said the following:

I think thirteen years is a lot, but I says it's all right. If God is willing I'll be home before I'm forty-four. Sixty-five you retire, right? So, I got twenty good years of labor or if I get a degree I don't have to flip burgers. I could start in a respectful position. . . . I would like to open a not-for-profit youth center somewhere, you know, that's my dream. . . . My door will always be open, 'cos, in my heart as a King, you know, I never give up.

CONTRIBUTORS

DR. LUIS BARRIOS is an Associate Professor at the Puerto Rican/Latin American Studies Department, John Jay College of Criminal Justice, New York City. He is the Principal Investigator and Director of Palenque-Family Life Center, a youth violence reduction program in the Washington Heights community, New York City. Dr. Barrios is a member of the American Psychological Association, and a Board Certified Forensic Examiner (American College of Forensic Examiners). Dr. Barrios is also an Episcopal priest in the diocese of New York.

DAVE BROTHERTON is an Associate Professor of Sociology and Criminal Justice at John Jay College of Criminal Justice and the Graduate Center, City University of New York. Dr. Brotherton cofounded the Street Organization Project in 1997 with Luis Barrios and directed two major conferences in 1998 and 2001 on the organization of street youth both nationally and internationally. Dr. Brotherton is currently working on the issue of school-age youth expelled from the United States and organizing a third international conference on resistance and youth street performance in Brazil to be held in 2004. Dr. Brotherton has two books forthcoming with Columbia University Press: the first written with Luis Barrios on the Latin Kings and Queens of New York City and the second coedited with Michael Flynn on cross-cultural perspectives on youth resistance.

RUSSELL CHABOT has a Ph.D. in Sociology from State University of New York at Buffalo. He is currently a "roads scholar" teaching at the University of Rhode Island, Providence College and Rhode Island School of Design. His areas of interest include the sociology of culture, deviance, and visual sociology. At present, he is working on a study of the response to video surveillance in everyday life, and a visual ethnography of a small island community in Rhode Island (focusing on the interaction between long-term residents and recent arrivals).

DR. RICHARD (RIC) CURTIS is an Associate Professor and Chair of the Anthropology Department at the John Jay College of Criminal Justice. He has more than twenty years of experience conducting ethnographic research in New York City neighborhoods. At John Jay College, he was the Project Director of the NIDA-funded "Heroin in the Twenty-first Century" project, a five-year ethnographic study of heroin users and distributors in New York City. He was also the Principal Investigator of the NIJ-funded "Lower East Side Trafficking" project, a two-year study examining the developmental trajectories and interactions between markets for different illegal drugs.

DONNA DECESARE is an award-winning freelance photographer and writer. Her photographs have appeared in many news and arts publications including the *New York Times Magazine*, *Life*, *DoubleTake*, and *Aperture*. Her awards include the Dorothea Lange Prize, an Alicia Patterson Fellowship, a Mother Jones International Photo Fund Award, an Independent Project Fellowship from the Soros Foundation, and in 2002, a top prize for her work on violence in Colombia from the National Press Photographers Pictures of the Year competition. DeCesare is currently Assistant Professor of Journalism at the University of Texas at Austin.

ALBERT DICHIARA earned his Ph.D. at the University of Missouri. He is Associate Professor of Sociology and Director of the Criminal Justice Program at the University of Hartford. He has published in the areas of drug use, drug education and drug policy, gangs, and crime policy. He has served as a consultant to the State of Connecticut and to private agencies on a variety of crime and justice issues. His current projects include research on the crime-police relationship in Hartford's North End, racism in the Connecticut criminal justice system, and he is project director of a school-based crime prevention program in several Hartford middle schools.

PHILLIP KASSEL is a staff attorney at Massachusetts Correctional Legal Services, with twenty-two years experience as a civil rights and poverty law advocate in Massachusetts, Washington State, and Minnesota. He has represented classes of poor persons and prisoners in numerous significant cases, has given voice to his clients' concerns in various governmental and public forums, and has written other articles for legal journals about his clients' problems, including the undue expulsion of children from school and police resistance to protecting women from domestic violence.

LOUIS KONTOS is Associate Professor of Sociology at Long Island University, C. W. Post Campus. He has published in the areas of ethnography and critical theory, and is completing a book on *The Politics of Deviance and Social Control* (Roman and Littlefield).

JUAN FRANCISCO ESTEVA MARTÍNEZ is a Mexico City–born Zapoteca from the indigenous community of Tehuantepec, Oaxaca. He immigrated to the San Francisco Bay Area in 1987 where he completed high school and obtained a dual degree in Chicano Studies and Sociology from the University of California at Berkeley. He is currently a doctoral candidate in Sociology at the State University of New York at Albany, a guest lecturer at the University of California at Berkeley's Sociology Department, and works as research assistant for the Alameda Alliance for Health, Cultural Competency Initiative.

KEVIN MCDONALD earned his Ph.D. in Sociology from the Ecole des Hautes Etudes en Sciences Sociales (Paris). He is Senior Lecturer in Sociology at the University of Melbourne. He is a specialist in ethnographic work focusing on action and identity, and is currently engaged in two areas of research. The first explores the social worlds and embodied subjectivities of young people who inject drugs; the second explores patterns of action and identity emerging in direct action groups involved in globalization conflicts. He can be contacted at <k.mcdonald@unimelb.edu.au>.

DANA NURGE recently joined the department of Public Administration and Urban Studies at San Diego State University as an assistant professor in criminal justice. She previously taught at Northeastern University College of Criminal Justice in Boston, where she completed a three-year study of female gangs and cliques and recently finished a project assessing local programs/services for "at-risk" adolescent girls. Dr. Nurge is currently completing a manuscript based on her female gang research and is teaching courses in the areas of juvenile justice and policy analysis.

RICHARD T. RODRÍGUEZ is Assistant Professor in the Department of Chicano Studies at California State University, Los Angeles. A graduate of the History of Consciousness program at UC Santa Cruz, he teaches, lectures, and writes on media and cultural studies.

CAMILA SALAZAR-ATIAS was a field researcher with the Street Organization Project between 1996 and 1999. She is currently studying for a graduate degree in Sociology at the University of Lund, Sweden.

LOREN SIEGEL is the former Director of Public Education for the American Civil Liberties Union.

DR. AVELARDO VALDEZ is a professor at the Graduate School of Social Work at the University of Houston. He obtained his Ph.D. in Sociology at the University of California, Los Angeles. Dr. Valdez was also a Fulbright Scholar at the Universidad Nacional Autónoma de Mexico, Mexico, D.F. His research and publications are on drugs, violence, adolescent gangs, drug markets, and sex workers in South Texas and the U.S./Mexico border. He is a recipient of National Institutes of Health (NIH), National Institute on Drug Abuse (NIDA), Center for Disease Control (CDC), and Substance Abuse Mental Health Services Administration (SAMHSA/CSAT) grants. He is currently Director of the Office for Drug and Social Policy at the UH.

SUDHIR VENKATESH is Associate Professor of Sociology and African-American Studies, Columbia University. He is the author of *American Project: The Rise and Fall of a Modern Ghetto* (Harvard University Press, 2000).

INDEX